Sussex Coroners'
Inquests
1603–1688

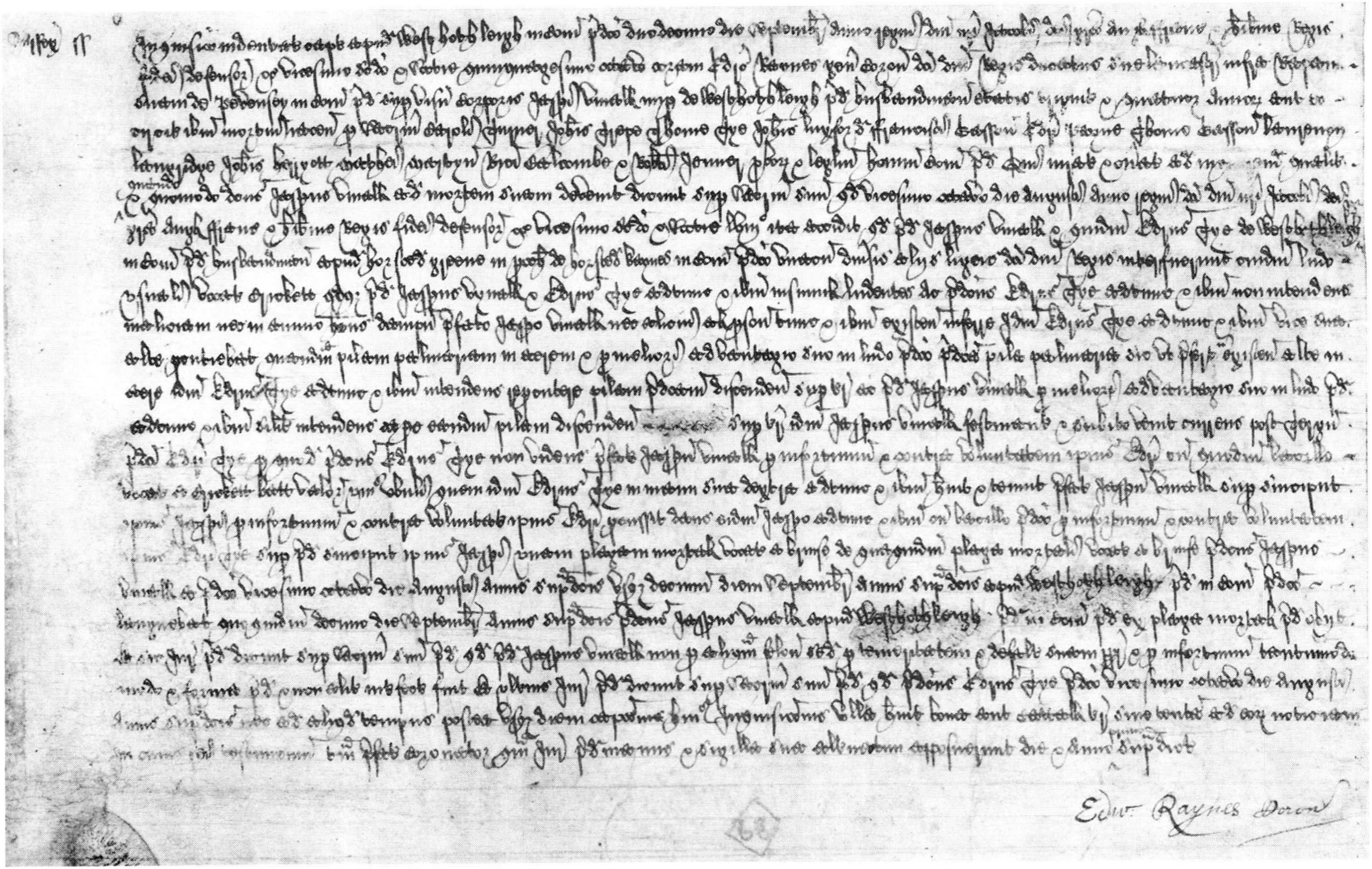

An early cricket fatality: inquest no 259.

Sussex Coroners' Inquests 1603–1688

Edited by
R F Hunnisett

PRO Publications
Public Record Office
Ruskin Avenue
Kew
Surrey
TW9 4DU

ISBN 1 873162 53 7

A catalogue card for this book
is available from the British Library

CONTENTS

PREFACE

Like its two forerunners, this volume owes more than is apparent to the help which I have always received from the staff of the Public Record Office, the East and West Sussex Record Offices and the Hastings Museum and Art Gallery. I am especially grateful to Elizabeth Hallam Smith and Aidan Lawes for their encouragement and to Melvyn Stainton and Millie Skinns for their cheerful cooperation. As always, this work would have been the poorer without the unfailing and expert assistance of Christopher Whittick and my wife.

Crown copyright material is published by permission of the Controller of Her Majesty's Stationery Office.

R.F.H.
July 1998

ABBREVIATIONS

ASSI 35	PRO: Assizes: Norfolk and Home Circuits: Indictments Files 1559–1688.
ASSI 94	PRO: Assizes: Norfolk and Home Circuits: Indictments Files 1689–1850.
C 202	PRO: Chancery: Petty Bag Office: Writ Files.
C 260	PRO: Chancery: Tower and Rolls Chapel Series: Recorda Files.
CAR	*Calendar of assize records: Sussex indictments, James I*, ed. J S Cockburn (London, 1975).
CAR Eliz	*Calendar of assize records: Sussex indictments, Elizabeth I*, ed. J S Cockburn (London, 1975).
CAR Introdn	J S Cockburn, *Calendar of assize records: Home Circuit indictments, Elizabeth I and James I: Introduction* (London, 1985).
CPR	*Calendar of the Patent Rolls preserved in the Public Record Office* (London, 1891–1986).
CSPD	*Calendar of State Papers, Domestic Series* (London, 1856–1998).
Complete peerage	G E C, *The complete peerage of England, Scotland and Ireland, Great Britain and the United Kingdom, extant, extinct or dormant*, revised edn (London, 1910–1959).
EP II/16/202A	WSRO: Archdeaconry of Lewes: Parish Register Transcripts: Withyham.
ESRO	East Sussex Record Office.
Edburton reg.	*S. Andrew's, Edburton, Sussex: copy of a parish register book, 1558–1673*, ed. C H Wilkie (Brighton, 1884).
HCA 1	PRO: High Court of Admiralty: Oyer and Terminer Records.
HMC, XIII	Historical Manuscripts Commission: *Thirteenth report* (London, 1892).
HASTINGS C/A(a)	Hastings Museum and Art Gallery: Court Books of the town and port of Hastings: Records of Sessions, Assemblies and Hundred Courts.
HASTINGS C/A(c)	Hastings Museum and Art Gallery: Court Books (duplicates) of the town and port of Hastings: Records of Sessions, Assemblies and Hundred Courts.
HASTINGS C/B(k)	Hastings Museum and Art Gallery: Coroners' Inquests.
Horsham millenium	W Albery, *A millenium of facts in the history of Horsham and Sussex 947–1947* (Horsham, 1947).
KB 9	PRO: Court of King's Bench: Crown Side: Indictments Files, Oyer and Terminer Files and Informations Files.
KB 11	PRO: Court of King's Bench: Crown Side: Out-Counties Indictments Files.
KB 27	PRO: Court of King's Bench: Plea and Crown Sides: Coram Rege Rolls.
KB 29	PRO: Court of King's Bench: Crown Side: Controlment Rolls and other Memoranda Rolls of the Clerk of the Crown.
PAR 92/1	WSRO: Goring Parish Registers.
PAR 203/1	WSRO: Warnham Parish Registers.
PAR 301/1	WSRO: Cuckfield Parish Registers.
PAR 430/1	ESRO: Ninfield Parish Registers.
PAR 442/1	WSRO: Petworth Parish Registers.
PAR 446/1	ESRO: Plumpton Parish Registers.
PRO	Public Record Office.
Par. reg. of Brighton	*The parish register of Brighton in the county of Sussex 1558–1701*, ed. H D Roberts (Brighton, 1932).
RYE 1	ESRO: Corporation of Rye: Hundred, Sessions and Assembly Books.
RYE 8	ESRO: Corporation of Rye: Indictments.
RYE 32	ESRO: Corporation of Rye: Inquisitions and Associated Papers.

RYE 47	ESRO: Corporation of Rye: Letters of Process, Letters Testimonial and Other Papers.
SAC	*Sussex Archaeological Collections* (1848–).
SCI	*Sussex coroners' inquests 1558–1603*, ed. R F Hunnisett (Kew, 1996).
SEA 6	ESRO: Corporation of Seaford: Court Book 1594–1654.
SNQ	*Sussex Notes and Queries* (1926–1971).
SP 18	PRO: Council of State, Navy Commission and related bodies: Orders and Papers.
SP 25	PRO: Council of State: Books and Accounts.
SRS, XIII	*The parish registers of Cuckfield, Sussex, 1598–1699*, ed. W C Renshaw (Sussex Record Society, XIII, 1911).
SRS, XV	*The parish registers of Bolney, Sussex, 1541–1812*, ed. E Huth (Sussex Record Society, XV, 1912).
SRS, XVII	*The parish registers of Ardingly, Sussex, 1558–1812*, ed. G W E Loder (Sussex Record Society, XVII, 1913).
SRS, XXI	*The parish register of Horsham in the county of Sussex 1541–1635*, ed. R G Rice (Sussex Record Society, XXI, 1915).
SRS, XXIV	*The parish register of East Grinstead, Sussex, 1558–1661*, ed. R P Crawfurd (Sussex Record Society, XXIV, 1917).
SRS, LIV	*Quarter Sessions Order Book 1642–1649*, ed. B C Redwood (Sussex Record Society, LIV, 1954).
SRS, LXXIV	*Sussex coroners' inquests 1485–1558*, ed. R F Hunnisett (Sussex Record Society, LXXIV, 1985).
WIN 55	ESRO: Corporation of Winchelsea: Court Book: Assemblies and Hundreds 1597–1627.
WIN 58	ESRO: Corporation of Winchelsea: Court Book: Assemblies, Hundreds and Sessions 1628–1691.
WIN 64	ESRO: Corporation of Winchelsea: Extracts from Court Books 1627–1765.
WSRO	West Sussex Record Office.
WSRO, MP	WSRO: Miscellaneous Papers.
WSRO, SAS	WSRO: Sussex Archaeological Society.

INTRODUCTION

The Records

Throughout the seventeenth century coroners continued to perform the two duties which had survived from the middle ages. The county coroners regularly attended the county court, which in Sussex was held every four weeks, at Lewes and Chichester alternately. Their presence there was essential for legalising and proclaiming outlawries. Outlawry — or waiver, the equivalent for women — was not a punishment but the last in a series of attempts to secure a person's attendance in court.[1] Large numbers of people were outlawed in every county every year and ten per cent of the inquests printed in this volume resulted in an outlawry or waiver for one reason or another, the same percentage as for the Elizabethan inquests.[2] In the middle ages and under the Tudors a coroner was occasionally outlawed.[3] Three of the seventeenth-century Sussex coroners — John Eagle, John Luck and Albany Stoughton — were outlawed, Stoughton on four occasions, always for failing to appear in the court of King's Bench to answer for defects in their inquests (**60, 93, 96, 131, 164, 199**).[4] That it seems not to have had any effect on their continuing in office shows that by that time outlawry was far removed from the serious sanction of the early middle ages.[5]

Even for county coroners the more onerous duty was that of holding inquests on view of dead bodies and it was the only one which borough and franchisal coroners performed by virtue of their office. Every homicide, suicide, accidental death and sudden and unexpected death should have resulted in an inquest as should every death of a prisoner in gaol. All are well represented in this volume, as is every category of homicide — murder, manslaughter, accidental homicide and homicide committed in self defence. Table IX, at the end of this introduction, shows the incidence year by year of each variety of death according to the inquest jurors' verdicts. The 520 inquests printed here are all that are known to survive, as either originals or copies, from the 85 years from 1603 to 1688, the beginning of James I's reign to the end of James II's. By contrast, there are 582 inquests extant from the 44 years of the reign of Elizabeth I and 243 from the 73 years of her Tudor precursors, from 1485 to 1558.[6] Of the seventeenth-century inquests 383 are from the years 1603 to 1642 and only 137 from 1643 to 1688. The wider picture is that there are 1,345 inquests surviving from the years 1485 to 1688: 146 from before 1550, an average of 2 a year; 137 from after 1642, an average of 3 a year; but 1,062 from 1550 to 1642, an average of over 11 a year.

There are three reasons which account for the smaller number of inquests surviving from the first half of the sixteenth century than from the second half. Two of them derive from the fact that the great majority that do survive owe their survival to a statute of 1487, 3 Henry VII c 2. That statute ordered that coroners should present their inquests regularly at the assizes, held normally in Lent and late summer. Those which related to homicides alleged to have been committed by persons who had been arrested and detained in the county gaol often served as indictments for the trial of the suspects at the assizes and were usually retained on the assize indictments files after the conclusion of the assizes. All other inquests — suicides, misadventures and natural deaths, as well as homicides for which no suspects were in gaol — were to be handed on to King's Bench, normally in the Easter and Michaelmas terms immediately following the assizes, and when that happened most of them are still on the King's Bench indictments files. Unfortunately, no assize indictments file survives from the Home Circuit from before 1559 which is one of the reasons for the paucity of Sussex inquests of the earlier sixteenth century: except for occasional copies sent to Chancery in connection with pardons, the inquests resulting in trials at assizes have been lost. Another reason is that the 1487 Act seems to have come into effect only slowly and the flow of inquests

---

1. R F Hunnisett, *The medieval coroner* (Cambridge, 1961), 61–68.
2. *SCI*, xi.
3. Hunnisett, *Medieval coroner*, 68; SRS, LXXIV, no 175; *SCI*, xi.
4. Throughout the volume figures in bold type refer to inquests as numbered in the text.
5. Hunnisett, *Medieval coroner*, 67–68.
6. The Sussex inquests from 1485 to 1603 are printed in SRS, LXXIV and *SCI*.

from assizes to King's Bench was weak and sporadic. Thirdly, of the Cinque Ports of Rye, Winchelsea, Hastings and Seaford, only Rye had just begun to copy some of its inquests into registers.[1]

For the reign of Elizabeth I the survival rate is far higher. Three-quarters of the assize indictments files are extant; from 1550 many more inquests were passed on to King's Bench, the vast majority of which are still on the indictments files of that court; and the copies of Rye inquests are much more numerous, with a few Winchelsea and Hastings ones towards the end of the reign.[2] The same pattern continued until the Civil War. Again only some twenty-five per cent of the assize indictments files have been lost from the years 1603 to 1642 and the survivors contain a similar number of inquests to the earlier ones. There were also a comparable number delivered to King's Bench and copied into Cinque Ports registers. Table I shows how many inquests from each year are now in the assize files, the files of King's Bench and the Cinque Ports records; just one inquest is known only as a copy sent into Chancery. In the Cinque Ports column the letters H, R, S and W stand for Hastings, Rye, Seaford and Winchelsea.

It is impossible to explain why so few Sussex inquests survive from the period 1643 to 1688. As can be seen from Table I, the numbers on the assize files do not substantially decrease and only a fifth of the files are lost; and although the number of Cinque Ports inquests declines after 1660, that does not substantially affect the overall picture. The vital difference was in the number of inquests preserved in King's Bench: 25 after 1642 as against 234 between 1603 and 1642. Not only that, but of the 25 inquests 20 were delivered into King's Bench directly by the coroners and only 5 via the assizes, the last being in Easter 1658. Even before 1643, 51 of the 234 inquests were delivered directly by the coroners. That was a new phenomenon. In the sixteenth century coroners rarely returned inquests directly into King's Bench and then usually when ordered by writ.[3] In the seventeenth century they seem to have made the returns on their own initiative, perhaps conscious that otherwise the records might never have reached King's Bench. However that may be, there can be no doubt that even before 1642 the procedure established by the statute of 1487 was slowly running down and that after that date it had virtually ceased to operate. The same pattern is true in varying degrees for all the counties of the Home Circuit, although for no other so markedly as for Sussex. It is in complete contrast to that of the other assize circuits, which continued to pass large numbers of inquests on to King's Bench, and they are still to be found on the indictments files.

Why some coroners returned some of their inquests into King's Bench themselves is unknown. If they had been ordered to do so by writ, the writs should be attached to the inquests. One would also expect to find a good reason for such returns to be ordered — a homicide case to be tried or a suicide or accidental death giving rise to forfeitures to the crown. But of the 71 inquests so returned only two had murder verdicts and one manslaughter; 18 were suicides and 40 misadventures, but many of them produced no forfeiture; and the remaining ten were natural deaths. They are therefore no different from the inquests delivered to King's Bench from assizes. Neither were direct returns to King's Bench a peculiarity of a few coroners or jurisdictions. Of the 16 Sussex jurisdictions outside the Cinque Ports 11 made such returns, the exceptions being the city of Chichester, the Lumley liberty, Rotherfield hundred and the liberties of Battle and Brede. John Teynton returned more inquests directly to King's Bench than any other coroner, 15 of the 31 which he held in Lewes rape and 16 of the 54 in Bramber rape, but there is no apparent pattern to his choice of assizes or King's Bench. He often returned some inquests to assizes and others to King's Bench in the same year so that his inquests arrived in King's Bench by two routes. The same is true of most of the other coroners who delivered some of their inquests into King's Bench. They are therefore unlikely to have adopted that practice from fear that otherwise their records would not arrive there. Indeed, they thereby exposed themselves to the peril, already mentioned, of being challenged as to the adequacy of the records and of consequent sanctions. Finally, the inquests delivered directly into King's Bench were seldom held more than a year before the date of delivery as can be seen in Table III. In Easter 1665 Edward Raines, a county coroner, delivered two inquests, one held in August 1661 and the other in August 1662 (**454, 458**); two others (**301, 325**) were retained by their coroners for two years and a third (**392**) for nearly

1. SRS, LXXIV, xiii–xxiii.
2. *SCI*, xi–xix.
3. e.g. *SCI*, xix.

as long; but the great majority were surrendered within a matter of months.

There was thus little difference between the rapidity with which inquests were delivered to King's Bench and to assizes. Table II shows what happened to all the latter with the exception of the one (**98**) known only from the copy sent on to Chancery. The first two columns give the numbers and dates of the inquests on the indictments files of the assizes noted in column 3; and the fourth and fifth columns give similar numbers and dates of those delivered from assizes to King's Bench in the terms listed in column 6, the inquests now being in the indictments files of those terms. It was highly unusual for inquests not to be delivered to the assizes held immediately after the date at which they were taken, one (**413**) even being taken on the day on which the assizes opened; the few exceptions were never held back for more than one assizes. The coroners' efficiency in this respect was equal to that of their Elizabethan forerunners.[1]

It is obvious that the inquests whose records survive from the second half of the seventeenth century are a very small proportion of those which must have been held and the position is only slightly better for the first half. The explanation cannot be that many records were lost after arriving in King's Bench. It has already been noted that the inquest records of other assize circuits survive in very large numbers on the King's Bench files. It would be extraordinary for those of the Home Circuit alone not to be preserved there if they had been handed in. There is proof that they did not arrive in King's Bench. If they had arrived there, they would have been recorded in the Controlment Rolls, but fewer than forty which are so recorded have not survived, because the indictments files of the relevant terms are either lost or incomplete. The 34 Sussex inquests which certainly arrived in King's Bench but are not extant are listed in Appendix I, at the end of the text, with any subsequent actions or other relevant information. It will be seen that 26 are earlier than 1643 and 8 later. Eleven were sent on to King's Bench from assizes and the other 23 were delivered directly by the coroners. Twenty were deaths by misadventure, 8 were suicides and 6 natural deaths.

Many more inquests — all, of course, with homicide verdicts — which should be on the assize indictments files no longer survive. Not only are more assize files missing but the contents of the existing ones are invariably incomplete. The files of James I's reign contain 50 inquests but there should be 21 more resulting from homicides of which the files contain either indictments by the grand jury or a record of the committal of suspects to gaol.[2] It would have been foolhardy of coroners not to bring to the assizes those inquests relating to people due to be tried. It is therefore probable that the inquests now on the Jacobean assize files are less than three-quarters of those originally there, and the position is similar for the rest of the century. Nevertheless, by far the greatest loss is of inquests which should have been surrendered at assizes and passed on to King's Bench. There are two possible explanations. One is that coroners did not hand in the majority of their inquests. That would certainly account for the long periods from which, for example, no inquest survives from Hastings rape; and for the fact that there are only 17 Hastings rape inquests between 1603 and 1688 compared with 131 for the reign of Elizabeth I[3] and compared with 27 from the half-hundred of Loxfield Camden which consisted merely of the parishes of Mayfield and Wadhurst and part of Lamberhurst.[4] It would, however, still be difficult to understand the apparently sporadic delivery of inquests to assizes. Another possibility is that the Home Circuit clerks of assize, with their greater familiarity with the machinery of the central courts, had a greater contempt for the more obscure and less vital parts of it than had their colleagues farther from Westminster. Knowing that nothing of value resulted from the vast number of written inquests, they largely ceased to pass them on or to preserve them themselves. Perhaps both explanations have some merit: both coroners and clerks of assize grew ever more lax in their record keeping. Even in the Cinque Ports the copying of inquests tailed off as the century wore on, not that it had ever been common in Winchelsea or Seaford; and very few of the originals survive. As with the body of the county, the Cinque Ports records contain many indictments of homicide for which inquests must have been held. One example is printed in Appendix II.[5]

1. *SCI*, xv.
2. *CAR*, passim; cf. *SCI*, xv–xvi.
3. *SCI*, xxvi-xxvii.
4. See Table VII.
5. See also, for example, WIN 55, f 213v.

There is therefore plenty of evidence in the legal records about deaths which should have resulted in inquests. The parish registers contain even more. They commonly describe how people came to their death accidentally and sometimes by suicide,[1] while the Horsham register contains the burial of many prisoners who had died in the county gaol.[2] Occasionally the registers even confirm that an inquest was held.[3] Only from such sources can a fuller picture of the coroners' activities be painted.

The Coroners and their Areas of Jurisdiction

From the early middle ages the Cinque Ports had been virtually autonomous and they had always been exempt from the jurisdiction of the Kent and Sussex coroners. In Sussex their annually elected chief officers were ex officio coroners: in Hastings, Rye and Winchelsea the mayors and in Seaford the bailiffs. The mayors and bailiffs of those four towns who held inquests between 1603 and 1688 which are known from surviving inquest records are listed in Table VI with any deputies who acted for them.[4]

Table V contains a list, by jurisdictions, of all the other coroners known to have held office in Sussex from 1603 to 1688. The two county coronerships, east and west, come first, followed by all the liberties which have left written inquests from that period arranged roughly from east to west. The 14 liberties were Hastings rape; the liberties of Battle and Brede within that rape; the duchy of Lancaster lands in Pevensey rape; the half-hundreds of Loxfield Camden and Loxfield Dorset and the hundred of Rotherfield, all in Pevensey rape; Lewes rape; Bramber rape; the honor of Arundel; the Lumley liberty in Chichester rape; the bishop of Chichester's liberty, often loosely called Manhood hundred, mainly in Chichester rape; the city of Chichester; and Bosham hundred in Chichester rape. Two of those liberties had not had their own coroners before 1603: Rotherfield hundred, which had coroners from 1614 to beyond 1686; and the liberty of the Lords Lumley which was carved from the honor of Arundel early in the seventeenth century. The latter consisted of the hundreds of Westbourne, Singleton, Box and Stockbridge. The honor of Arundel was left with the five hundreds of Arundel rape and Easebourne hundred in Chichester rape. In addition, the liberty of Bosham, whose chamberlain was ex officio coroner and which had left one earlier extant inquest, from 1555,[5] but none from Elizabeth I's reign, is represented by ten in this volume. On the other hand the liberty of Bexhill and the hundred of Eastbourne, which at least sometimes had coroners under Elizabeth,[6] are not known to have had any later; and three liberties from which only pre-Elizabethan inquests survive — that of the bishop, dean and chapter of Chichester, the parish of Apuldram and the Sussex liberty of King's College, Cambridge[7] — again left none. Eton College, which had the right to appoint its own coroners, is not known ever to have exercised it in its Sussex lands.[8] In one early seventeenth-century inquest (**20**) George Ardern is described as coroner of Arundel town, but that does not imply that the borough coronership, known in earlier centuries,[9] had been restored. Ardern, the coroner of the honor of Arundel, was commonly described as the coroner of the hundred or town in which he was acting, for example as coroner of Rotherbridge hundred (**26**). That does not mean that Rotherbridge hundred had its own coroner. In none of the other inquests taken in Arundel is the coroner called the borough coroner (e.g. **34, 295**). The earlier conclusion that the Arundel borough coronership had been

1. e.g. *Par. reg. of Brighton*, 180, 354, 373.
2. SRS, XXI, passim.
3. e.g. *Par. reg. of Brighton*, 358; *SAC*, IV, 257–258.
4. Other Rye mayors of the period are listed in L A Vidler, *A new history of Rye*, 2nd edn (Rye, 1971), 160–161; and a list of Winchelsea mayors, compiled by Mr Malcolm Pratt, the present town clerk of Winchelsea, has been deposited at the East Sussex Record Office.
5. SRS, LXXIV, no 199.
6. *SCI*, xx.
7. SRS, LXXIV, nos 88, 209, 212; *SAC*, XCV, 55–56; XCVIII, 70.
8. *SAC*, XCVIII, 48.
9. *SAC*, XCVIII, 68–69; SRS, LXXV, xxxvi.

subsumed in that of the honor by the reign of Elizabeth I is thereby reinforced.[1] In 1614 quo warranto proceedings began in King's Bench against the bailiffs and burgesses of Horsham who were accused of having usurped and exercised many rights for over three years, including the right to have their own coroner,[2] but it is certain that there was never a Horsham borough coroner.

The lords of the liberties are usually named in the records of their inquests, but to avoid tedious repetition they have been omitted from the calendared versions printed here. Instead they are listed in Table VIII. The dates given against each lord are derived from the surviving inquests and from the lists of coroners on the assize indictments files. The latter are less reliable because the assize lists seem sometimes to have been copied from those of previous assizes. They have been disregarded when they conflict with data from the inquests or when they can be otherwise shown to be wrong. Thus at the assizes of 17 July 1609 George Sayers was listed as coroner of John Lumley, Lord Lumley, but Lumley had died on 11 April.[3] The July date is therefore not included in Lumley's entry. Similarly, at the assizes of 17 July 1620 Samuel Harsnett is given as the bishop of Chichester, although he had been translated to Norwich in the previous year and an inquest (207) had been held in the bishop's liberty on 30 September 1619 by John Adams as coroner of Harsnett's successor, George Carlton.[4]

It is the inquests which present a cognate problem concerning the liberty of the duchy of Lancaster in Pevensey rape, surprisingly given that the duchy always belonged to the crown except, of course, during the Interregnum. One (162), of 1615, describes John Butcher as coroner of Richard earl of Dorset of his duchy of Lancaster in his rape of Pevensey; and in his two other inquests (186, 191), of 1617, Butcher is called coroner of Richard earl of Dorset in or of his rape of Pevensey. During those years, however, the assize lists correctly call him, as they do all his predecessors and successors, the king's coroner of his duchy of Lancaster within his rape of Pevensey. Richard Sackville, earl of Dorset, was never lord of the duchy or of its Pevensey rape lands. From 1609 until his death in 1624, however, he was steward, feodary and bailiff of the duchy liberties in Sussex and as such also titular coroner there, as was Thomas Pelham, earl of Chichester, when steward and feodary in the early nineteenth century.[5] That is proved by five other inquests: four (134, 135, 137, 140), held by Richard Rickward in 1613, call him under-coroner of Richard earl of Dorset of the liberty of the duchy of Lancaster in Pevensey rape; and the other (225), of 1621, calls Edward Raines deputy coroner of Richard earl of Dorset, the king's coroner of his duchy of Lancaster in Pevensey rape. Only the king is therefore named in Table VIII as lord of the duchy. There are no other duchy inquests extant from between 1613 and 1621, but all the earlier and later inquests state that the duchy belonged to the king. The earl of Dorset was never an active coroner and has therefore not been included among the duchy coroners in Table V where Rickward is entered as a full coroner. John Teynton, however, is listed as a deputy coroner in respect of the inquest (241) which he held in 1622 for the coroner, Edward Raines.

A number of coroners who took up office towards the end of Elizabeth's reign continued to serve under James I: John Aylwin as a county coroner and as coroner of Lewes and Bramber rapes; Henry Peckham as the other county coroner and in the bishop of Chichester's liberty; Samuel Playfair in Hastings rape; Thomas Woodgate as the duchy coroner in Pevensey rape; John Eagles in Loxfield Camden half-hundred; George Ardern as coroner of the honor of Arundel; and Thomas Bird and John Exton as Chichester city coroners.[6] One can at least be confident that those coroners were in office on 24 March 1603. For the rest, it is impossible to say exactly when they began or ceased to be coroners. County coroners were elected on writs de coronatore eligendo, but no writ for a Sussex election survives from the seventeenth

1. *SCI*, xxv.
2. KB 9/743, m 8.
3. ASSI 35/51/9, m 44; *Complete peerage*, VIII, 278.
4. ASSI 35/62/7, m 48; J Le Neve, *Fasti Ecclesiae Anglicanae 1541–1857*: II, *Chichester diocese*, ed. J M Horn (London, 1971), 2–3.
5. R Somerville, *Office-holders in the duchy and county palatine of Lancaster from 1603* (Chichester, 1972), 217–218.
6. *SCI*, xx–xxii.

century. There is, however, one which issued on 18 November 1710, ordering the sheriff to cause a coroner to be elected in the place of Alexander Luxford who had died. It is endorsed with a note of the election of John Mitchell in the county court at Lewes on 30 November.[1] Luxford had been coroner in the eastern part of the county since 1669. Most franchisal coroners were appointed by the lords of the liberties, but again no such appointment is known. In the absence of firm dates for taking up and laying down his office, Table V lists for each coroner those on or between which he is known to have held inquests and those on or between which he is recorded as having attended or, less frequently, as having failed to attend assizes. The inquest dates are the more reliable, although for some coroners few inquests or none survive. As already mentioned, the lists of coroners in the assize indictments files seem sometimes to have been copied from those of earlier assizes, with the result that a coroner may occasionally appear from them to have been in office slightly longer than he really had been. As against that, some of the assize lists are illegible or partly or completely missing and a number of the assize files are lost, so that some coroners may have been in office earlier than they reveal or have remained in office beyond their last known mention at assizes. That is particularly the case with franchisal coroners of the second half of the century, because after the early 1650s very few franchisal coroners were listed and after 1660, except at two assizes, only the two county coroners are named.

Like their sixteenth-century predecessors,[2] many of the seventeenth-century coroners held more than one coronership at the same time. Of the county coroners of the eastern district only the last one, Alexander Luxford, is not known to have done so, and the lack of knowledge of who served in liberties during his long life as a coroner makes it impossible to say confidently that he did not. John Aylwin, who had been a county coroner and coroner of Lewes and Bramber rapes before 1603, continued in those offices under James I, probably until 1612 in them all; and he was also coroner of Loxfield Dorset half-hundred in 1605, again possibly until 1612. Thomas Rickward was county coroner in 1612 and 1613, coroner of the duchy of Lancaster and of Loxfield Dorset in 1613, and coroner of Lewes and Bramber rapes in 1613 and 1614. John Eagles served as county coroner in 1613, after Rickward, and as Loxfield Camden half-hundred coroner from 1600 to 1612. He may have held the latter office in 1613 also, because the William Eagles who is recorded as having defaulted at the assizes of 4 July 1613 may never have been coroner, William being an error for John.[3] On the other hand, John Eagles may have had to give up the Loxfield Camden coronership in Trinity term 1613 when he was accused in King's Bench of having usurped it.[4] John Butcher, the East Sussex coroner between 1617 and 1627 (and possibly for some time both earlier and later) was also coroner of Hastings rape from 1614 to 1617, of the duchy from 1615 to 1617, of Loxfield Camden from 1614 to 1617, and of Loxfield Dorset in 1619. Edward Raines was county coroner from 1629 until 1668, coroner of the duchy of Lancaster between 1621 and 1653, and coroner of Loxfield Dorset half-hundred at least from 1656 to 1659. George Courthope, the Hastings rape coroner of 1646–1654 and Loxfield Camden coroner 1647–1664, was also a county coroner between 1648 and 1654 although, as will appear below, an abnormal one.

The pattern for the western county coroners is remarkably similar. The three who held office from 1651 onwards are not known ever to have held other coronerships, but the others held at least one. Henry Peckham, who had been a county coroner and coroner of the bishop of Chichester's liberty under Elizabeth, remained in the first office until 1616 and the second until at least 1613. In 1616 he also held one inquest (**168**) as coroner of the honor of Arundel pro hac vice. Richard Williams, county coroner from 1617 to 1622, was subsequently Arundel honor coroner, from 1624 to 1649, and also jointly held one inquest (**286**) in 1628 as one of the two coroners of the city of Chichester. By contrast, John Eagle was county coroner between 1623 and 1636, having been coroner of Arundel honor in 1618 and 1619, a position which he seems to have resumed briefly in 1623, shortly after taking up his county coronership. The other West Sussex coroners, Albany Stoughton and Anthony Smith, occupied a similarly anomalous position in the

1. C 202/97, no 4.
2. *SCI*, xxiii–xxv.
3. ASSI 35/55/7, m 41.
4. KB 9/738, m 36.

west to that of George Courthope in the east and will likewise be discussed below. Stoughton, who held one inquest (112) as county coroner in 1612, was coroner of the honor of Arundel from 1605 to 1617; and Smith, county coroner in 1620 and 1621, was a Chichester city coroner between 1605 and 1620 (holding his last known city inquest (216) the day before his first known inquest (217) as county coroner) and coroner of the liberty of the bishop of Chichester in 1612.

Hastings rape conformed to the same pattern. Its last two coroners, after 1660, probably held no other coronerships, but their five known predecessors all did. Samuel Playfair, who had been appointed before 1603, seems not to have served elsewhere until 1610. He was coroner of the duchy of Lancaster in Pevensey rape from then until 1612, and possibly until 1613, the last year of his period of office in Hastings rape when his right to be coroner of the rape was challenged in King's Bench.[1] His successor, John Butcher, has already been mentioned as county coroner and coroner of the duchy and of the two Loxfield half-hundreds. John Butcher was Hastings rape coroner from 1614 to 1617, if not longer, but an Alexander Butcher is listed as having attended the assizes of 17 July 1615.[2] It is tempting to assume that Alexander was written in error for John (although it would be a strange error), especially as John Butcher is recorded as having attended the other assizes between 25 July 1614 and 21 July 1617 as coroner of the rape. But Alexander is also said to have attended the same 1615 assizes as coroner of the duchy of Lancaster. The 1615 assizes were held shortly before John Butcher is known to have been duchy coroner and some 18 months after the last known reference to the previous duchy coroner. It is therefore possible that Alexander Butcher was briefly coroner of the duchy and not completely impossible that he had a few months as coroner of Hastings rape, John Butcher's period of office there having been interrupted for some reason. The next known Hastings rape coroner, Thomas Butcher, was coroner there from 1622 until 1645, during which time he had two spells as coroner of the half-hundred of Loxfield Camden, from 1622 to 1623 and from 1641 to 1644. The other Hastings rape coroner, George Courthope, was mentioned in his capacity as county coroner and will be discussed again.

Thomas Woodgate, coroner of the duchy of Lancaster in Pevensey rape from 1589 until 1609, had also been coroner of the liberty of Bexhill before 1603 and may well have been later although there is no evidence for or against it.[3] His successors as duchy coroner have already been discussed in respect of their other coronerships: Samuel Playfair in Hastings rape; Thomas Rickward in the eastern district of the county, Lewes and Bramber rapes and Loxfield Dorset; Alexander Butcher, if he really existed, in Hastings rape; John Butcher in the eastern district, Hastings rape and both Loxfield half-hundreds; and Edward Raines in the eastern district and Loxfield Dorset. John Teynton, who deputised for Raines on one occasion (241) in 1622, was coroner of Lewes and Bramber rapes from 1615 to 1636 and held one inquest (239) in 1622 as deputy coroner of the honor of Arundel; but John Spillett, who held a single inquest (325) in 1633 as duchy coroner pro hac vice, is otherwise unknown.

Of the Loxfield Camden coroners only Thomas Houghton and, unless he is a ghost, William Eagles never held office elsewhere. John Eagles was a county coroner; John Butcher county, Hastings rape, duchy and Loxfield Dorset coroner; Thomas Butcher coroner of Hastings rape; and George Courthope county and Hastings rape coroner. All five known coroners of Loxfield Dorset were also pluralists. John Butcher has just been mentioned; John Aylwin served in the county and in Lewes and Bramber rapes; Thomas Rickward was also coroner of the county and of Lewes and Bramber rapes as well as of the duchy; Edward Raines was county and duchy coroner; and Robert Shoebridge, Loxfield Dorset coroner in 1659 and possibly later, was coroner of Rotherfield hundred between 1657 and 1665 at least. Shoebridge was the only one of the three known Rotherfield hundred coroners who is recorded as having held another coronership.

Under Elizabeth I the same man was usually, but not invariably, coroner of Lewes and Bramber rapes.[4] From 1603 until at least 1653 those two rapes always had the same coroner who was often described in terms of both rapes in the inquests and at assizes; and all but one of the coroners during that period were

1. KB 9/738, m 37.
2. ASSI 35/57/7, m 66.
3. *SCI*, xx.
4. *SCI*, xxv.

also coroners elsewhere. John Aylwin was a county coroner for the eastern district and coroner of Loxfield Dorset; Thomas Rickward was also an eastern district coroner and coroner of the duchy of Lancaster and of Loxfield Dorset; John Teynton, coroner of the two rapes from 1615 to 1636, held two inquests in 1622 as a deputy coroner, one (**239**) in the honor of Arundel and the other (**241**) in the duchy lands in Pevensey rape; and William Baldwin, Lewes and Bramber coroner between 1650 and 1653, was coroner of Arundel honor in the same years. Francis Coomber, coroner of the rapes from 1636 to 1645, is the one exception, although nothing more is known of the official positions of Leonard Crook who held an inquest (**386**) as deputy coroner of Bramber rape in 1644. After 1653 no coroner's name has survived before John Howes. He is called coroner of Arundel and Bramber rapes in the records of his first three inquests, held in 1670 and 1672, but only coroner of Arundel rape for the later ones (1679 to 1683) and on the two occasions, in 1671 and 1679, when he is noted as having attended assizes. All his extant inquests were held in Arundel rape, but it is certain that he was also Bramber rape coroner throughout that time because Henry Chatfield was described as coroner of Arundel and Bramber rapes in his one surviving inquest (**515**), held in 1686 in Bramber rape. The fact that Lewes rape was never mentioned suggests that Howes and Chatfield were not coroners there.

    If one regards Arundel and Bramber rapes as separate coronerships held by the same coroners from 1670, all the coroners of the honor of Arundel were pluralists. George Ardern, coroner of the honor until 1605, was also listed at assizes as coroner of the bishop of Chichester's liberty in July 1604. That is surprising because it would otherwise seem from the assize lists that Henry Peckham had been the bishop's coroner from 1601 to 1613. It is probable, however, that there was a short break in Peckham's coronership in 1604 just as there was in 1612 when Anthony Smith held an inquest (**111**) as the bishop's coroner. As already noted, the next two coroners of the honor, Albany Stoughton and John Eagle, were also county coroners; Richard Williams was both a county and a Chichester city coroner; and William Baldwin was coroner of Lewes and Bramber rapes. The only other coroner of Arundel honor, John Adams, who served there from 1619 to 1621, was coroner of the bishop's liberty from 1617 to 1620. Henry Peckham, who was the honor coroner pro hac vice in 1616, was a county coroner until 1616 and the bishop's coroner until at least 1613, having entered upon both offices before 1603; and John Teynton, who held one inquest (**239**) as deputy coroner in the honor in 1622, held another (**241**) as deputy coroner in the duchy of Lancaster in the same year, during his main coronership of Lewes and Bramber rapes.

    Only three coroners of the Lumley liberty are known and only the last of them, Eusebius Hayes, who was in office there between 1631 and 1642, was coroner elsewhere — in the bishop of Chichester's liberty from 1626 until 1642, or more probably 1644. The last two known coroners of the bishop's liberty, who were in office from 1650, seem not to have held other coronerships, but their five predecessors all did: George Ardern and John Adams in the honor of Arundel; Henry Peckham in the western part of the county and, pro hac vice, in Arundel honor; Anthony Smith in the county and Chichester; and Eusebius Hayes in the Lumley liberty. It is surprising to find any Chichester city coroners holding coronerships in other jurisdictions, but two of the known nine did. Anthony Smith was county coroner and coroner of the bishop's liberty and Richard Williams county and Arundel honor coroner, but William Baldwin was not the earlier coroner of that name in Lewes and Bramber rapes and Arundel honor.

    Under Elizabeth the liberties of Battle and Brede at least sometimes shared a coroner, but that must have been because the same person was lord of both.[1] At the time of their surviving seventeenth-century inquests they were tenurially separate and none of their officiating coroners held office outside his liberty. Similarly the Bosham hundred coroners held no other coronerships, doubtless because the Bosham chamberlains were ex officio coroners and had little leisure for duties elsewhere; and it would have been unthinkable for the cherished administrative isolation of the Cinque Ports to be breached by their officers serving as coroners anywhere but within the confederation. Nevertheless, more than a third of Sussex coroners had two or more jurisdictions in the seventeenth century, so that at any one time there were fewer active coroners than there were coroners' jurisdictions. The result is that there was a group of officials who can be regarded as professional coroners. Not only did they operate over wide areas, but many of them

---

1. *SCI*, xxiii–xxv.

remained in office for many years: Edward Raines for 47 years, Alexander Luxford for 41, Richard Williams 32, John Peachey 30, John Luck 27, John Teynton and John Purfield 21, and Thomas Woodgate 20. In some cases their periods of office may have been slightly longer. Of the eight coroners who certainly served for 20 years or more only John Luck was the coroner of a small area. Thomas Houghton may have had an official life lasting from 1623 to 1649, but his period of office as Loxfield Camden coroner more probably ended in 1641, after 18 years. His only mention as coroner thereafter is as having attended the assizes of 12 March 1649, but that may have been the result of a careless copying of an earlier list. Overall, though, the combination of wide jurisdictions and long working lives must have meant that many of the coroners built up considerable expertise and knowledge. Only the lack of a salary can prevent them from being considered in every respect professional.[1]

When one considers how many coroners held two or more coronerships, it is surprising that they were not sometimes described in terms of a jurisdiction other than the one in which an inquest was held. Some were called coroners of Lewes and Bramber rapes or, later, of Arundel and Bramber rapes, but the two rapes were obviously regarded as a single liberty. The records of the inquests held by Thomas Rickward in the duchy all call him under-coroner of Richard earl of Dorset of the liberty of the duchy of Lancaster in Pevensey rape and of his half-hundred of Loxfield Dorset. The last part of the description is not wrong, merely irrelevant. The only comparable inquest is one (405) held by George Courthope for which he is described as county coroner and coroner of Hastings rape. It will be discussed more fully below.

It is equally surprising how seldom coroners acted outside their jurisdictions. One such occasion was in 1623 when a Mayfield inquest (249) was held jointly by John Butcher as county coroner and Thomas Houghton, coroner of Loxfield Camden half-hundred. It is interesting that Butcher had held the previous inquest (232) there alone, as county coroner in 1622 and Houghton took the next (262) in 1624 as coroner of the half-hundred. The 1623 inquest was the only one taken by two coroners other than in the city of Chichester which always had two coroners. Eleven of the 13 known Chichester inquests were held by both. No franchisal coroner held an inquest outside his liberty as coroner of that liberty with the exception of John Purfield. He held one (516) in 1686 as coroner of Hastings rape at Sedlescombe. Sedlescombe is in Hastings rape but also within the liberty of Battle and Battle coroners had earlier taken two of their four surviving inquests there (201, 236). There must have been a special reason for Purfield's acting there in 1686.

The two county coronerships warrant more detailed consideration. Ever since the thirteenth century Sussex had had two county coroners, one for the three eastern rapes of Hastings, Pevensey and Lewes and the other for Bramber, Arundel and Chichester rapes in the west.[2] That division of the county persisted after 1603 until 1639, from which year the 12 surviving inquests held by county coroners in Bramber rape were all taken by those of the east, the jurisdiction of their western colleagues being limited to Arundel and Chichester rapes. The fact that the new boundary between the two jurisdictions is not known ever to have been disregarded before 1688 suggests that it was established by a formal arrangement. Indeed, there is only one instance in the seventeenth century of a county coroner holding an inquest in the wrong half of the county, possibly because the usual coroner was for some reason unable to attend. That was in 1612 when John Aylwin, coroner for the eastern part, held an inquest (117) at Westhampnett in the far west. It was said to have been taken on the day of the death. Unless the same date was erroneously written twice, Aylwin must have been near to Westhampnett at that time, possibly at Chichester for the county court. There was nothing improper in his acting outside his district: county coroners were elected for the whole county; it was merely for their convenience that the county was divided into two parts.[3]

More unexpected is the fact that both districts seem to have had supernumerary coroners from time to time. One such was George Courthope. He held five inquests as a county coroner, all in Hastings rape of which he was also coroner. The record of the first (405), in 1648, called him county coroner and coroner

1. Coroners were allowed a fee of 13s 4d for holding an inquest, but only if the verdict was murder or manslaughter: *Wiltshire coroners' bills 1752–1796*, ed. R F Hunnisett (Wilts Rec. Soc., XXXVI, 1981 for 1980), xxix.
2. *SAC*, XCVIII, 44–45; SRS, LXXIV, xxiii–xxvii; *SCI*, xix.
3. *SCI*, xix.

of Hastings rape. Two months later he held another (**407**) as Hastings rape coroner, and then four others (**410, 411, 413, 431**), between 1649 and 1654, as county coroner. But for his double description in the first inquest it might have been thought that he had been misdescribed, especially as he was ever listed only as Hastings rape coroner at assizes and Edward Raines was the county coroner of East Sussex and held inquests as such throughout Courthope's period of office. Courthope was therefore an unusual county coroner, but not unique. John Eagles and Thomas Rickward were similar. Neither was listed at assizes as a county coroner but both held inquests in that capacity, although during John Aylwin's period as East Sussex county coroner. Eagles had had a lengthy tenure of office as Loxfield Camden half-hundred coroner, from 1600 to 1612, after which he held one more inquest (**130**) in 1613 at Mayfield in the half-hundred as a county coroner. As already mentioned, it was in 1613 that Eagles's right to act as coroner of the liberty was challenged. Rickward held two inquests as county coroner, both at Cuckfield, one (**114**) on 15 August 1612 and the other (**121**) on 15 February 1613. Cuckfield is in Lewes rape and between 29 March 1613 and 7 February 1614 Rickward held seven inquests as coroner of the rape, one of them (**129**) at Cuckfield.

Albany Stoughton and Anthony Smith were the supernumerary county coroners in West Sussex. Like their eastern counterparts they were never listed as such at assizes. Stoughton took only one inquest (**112**) in that capacity — at Easebourne on 16 April 1612 when Henry Peckham was the traditional county coroner. Easebourne was in the Chichester rape part of the honor of Arundel, and Stoughton held many inquests as coroner of the honor between 1605 and 1617, including one (**93**) in 1610 at Easebourne, but none has survived from July 1610 until September 1612. Anthony Smith's three inquests as county coroner (**217, 226, 229**) were taken on 23 March 1620 and in June 1621, also in the honor of Arundel, during Richard Williams's West Sussex county coronership. Smith is not known ever to have served as coroner of the honor. No inquest held by an honor coroner survives between 15 March 1620, the date of John Adams's last inquest (**215**), and 1628, although John Teynton held one (**239**) as deputy coroner in 1622. Adams defaulted at the assizes of July 1621 because he was sick[1] and it seems that special arrangements had to be made for Arundel honor in the early 1620s. The incapacity of the franchisal coroners cannot account for the four other supernumerary county coroners acting within liberties because they were, or had been, the franchisal coroners. Whatever the reasons for their temporary county coronerships, they clearly occupied them for a particular purpose and their activities were limited to one liberty. That suggests that quo warranto proceedings may have been the reason. Almost certainly the coroners were not elected to their county offices.

The activities of the traditional, elected county coroners remain to be considered. The geographical patterns presented by their surviving inquests vary markedly. Apart from his excursion to Westhampnett discussed above, John Aylwin, the first coroner in the eastern rapes, has left only three inquests (**82, 107, 110**), all held at Framfield which was in Pevensey rape but not part of the duchy of Lancaster. John Butcher's four inquests, however, were all taken within liberties. The first (**188**) was at Eastbourne in March 1617. Eastbourne was within the duchy and duchy coroners normally operated there (e.g. **256, 271**); and Butcher himself held inquests elsewhere as duchy coroner, including one (**186**) earlier and one (**191**) later in 1617. His second inquest (**222**) as county coroner was at Northiam in Hastings rape in 1621. He had earlier been Hastings rape coroner. The other two (**232, 249**) were taken at Mayfield, the second with Thomas Houghton, coroner of the half-hundred of Loxfield Camden in which Mayfield lies. Once again, Butcher himself had earlier been coroner of the half-hundred. Edward Raines and Alexander Luxford ranged more widely. As well as those which they held outside liberties, they took a few inquests in Loxfield Dorset and a considerable number in the duchy lands in Pevensey rape and also in Lewes and Bramber rapes, although most of them in years in which no liberty coroner is known to have acted and, with one exception (**369**), the Bramber inquests do not begin until 1646.

The pattern for the west is similar. Again the first county coroner, Henry Peckham, acted only outside liberties, as did his successor, Richard Williams. John Eagle's first inquest (**255**) was held in the honor of Arundel, but that was in 1624 when the unsettled state of the honor coronership, already mentioned in connection with the operation of a supernumerary county coroner and a deputy coroner in the honor, still

---

1. ASSI 35/63/6, m 56.

persisted. Eagle's other inquests were all taken outside liberties. So was the first (**391**) held by Richard Smith, but of his other three, two (**400, 409**) were held in the honor of Arundel and the third (**403**) in the Lumley liberty. Of the last two coroners whose records survive, Richard Aylwin held all his inquests in Arundel honor and John Peachey most of his there and in the Lumley liberty but also one (**505**) in the bishop of Chichester's liberty, in 1680 when there was no vacancy.[1] No Lumley coroners' inquests survive beyond 1633 and none held by Arundel honor coroners between 1638 and 1670. Those held by Smith, Aylwin and Peachey are all from between 1648 and 1670 and therefore fill those gaps.

It would require a detailed study of the relevant liberties to attempt to ascertain why county coroners operated within some of them at certain times and why, at others, supernumerary county coroners carried out the duties of franchisal coroners. Here it must suffice to note the extreme complexity of the overlapping nature of the coronerships in the seventeenth century.

The Inquests

Table IX lists year by year the various verdicts returned by the jurors at the 520 inquests. The verdicts total 521 because one inquest (**54**) resulted from the murder of her three children by a mother followed by her suicide. Another inquest (**234**) was held on view of six bodies, a third (**42**) on three and six (**126, 204, 257, 330, 336, 456**) on two. The 520 inquests thus resulted from 536 deaths. When one counts all the dead bodies, the number of murders increases to 100 and the accidental deaths to 180, the other totals remaining the same.

There would be little to gain by comparing the total numbers of each category of verdict. Not only are the surviving records an unknown, although certainly small, percentage of the inquests that must have been held, but the proportion of homicide verdicts is inflated by the fact that there are more records of inquests on the assize files than on the files of King's Bench during the later decades of the century. Nevertheless a few interesting statistics emerge. No fewer than 37 of the 96 murder verdicts were for infanticide and, because two inquests (**126, 456**) were on twins, 39 of the 100 murder victims were new-born babies. Between 1650 and 1688 17 of the 39 murder inquests and 18 of the 40 deaths were from infanticide. There are a few other cases in which the inquest juries returned verdicts other than murder or failed to agree on a verdict when a baby had died shortly after birth but the grand jury indicted the mother for murder (e.g. **506**). In addition, two children, of 8 weeks and 6 months, were found at the inquests (**81, 512**) to have been murdered by men, one of whom was called the father and the other almost certainly was. The 37 definite infanticides were, with a single exception, committed by unmarried mothers, with spinsters greatly outnumbering widows; and all but one killed their children on the day of their birth. There are indictments for infanticide on the assize files for which no record of an inquest survives.[2]

Only five (**8, 280, 448, 510, 511**) of the 73 suicides were found to have been committed by persons whose minds were unbalanced. The rest were felonious. One case (**295**) is listed among the murders, not the suicides, because the inquest jurors' verdict was murder by John Beyond the Moon, one of the more exotically named of the fictitious killers. That verdict was not believed and the court of King's Bench ordered the sheriff to hold an inquisition to ascertain if the deceased had committed suicide. It found that he had and his goods and chattels were valued at over £100, which probably accounts for the inquest verdict. Local men were reluctant to assist in the forfeiture of a neighbour's possessions. Table X lists the 73 suicide inquests by the methods by which the suicides were committed and also by the sex of the deceased. The total of 74 results from one woman — the one who had just murdered her three children — having first cut her throat and then drowned herself (**54**). Hanging and drowning were by far the most common methods of committing suicide, as they had been in the previous century, with drowning the method most popular with women. Both in Elizabeth I's reign and during the whole of the sixteenth

1. Le Neve, *Fasti 1541–1857: Chichester*, 3.
2. e.g. *CAR*, nos 200, 221, 647.

century almost exactly twice as many men as women killed themselves.[1] There were relatively fewer female suicides in the seventeenth century, although the smaller totals make the variation of no significance. The seasonal pattern of the suicides is quite different from that of the earlier ones. In the sixteenth century there were nearly twice as many from March to August as from September to February[2] whereas in the seventeenth the numbers were virtually equal — 37 between March and August, 36 between September and February. The seventeenth century saw 44 suicides in the first six months of the year but only 29 in the second half. A full break-down by months will be found in Table XI.

Coroners were required to hold inquests into all deaths occurring in gaol. The verdict was usually death by the visitation of God, which meant from natural causes. The 520 surviving inquests include 72 whose verdicts were natural death, 38 of which, slightly more than half, occurred in gaol. The picture is distorted by the absence of inquest records on the King's Bench files in the second half of the century. There are only ten natural deaths from between 1642 and 1688 and only two of those occurred in gaol. Three other deaths occurred in gaol: one suicide (**34**), one accidental death (**238**) and one homicide (**386**). One death occurred in Arundel gaol (**34**), one in Hastings gaol (**499**), two in Rye gaol (**147, 238**), two more in Lewes gaol, both in January 1610 (**84, 85**), and all the others in the county gaol at Horsham. It was doubtless because infectious diseases spread rapidly among prisoners, whose resistance was likely to be low, that coroners sometimes held more than one inquest on dead prisoners on the same day. They once held three with the same jurors (**1–3**), once three with different jurors (**47–49**), once two with different jurors (**318, 319**) and twice two with the same jurors (**29, 30, 316, 317**). They never held a single inquest for more than one prisoner as their Elizabethan predecessors had sometimes done.[3] Two still-births were categorized as natural deaths (**19, 506**) and therefore those two and a third which resulted in an inquest (**10**) although not expressly so called are counted among the 34 deaths from natural causes other than those of prisoners.

This is not the place to analyse the homicides and accidental deaths or the inventories of the goods and chattels of felons and suicides which are sometimes included in or attached to the records of the inquests. To do so would entail the writing of part of the social and economic history of the period. The framework of such a study will be found under the relevant headings of the subject index. But three inquests of particular interest demand a brief mention here. One (**259** and frontispiece) was held in 1624 as a result of a cricketing accident. It is one of a number resulting from sporting activities, including football (**145, 320**) and trap-ball (**112**). Its importance lies not only in the fact that it is one of the earliest references to cricket and that by 1624 it was regarded as a 'customary game' but also in the information it provides about the rules by which it was played, at least in Sussex. Today a batsman is given out if he hits the ball twice except in defence of his wicket, but in early seventeenth-century Sussex a batsman could legally pursue the ball which he had hit into the air and strike it again before it had fallen to the ground; and from the account in the inquest it was clearly to his advantage to do so. It was equally clearly dangerous, and it may well be that this and similar fatalities led to a change in the rules. The present editor has commented on this case at greater length elsewhere.[4]

The second inquest (**127**) was taken at Rye in 1613. The death had been occasioned by a quarrel over a game of cards called 'the new cut'. The evidence of a number of witnesses given at the inquest has survived, including that of four surgeons. One was an 87-year-old Londoner and the others were of Rye. They had opened the skull of the deceased, found it to be cracked and broken and concluded that death had occurred by reason of the great amount of 'contused or bruised blood' that lay upon the brain. This is the earliest Sussex case of medical evidence being presented at an inquest and of an autopsy having been performed in preparation for it. Similar evidence survives from 1618 (**542**), although the inquest at which it was presented was not copied into the Rye registers and the original is not extant. The inquest would have been upon the bodies of a married woman and her unborn child. It was alleged that the woman had

1. *SCI*, xxxv–xxxvi.
2. *SCI*, xxxvii.
3. *SCI*, xxxv.
4. *SNQ*, XVI, 217–221, 319–320. See also *The Cricket Quarterly*, IV, 249–253.

been kneed in the abdomen before her death. One of the surgeons who testified, John Keevil, had also given evidence in 1613. He deposed that, on the opening of the woman's body, he found that the female child in her womb had her skull broken in one place and bruised in another and that the right side of the head near the ear was bruised in three places and the skin was off, but he could not say how mother or child had come to her death. Another Rye surgeon agreed with Keevil concerning the findings on view of the child, but he had not been present when the mother's body was opened; and a woman testified that the child was dead when removed from her body. There was medical evidence at two slightly later Rye inquests. In 1637 two physicians of the town testified concerning a woman who had died of dropsy and whom they had attended during her last illness (**358**). Once again, John Keevil was one of the witnesses. In 1641 it was Francis Keevil, also a Rye surgeon, who gave evidence, although not on the day of the opening of the inquest (**376**), concerning his examination of a man killed during a quarrel over a tavern bill. It is, however, the first two cases that are of greatest interest. To find such autopsies two centuries later in some parts of the country would be noteworthy.[1] To find them so early in Rye shows a degree of sophistication probably unknown in the rest of the county. Witnesses were, however, increasingly common at inquests in the county at large, their names being endorsed on the inquest records.

The third inquest demanding attention was also taken at Rye, in September 1652 (**424**). The Rye officials held it although the death had occurred on board a frigate on the high sea; but, although the case ultimately went to the High Court of Admiralty, the legality of the inquest was never challenged because the Cinque Ports were unique in having long since established their right to act in lieu of the Admiralty coroner.[2] That a death dealt with at a Sussex inquest resulted in a trial in the High Court of Admiralty, rather than, as usual, at assizes, in King's Bench or, earlier, in Star Chamber, is interesting in itself, but its nature and circumstances are more so. The frigate was at the time engaged in action against the Dutch fleet during the first Anglo-Dutch war and the evidence given in the Admiralty court goes into considerable detail about the engagement. The death was caused by a shot fired by the captain of the frigate. He either fired his pistol accidentally while trying to quell an incipient mutiny, according to his own account, or was guilty of murder as evidence given at Rye by other officers of the ship implies. Exceptionally, the inquest is of more than local concern.

It is difficult to assess how efficiently the Sussex coroners performed their duties in the seventeenth century. No doubt they regularly attended the monthly meetings of the county court: their absence could not have passed unnoticed and their presence was essential for the promulgation of outlawries. It was also unusual for the county coroners and the coroners of the larger liberties not to attend the half-yearly assizes, at least during the first half of the century. It is impossible to know how many inquests each coroner held because relatively few of the records survive; and it is therefore impossible to guess how many he should have held and did not. However, coroners continued to act when deaths obviously had no administrative or financial ramifications, even in the second half of the century after the system for preserving the records had broken down. The inquests seem generally to have been properly conducted and the records to have been presented in an acceptable form, probably with the use of formularies as their reasonable uniformity would suggest. Few of the records were found to have defects, and then they were mostly corrected with minor additions or changes. Just two (**102, 171**) were declared void at assizes because of their insufficiency. The first was redrafted in a more conventional form and the second was replaced for the purposes of a possible trial by a grand jury indictment. The inquest (**295**) mentioned above, which found that a murder had been committed by John Beyond the Moon, was followed by a further inquisition taken by the sheriff not because of procedural or verbal irregularities but presumably because the verdict was not considered to be credible.

Perhaps the most telling evidence as to the coroners' efficiency is the length of time which elapsed between the death, or the finding of the body, and the inquest. For 30 of the 520 inquests one or, occasionally,

1. J D J Havard, *The detection of secret homicide* (London, 1960), 1–10.
2. K M E Murray, *The constitutional history of the Cinque Ports* (Manchester, 1935),126–128, 137. See also *Select pleas in the court of Admiralty*, ed. R G Marsden, II (Selden Soc., XI, 1897), xxi–xxxii; *Hale and Fleetwood on Admiralty jurisdiction*, ed. M J Prichard and D E C Yale (Selden Soc., CVIII, 1993 for 1992), 89, 111, 146–149.

both dates are unknown. In the remaining 490 cases the inquests were held on average 8 days after the deaths. That average, however, is inflated by a few instances of exceptionally long delays. If one excludes the eight cases (**106, 120, 141, 232, 295, 306, 342, 344**) when the inquest was delayed for more than 100 days, ranging from 102 to 348, the average for the rest is reduced to 5 days. Even that figure may underestimate the coroners' speed of action. The only relevant dates normally supplied are those of death and inquest, but in some cases the body might not have been found on the day of death. That is particularly likely when death occurred by drowning, which accounts for some of the exceptional delays (e.g. **120**). In other cases the coroners may not have been summoned on the day of death or of the discovery of the body. County coroners might have been at the county court, perhaps in the other half of the county; any coroner might have been at assizes; and those with more than one jurisdiction could well have been occupied elsewhere. Some dates, either of death or of inquest, may have been copied incorrectly. Finally, the date assigned to the inquest is almost certainly sometimes the day of the last sitting, there having been one or more earlier sessions which are unrecorded.[1] The only inquest certainly known to have been adjourned is one whose records survive merely in the form of draft notes (**475**). Given such imponderables, what is surprising is not that a lengthy period seems sometimes to have elapsed between death and inquest but that so many inquests were held either on the day of death or within one or two days of it. The evidence of the inquests therefore reinforces the general impression of the coroners' conscientiousness.

Table XII lists the minimum, maximum and average number of days between death, or the finding of the body, and inquest for every jurisdiction. As might be expected, the lowest averages are for the towns and smaller liberties where no great distances were involved. Brede is the exception, but it is represented by only three inquests, two of which experienced extreme delays, of 77 and 211 days (**298, 342**). The larger liberties show fairly uniform figures, the bishop of Chichester's average being inflated by the 348 days' delay in one case (**120**). Because of the imponderables mentioned above, it would be unfair to single out individual coroners for praise or blame on the basis of these figures.

One vital element of the inquest system requires a brief discussion: the jurors. A panel of 24 men was usually summoned.[2] In two cases (**197, 229**), both in the honor of Arundel, all 24 served, as did more than 20 on rare occasions elsewhere; but the average size of juries for the county as a whole was 14. As shown by Table XIII, which gives the minimum, maximum and average number of jurors, there were no great variations in average size between jurisdictions. Individual coroners could, however, make a difference. For example, until 1668 the county coroners of the three eastern rapes held inquests attended by an average of 13 jurors whereas those of the last coroner, Alexander Luxford, were served on average by 17. The rare occasions when fewer than 12 are recorded — 9 was the smallest number (**56**) — can almost certainly be explained by the omission of one or more names in copying. They are probably balanced by a juror being occasionally included twice, as when a name is repeated with no occupation, residence or other qualification provided to indicate that there are two different people of the same name (e.g. **69**). When a juror was described by his residence or occupation, which occurred much less commonly than under Elizabeth I,[3] there was more often than not no one else of the same name serving with him (e.g. **21, 146**), although there might have been one on the full panel. In other cases such descriptions distinguished two similarly named jurors (e.g. **203**). There were three men named Richard Bridger on one jury (**229**), distinguished as senior, junior and of Tye House. Gentlemen seem to have been usually so styled. The first juror, the foreman, was often a gentleman; sometimes the first two (e.g. **26**) and once the first three (**505**) were. One foreman was a physician (**504**). Two Rye inquests (**414, 415**) are exceptional in that the foreman is entered apart from the other jurors who are arranged in groups of from two to four, doubtless according to the wards which they represented. That was a more common feature of Rye inquests of the sixteenth century.[4]

Rye and the other towns of the Cinque Ports would never have recruited jurors from beyond their boundaries, although Rye jurors are expressly stated as being Rye men on only seven occasions (**376, 379, 382–384, 387, 402**) and only once was a Hastings jury said to comprise men of Hastings (**103**). Winchelsea

1. *SCI*, xxxviii.
2. *SCI*, xli.
3. *SCI*, xliv–xlv.
4. SRS, LXXIV, xli; *SCI*, xliv.

and Seaford jurors were never so defined. Half of the Chichester inquests describe their jurors as being of the city, which must also have been the case with the others. The records of two Battle inquests (**236, 243**), one Lumley liberty (**326**) and one Loxfield Dorset inquest (**451**) describe the jurors as men of the liberty. At one Bosham inquest (**284**) the jurors were of Bosham and three named neighbouring townships which were in the parish of Bosham. Brede showed greater variation. One set of jurors was said to be of Brede (**298**), one of the hundred of Brede (**342**) and a third of Brede and three neighbouring townships (unnamed) in the county and the liberty (**502**). The wording of the last suggests that some of the jurors were from outside the liberty. Similarly, while some juries for inquests held in Rotherfield hundred were described as consisting of men of the hundred (e.g. **276, 518**), others were apparently empanelled from the hundred and the county (e.g. **332, 354**), presumably from within and outside the liberty. Loxfield Camden half-hundred shows even greater variations. Some juries were said to be of the half-hundred (e.g. **108**) and others of the half-hundred and the county (**463, 464**). There were only three parishes in the half-hundred — Mayfield, Wadhurst and part of Lamberhurst. Sometimes the jurors were all from one of those places, that at which the inquest was held (e.g. **32**, Wadhurst; **51**, Mayfield). At other times they came from two of the parishes and the record states in which parish each juror lived (e.g.**71**, Wadhurst and Lamberhurst; **79**, Mayfield and Wadhurst) and on one occasion (**88**) they were from all three. For one Loxfield Camden inquest (**109**) the jurors were each described as from Mayfield, Wadhurst or Burwash. Burwash was not in the half-hundred but in Hastings rape.

For only three inquests held in the bishop of Chichester's liberty is it known from where the jurors came. On one occasion they were all from Oving, the place at which the inquest was held (**207**). The other two records specify the places of residence of each juror — three places in one (**212**) and six in the other (**187**). The coroner was John Adams who took four inquests as coroner of the honor of Arundel and again the records state the places the jurors came from, ranging from as few as two (**206**) to as many as six (**213**). Some of the inquests held by Richard Williams as coroner of the honor record that the jurors were of Rotherbridge hundred (**365**), Easebourne hundred and the county (**362**) and the liberty of Arundel and the county (**360**). It is surprising to find that a liberty as large as the honor of Arundel needed to recruit jurors from beyond its borders, if that is how 'the county' should be interpreted. In another inquest, of 1683 (**507**), the jurors were recorded as from Arundel rape and the county. That was held by John Howes, some of whose other juries were from the rape alone (e.g. **506**). There were special reasons for jurors at two Hastings rape inquests to be taken from the rape and the body of the county. One (**356**) was held at Wadhurst, presumably in that small part of the parish which was in Hastings rape, the rest being in Loxfield Camden half-hundred in Pevensey rape. The other (**405**) was taken by George Courthope and was the occasion, mentioned above, when he officiated as county and Hastings rape coroner. In some of the later inquests the jurors are described as of the rape (e.g. **516**). Francis Coomber held four inquests as Bramber rape coroner. At two of them the jurors were called jurors of the rape (**364, 372**). The second was held at Horsham, as were the other two (**371, 375**) when the jurors came from Horsham alone. The jurors for the inquests which Coomber took as coroner of Lewes rape were sometimes said to be of that rape (e.g. **367**) but on other occasions were not described.

The records of the county coroners' inquests seldom state from where the jurors came. The exceptions were two (**255, 258**) held by John Eagle when it was the venue and three neighbouring townships, which were named; one (**421**) by Richard Aylwin when it was the venue, Petworth, alone; and one (**448**) by John Peachey when it was the venue and five neighbouring townships, again named. It is for only 15 per cent of the 520 inquests that we are told where the jurors lived, and then only loosely in many cases. Nevertheless it is clear that they lived either in the town or village where the inquest was held or there and in the immediate neighbourhood — in the neighbouring townships, as in the middle ages.[1] Naturally, the more limited the area and the more frequent the inquests the more often men had to serve as jurors. The inhabitants of Rye, Hastings and Horsham were called upon most often and the same jurors can be found on a fair number of their inquests. Two or three Horsham inquests were sometimes held on dead prisoners on the same day when the same jury might be used throughout (e.g. **1–3**), although one or two jurors might be

---

1. Hunnisett, *Medieval coroner*, 13–19.

SUSSEX INQUESTS

changed from inquest to inquest (e.g. **47–49**). The only other places at which coroners held two inquests on the same day were Duncton (**94, 95**), when the juries were slightly different, and Hailsham, (**418, 419**), when the same jurors were used. Having held the Duncton inquests, the coroner, Albany Stoughton, made a lengthy journey to Slinfold where he held another (**96**) on the same day, but naturally with a different jury. Edward Raines took one inquest (**351**) at Framfield on 7 October 1636 and another (**352**) at Uckfield on 26 October. Uckfield and Framfield are close together, but it is still surprising, given the lapse of time, that the same jurors were used on both occasions. They were even recorded in the same order. There was probably a limited number of suitable people from whom juries could be constituted, and even fewer who were content to serve. Local historians will doubtless recognize many of the jurors. It would, for instance, be good to know if the Thomas Boorer who was the subject of a Warnham inquest (**160**) on 2 September 1615, after being killed in an accident at Capel, was the man of that name who had been a juror on another Warnham inquest (**152**) less than three months before; and if Francis Pankhurst, a Mayfield juror in 1629 (**306**), was the Francis Pankhurst of Mayfield, mercer, who had been acquitted at the East Grinstead assizes of July 1623 of negligently selling poison instead of medicine to a woman with the result that her husband died.[1]

Editorial Note

The inquests printed below are presented in the same form as were those in the previous volume.[2] They are fully calendared, which means that nothing has been omitted apart from unnecessary repetition and some common form. The more long-winded the originals, the more they have been curtailed; the more succinct ones have been pruned less. The inevitable result is that the calendared text suggests that the original records are more uniform than they really are. On average, the length of the inquests has been reduced by about three-quarters. Most of the originals are in Latin with occasional words or phrases in the vernacular, in some cases following the Latin equivalent and in others in place of it. All such vernacular words and phrases are preserved in the calendared text and printed in single inverted commas. An Act of November 1650 abolished the use of Latin and French for all formal documents from 1 January 1651 and it remained in force until abrogated at the Restoration.[3] The first two Sussex inquests surviving from 1651 (**418, 419**), both held on 11 March, were nevertheless written in Latin; but the records of the next 33 (**420–452**), held between 21 May 1651 and 15 November 1659, are entirely in English. One earlier Winchelsea inquest (**385**) is also wholly in English, as are the verdicts of 30 Rye and 2 Hastings inquests. They have all been calendared in modern English, with only occasional words and phrases kept as in the records, within single inverted commas, either because of their unusual interest or, when space would not have been saved by changing them, to give the flavour of the originals.

Just as no matter of substance, however small or seemingly unimportant, has been omitted from the calendared text, so every person and place has been included, with one exception. As already noted, the names of lords of liberties have been excluded when they are mentioned merely to describe the coroners, as in the regular formula 'Inquest taken … before A, coroner of B of his liberty of C'. Instead, the lords of all relevant liberties are listed in Table VIII. Witnesses are, however, printed, immediately after the names of the jurors, although they are never in the body of the original inquest but written on the dorse. Surnames of all persons are printed in their manuscript forms, except that when a name occurs with two or more different spellings in the same record the one closest to the most common modern spelling has been adopted. The spellings used in the text of an inquest have also been used in the note which follows it. Forenames have been translated from the Latin into the forms most common today. Wherever possible places have been given their modern spellings. Those which could not be identified or whose names have not survived — usually minor features such as fields, streams and woods — have been left in their manuscript

1. ASSI 35/67/7, m 44; *CAR*, no 648.
2. *SCI*, xlvi–xlviii.
3. L C Hector, *The handwriting of English documents*, 2nd edn (London, 1966), 22–23.

spellings, or what appear to be the least aberrant of those spellings, within single quotes.

If an inquest record is damaged or is written wholly or partly in English, those facts are noted in square brackets immediately after the calendared version. There then follows the document reference and, again in square brackets, any work in which the inquest has previously been published. Most inquests were delivered to assizes or King's Bench where quite a lot of them gave rise to subsequent proceedings. All such information is summarized, in square brackets, in one or more paragraphs beneath the inquest. References to the sources of this information are listed at the end of each note. Cross-references to other inquests in the volume come first in bold type, then references to other manuscripts in alpha-numerical order, and finally printed works in alphabetical order.

There are three indexes. By far the largest is the Index of Persons. People have been entered under the most common modern spellings of their surnames or, for names now largely restricted to Sussex, the spellings now most popular there. Inevitably a few names have had to be left in their manuscript forms because they seem not to have survived or because their spellings are too outlandish to be recognizable. There are cross-references from all spellings occurring in the calendar to the chosen modern form unless they would have been adjacent to it. All forms used in the calendar and any others occurring in the original inquests, but not those found solely in supporting documents, are printed in alphabetical order in round brackets after the chosen modern spelling. The index has separate subentries for different people with the same surname and forename. Inevitably, local historians and genealogists will discover that occasionally two or even more people have been conflated or references to the same person have been wrongly separated.

In the Index of Places all cities, towns and ancient parishes have their own entries. So have all other substantial settlements — hamlets, townships and manors — and they have cross-references from their town or parish. Lesser place names, such as fields, woods and streams, are indexed as subentries under the towns or parishes in which they lie, with cross-references from their own names if it is not clear from the text where they should be found. Spellings used in the inquest records, but not those occurring only in supporting documents, are printed in alphabetical order in round brackets after the modern forms of each name. Because only the modern spellings appear in the text, there are no cross-references from obsolete to modern ones. Unidentified places and minor places with no known modern forms are indexed under their manuscript spellings in single inverted commas, under a town or parish when that is known, otherwise with entries of their own. When the records contain two or more spellings of such a place, it is indexed under that which looks the most modern, the others following in round brackets. Only places outside Sussex are assigned their counties. There are references from those counties to all the places within them.

The Index of Subjects has already been discussed. It is preceded by a note listing the main headings under which most subjects are grouped.

TABLE I

Present whereabouts of the inquests

Year	Assizes	Chancery	King's Bench	Cinque Ports	Total
1603	–	–	10	1 (H)	11
1604	4	–	5	1 (H)	10
1605	3	–	15	2 (H, R)	20
1606	–	–	16	3 (R)	19
1607	1	–	7	2 (H, R)	10
1608	1	–	4	–	5
1609	3	–	5	–	8
1610	–	1	14	–	15
1611	1	–	4	2 (H)	7
1612	3	–	10	–	13
1613	4	–	15	3 (R, R, H)	22
1614	2	–	4	1 (R)	7
1615	4	–	14	2 (R)	20
1616	2	–	14	1 (H)	17
1617	5	–	2	–	7
1618	1	–	6	–	7
1619	–	–	12	–	12
1620	–	–	9	1 (H)	10
1621	4	–	6	1 (R)	11
1622	7	–	3	3 (R, R, S)	13
1623	1	–	5	3 (R, H, H)	9
1624	4	–	6	2 (R)	12
1625	1	–	1	1 (H)	3
1626	5	–	6	2 (H)	13
1627	–	–	3	–	3
1628	8	–	4	4 (R, R, H, H)	16
1629	1	–	3	2 (R, H)	6
1630	–	–	5	3 (R, H, W)	8
1631	1	–	4	2 (R, H)	7
1632	–	–	2	1 (H)	3
1633	3	–	2	–	5
1634	3	–	9	1 (R)	13
1635	3	–	1	–	4
1636	3	–	2	2 (R, W)	7
1637	7	–	–	1 (R)	8
1638	4	–	1	1 (W)	6
1639	1	–	2	–	3
1640	2	–	1	–	3
1641	2	–	2	1 (R)	5
1642	2	–	–	3 (R)	5
1643	–	–	–	1 (R)	1
1644	1	–	–	1 (W)	2
1646	4	–	2	1 (R)	7
1647	3	–	2	–	5
1648	9	–	1	1 (R)	11
1649	–	–	2	–	2
1650	4	–	–	2 (R)	6
1651	5	–	–	1 (R)	6
1652	–	–	–	1 (R)	1
1653	2	–	–	3 (R)	5
1654	2	–	1	2 (R)	5
1655	2	–	–	1 (R)	3
1656	1	–	–	2 (H, R)	3

TABLE I (contd)

Year	Assizes	Chancery	King's Bench	Cinque Ports	Total
1657	3	–	1	2 (R)	6
1658	2	–	1	–	3
1659	1	–	1	1 (R)	3
1661	–	–	3	–	3
1662	2	–	2	–	4
1663	1	–	–	1 (H)	2
1664	1	–	2	–	3
1665	2	–	1	1 (H)	4
1666	3	–	2	1 (H)	6
1667	2	–	–	1 (H)	3
1668	1	–	–	–	1
1670	3	–	–	–	3
1671	1	–	1	1 (H)	3
1672	4	–	–	–	4
1673	1	–	–	–	1
1674	1	–	–	1 (H)	2
1676	1	–	–	2 (R, H)	3
1677	2	–	–	–	2
1778	1	–	–	1 (H)	2
1679	2	–	–	1 (H)	3
1680	3	–	–	1 (H)	4
1682	–	–	1	–	1
1683	1	–	–	–	1
1684	1	–	–	–	1
1685	2	–	2	–	4
1686	6	–	–	–	6
1687	1	–	–	–	1
1688	1	–	–	–	1
Total	178	1	259	82	520

TABLE II

Inquests delivered to assizes

Inquest numbers	Inquest dates	Assizes	Inquest numbers	Inquest dates	King's Bench
–	No file	3 Oct 1603	1–7	3 Apr – 30 Sept 1603	Mich 1603
12–14	16 May – 1 June 1604	Lent 1604	9, 10	1 Oct, 20 Dec 1603	Easter 1604
20	19 Nov 1604	13 July 1604	15–17	17 June – 11 July 1604	Mich 1604
26, 27, 31	9 Mar – 16 Apr 1605	8 Mar 1605	18, 19, 22	9 Sept 1604 – 5 Jan 1605	Easter 1605
–	No file	8 July 1605	23, 28–30, 32, 33	19 Feb – 26 June 1605	Mich 1605
–	No file	Lent 1606	34–41, 43–49	20 July 1605 – 17 Mar 1606	Easter 1606
–	No file	Summer 1606	51–55	9 Apr – 18 July 1606	Mich 1606
–	–	13 Mar 1607	56, 58, 59	27 July – 24 Oct 1606	Easter 1607
–	–	13 Mar 1607	60	29 Dec 1606	Mich 1607
	No file	13 July 1607	61	29 Apr 1607	Easter 1608
65, 73	3 Aug 1607, 19 Feb 1608	22 Feb 1608	62, 63, 67–72, 74	27 May 1607 – 21 Feb 1608	Easter 1608
	No file	Summer 1608	75	9 Mar 1608	Mich 1608
77	25 Apr 1609	17 July 1609	76, 78, 80, 81	26 Mar – 30 June 1609	Mich 1609
82, 83	28 July, 27 Aug 1609	23 Mar 1610	84, 85	11, 13 Jan 1610	Easter 1610
–	No file	Summer 1610	86–91, 93–96	20 Feb – 27 July 1610	Mich 1610
	–	18 Feb 1611	92, 99	13 July 1610, 8 Jan 1611	Easter 1611
102	26 Mar 1611	24 June 1611	101	12 Mar 1611	Mich 1611
107, 108	30 Jan, 6 Feb 1612	24 Feb 1612	104–106, 109	31 July 1611 – 17 Feb 1612	Easter 1612
112	16 Apr 1612	13 July 1612	110, 111, 113	19 Mar – 12 July 1612	Mich 1612
122	19 Feb 1613	8 Mar 1613	114, 116, 117, 119–121	15 Aug 1612 – 15 Feb 1613	Easter 1613
123, 126, 129	29 Mar – 27 May 1613	4 July 1613	115, 118, 124, 125, 128, 130, 131	20 Sept 1612 – 30 June 1613	Mich 1613
	No file	Lent 1614	133–137, 139–143	29 July 1613 – 21 Feb 1614	Easter 1614
145, 146	8 June, 1 July 1614	25 July 1614	144	27 Mar 1614	Mich 1614
148	5 Jan 1615	27 Feb 1615	–		Easter 1615
150	8 June 1615	17 July 1615	149, 151–153, 155, 156	30 May – 11 July 1615	Mich 1615

TABLE II (contd)

Inquest numbers		Inquest dates	Assizes	Inquest numbers	Inquest dates	King's Bench
157, 166		19 July, 20 Nov 1615	26 Feb 1616	159–161	31 Aug – 26 Dec 1615	Easter 1616
			26 Feb 1616	163, 167		Mich 1616
170, 171		18 Mar, 24 Apr 1616	8 July 1616	158, 162	20 July, 9 Oct 1615	Mich 1616
185, 186		8, 26 Jan 1617	3 Mar 1617	164, 168, 172, 174	23 Oct 1615 – 20 May 1616	Easter 1617
188, 189		7 Mar, 12 Apr 1617	21 July 1617	179, 180, 182–184, 187	13 Sept 1616 – 29 Jan 1617	Mich 1617
191, 193		3 Dec 1617, 21 Jan 1618	23 Feb 1618	181	8 Oct 1616	Easter 1618
	No file		Summer 1618	192	10 Jan 1618	Mich 1618
	No file		Lent 1619	195–198	30 Apr – 25 May 1618	Easter 1619
	No file		Summer 1619	199	17 Feb 1619	Mich 1619
			Lent 1620	200, 201, 203	22 Mar – 19 June 1619	Easter 1620
–			17 July 1620	204, 206, 207, 210, 212, 213	6 July 1619 – 18 Jan 1620	Mich 1620
222, 224–226		2 Apr – 9 June 1621	2 July 1621	215–217	15–23 Mar 1620	Mich 1621
–			4 Mar 1622	223, 229	3 May, 22 June 1621	Easter 1622
235–237, 239		19 Apr – 28 June 1622	22 July 1622	233	9 Feb 1622	Mich 1622
232, 242, 243		14 Jan – 12 Nov 1622	3 Mar 1623	–	28 Oct 1622 – 14 Feb 1623	Easter 1623
	No file		14 July 1623	241, 244, 245, 249, 250	23 Apr, 10 June 1623	Mich 1623
253		8 Nov 1623	8 Mar 1624	–		Easter 1624
258, 259, 263, 264		10 Sept – 13 Dec 1624	7 Mar 1625	262	3 Nov 1624	Easter 1625
	No file		Lent 1626	267	21 Sept 1625	Easter 1626
268, 271–273, 275, 278		12 Oct 1625 – 6 July 1626	10 July 1626	274, 276	24 Apr, 29 May 1626	Mich 1626
–			5 Mar 1627	279–281	7 Aug – 26 Dec 1626	Easter 1627
	No file		Summer 1627	282	12 June 1627	Mich 1627
286, 287, 290, 292		Mar – 9 July 1628	Lent 1628	283, 285.	5 July 1627, 22 Feb 1628	Easter 1628
294, 296, 298, 300		30 July – 14 Nov 1628	14 July 1628	–	–	Mich 1628
			9 Mar 1629	297	30 Sept 1628	Easter 1629
302		15 May 1629	6 July 1629	293	28 July 1628	Mich 1629
	No file		Lent 1630	303, 306, 307	27 May 1629 – 4 Feb 1630	Easter 1630
	No file		Lent 1631	312, 314, 316–319	16 Nov 1630 – 25 Feb 1631	Mich 1631
320		26 Apr 1631	18 July 1631	–	–	Mich 1631
	No file		Lent 1632	322, 323	11 Jan, 27 Feb 1632	Easter 1632

TABLE II (contd)

Inquest numbers	Inquest dates	Assizes	Inquest numbers	Inquest dates	King's Bench
326	11 July 1633	29 July 1633	–		Mich 1633
327, 328	23 Aug, 23 Oct 1633	6 Mar 1634	331, 332, 337	28 Mar – 26 Aug 1634	Easter 1634
339, 341, 342	21 Oct – 20 Dec 1634	2 Mar 1635	No file		Easter 1635
344	21 May 1635	6 July 1635	No file		Mich 1635
345, 346, 348	20 July 1635 – Feb 1636	29 Feb 1636	No file		Easter 1636
353–356	21 Dec 1636 – 20 Feb 1637	27 Feb 1637	No file		Easter 1637
350, 357	15 Sept 1636, 7 Apr 1637	17 July 1637	No file		Mich 1637
359–362	23 Aug 1637 – 16 Jan 1638	26 Feb 1638	No file		Easter 1638
364	17 June 1638	5 July 1638	–	–	Mich 1638
365, 367, 368	12 July 1638 – 4 Jan 1639	4 Mar 1639	–		Easter 1639
–	–	2 Mar 1640	371	20 Jan 1640	Easter 1640
372, 373	3 Apr, 18 May 1640	11 July 1640	–	–	Mich 1640
375	9 Feb 1641	6 Mar 1641	–		Easter 1641
378	18 Sept 1641	17 Mar 1642	No file		Easter 1642
380, 381	29 June, 16 July 1642	29 July 1642	No file		Mich 1642
386	Dec 1644	12 Aug 1645	No file		Mich 1645
	No file	Summer 1646	388	15 May 1646	Mich 1646
389–391, 393, 394	11 Aug 1646 – 3 Mar 1647	16 Mar 1647	–		Easter 1647
397	29 June 1647	2 Aug 1647	395, 396	22 Apr, 11 June 1647	Mich 1647
398, 399	22 Dec 1647, 21 Feb 1648	13 Mar 1648	–	–	Easter 1648
400, 401, 403, 404, 406	4 Mar – 29 Aug 1648	1 Sept 1648	–		Mich 1648
407–409	8 Sept – 30 Oct 1648	12 Mar 1649	No file		Easter 1649
412	14 Mar 1650	21 Mar 1650	–		Easter 1650
413	1 Aug 1650	1 Aug 1650	–		Mich 1650
416–419	3 Dec 1650 – 11 Mar 1651	15 Mar 1651	–		Easter 1651
420	21 May 1651	14 July 1651	–		Mich 1651
421, 422	6 Aug, 15 Sept 1651	13 Mar 1652	–		Easter 1652
427	9 July 1653	21 July 1653	–		Mich 1653
428	30 Sept 1653	2 Mar 1654	–		Easter 1654
432	28 May 1654	28 July 1654	–		Mich 1654
433, 435	27 Oct 1654, 8 Mar 1655	14 Mar 1655	431	13 May 1654	Easter 1655
437	20 Nov 1655	11 Mar 1656	–		Easter 1656
440–442	15 Dec 1656 – 10 Mar 1657	21 Mar 1657	–		Easter 1657
443	4 Apr 1657	11 July 1657	445	27 July 1657	Mich 1657
–	–	26 Mar 1658	–		Easter 1658
447	26 May 1658	17 July 1658	–		Mich 1658

TABLE II (contd)

Inquest numbers	Inquest dates	Assizes	Inquest numbers	Inquest dates	King's Bench
449, 450	26 Nov 1658, 1 Jan 1659	22 July 1659	—	—	Mich 1659
455, 456	12, 28 Mar 1662	10 July 1662	—	—	Mich 1662
461	29 June 1663	4 Aug 1663	No file	—	Mich 1663
462	21 June 1664	28 July 1664	—	—	Mich 1664
465	15 Apr 1665	1 July 1665	—	—	Mich 1665
466	18 July 1665	22 Mar 1666	—	—	Easter 1666
472, 474	28 Sept, 24 Dec 1666	7 Mar 1667	—	—	Easter 1667
473, 476	17 Dec 1666, 27 Aug 1667	5 Sept 1667	No file	—	Mich 1667
?477, 478	26 Sept 1667, 11 Feb 1668	28 Feb 1668	—	—	Easter 1668
479, 480	23, 30 Mar 1670	7 July 1670	—	—	Mich 1670
481	22 Sept 1670	27 Mar 1671	—	—	Easter 1671
484, 485	4 Dec 1671, 11 Mar 1672	16 Mar 1672	No file	—	Easter 1672
486	22 July 1672	27 July 1672	—	—	Mich 1672
487, 488	24 Sept, 2 Oct 1672	14 Mar 1673	—	—	Easter 1673
489	6 Dec 1673	2 Apr 1674	—	—	Easter 1674
491	2 May 1674	23 July 1674	—	—	Mich 1674
493	11 May 1676	17 July 1676	—	—	Mich 1676
495–497	3 Oct 1677 – 21 Jan 1678	16 Mar 1678	No file	—	Easter 1678
500	29 Jan 1679	27 Mar 1679	—	—	Easter 1679
501	12 July 1679	24 July 1679	No file	—	Mich 1679
502	8 Mar 1680	18 Mar 1680	—	—	Easter 1680
503	12 June 1680	22 July 1680	—	—	Mich 1680
505	17 Oct 1680	11 Mar 1681	—	—	Easter 1681
507	13 Mar 1683	23 July 1683	No file	—	Mich 1683
508, 509	Nov 1684, Feb 1685	16 Mar 1685	No file	—	Easter 1685
512	24 Aug 1685	Summer 1685	—	—	Mich 1685
513–515	5 Jan – ?1 Feb 1686	22 Mar 1686	—	—	Easter 1686
516	21 July 1686	22 July 1686	—	—	Mich 1686
517, 518	5 Nov, 13 Dec 1686	28 Feb 1687	No file	—	Easter 1687
519	5 Apr 1687	14 July 1687	—	—	Mich 1687
520	17 Sept 1688	20 July 1689	No file	—	Mich 1689

TABLE III

Inquests delivered directly to King's Bench

Inquest numbers	Inquest dates	King's Bench
8	1 Oct 1603	Mich 1603
79	31 May 1609	Mich 1609
97	10 Aug 1610	Easter 1611
169, 173, 175–177	8 Mar – 16 June 1616	Mich 1616
190	25 Aug 1617	Mich 1617
194	10 Feb 1618	Trin 1618
202, 208, 209, 211, 214	31 May 1619 – 19 Jan 1620	Easter 1620
205	3 Sept 1619	Trin 1620
218	Apr 1620	Mich 1620
219, 221, 228, 230, 231	30 July 1620 – 16 July 1621	Mich 1621
247, 251	11 Apr, 2 Aug 1623	Mich 1623
255	16 Mar 1624	Easter 1624
256	13 May 1624	Easter 1625
257, 261, 265	21 July – 31 Dec 1624	Trin 1625
270	9 Feb 1626	Trin 1626
284	14 Aug 1627	Easter 1628
295	31 July 1628	Mich 1628
309, 313	25 June, 7 Dec 1630	Easter 1631
301	10 Feb 1629	Trin 1631
329, 333	5 Nov 1633, 17 May 1634	Trin 1634
336	15 Aug 1634	Hil 1635
334, 335, 338, 340, 343	24 June 1634 – 23 Apr 1635	Easter 1635
325	25 Mar 1633	Trin 1635
351, 352	7, 26 Oct 1636	Trin 1637
363	18 Apr 1638	Hil 1639
369, 370	28 May, 29 Sept 1639	Mich 1639
374, 377	27 Jan, 10 July 1641	Mich 1641
392	15 Oct 1646	Trin 1648
405, 410, 411	30 June 1648 – 17 Mar 1649	Trin 1649
448	21 June 1658	Mich 1658
451	4 July 1659	Hil 1660
453	19 July 1661	Hil 1662
457	23 May 1661?	Easter 1662
459	1 Sept 1662	Mich 1662
463, 464	30 June, 21 July 1664	Mich 1664
454, 458	13 Aug 1661, 16 Aug 1662	Easter 1665
468	3 Nov 1665	Easter 1666
470, 471	28 May, 20 June 1666	Mich 1666
483	27 Feb 1671	Easter 1671
506	4 Feb 1682	Trin 1682
510, 511	23 Mar, 3 Apr 1685	Trin 1685

TABLE IV

Delivery of inquests

To assizes	178
To assizes and on to Chancery	1
To assizes and on to King's Bench	188
To King's Bench	71

TABLE V

Sussex Coroners 24 Mar 1603 – 11 Dec 1688

Coroner	Held inquests	Attended assizes
County, East		
John Aylwin	28 July 1609 – 25 Nov 1612	13 July 1604 – 25 July 1614
Thomas Rickward	15 Aug 1612, 15 Feb 1613	–
John Eagles	5 June 1613	–
John Butcher	7 Mar 1617 – 23 Apr 1623	21 July 1617 – 5 Mar 1627
Edward Raines	23 Aug 1633 – 11 Feb 1668	9 Mar 1629 – 2 July 1668 Defaulted 12 Mar 1669
George Courthope	30 June 1648 – 13 May 1654	–
Alexander Luxford	27 Mar 1671 – 17 Sept 1688	22 July 1669 – 14 July 1687
County, West		
Henry Peckham	1 June 1610 – 20 May 1616	13 July 1604 – 8 July 1616
Albany Stoughton	16 Apr 1612	–
Richard Williams	21 Jan 1618, 3 Sept 1619	21 July 1617 – 22 July 1622
Anthony Smith	23 Mar 1620 – 22 June 1621	–
John Eagle	16 Mar 1624 – Feb 1636	3 Mar 1623 – 29 Feb 1636
Richard Smith	3 Sept 1646 – 30 Oct 1648	18 July 1636 – 14 July 1649
Richard Aylwin	6 Aug 1651 – 28 May 1654	15 Mar 1651 – 4 Aug 1655
William Reynolds	–	11 Mar 1656 (possibly defaulted)
John Peachey	3 Feb 1657 – 17 Oct 1680	21 Mar 1657 – 28 Feb 1687
Hastings rape		
Samuel Playfair	1 Oct 1603 – 12 Mar 1611	13 July 1604 – 4 July 1613
John Butcher	–	25 July 1614 – 21 July 1617
Alexander Butcher	–	17 July 1615
Thomas Butcher	30 Sept 1628 – 18 Sept 1641	4 Mar 1622 – 12 Aug 1645
George Courthope	15 May 1646 – 8 Sept 1648	16 Mar 1647 – 28 July 1654
William Cook	19 July 1661, 28 Mar 1662	26 Mar 1658
John Purfield	17 Dec 1666 – 5 Apr 1687	–
Battle liberty		
John Aynscombe	4 May 1619	–
George Cole	17 May – 12 Nov 1622	–
Henry Cole	14 Nov 1628	–
Brede liberty		
Anthony Tuttesham	1 Oct 1628	–
Nathaniel Powell	20 Dec 1634	–
Richard Coleman	8 Mar 1680	–
Duchy of Lancaster in Pevensey rape		
Thomas Woodgate	16 May 1604 – 9 Feb 1608	13 July 1604 – 17 July 1609
Samuel Playfair	–	23 Mar 1610. Defaulted (sick) 24 Feb 1612
Thomas Rickward	15 Sept – 29 Dec 1613	–
Alexander Butcher	–	17 July 1615
John Butcher	9 Oct 1615 – 3 Dec 1617	8 July 1616 – 21 July 1617
Edward Raines	19 May 1621 – 24 Oct 1634	22 July 1622 – 9 Mar 1653
John Teynton, deputy	28 Oct 1622	–
John Spillett, pro hac vice	25 Mar 1633	–

TABLE V (contd)

Coroner	Held inquests	Attended assizes
Loxfield Camden half-hundred		
John Eagles	30 July 1603 – 12 July 1612	13 July 1604 – 24 Feb 1612
William Eagles	–	Defaulted (sick) 14 July 1613
John Butcher	8 June 1614	8 July 1616 – 21 July 1617
Thomas Butcher	–	4 Mar 1622 – 3 Mar 1623
Thomas Houghton	23 Apr 1623 – 21 Sept 1629	14 July 1623 – 6 Mar 1641
Thomas Butcher	10 July 1641	29 July 1642 – 18 Sept 1644
George Courthope	20 Apr 1647 – 21 July 1664	14 July 1649 – 22 July 1659
Thomas Houghton	–	12 Mar 1649
Loxfield Dorset half-hundred		
John Aylwin	16 Apr 1605	–
Thomas Rickward	15 Sept – 29 Dec 1613	–
John Butcher	6 July 1619	–
Edward Raines	–	11 Mar 1656 – 22 July 1659
Robert Shoebridge	4 July 1659	–
Rotherfield hundred		
John Luck	1 July 1614 – Jan 1637	25 July 1614 – 6 Mar 1641
		Name deleted 29 July 1642,
		18 Sept 1644
Robert Shoebridge	4 Apr 1657, 15 Apr 1665	11 July 1657
Thomas Hooper	13 Dec 1686	–
Lewes rape		
John Aylwin	1 June 1604 – 13 Jan 1610	13 July 1604 – 24 Feb 1612
Thomas Rickward	4 Jan 1613 – 21 Feb 1614	4 July 1613
John Teynton	5 Jan 1615 – 24 June 1634	3 Mar 1617 – 29 Feb 1636
Francis Coomber	15 Sept 1636 – 16 July 1642	18 July 1636 – 18 Sept 1644
		Defaulted (sick) 12 Aug 1645
William Baldwin	–	1 Aug 1650 – 9 Mar 1653
Bramber rape		
John Aylwin	3 Apr 1603 – 3 Dec 1610	13 July 1604 – 8 July 1605
		Defaulted (sick) 17 July 1609
Thomas Rickward	4 Jan 1613 – 21 Feb 1614	4 July 1613
John Teynton	5 Jan 1615 – 23 Apr 1635	17 July 1615 – 29 Feb 1636
Francis Coomber	17 June 1638 – 9 Feb 1641	18 July 1636 – 18 Sept 1644
		Defaulted (sick) 12 Aug 1645
Leonard Crook, deputy	Dec 1644	
William Baldwin	–	1 Aug 1650 – 9 Mar 1653
John Howes	23 Mar 1670 – 2 Oct 1672	–
Henry Chatfield	Feb 1686	–
Arundel honor		
George Ardern	30 May 1604 – 9 Mar 1605	13 July 1604, 8 Mar 1605
		Defaulted (in prison) 8 July 1605
Albany Stoughton	20 July 1605 – 8 Jan 1617	22 Feb 1608 – 21 July 1617
Henry Peckham, pro	23 Jan 1616	–
hac vice		
John Eagle	21 May 1618, 17 Feb 1619	23 Feb 1618, 14 July 1623
John Adams	25 Sept 1619 – 15 Mar 1620	Defaulted (sick) 2 July 1621
John Teynton, deputy	28 June 1622	–
Richard Williams	30 July 1628 – 12 July 1638	8 Mar 1624 – 14 July 1649
William Baldwin	–	1 Aug 1650 – 9 Mar 1653
John Howes	23 Mar 1670 – 13 Mar 1683	27 Mar 1671, 24 July 1679

TABLE V (contd)

Coroner	Held inquests	Attended assizes
Arundel honor (contd)		
Henry Chatfield	Feb 1686	–
Lumley liberty		
George Sayers	15 Aug 1605 – 26 Mar 1611	17 July 1609 – 4 July 1613
George Matthew	20 Dec 1622	10 July 1626 – 15 July 1630
Eusebius Hayes	11 July 1633	18 July 1631 – 29 July 1642
		Noted as dead 18 Sept 1644
Bishop of Chichester's liberty		
George Ardern	–	13 July 1604
Henry Peckham	13 May 1603 – 17 Jan 1613	8 Mar 1605 – 24 Feb 1612
Anthony Smith	7 Apr 1612	–
John Adams	29 Jan 1617 – 17 Jan 1620	Defaulted (sick) 17 July 1620
Eusebius Hayes	24 Apr 1626, 1 Apr 1628	10 July 1626 – 29 July 1642
		Noted as dead 18 Sept 1644
George Copperthwaite	14 Mar 1650	1 Aug 1650, 15 Mar 1651
Edmund Crisp	28 May 1666	–
Chichester city		
Thomas Bird	16 Sept 1604	–
John Exton	16 Sept 1604 – 26 Mar 1609	–
Anthony Smith	5 Jan 1605 – 22 Mar 1620	–
Thomas Greenfield	28 Apr 1616 – 22 Mar 1620	–
John ?Pannett	Mar 1628	–
Richard Williams	Mar 1628	–
Richard Bragg	15 Sept 1651	–
Thomas Wheeler	15 Sept 1651	–
William Baldwin	11 May 1676	–
Bosham hundred		
William Holland	20 June 1603	–
Thomas Holmes	17 June, 9 Sept 1604	–
Zacchaeus Gittins	14 Apr 1605	–
Thomas Fielder	27 Aug 1609	–
Richard Jelly	31 July 1611	–
Thomas Holmes	27 Mar 1614	–
Thomas Fielder	3 May 1621	–
William Kimber	14 Aug 1627	–
John Edsall	15 Aug 1634	–

TABLE VI

Cinque Ports Coroners 24 Mar 1603 – 11 Dec 1688

Coroner	Deputy	Held inquests
Hastings		
Richard Life	–	26 Dec 1603
William Bishop	–	6 Dec 1604, 1 Mar 1605
James Lasher	–	16 July 1607
Richard Withers	–	17 Jan 1611
Martin Life	–	15 May 1611
Thomas Young	–	10 Dec 1613
Richard Waller	–	3 Aug 1616, 16 Oct 1620
Richard Boys	–	23 Apr, 25 Sept 1623
John Barley		25 Apr 1625
	William Bishop	2 Feb 1626
John Brett	–	27 June 1626
Thomas Brian	–	2 June, 5 Nov 1628
William Barker	–	13 Sept 1629, 12 July 1630
John Dunk	–	25 Aug 1631, 4 Mar 1632
Thomas Delves		–
	William Parker	22 July 1656
William Parker	–	7 Mar 1663
John Cox	–	24 July 1665, 2 Mar 1666
Thomas Jarrett	–	10 Feb 1671
John Lunsford	–	9 Feb 1674
William Parker sen.	–	28 May 1676
Thomas Carleton	–	4 Mar 1678
Thomas Lovell	–	4 Jan 1679
Samuel Smersall	–	17 Aug 1680
Rye		
John Fowtrell	–	3 Mar 1605
Thomas Hamon	–	6 Jan – 9 Aug 1606
Thomas Higgons	–	18 Aug 1607
Richard Fowtrell	–	15 May, 13 July 1613
Matthew Young	–	28 Dec 1614, 3 July 1615
Mark Thomas		–
	Thomas Ensinge	8 Nov 1615
John Palmer	–	11 June 1621 – 28 June 1622
Richard Fowtrell	–	11 Mar 1623
Mark Thomas		25 Feb 1624
	Richard Gibbridge	4 Oct 1624
John Sharp		–
	Richard Mills	14, 18 May 1628
John Nowell		7 Sept 1629, 8 Mar 1630
	Alan Gribell	5 Jan 1631
Mark Thomas	–	24 Mar 1634
Richard Mills		–
	Mark Thomas	21 Jan 1636
Richard Cockram		–
	Mark Thomas	3 July 1637
Robert Urwin	–	6 Mar 1641 – 19 July 1642
John Fagg	–	15 Oct 1642 – 11 Feb 1643
Alan Gribell	–	16 Mar 1646
Thomas Palmer	–	15 Apr 1648
Samuel Lansdale	–	30 Sept, 9 Oct 1650
Thomas Greenfield	–	29 Sept 1651

TABLE VI (contd)

Coroner	Deputy	Held inquests
Rye (contd)		
William Burwash		30 May 1653
	Alan Gribell	22 Sept 1652 – 10 Jan 1654
Alexander Bennet	–	23 Dec 1654, 9 Oct 1655
Thomas Marshall	–	24 Nov 1656 – 10 Dec 1657
Thomas Greenfield		–
	Thomas Marshall	15 Nov 1659
Michael Cadman	–	11 Feb 1676
Seaford		
Samuel Hide	–	17 Aug 1622
Winchelsea		
John Pettit	–	10 Sept 1630
George Sampson	–	30 May 1636
Daniel White	–	29 Oct 1638
Hugh Berisford	–	1 June 1644

TABLE VII

Inquests by coroners' jurisdictions

Year	County East	County West	Hastings rape	Battle	Brede	Duchy of Lancaster	Loxfield Camden	Loxfield Dorset	Rotherfield	Lewes rape	Bramber rape	Arundel honor	Lumley	Bishop of Chichester	Chichester city	Bosham	Cinque Ports	Total
1603	–	2	–	–	–	–	1	–	–	–	5	5	–	1	1	1	1 (H)	11
1604	–	–	–	–	–	1	1	–	–	1	1	2	–	–	1	2	1 (H)	10
1605	–	–	–	–	–	1	1	–	–	3	2	6	2	–	1	1	2 (H, R)	20
1606	–	–	1	–	–	1	1	1	–	3	4	3	1	2	1	–	3 (R)	19
1607	–	–	1	–	–	1	1	–	–	–	–	5	–	1	1	–	2 (H, R)	10
1608	–	–	–	–	–	–	–	–	–	1	1	–	–	–	1	–	–	5
1609	1	1	–	–	–	–	2	–	–	1	2	–	1	–	1	1	–	8
1610	–	1	1	–	–	–	4	–	–	2	1	5	–	1	–	–	–	15
1611	–	1	1	–	–	–	2	–	–	2	–	5	1	–	–	1	2 (H)	7
1612	4	3	–	–	–	4	3	–	–	–	–	2	–	–	–	–	–	13
1613	2	–	–	–	–	4	1	1	–	6	2	4	–	1	–	–	3 (H, R, R)	22
1614	–	–	–	–	–	1	1	–	1	7	2	–	–	1	–	1	1 (R)	7
1615	–	1	–	–	–	–	–	–	2	7	8	–	–	–	–	–	2 (R)	20
1616	–	1	–	–	–	2	–	–	–	5	6	3	–	1	1	–	1 (H)	17
1617	1	1	–	–	–	–	2	–	–	1	–	1	–	–	1	–	–	7
1618	–	1	–	–	1	–	–	1	–	1	4	–	–	1	1	–	–	7
1619	–	1	–	–	1	–	–	–	1	2	2	3	–	1	–	–	–	12
1620	–	1	–	–	–	1	–	–	–	3	2	2	–	–	–	–	1 (H)	10
1621	1	2	–	2	–	1	1	–	–	–	2	–	1	–	–	1	1 (R)	11
1622	1	1	–	–	–	3	2	–	–	2	3	1	1	–	–	–	3 (R, R, S)	13
1623	–	–	–	–	–	2	1	–	–	2	2	–	–	–	–	–	3 (H, H, R)	9
1624	–	2	–	–	–	2	2	–	–	2	1	–	–	–	–	–	2 (R)	12
1625	–	–	–	–	–	–	1	–	–	–	5	–	–	–	–	–	1 (H)	3
1626	–	1	–	–	–	2	1	1	–	1	1	–	–	1	1	1	2 (H)	13
1627	–	–	–	–	–	–	–	1	–	1	2	–	–	–	–	–	–	3
1628	–	–	1	–	1	1	1	–	–	2	2	2	–	–	1	–	4 (H, H, R, R)	16
1629	–	–	–	–	–	–	1	–	–	1	1	1	–	–	–	–	2 (H, R)	6
1630	–	–	–	–	–	–	–	–	–	1	4	–	–	–	–	–	3 (H, R, W)	8
1631	–	–	2	–	–	–	–	–	–	–	4	1	–	–	–	–	2 (H, R)	7
1632	–	–	–	–	–	–	–	–	–	–	2	–	–	–	–	–	1 (H)	3
1633	1	–	–	–	–	1	1	–	–	2	2	–	1	–	–	–	–	5
1634	2	–	–	1	–	2	2	–	3	2	1	–	–	–	–	1	1 (R)	13
1635	2	–	–	–	–	–	–	–	1	–	1	–	–	–	–	–	–	4
1636	2	1	–	–	–	–	–	–	–	2	–	–	–	–	–	–	2 (R, W)	7

TABLE VII (contd)

Year	County East	County West	Hastings rape	Battle	Brede	Duchy of Lancaster	Loxfield Camden	Loxfield Dorset	Rotherfield	Lewes rape	Bramber rape	Arundel honor	Lumley	Bishop of Chichester	Chichester city	Bosham	Cinque Ports	Total
1637	1	–	1	–	–	?1	–	–	1	1	1	2	–	–	–	–	1 (R)	8
1638	1	–	–	–	–	–	–	–	–	1	1	2	–	–	–	–	1 (W)	6
1639	3	–	–	–	–	–	–	–	–	–	–	–	–	–	–	–	–	3
1640	1	–	1	–	–	–	1	–	–	–	–	–	–	–	–	–	–	3
1641	1	–	1	–	–	–	–	–	–	2	–	–	–	–	–	–	1 (R)	5
1642	–	–	–	–	–	–	–	–	–	2	–	–	–	–	–	–	3 (R)	5
1643	–	–	–	–	–	–	–	–	–	–	–	–	–	–	–	–	1 (R)	1
1644	–	–	–	–	–	–	–	–	–	1	–	–	–	–	–	–	1 (W)	2
1646	4	1	1	–	–	–	–	–	–	–	–	–	–	–	–	–	1 (R)	7
1647	3	1	1	–	–	–	–	–	–	–	–	–	–	–	–	–	–	5
1648	5	3	2	–	–	–	–	–	–	–	–	–	–	–	–	–	1 (R)	11
1649	2	–	–	–	–	–	–	–	–	–	–	–	–	–	–	–	–	2
1650	3	–	–	–	–	–	–	–	–	–	–	–	–	1	–	–	2 (R)	6
1651	3	1	–	–	–	–	–	–	–	–	–	–	–	–	1	–	1 (R)	6
1652	–	–	–	–	–	–	–	–	–	–	–	–	–	–	–	–	1 (R)	1
1653	1	1	–	–	–	–	–	–	–	–	–	–	–	–	–	–	3 (R)	5
1654	2	1	–	–	–	–	–	–	–	–	–	–	–	–	–	–	2 (R)	5
1655	2	–	–	–	–	–	–	–	–	–	–	–	–	–	–	–	1 (R)	3
1656	1	–	–	–	–	–	–	–	–	–	–	–	–	–	–	–	2 (H, R)	3
1657	1	2	–	–	–	–	–	–	1	–	–	–	–	–	–	–	2 (R)	6
1658	1	1	–	–	–	–	–	1	–	–	–	–	–	–	–	–	–	3
1659	–	1	1	–	–	–	–	–	–	–	–	–	–	–	–	–	1 (R)	3
1661	2	–	1	–	–	–	–	–	–	–	–	–	–	–	–	–	–	3
1662	3	–	–	–	–	–	–	–	–	–	–	–	–	–	–	–	1 (H)	4
1663	–	–	–	–	–	–	2	–	–	–	–	–	–	–	–	–	–	2
1664	1	–	–	–	–	–	–	–	1	–	–	–	–	–	–	–	1 (H)	3
1665	1	2	–	–	–	–	–	–	–	–	–	–	–	–	–	–	1 (H)	4
1666	1	2	1	–	–	–	–	–	–	–	–	–	–	1	–	–	1 (H)	6
1667	1	2	–	–	–	–	–	–	–	–	–	–	–	–	–	–	–	3
1668	1	–	–	–	–	–	–	–	–	–	–	–	–	–	–	–	–	1
1670	–	1	–	–	–	–	–	–	–	–	–	2	–	–	–	–	–	3
1671	2	–	–	–	–	–	–	–	–	–	–	1	–	–	–	–	1 (H)	3
1672	3	1	–	–	–	–	–	–	–	–	–	–	–	–	–	–	–	4
1673	1	–	–	–	–	–	–	–	–	–	–	–	–	–	–	–	1 (H)	1
1674	–	1	–	–	–	–	–	–	–	–	–	–	–	–	–	–	1 (H)	2
1676	–	–	–	–	–	–	–	–	–	–	–	–	–	–	1	–	2 (H, R)	3
1677	2	–	–	–	–	–	–	–	–	–	–	–	–	–	–	–	–	2
1678	1	–	–	–	–	–	–	–	–	–	–	–	–	–	–	–	1 (H)	2

TABLE VII (contd)

Year	County East	County West	Hastings rape	Battle	Brede	Duchy of Lancaster	Loxfield Camden	Loxfield Dorset	Rotherfield	Lewes rape	Bramber rape	Arundel honor	Lumley	Bishop of Chichester	Chichester city	Bosham	Cinque Ports	Total
1679	1	–	–	–	–	–	–	–	–	–	–	1	–	–	–	–	1 (H)	3
1680	–	1	–	–	1	–	–	–	–	–	–	1	–	–	–	–	1 (H)	4
1682	–	–	–	–	–	–	–	–	–	–	–	1	–	–	–	–	–	1
1683	–	–	–	–	–	–	–	–	–	–	–	1	–	–	–	–	–	1
1684	?1	–	–	–	–	–	–	–	–	–	–	–	–	–	–	–	–	1
1685	3	?1	–	–	–	–	–	–	–	–	–	–	–	–	–	–	–	4
1686	3	–	1	–	–	–	–	–	1	–	1	–	–	–	–	–	–	6
1687	–	–	1	–	–	–	–	–	–	–	–	–	–	–	–	–	–	1
1688	1	–	–	–	–	–	–	–	–	–	–	–	–	–	–	–	–	1
Total	81	34	17	4	3	23	27	3	15	55	80	53	6	14	13	10	82	520

TABLE VIII

Lords of liberties at the time of the surviving inquests
and of their coroners' attendance at assizes

Hastings rape
1 Oct 1603 to 5 July 1624, Thomas Pelham, esq., later bt (d. 1624).
10 July 1626 to 1 Aug 1650, Thomas Pelham, bt (d. 1654).
26 Mar 1658 to 5 Apr 1687, John Pelham, bt.

Battle liberty
4 May 1619, Richard Sackville, earl of Dorset, George Moore, kt, John Walter, esq., and Thomas Spencer, esq.
17 May 1622, George Moore, kt, John Walter, kt, and Thomas Spencer, esq.
17 Nov 1622 to 14 Nov 1628, not named.

Brede liberty
1 Oct 1628 to 20 Dec 1634, Henry English, gent.
8 Mar 1680, not named.

Duchy of Lancaster in Pevensey rape
The king.

Loxfield Camden half-hundred
30 July 1603 to 21 July 1617, Thomas May, kt.
4 Mar 1622 to 5 July 1638, John Baker, esq. (d. 1638).
4 Mar 1639 to 18 Sept 1644, John Baker, esq. (d. 1644).
22 Apr 1647 to 22 July 1659, John Baker, esq. (d. 1688).
30 June to 21 July 1664, not named.

Loxfield Dorset half-hundred
16 Apr 1605, the king.
6 July 1619, Richard Sackville, earl of Dorset (d. 1624).
11 Mar 1656 to 4 July 1659, Richard Sackville, earl of Dorset (d. 1677).

Rotherfield hundred
1 July 1614 to 22 July 1622, Edward Nevill, Lord Abergavenny.
3 Mar 1623 to 6 Mar 1641, Henry Nevill, Lord Abergavenny.
29 July 1642 to 11 July 1657, John Nevill, Lord Abergavenny.
15 Apr 1665, George Nevill, Lord Abergavenny.

Lewes and Bramber rapes
3 Apr 1603 to 3 Dec 1610, feoffees of Thomas Howard, duke of Norfolk.
4 Jan 1613 to 12 Aug 1645, Thomas Howard, earl of Arundel and Surrey.
?1 Feb 1686, Henry Howard, duke of Norfolk.

Arundel honor
30 May 1604 to 8 July 1605, John Lumley, Lord Lumley.
20 July 1605 to 12 Aug 1645, Thomas Howard, earl of Arundel and Surrey.
14 July 1649 to 14 July 1651, Henry Howard, earl of Arundel and Surrey.
23 Mar 1670 to 2 Oct 1672, Thomas Howard, duke of Norfolk.
12 July 1679 to 13 Mar 1683, Henry Howard, duke of Norfolk (d. 1684).
?1 Feb 1686, Henry Howard, duke of Norfolk (d. 1701).

Lumley liberty
13 July 1604 to 18 July 1606, John Lumley, Lord Lumley.
26 Mar 1611 to 4 July 1613, Elizabeth Lumley, Lady Lumley.
22 Dec 1622 to 18 Sept 1644, Richard Lumley, kt, later Viscount Lumley.

Bishop of Chichester's liberty
13 May 1603 to 8 July 1605, Anthony Watson, bishop.

TABLE VIII (contd)

Bishop of Chichester's liberty (contd)
27 Jan 1606 to 30 Dec 1607, Lancelot Andrews, bishop.
26 June 1610 to 29 Jan 1617, Samuel Harsnett, bishop.
30 Sept 1619 to 5 Mar 1627, George Carlton, bishop.
15 July 1630 to 26 Feb 1638, Richard Montagu, bishop.
2 Mar 1640 to 6 Mar 1641, Brian Duppa, bishop.
29 July 1642 to 18 Sept 1644, Henry King, bishop.
16 Mar 1647 to 15 Mar 1651, in sequestration.
28 May 1666, Henry King, bishop.

Bosham hundred
20 June 1603 to 31 July 1611, Henry Berkeley, Lord Berkeley.
27 Mar 1614 to 15 Aug 1634, Elizabeth Berkeley, Lady Berkeley.

TABLE IX

Verdicts of the inquest jurors

Year	Murder	Manslaughter	Accidental Homicide	Self Defence	Uncertain Homicide	Suicide	Accidental Death	Natural Death	Unknown or Uncertain	Total
1603	–	–	–	–	–	1	4	6	–	11
1604	1	3	–	–	–	1	3	2	–	10
1605	2	–	–	1	–	7	8	2	–	20
1606	1	1	–	–	–	4	10	4	–	20
1607	1	1	–	–	–	3	5	–	–	10
1608	–	–	1	–	–	1	2	1	–	5
1609	2	2	–	–	–	2	1	1	–	8
1610	–	1	–	1	–	4	7	2	–	15
1611	2	1	–	–	–	1	–	3	–	7
1612	1	–	2	–	–	3	5	2	–	13
1613	3	2	–	1	–	7	7	2	–	22
1614	1	1	–	–	–	2	1	2	–	7
1615	1	4	–	–	–	1	12	1	1	20
1616	1	2	–	–	–	5	7	1	1	17
1617	2	3	–	–	–	1	1	–	–	7
1618	–	–	–	1	–	1	1	4	–	7
1619	–	–	–	–	–	–	11	1	–	12
1620	–	–	–	–	–	1	5	3	1	10
1621	2	1	1	–	–	1	6	–	–	11
1622	2	4	2	–	–	–	3	2	–	13
1623	–	1	1	–	–	1	2	4	–	9
1624	3	1	1	–	–	2	5	–	–	12
1625	–	1	–	–	–	–	1	1	–	3
1626	2	3	–	–	–	3	3	2	–	13
1627	–	–	–	–	–	1	2	–	–	3
1628	4	4	3	–	–	–	4	1	–	16
1629	1	–	–	–	–	2	3	–	–	6
1630	–	–	–	–	–	1	4	3	–	8
1631	–	–	1	–	–	1	–	5	–	7
1632	–	–	–	–	–	1	–	2	–	3
1633	1	1	1	–	–	1	1	–	–	5
1634	2	–	1	–	–	–	8	2	–	13

TABLE IX (contd)

Year	Murder	Manslaughter	Accidental Homicide	Self Defence	Uncertain Homicide	Suicide	Accidental Death	Natural Death	Unknown or Uncertain	Total
1635	3	–	–	–	–	–	1	–	–	4
1636	2	–	–	–	–	–	5	–	–	7
1637	4	3	–	–	–	–	–	1	–	8
1638	1	–	3	–	–	–	2	–	–	6
1639	1	–	–	–	–	1	1	–	–	3
1640	2	–	–	–	–	–	–	1	–	3
1641	1	1	–	–	–	–	2	1	–	5
1642	–	1	1	–	–	1	2	–	–	5
1643	–	–	–	–	–	1	–	–	–	1
1644	–	–	–	–	1	–	1	–	–	2
1646	4	–	1	–	–	1	1	–	–	7
1647	–	2	1	–	–	–	2	–	–	5
1648	4	3	1	–	–	–	2	1	–	11
1649	–	–	–	–	–	1	1	–	–	2
1650	4	–	2	–	–	–	–	–	–	6
1651	2	1	2	–	–	–	1	–	–	6
1652	1	–	–	–	–	–	–	–	–	1
1653	1	1	–	–	–	–	3	–	–	5
1654	–	3	1	–	–	–	–	1	–	5
1655	–	2	–	–	–	–	1	–	–	3
1656	–	1	–	–	–	–	–	1	1	3
1657	2	1	–	–	1	1	1	–	–	6
1658	1	1	–	–	–	1	–	–	–	3
1659	1	–	–	–	–	–	2	–	–	3
1661	–	–	–	–	–	1	2	–	–	3
1662	2	–	–	–	–	–	2	–	–	4
1663	1	–	1	–	–	–	–	–	–	2
1664	–	–	1	–	–	–	1	1	–	3
1665	1	1	–	–	–	1	1	–	–	4
1666	2	–	1	–	–	1	–	2	–	6
1667	–	1	1	–	–	–	–	–	1	3
1668	1	–	–	–	–	–	–	–	–	1
1670	–	2	–	–	–	–	–	–	1	3
1671	–	1	–	–	–	1	–	1	–	3
1672	3	1	–	–	–	–	–	–	–	4
1673	1	–	–	–	–	–	–	–	–	1
1674	1	–	–	–	–	1	–	–	–	2
1676	1	–	–	–	–	–	1	1	–	3
1677	2	–	–	–	–	–	–	–	–	2
1678	1	–	–	–	–	–	1	–	–	2
1679	2	–	–	–	–	–	–	1	–	3
1680	–	3	–	–	–	–	1	–	–	4
1682	–	–	–	–	–	–	–	1	–	1
1683	1	–	–	–	–	–	–	–	–	1
1684	1	–	–	–	–	–	–	–	–	1
1685	1	1	–	–	–	2	–	–	–	4
1686	4	2	–	–	–	–	–	–	–	6
1687	1	–	–	–	–	–	–	–	–	1
1688	1	–	–	–	–	–	–	–	–	1
Total	96	69	30	4	2	73	169	72	6	521

TABLE X

Methods of committing suicide

Method	Men	Women	Total
Hanging	30	6	36
Drowning	17	10	27
Cutting throat	3	2	5
Poisoning	–	3	3
Cutting body	2	1	3
Total	52	22	74

TABLE XI

Suicide by months

Month	Men	Women	Total
January	5	3	8
February	6	1	7
March	5	2	7
April	7	–	7
May	4	1	5
June	6	4	10
July	3	2	5
August	1	2	3
September	3	2	5
October	7	1	8
November	2	1	3
December	3	2	5
Total	52	21	73

TABLE XII

Days elapsing between death or finding body and inquest

Jurisdiction	Number of days		
	Minimum	Maximum	Average
County (east)	0	205	11
County (west)	0	156	10
Hastings rape	1	34	10
Battle liberty	1	2	2
Brede liberty	1	211	96
Duchy of Lancaster in Pevensey rape	1	44	8
Loxfield Camden half-hundred	0	146	13
Loxfield Dorset half-hundred	3	41	18
Rotherfield hundred	0	75	10

TABLE XII (contd)

Jurisdiction	Number of days		
	Minimum	Maximum	Average
Lewes rape	0	28	5
Bramber rape	0	102	5
Arundel honor	0	194	8
Lumley liberty	1	12	4
Bishop of Chichester's liberty	0	348	31
Chichester city	0	25	4
Bosham hundred	0	2	1
Hastings	0	20	2
Rye	0	3	1
Seaford	1	1	1
Winchelsea	1	2	2
Whole of Sussex	0	348	8

TABLE XIII

Number of jurors by jurisdictions

Jurisdiction	Number of jurors		
	Minimum	Maximum	Average
County (east)	10	23	14
County (west)	12	21	16
Hastings rape	12	20	15
Battle liberty	12	15	13
Brede liberty	13	17	15
Duchy of Lancaster in Pevensey rape	12	16	14
Loxfield Camden half-hundred	12	17	14
Loxfield Dorset half-hundred	12	13	12
Rotherfield hundred	12	19	16
Lewes rape	9	19	14
Bramber rape	11	20	14
Arundel honor	12	24	16
Lumley liberty	12	16	13
Bishop of Chichester's liberty	13	22	16
Chichester city	15	21	18
Bosham hundred	14	21	17
Hastings	12	18	14
Rye	12	18	13
Seaford	15	15	15
Winchelsea	12	18	14
Whole of Sussex	9	24	14

1   3 Apr 1603. Horsham. John Aylwin, gent., coroner of the feoffees of Thomas late duke of Norfolk. Jurors: George Morgaine, Henry Puttucke, Thomas Rouland, Thomas Pyke, Arthur Woodgate, Richard Hunt, Thomas Tedcroft, John Penfold, Thomas Whitheade, 'Heug' Deane, William Grenfeild, Richard Grenfeild. On 3 Apr Thomas Barker [*later written* Baker] died a natural death in Horsham gaol. No one else was privy to his death to the jurors' knowledge. KB 9/714, m 145.
[Delivered to East Grinstead assizes on 3 Oct and on to King's Bench in Michaelmas. Barker had been committed to gaol by Richard Blount, esq., JP, before whom on 30 May 1602 John Radford of Fulham, Middlesex, yeoman, had entered a recognizance in £20 to appear at the next assizes to prefer a bill of indictment and give evidence against Barker concerning his stealing a grey gelding from John Challenor of London, merchant. At Horsham assizes on 12 July 1602 the grand jury presented an indictment which charged Barker late of Billingshurst, glover, with feloniously taking and carrying away a dark grey gelding worth £7 belonging to Challenor, gent., at Billingshurst on 26 May 1602. Barker pleaded not guilty but was convicted; he had no chattels. He was remanded in custody after sentence to await consideration for the queen's service. He is not listed among the prisoners at the assizes of 25 Feb 1603. ASSI 35/44/10, mm 21, 22, 44, 86; ASSI 35/45/7, m 83; KB 9/714, m 174d; KB 29/243, m 35d; *CAR Eliz*, nos 2050, 2059, 2063, 2079; *CAR Introdn*, 171.]

2   Same date, place, coroner and jurors as 1 (*but* Tedcroft *is written* Tredcroft). On 3 Apr Thomas Burchall died a natural death in Horsham gaol. No one else was privy to his death to the jurors' knowledge. KB 9/714, m 146.
[Delivered with 1. Burchall had been committed to gaol by Henry Shelley, esq., JP, before whom on 4 Feb 1602 Robert Haler of Billingshurst, yeoman, had entered a recognizance in £10 to prefer a bill of indictment and give evidence against Burchall at the next assizes for stealing his ox. On 6 Feb William Wastlen alias Saunders and Richard Norman, both of Clayton, yeomen, entered a recognizance in £10 each before Walter Covert, kt, and Thomas Ersfeild, esq., JPs, for the appearance at the assizes of John Wastlen alias Saunders of Clayton, labourer, who had been arrested and imprisoned suspected of felony; and Henry Haler of Shipley, yeoman, entered a recognizance in £10 before Covert alone to appear at the assizes to prefer a bill of indictment and give evidence against John Wastlen alias Saunders. At East Grinstead assizes on 26 Feb 1602 the grand jury presented an indictment which charged Burchall late of Billingshurst, weaver, with feloniously taking and driving away a 'brinded' ox worth £4 belonging to Haler at Shipley on 29 Jan; and John Wastlen alias Saunders with feloniously receiving and harbouring him at Clayton on 1 Feb, knowing that he had committed the felony. Burchall and John Wastlen alias Saunders both pleaded not guilty but were convicted; they had no chattels. They then successfully pleaded benefit of clergy and were branded. There is no record of Burchall being remanded in custody and he is not listed among the prisoners at subsequent assizes. He must have been rearrested shortly before his death. ASSI 35/44/9, mm 11, 19, 60, 90, 97, 108; KB 9/714, m 174d; KB 29/243, m 35d; *CAR Eliz*, nos 2014, 2022, 2023; *CAR Introdn*, 171.]

3   Same date, place, coroner and jurors as 1 (*but* Tedcroft *is written* Tredcroft). On 3 Apr John Umfry died a natural death in Horsham gaol. No one else was privy to his death to the jurors' knowledge. KB 9/714, m 147.
[Delivered with 1. KB 9/714, m 174d; KB 29/243, m 35d; *CAR Introdn*, 171.]

4   13 May 1603. Ferring. Henry Peckham, gent., coroner of the bishop of Chichester's liberty. Jurors: John Barnard, Thomas Cooke, John Whitgrove, John Yonge, John Whittington, Thomas Sewell, John Frogbrooke, William Wright, Richard Penfold, Richard Parker, Robert Marten, Richard Snellinge, Henry Tayler, John Woolvin, William Woolvin. On 13 May, when John Robinut late of Ferring, 'labourer', was getting water in 'a water cart' at 'Weres Bridge' in Ferring, he fell from the cart from the movement of a horse which was in the tail of the cart and broke his neck, dying immediately. The horse and cart are worth 46s 8d and are sold by Anthony bishop of Chichester. KB 9/714, m 167.
[Delivered with 1. The note *pro bonis* on the inquest is cancelled by a cross and there is nothing about the deodands on the Controlment Roll. KB 9/714, mm 167, 174d; KB 29/243, m 35d.]

5   20 June 1603. Funtington. William Holland, Bosham hundred chamberlain and coroner. Jurors:

Christopher Corderoy, gent., Richard Jellye, John Tilley, William Trymlet, Thomas Martin, Edward Lucas, John Greene, Thomas Feelder, Henry Jellye, Thomas Colden, John White, John Clemens, Richard Figg, Oliver Mathewe, John Cunstable, Richard Woodes. About 8 a.m. on 20 June, when William Scardvyle was working in 'a marlepitt' of Michael Marchaunt at Funtington digging 'marle stones', by misadventure about 'three score loades' of the stones worth 8d which were hanging over him fell on him and crushed his body whereby he immediately died. No one else was privy to his death. KB 9/714, m 168.
[Delivered with 1. KB 9/714, m 174d; KB 29/243, m 35d.]

6   30 July 1603. Wadhurst. John Egles, gent., Loxfield Camden half-hundred coroner. Jurors: Henry Beale, Alexander Mudle, John Relfe, Robert Parris, John Lewes, Reynold Weston, Thomas Markwicke, John Pollye, Richard Markwicke, William Barham, Thomas Butcher, Thomas Longlye. About 1 p.m. on 13 July, when Thomas Allen late of Wadhurst, 'laborer', was in 'a marlepett' at Wadhurst, by misadventure a piece of marl fell upon his body, threw him to the ground and so crushed and wounded his body that he languished thereof until 21 July and then died. KB 9/714, m 166.
[Delivered with 1. KB 9/714, m 174d; KB 29/243, m 35d.]

7   30 Sept 1603. Horsham. John Aylwin, gent., coroner of the feoffees of Thomas late duke of Norfolk. Jurors: Thomas Clarcke, John Steere, Arthur Woodgate, William Chambers, William Hilton, Thomas Galpin, William Michell, John Mose, John Hudson, Edward Juppe, George Forde, Richard Mare. On 30 Sept William Harvie died a natural death in Horsham gaol. No one else was privy to his death to the jurors' knowledge. KB 9/714, m 144.
[Delivered with 1. Harvie had been committed to gaol by John Colepeper, esq., JP, before whom on 11 May 1602 Edward Russell of Goudhurst, Kent, gent., had entered a recognizance in £20 to appear at the next assizes to prefer a bill of indictment and give evidence against Harvie. At Horsham assizes on 12 July 1602 the grand jury presented 2 indictments against Harvie late of Icklesham, labourer: one charging him with feloniously taking and carrying away 2 pewter porringers worth 12d, 4 saucers worth 16d and a pair of shoes worth 22d belonging to Thomas Russell at Icklesham on 25 Mar 1602; and the other with feloniously taking and carrying away a pair of stockings worth 12d and a cambric band worth 12d belonging to Edward Russell and a silver spoon worth 8s belonging to Deborah Russell at Icklesham on the same day. Harvie pleaded not guilty but was convicted on both; he had no chattels. He was remanded in custody after sentence to await consideration for the queen's service. He was still in gaol at the East Grinstead assizes of 25 Feb 1603 when the grand jury presented an indictment which charged him under the name of William Harvy of Goudhurst, labourer, with feloniously taking and carrying away goods and chattels belonging to George Tyler at Ardingly on ?22 ... 1602 or 1603. The indictment is badly damaged, but the goods included 2 doublets worth 6s, a coat worth 2d, 2 pairs of venetians (*sc.* hose *or* breeches) worth 1s, 3 pairs of stockings worth 1s, a hat worth 6d, a pair of belts worth 1d, 3 silk girdles worth 1s, a linen sheet worth 6d, a shirt worth 2d, 2 pillows worth 10d, 5 neck-bands worth 2s, 9 neck-bands worth 2s, 8 ... worth 1s, 2 handkerchiefs worth ..., a ?coif worth 2d, 2 pairs of shoes worth 1s and 2 ... Harvie pleaded not guilty to the indictment but was convicted; he had no chattels. He then successfully pleaded benefit of clergy and was branded, but was remanded in gaol. A recognizance was delivered to the assizes of 25 Feb 1603 which had been entered on 28 Jan 1603 before Henry Bowyer, esq., JP, by Charles Stiller of Goudhurst, iron-founder, in £20 to appear at the assizes and there to prefer, or cause to be preferred, a bill of indictment and also to give evidence against Harvie (called late of Taunton in Somerset) who had been brought before Bowyer by Stiller and charged by him with feloniously breaking and entering his house in daytime and taking some of Stiller's goods, whereupon Bowyer had sent Harvie to Horsham gaol. No such indictment survives. Harvie had died before the next assizes, that of 3 Oct. ASSI 35/44/10, mm 18, 19, 22, 50, 86; ASSI 35/45/7, mm 19, 67, 83; KB 9/714, m 174d; KB 29/243, m 35d; *CAR Eliz*, nos 2050, 2059, 2062, 2079, 2084; *CAR Introdn*, 171.]

8   1 Oct 1603. New Shoreham. John Aylwyn, gent., coroner of the feoffees of Thomas late duke of Norfolk. Jurors: Henry Halle, Richard Gravesend, John Thomas, Henry Wolven, John Dawe, Richard Wolven, William [*Gulielmus*] Gardiner, Richard Coke, Thomas Freman, Lawrence Farley, Thomas Burgis, Henry Fynche. On 1 Oct, when John Paige was of unsound mind, he wilfully drowned himself in the harbour of New Shoreham. KB 9/714, m 6.
[Delivered into King's Bench at Winchester by the coroner in Michaelmas. The inquest has a note *felo de se*,

lunaticus and it is classified as a suicide *non compos mentis* on the Controlment Roll. KB 9/714, mm 6, 7d; KB 29/243, m 40d.]

9 1 Oct 1603. Hooe. Samuel Playfere, Hastings rape coroner. Jurors: John Elvery, John Ellys, George Colman, William Eglesden, John Goodden, Richard Harte, John Brigden, Richard Cockshoote, William Pickket, John Newen, Richard Nashe, Thomas Turle, James Goodden. On 27 Sept Bridget Weekes late of Hooe, 'spynster', being weak, died a natural death at Hooe. KB 9/1074, m 77.
[Delivered to the Sussex Lent assizes and on to King's Bench in Easter 1604. KB 9/1074, m 60d; KB 29/244, m 4.]

10 20 Dec 1603. Ticehurst. Samuel Playfere, Hastings rape coroner. Jurors: James Markewick, Robert Mauncer, John Holland, Richard Ha[?r]te, John Stephen, Thomas Wyldinge, Richard Apse, Isaac Alchyn, Philip Danyell, Edward Hodelye, Edward Burcombe, Goddard Oxenbridge, William Hunt, William Apse, Henry Jervis, Thomas Mills, John Apse. On 8 Dec Alice Lyghe of Ticehurst, 'spinster', was delivered prematurely at Ticehurst of a still-born male child. KB 9/1074, m 73.
[Delivered with **9**. Both the note on the inquest and the Controlment Roll entry, which is separate from the natural deaths, classify this as a still-birth. KB 9/1074, mm 60d, 73; KB 29/244, m 4.]

11 26 Dec 1603. Hastings. Richard Lyfe, Hastings mayor and coroner, and other jurats. Jurors: Thomas Lasher sen., Thomas Mannington, Robert Parkes, Thomas Rolfe, Thomas Wynter, Thomas Thistlethwaites, George Bradbury, Edward Stace, Christopher Salter, Nicholas Willard, John Rygat, James Furner, John Brymsted, Abraham Yelding. About 9 a.m. on 25 Dec William Emes late of Hastings, 'weaver', aged about 14, apprentice of Richard Dyer of Hastings, 'weaver', went out of Dyer's dwelling-house in Hastings and, going towards the priory near Hastings and intending to cross a bridge called 'le Clappers' near the priory, he suddenly and accidentally fell from the bridge and was drowned in the water flowing under it. HASTINGS C/A(a) 1, f 86v.

12 16 May 1604. East Grinstead. Thomas Woodgate, gent., duchy of Lancaster coroner in Pevensey rape. Jurors: Edmund Harman, John Lee, Abraham Lullingden, John Kyppynge, Solomon Cole, Robert Johnson, Nicholas Wythier, Henry Browne, Henry Arlington, George Harris, Nicholas Meere, Thomas Lyntot, John Underhill. On 14 May, when Oliver Mockett and John Palmer late of Angmering, esq., were with many others in the dwelling-house of Edward Kippynge, 'vitler', at East Grinstead, Palmer, seeing that Mockett was being 'very unrulye', caused him to withdraw and to go up into a room in the house where he slept and followed him into the room. Thereupon Palmer feloniously killed Mockett with a sword worth 12d which he held in his right hand, giving him 'a thurst' [*sc.* thrust] in the left side of the abdomen 3 inches deep and 1 inch wide of which he languished at East Grinstead until the next day and then died. Palmer did not flee. He had no goods or chattels, lands or tenements at the time of the felony or ever after to the jurors' knowledge. ASSI 35/46/3, m 27. [*Calendared in CAR, no 15.*]
[Delivered to East Grinstead assizes on 13 July when Palmer, who had been committed to gaol by the coroner, pleaded not guilty but was convicted; he had no chattels. He then successfully pleaded benefit of clergy and was remanded in gaol without being branded. He was still in gaol at the assizes of 8 Mar and 8 July 1605. Oliver Mockett of Ditchling was buried at East Grinstead on the day of the inquest. ASSI 35/46/3, mm 27, 32, 40; ASSI 35/47/6, m 50; ASSI 35/47/7, m 81; *CAR*, nos 9, 14, 15, 36, 61; SRS, XXIV, 154.]

13 30 May 1604. Linchmere. George Ardern, gent., Easebourne hundred coroner. Jurors: Roger Shotter, Thomas Cover, William Shotter sen., William Shotter jun., John Collens, Stephen Willard, Edward Collyer, William Ide, Walter Scudmore, William Standishe, Walter Sturte, Richard Hogesfleshe, John Weste, Andrew Clarke, Anthony Aylynge, William Boxhall, John Hudson, Richard Collyn. About 3 p.m. on 27 May William Coggyn late of Kirdford, 'glasseman', feloniously killed Nicholas Oulde on the road at Linchmere with 'a sworde' worth 6d which he held in his right hand, giving him a wound on the left side 2 inches wide and 4 inches deep of which he languished at Linchmere until the next day and then died. After committing the felony Coggyn fled. At that time he had no goods or chattels,

lands or tenements to the jurors' knowledge. ASSI 35/46/3, m 25. [*Calendared in CAR, no 11.*]
[Delivered with **12**. At the assizes the grand jury, to which Thomas Erne, Elizabeth Farnden and Rose Oulde gave evidence, presented an indictment which charged Coggyn, called a glazier, with murdering Oulde at Linchmere on 28 May with a dagger worth 12d which he held in his right hand, giving him a wound under the left arm 3 inches deep and 2 inches wide of which he immediately died. Coggyn, who had been committed to gaol by Peter Barton, kt, JP, pleaded not guilty to the indictment and was acquitted of murder but convicted of manslaughter and hanged; he had no chattels. ASSI 35/46/3, mm 24, 26, 40; *CAR*, nos 9–11.]

14   1 June 1604. Southover. John Aylwyn, gent., coroner of the feoffees of Thomas late duke of Norfolk. Jurors: John Knowles, gent., Edward Hart, William Addams, Nicholas Russell, Dominic Monger, Thomas Earle, Nicholas Wilson, Thomas Harwarde, John Hatcher, Abraham Umfry, Robert Lepparde, Nicholas Virgo, Lancelot Howarde. On 29 May Thomas Alderton late of Ringmer, gent., murdered his wife Joyce at Southover with a knife worth 2d which he held in his right hand, giving her 5 fatal wounds under the right arm ½ inch wide and 3 inches deep of which she immediately died. Thomas did not flee. At that time he had no lands or tenements, but he had goods and chattels worth 3s 1d [*sic*], viz 'ij quaves [*sc.* coifs] [worth] xij d, one ruff band xij d, one paier of gloves ij d, j grene apron vj d, the murdering knife j d, one cloth jerkin xvj d'. ASSI 35/46/3, mm 1, 2. [*Calendared in CAR, nos 23, 24.*]
[Delivered with **12**. At the assizes Alderton, who had been committed to gaol by Herbert Morley, esq., JP, confessed and was hanged. ASSI 35/46/3, mm 1, 40; *CAR*, nos 9, 23.]

15   17 June 1604. Funtington. Thomas Holmes, Bosham hundred chamberlain and coroner. Jurors: John Combes, William Trimlet, William Wepham, William Jellye, Richard Ayling, John Button, Stephen Gratwicke, John Colden, Richard Churcher, William Kember, Robert Trowe, Michael Marchaunte, Richard Woodes, William Goldocke, Richard Harding, Thomas Colden, John White, John Baker. About 2 p.m. on 16 June, when Thomas Wedgewood was working in 'a marle pitt' on 'the common heath' at Funtington digging 'marle stones', by misadventure about 'fortye loades' of 'le upper earth or greete' of the pit, worth 4d, which was hanging over him, fell on him and crushed his body whereby he immediately died. No one else was privy to his death. KB 9/1075, m 136.
[Delivered with **12** and on to King's Bench in Michaelmas. KB 9/1075, m 130d; KB 29/244, m 69d.]

16   30 June 1604. Wadhurst. John Egles, Loxfield Camden half-hundred coroner. Jurors: Henry Beale, Edward Chapman, Geoffrey Beale, Francis Enge, John Beale, William Upton, Robert Enge, Richard Ford, Richard Burges, John Pollye, Robert Beale, all of Wadhurst; John Hale of Lamberhurst. About 11 a.m. on 16 June, when Elizabeth Collen late of Wadhurst, 'spinster', was alone in a close called 'Kitchem Meade' at Wadhurst, she feloniously hanged herself with 'a halter' worth 1d which she held in both hands, tying one end round 'one bough of an apletree' and the other round her neck. At that time she had no goods or chattels, lands or tenements. KB 9/1075, m 133.
[Delivered with **15**. KB 9/1075, m 130d; KB 29/244, m 69d.]

17   11 July 1604. Horsham. John Aylwin, gent., coroner of the feoffees of Thomas late duke of Norfolk. Jurors: Thomas Rouland, John Hudson, Arthur Woodgate, John Comber, Thomas Pike, Thomas Wood, Edward Bristowe, Richard Stere, William Waterton, Thomas Lamberd, James Slater, George Hilton, Richard Hatt, James Vera. On 11 July Elizabeth Jellett died a natural death in Horsham gaol. No one else was privy to her death to the jurors' knowledge. KB 9/1075, m 144.
[Delivered with **15**. Jellett was listed among the prisoners in gaol at the East Grinstead assizes of 13 July 1604, having been sentenced to death but remanded in gaol at a previous assizes. ASSI 35/46/3, m 40; KB 9/1075, m 130d; KB 29/244, m 69d; *CAR*, no 9; *CAR Introdn*, 171.]

18   9 Sept 1604. Bosham. Thomas Holmes, chamberlain and coroner of the manor and liberties of Bosham. Jurors: John Combes, Richard Jelly, Robert Trymlet, Nicholas Pen, William Barnham, Thomas Michelborne, Richard Nonington, William Grigg, William Goldocke, William Foster, Stephen Barret,

William Barret, John Greene, William Skerle, John Bartilmewe. About 5 p.m. on 7 Sept Thomas Trymlet of Bosham, 'yeoman', climbed 'at plumbe tree', which was growing in his garden at Bosham, to pick its fruit and, being alone in the tree about 10 feet above the ground, by misadventure he fell from the tree to the ground whereby he 'did crushe and bruse' the left side of his body of which he languished at Bosham until the next day and then died. KB 9/717, m 217.
[Delivered with **20** and on to the King's Bench in Easter 1605. KB 9/717, m 222ad; KB 29/246, m 5.]

19 16 Sept 1604. Chichester. Thomas Birde and John Exton, Chichester city coroners. Jurors: John Steevenson jun., Richard Michell, gent., Gilbert Miller, Richard Butcher sen., Thomas Diggens, William Bartlet, Thomas Hushe, Robert Jenman, Raymond King, Thomas Swayne, Nicholas Wild, Ralph Tolpat, Clement Tompson, John Johnson, Richard Ayling, William Whetham, Thomas Grigg. On 7 Sept Helen Gates late of Chichester, 'spinster', was delivered of a dead male child at Chichester. KB 9/717, m 231.
[Delivered with **18**. This is classified as a natural death both in the note on the inquest and on the Controlment Roll. KB 9/717, mm 222ad, 231; KB 29/246, m 5.]

20 19 Nov 1604. Arundel. George Ardern, gent., Arundel town coroner. Jurors: Richard Forgouse, James Wilson, Henry Hobbs jun., William Washer, John Wolvyn, Christopher Bridger, Thomas Campion, Adam Kelsam, Thomas Moone, William Maicham, Thomas Mothe, Robert Yonge, William Cooper, Richard Hesman, John Hollyer, Thomas Selden, Richard Oliver, John Warne. About 2 p.m. on 18 Nov Richard Gattes of [apud *in error for* de] Arundel, 'glover', feloniously killed Paul Abrare at Arundel with 'a staffe' worth ½d which he held in both hands, giving him a wound on the head 2 inches long and about [*blank*] inch deep of which he languished at Arundel until 7 p.m. and then died. Gattes had no goods or chattels to the jurors' knowledge. ASSI 35/47/6, m 1. [*Calendared in CAR, no 38.*]
[Delivered to East Grinstead assizes on 8 Mar 1605 when Gattes, who had been committed to gaol by the coroner, pleaded not guilty and was acquitted, Abrare having died a natural death; Gattes had not fled. ASSI 35/47/6, mm 1, 17, 50; *CAR*, nos 36–38.]

21 6 Dec 1604. Hastings. William Bysshop, Hastings mayor and coroner, and other jurats. Jurors: John Fissenden, Thomas Mannington, Robert Jenkyn, Grimbald Standbynorth, Richard Wynckfeld, John Wood, 'shomaker', Nicholas Willard, Thomas Badcock, John Coombes, George Bradbury, Denis Dufford, Robert Wright. Richard Waller of St Mary Magdalen within the liberty of Hastings, 'yoman', recently contracted with William Godfrey, 'mason', to dig and construct 'a well' at Waller's dwelling-house, and Godfrey dug the well according to the agreement to a depth of about 13 'fadoms' [*sc.* fathoms]. About 7 a.m. on 6 Dec Edward Abbot, Godfrey's servant, with the assistance of Griffin Snow, late Waller's servant, and in the absence of Godfrey, descended into the well to dig and work there and immediately began to become ill and suffocate from the strength of the vapour of the soil, in English 'the damp'. In order to get him help Snow went quickly to Waller, strongly urging him to help him to go down into the well with a rope which was hanging there. So Snow, with Waller's assistance, descended into the well and tied the rope around Abbot and so Waller recovered Abbot from the well. In the meantime Snow became very ill from the strength of the damp so that he could not help himself by means of the rope which was lowered into the well for that purpose but was suddenly suffocated, thus dying by misadventure. HASTINGS C/A(a) 1, f 99v.

22 5 Jan 1605. Chichester. John Exton and Anthony [?Smyth], Chichester city coroners. Jurors: John Lenerd, Richard Trigges, John Pickering, Richard Michell, John Stempe, Robert Foorde, John Wardoure, Thomas Diggens, Richard Brooker, John Hobson, Roger Horly, John Fullicke, Humphrey Colbrooke, Ralph Tolpat, Robert Cole, Robert Wallis, Thomas Swayne, Roger Rawlyn, Daniel Allen, John Wright, George Burrell. About 4 p.m. on 4 Jan William Pymble of Chichester, 'husbandman', feloniously hanged himself in 'a garden' at Chichester with 'a little rope or coarde' worth 1d which he held in both hands, putting one end round his neck and tying the other end round 'the wynch of a well'. He had goods and chattels worth 3s 2d which remain with the city steward for the use of the mayor and citizens of Chichester. He had no lands or tenements. [*Faded.*] KB 9/717, m 220.

[Delivered with **18**. The steward was summoned to King's Bench to answer for the goods and chattels, said to be worth 3s 4d; he was outlawed at Lewes on 24 Apr 1606. Process was resumed in 1626 but the outcome is unknown. KB 9/717, mm 220, 222ad; KB 29/246, m 5.]

2 3   19 Feb 1605 [*MS* 3 *in error for* 2 James I]. Balcombe. John Aylwin, gent., coroner of the feoffees of Thomas late duke of Norfolk. Jurors: Edmund Bechely, John Gaston, Richard Burt, Nicholas Burt, William Ilman, Ellis Juner, John Skiell, Edmund Tomson, William Bancke, William Jupp, Richard Warde, Roger Hoder. George White feloniously drowned himself in Nicholas Burt's pond in Balcombe. At that time he had no goods or chattels. KB 9/718, m 128.

[Delivered with **26** and on to King's Bench in Michaelmas. KB 9/718, mm 121, 128d; KB 29/246, m 77.]

2 4   1 Mar 1605. Hastings. William Bysshop, Hastings mayor and coroner, and other jurats. Jurors: Robert Jenkyn, John Wood, Thomas Thistlethwaites, George Bradbury, Daniel Downe, Toby Parson, William Barker, Henry Norrys, Nicholas Wyllard, Thomas Badcock, Thomas Stevenson jun., John Rygat. On 9 Feb Michael Byrchet late of Hastings, 'baker', went from his dwelling-house in Hastings and rode on the sea-shore towards Eastbourne in the company of Robert Whate until they came to Bulverhythe 'haven' beneath Gensing cliffs where they tried to ride across the water of 'le haven', but because 'le haven' had shortly before been opened the water was flowing from it with such force that Byrchet and his horse were violently and suddenly thrown into the sea by it and washed away and Byrchet was drowned in the sea by misadventure. HASTINGS C/A(a) 1, f 102.

2 5   3 Mar 1605. Rye. John Fowtrell, Rye mayor and coroner, and the jurats. Jurors: Quintin Pye, [John Engram did not appear], John Nicholson, John Duffett, Richard Franck, Thomas Byshopp, William Apprice, John Ivy, William Hackelton, George Reynoldes, Michael Colgate, George Tuggett, Robert Gladishe, [Richard Cheverell did not appear], Thomas Starky, Thomas Wattes. Between 4 and 5 p.m. on 2 Mar, when Judith daughter of William Barram of Rye, 'blacksmith', aged about 8, was resting under the window of John Sole of Rye, 'shomaker', in Lower Street in Rye with her sister Susanna, aged about half a year, in her arms, 'there came by the horse and beare [*sc.* beer] carte of Mr Richard Portriffe of Rye aforesaid, juratt, and by mysfortune the said Susanna, beinge lett fall by the violent goinge of the horse and carte, the further wheale rone over' her head, whereby she died. The cart is worth 13s 4d and the horse 26s 8d. [*Verdict in English.*] RYE 1/7, ff 559–559v.

[The words 'did not appear' are marked for insertion after the names in square brackets, but possibly apply to the following names, above which they are written. At the Rye assembly of 25 Jan 1606 it was decided at the special request of Richard Portriffe that the 40s, the value of the horse and cart which were forfeit to Rye as deodand, should be reduced to 20s which Portriffe was to pay to the chamberlain and so regain his horse and cart. RYE 1/7, f 611v.]

2 6   9 Mar 1605. Stopham. George Ardern, gent., Rotherbridge hundred coroner. Jurors: William Westdeane, gent., John Sarys, gent., John Lane, John Sergante, John Edsawe, Miles Sutor, John Boode, Henry Campian, Thomas Brabye, William Colle, William White, Thomas Dunch, Thomas Pyper. About 10 a.m. on 4 Mar John Maskall not only violently assaulted John Nitingall late of Kirdford, 'carpenter', at Pallingham Quay near the river with 'a walkinge bill' worth 6d which he held in both hands but also violently assaulted him near 'le brinke' of the river with both hands extended, took him by the throat with both hands and tried to throw him into the river with all his strength. Thereupon Nitingall fled backwards as far as he could to 'the farthest syde' of the river at Pallingham Quay, beyond which he could not flee. Then Nitingall, seeing that he was in danger of losing his life, killed Maskall in lawful self defence with 'a walkinge byll' worth 6d which he held in both hands, reaching out towards him and feloniously giving him a wound under the left eye ½ inch long and about 2 inches deep of which he languished until 8 Mar and then died at Stopham. Nitingall had no goods or chattels. ASSI 35/47/7, m 1. [*Calendared in CAR, no 81.*]

[Delivered to East Grinstead assizes on 8 July. A copy of the inquest was sent into Chancery by the coroner on a writ of 12 June. C 260/179, no 20.]

27   11 Mar 1605. Heathfield. Thomas Woodgate, gent., duchy of Lancaster coroner in Pevensey rape. Jurors: Thomas Eyherst, Francis Wood, Thomas Kent, Jonah Fuller, William Hurrier, Walter Usborne, John Wackett, Thomas Wood, Thomas Iden, John Moore, John Gay, Robert Pryor, John Tysherst, Richard Meppham, John Sherwood. On 7 Mar Abraham Chilley late of Heathfield, 'laborer', murdered John Hobjohn at Heathfield with 'a hedgingbill' worth 6d which he held in both hands, giving him 7 fatal wounds on various parts of his body — one on the left shoulder 7 inches long and 4 inches deep, two on the left arm of which one was 4 inches long and 3 inches deep and the other 6 inches long and 3 inches deep, another on the left shin [*crus*] and knee 8 inches long and 4 inches deep, another on the left shin [*tibia*] 4 inches long and 2 inches deep, one on the right shoulder 3 inches long and 2 inches deep, and one on the right hand 3 inches deep — of which he languished at Heathfield until 10 Mar and then died. At the time of the felony Chilley had no goods or chattels, lands or tenements to the jurors' knowledge. ASSI 35/47/7, m 2. [*Calendared in CAR, no 63.*]
[Delivered with **26**. At the assizes an indictment was preferred which charged Chilley, called a husbandman, with murdering Hobjohn on 7 Mar at Heathfield with 'a bearinge bill' worth 6d which he held in both hands, giving him 2 fatal wounds — one on the left shoulder 7 inches long and 4 inches deep, the other on the left arm 4 inches long and 3 inches deep — of which he languished at Heathfield until 10 Mar and then died; and Joan wife of Richard Chilley late of Heathfield with feloniously inciting and procuring Abraham Chilley on 5 Mar at Heathfield to commit the murder. The grand jury affirmed the indictment of Abraham Chilley but rejected the charge against Joan. Abraham, who was said to have been committed to gaol after confessing, pleaded not guilty to the inquest verdict but was convicted and hanged; he had no chattels. ASSI 35/47/7, mm 2, 3, 13, 81; *CAR*, nos 61–63.]

28   14 Apr 1605. East Ashling. Zacchaeus Gyttins, Bosham hundred chamberlain and coroner. Jurors: Christopher Corderoy, John Button, John Scardvyle, Thomas Martyn, Robert Trowe, William Goledocke, Stephen Gratwicke, Michael Marchaunt, Robert Nonington, Edmund Goter, Christopher Graynge, Humphrey Penbrooke, Richard Luckyn, John Ingles. About 11 a.m. on 13 Apr, when Elizabeth, aged 2 or thereabouts, daughter of John White of East Ashling, 'husbandman', was playing alone at East Ashling near 'a keever of the depthe of eight inches or thearaboutes', by misadventure she 'did fall into' 'le keever' [*sc.* kiver, a tub] and was drowned. KB 9/718, m 124.
[Delivered with **23**. KB 9/718, mm 121, 128d; KB 29/246, m 77.]

29   15 Apr 1605. Horsham. John Aylwin, gent., coroner of the feoffees of Thomas late duke of Norfolk. Jurors: Richard Harrison, William Champion, Edward Bristowe, Humphrey Eaton, Arthur Woodgate, John Pylfold, John Stere, Thomas Pyke, Thomas Davie, Edward Jupp, James Slaughter, John Eve. On 15 Apr Thomasin Newton died a natural death in Horsham gaol. No one else was privy to her death to the jurors' knowledge. KB 9/718, m 122.
[Delivered with **23**. Newton was in gaol at the assizes on 8 Mar, having been sentenced at Chichester quarter sessions and remanded in gaol by the JPs. ASSI 35/47/6, m 50; KB 9/718, mm 121, 128d; KB 29/246, m 77; *CAR*, no 36.]

30   Same date, place, coroner and jurors (in the same order) as **29**. On 15 Apr Joan Wise died a natural death in Horsham gaol. No one else was privy to her death to the jurors' knowledge. KB 9/718, m 123.
[Delivered with **23**. At East Grinstead assizes on 13 July 1604 the grand jury had presented an indictment which charged Wise, Alice Growte, Margaret Squyer, Mary Baker and Margaret Kynge, all late of St John sub Castro, spinsters, who had been committed to gaol by Walter Covert, kt, JP, (Kynge under the name of Kynge alias Johnson), with burglary in that on 28 May 1604 they feloniously broke and entered the dwelling-house of Edward Hyde, clerk, at Poynings and took and carried away 2 pairs of flaxen sheets worth 20s, 3 hempen sheets worth 10s, 2 tablecloths worth 4s, 3 hats worth 6s 8d, a child's coat worth 12d, 2 bands and gorgets worth 2s 6d and a flaxen shirt worth 2s 6d belonging to Hyde. They all pleaded not guilty but were convicted; they had no chattels. Growte was hanged; Squyer was remanded in gaol after sentence because she was pregnant; and the others were remanded in gaol without sentence.

Wise, Squyer, Baker and Kynge were said to be still in gaol at the assizes of 8 Mar and 8 July 1605, although by the latter date Wise was dead. Kynge died a natural death in gaol on 17 Mar 1606. Squyer was executed on 29 July 1606 and buried at Horsham on the same day. 47; ASSI 35/46/3, mm 31, 32, 40; ASSI 35/47/6, m 50; ASSI 35/47/7, m 81; KB 9/718, mm 121, 128d; KB 29/246, m 77; *CAR*, nos 9, 14, 19, 36, 61; *CAR Introdn*, 171; SRS, XXI, 336.]

31   16 Apr 1605. Cliffe. John Aylwyn, gent., Loxfield Dorset half-hundred coroner. Jurors: Gargan [*Garganus*] Archer, Richard Norman, Hamon Hardiman, Richard Faucknor, Henry Martin, John Floyde, Henry Hulle, Henry Biggard, John Adames, John Grover, John Bexly, John Sharp. On 5 Apr Robert Emery late of Cliffe, 'shomaker', murdered Robert Martin at Cliffe with a knife worth 2d which he held in his right hand, giving him a wound in the left side of the chest 1 inch wide and 4 inches deep of which he immediately died. At that time Emery had no goods or chattels, lands or tenements to the jurors' knowledge. ASSI 35/47/7, m 6. [*Calendared in CAR, no 65.*]
[Delivered with **26**. At the assizes Emery, who had been committed to gaol by John Shurly, kt, and Herbert Morley, JPs, pleaded not guilty but was convicted and hanged; he had no chattels. ASSI 35/47/7, mm 6, 13, 81; *CAR*, nos 61, 62, 65.]

32   17 May 1605. Wadhurst. John Egles, Loxfield Camden half-hundred coroner. Jurors of Wadhurst: Alexander Butcher, John Barham, William Briant, Richard Marckwicke, Richard Burges, Nicholas Tayler, William Barham, 'Davi' Barham, Thomas Marckwicke jun., Peter Marckwicke, John Lewes, Nicholas Barham, Thomas Wenborne, William Terrye, George Collen. About 4 p.m. on 16 May, when Rose, one of the daughters of Thomas Porter of Wadhurst, gent., was looking into 'a drawwell' in her father's close at Wadhurst, by misadventure she suddenly fell into the well and was suffocated in the water, dying immediately. KB 9/718, m 125.
[Delivered with **23**. KB 9/718, mm 121, 128d; KB 29/246, m 77.]

33   26 June 1605. Slaugham. John Aylwyn, gent., coroner of the feoffees of Thomas late duke of Norfolk. Jurors: William Merry, William Burstie, Edmund Tomsett, John Codford, 'Randell' Bennett, Nicholas Write, George Moggeridg, Henry Moggeridge, John Scrace, Robert Archpole, John Ashfold, John Ellizander. On 2 June Joan Hockham alias Anstie feloniously hanged herself with 'a corde' worth 1d, tying it round her neck and round 'a birche tree' on the land of Agnes Gatforde, widow, in Slaugham. At that time she had no goods or chattels except those with Edmund Tomset, viz 'three paier of old sheetes [worth] viij s, item j old flockbedd, thre bolsters, j old pillowe v s, item fower peuter dishes and sawcers ij s iiij d, item j litle ketle, j canstick [*sc.* candlestick], j salt seller, j peuter cup xviij d, item her wearing apparell, lynen and wollen iiij s', total value 20s 10d. [*Inventory in English.*] KB 9/718, mm 126, 127.
[Delivered with **23**. Edmund Tompson (*sic*) was summoned to King's Bench to answer for the goods and chattels; he was outlawed at Lewes on 9 Oct 1606. KB 9/718, mm 121, 126, 128d; KB 29/246, m 77.]

34   20 July 1605. Arundel. Albany Stoughton, gent., Arundel liberty coroner. Jurors: Nathan [*Nethania*] Fenne, Henry Hobs jun., John Wulvin, Richard Heseman, Adam Kelsam, Thomas Thorne, Thomas Reading, James Voys, Benjamin Blundell, Silas [*Silvanus*] Paine, William Cooper, Richard Page, John Kendall, William Merchant, Thomas Moth. About 7 p.m. on 19 July, when John Johnes was alone in a 'prison house' at Arundel, he feloniously hanged himself with a leather girdle of no value which he held in both hands, putting one end round his neck and tying the other round 'an iron staple' fixed to the wall of the building. He had no lands or tenements nor any goods or chattels except a purse worth 1d and 3 halfpennies in it which were delivered to Nicholas Bell, one of the borough constables, who will answer for them to Thomas earl of Arundel and Surrey, lord of the liberty. KB 9/720, m 272.
[Delivered to the Sussex Lent assizes and on to King's Bench in Easter 1606. KB 9/720, m 277d; KB 29/247, m 5.]

35   30 July 1605. [*Place omitted.*] Albany Stoughton, gent., coroner of Chichester and Arundel rapes. Jurors: Nicholas Todman, William Philpe, Daniel Collyer, John Hopkin, Owen Typp, Anthony

Neale, John Trybe, Richard Asten, Nicholas Ide, Roger Bawcomb, John Dubbing, Thomas Ewen, John Ewen, Richard Ewen, Richard Hammond, Richard Saunders, Thomas Mersh, Thomas Wickman. On 22 July, when John Bradbridge late of Heyshott, 'taylor', was digging in 'a marlepitt' near the road in Heyshott between 11 a.m. and noon 'in the forenoone of ye same daie', a quantity of soil estimated at 'two loades of rubbish and greet' of no value fell on his head and body and so severely crushed him upon the ground that it killed him. KB 9/720, m 263.
[Delivered with 34. KB 9/720, m 277d; KB 29/247, m 5d.]

36   13 Aug 1605. [*Place omitted.*] Albany Stoughton, gent., Arundel liberty coroner. Jurors: Richard Butterwick, gent., Clement Tupper, Christopher Parham, Zachariah [*Zachia*] Gittens, William Grantham, Henry Scutt, John Sergeant, Henry Pricklowe, Robert Henly, Edward Rawson, Richard Bennet, William Lucas, John Elyott, Edmund Vallor, Thomas Grantham jun. On 10 Aug, when John Smith late of Bury, 'husbandman', was working in 'a chawlkpit upon Bury Hill' at Bury, by misadventure 'certaine chawlk and greete' amounting to 20 cartloads and a large stone of no value fell from the top of the pit upon his right shin and other inner parts of his body so that they broke his right shin and 'one of his thighes' and so severely 'did crush' the inner parts of his body that he languished for 3 hours afterwards and then died at Bury about 1 p.m. KB 9/720, m 260.
[Delivered with 34. KB 9/720, m 277d; KB 29/247, m 5d.]

37   15 Aug 1605. Compton. George Sarys, Westbourne hundred coroner. Jurors: Thomas Randall, Arthur Lodger, Robert Trevett, Clement Paddock, George Trevett, John Pay, Nicholas Cresseller, William Leiffe, William Lodger, Richard Lodger, Thomas Mylles, Edmund Fayremanner. On 9 Aug, when Christopher Cook was driving 'his carte' in 'Greenhill' at Compton, he fell under the further wheel of the cart, which was pulled violently by a horse and 2 oxen, and was wounded in 'his right legg' which was run over by the wheel whereof he died at Compton on 14 Aug. The horse, oxen and cart with its 2 wheels were the cause of his death and were delivered to Richard Mathewe, gent., hundred bailiff; they are worth 40s. KB 9/720, m 259.
[Delivered with 34. The bailiff was summoned to King's Bench to answer for the deodands; he had licence to imparl in Michaelmas 1607. KB 9/720, mm 259, 277d; KB 29/247, m 5d.]

38   16 Aug 1605. Sutton. Albany Stoughton, gent., Arundel liberty coroner. Jurors: Thomas Smart, Richard Bealle, Thomas Rhodes, Michael Gittens, John West, John Gunter, Thomas Legatt, Robert Bridges, William Langley, Robert Ford, John Blundell, James Coote, William Spicer, Thomas Etherton, Thomas Smythe, Richard Shottyer. About 1 p.m. on 8 July, when Mary, one of the daughters of Richard Ford of Sutton, 'husbandman', was in a pit on 'Forehill' at Sutton, by misadventure a quantity of soil and grit to the amount of 1½ cartloads, of no value, fell from the top of the pit on her head, burying her body, breaking her head and one of her shins and so severely crushing the whole of her body that she immediately died. KB 9/720, m 261.
[Delivered with 34. KB 9/720, m 277d; KB 29/247, m 5d.]

39   25 Aug 1605. Lindfield. John Aylwin, gent., coroner of the feoffees of Thomas late duke of Norfolk. Jurors: John Bartlett, John Garrett, John Martin, John Nutfeild, John Uden, William Neale, William Joye, William Tabbe, Thomas Davies, Robert Burt, Thomas Mascull, William Sayers, Henry Beldam. About 9 a.m. on 18 Aug Joan Drudge feloniously killed herself at Wivelsfield, drinking poison called 'rattes bane' mixed with a drink of which she died at 9 p.m. At the time of the felony she had goods and chattels worth 19s which remain with John Drudge of Edburton, viz 'a red peticote [worth] x s, two wastcotes iij s, a hatt xx d, an old peticote xij d, certein lynen iij s iiij d'. [*Inventory in English.*] KB 9/720, mm 273, 274.
[Delivered with 34. John Drudge was summoned to King's Bench to answer for the goods and chattels; he was outlawed at Lewes on 26 Mar 1606 (*recte* 1607: *MS* 4 *in error for* 5 James I). KB 9/720, mm 274, 277d; KB 29/247, m 5.]

40   11 Sept 1605. Petworth. Albany Stoughton, gent., Arundel liberty coroner. Jurors: Richard Norris, Thomas Stradlinge, gent., Edward Goble, Geoffrey Hawkins, Richard Hammond, Reynold Harrison, John Butcher, George Fry, John Shorter, Edward Crosse, Thomas Pimble, William Seamere, John Poling, Thomas Lucas, Edward Morley, John Michener, Thomas Alderton. Between noon and 1 p.m. on 10 Sept, when William Belchamber was alone in 'le staulhouse' next to 'le stoneheeld barne' which was in the occupation of Robert Sadler of Petworth, 'yeoman', he feloniously hanged himself with 'a peice of an hempen traice' of no value which he held in both hands, placing one end round his neck and tying the other round a piece of timber called 'a gueiste' [*sc.* joist] which was fixed in the stallhouse. He had no lands or tenements, but he had goods and chattels worth £11 2s [*sic*] which were seized by Nicholas Tompson, gent., for the use of Thomas earl of Arundel and Surrey, lord of the liberty, viz 'iij kine, 24 sheape [worth] vj li, item iij young hogges and one pigg xv s, item a parcell of rie and oates xlvj s viij d, item vj wattells xvj d, item certaine woodc xij d, item x pultry ij s, item foure load of dunge xij d, item sythes ij and ij lettell laderes ij s, item ij litle rackes iij d, item j lader xij d; in the hall, item an old cobbard and tabell, one forme, iiij platters, one shellfe, iiij cheastes iiij s iiij d, one [*word erased*], one possenet, j baskett, an iron pot and pott hangeres xij d, item ij candelstickes, j salt, j pronge, iiij bucketes, j share, ij bills, j axe, j hatchet ij s vj d, item ij seckells, j iron weadge, ij cheires, j stole, 4 trudges [*sc.* trugs] xij d, item one fringe panne, iij panches [*sc.* paunches: mats or coverings], j tableclothe viij d; in the rome next to the hall, item ij earnes [*sc.* urns], j table, ij ferkines and other tubes, j kettell, j kiver and other ould thinges v s; in the chamber, item ij ould bedes, ij coverlites, ij blancketes, ij paire of sheates, ij steadells [*sc.* bedsteads], ij boulsters x s, item iiij cheastes, j chaire and iiij cheses ij s vj d, item j dublet, jerkine, hose and hatt iij s, item j bushell of mault ij s'. [*Inventory in English.*] KB 9/720, mm 270, 271.

[Delivered with **34**. Tompson, called the earl's bailiff, was summoned to King's Bench to answer for the goods and chattels; he had licence to imparl in Trinity 1613. KB 9/720, mm 271, 277d; KB 29/247, m 5.]

41   14 Oct 1605. Westhampnett. George Sarys, Box hundred coroner. Jurors: William Rose, Jerome [*Jerominus*] Legate, John Skarvile, James Flote, John Salter, Thomas Court, Edmund Bridger, Richard Gage, William Clark, Henry Aylmer, William Joyes, William Aylmer. On 13 Oct David Marland feloniously hanged himself on 'a hasell tree' in 'Hasell Corner' at Westhampnett with 'a hasell with' which he placed on [*super*] his neck. At that time he had 46s 8d in money belonging to himself which was delivered to Richard Mathewe, gent., hundred bailiff. KB 9/720, m 275.

[Delivered with **34**. The bailiff was summoned to King's Bench to answer for the goods and chattels; he had licence to imparl in Michaelmas 1607. KB 9/720, mm 275, 277d; KB 29/247, m 5.]

42   6 Jan 1606. Rye. Thomas Hamon, Rye mayor and coroner, and the jurats. Jurors: Thomas Standen, William Halliard jun., James Mackett, Peter Cooper, Philip Williams, Thomas Beale, Richard Chauntler, Thomas Ceeley, Edward Jones, Richard Barker, Henry Davys, Thomas Humfrey, Robert Overington, John Carmon. On 4 Jan, when Robert Thomas, merchant, John Ferne, 'fysherman', and William Style, 'cockman', all of Rye, were with Stephen Harrison of Rye, 'jurat', John Burdett of Udimore, 'yeoman', and George Wood of Rye, 'taylor', in a cock-boat laden with barley in Wainway Creek, intending to sail and row to Rye, as they sailed towards Rye between Camber and the town 'by extreamatie of fowle wether' the boat 'was sunck and turned over' and the 6 men 'by mysfortune beinge turned over borde were all drowned'. The inquest was on view of the bodies of Thomas, Ferne and Style only. [*Verdict in English.*] RYE 1/7, ff 607–607v.

43   21 Jan 1606. Horsham. John Aylwin, gent., coroner of the feoffees of Thomas late duke of Norfolk. Jurors: Thomas Smith, Edward Bristowe, Edward Jupp, William Hilton, Henry Whitall, William Chambers, Henry Salter, Thomas Jupp, Thomas Galpin, John Steere, William Waterton, Richard Gates. On 21 Jan John Hubberd died a natural death in Horsham gaol. No one else was privy to his death to the jurors' knowledge. KB 9/720, m 244.

[Delivered with **34**. KB 9/720, m 277d; KB 29/247, m 6; *CAR Introdn*, 171.]

44   27 Jan 1606. Birdham in Manhood hundred. Henry Peckham, gent., coroner of the bishop of Chichester's liberties. Jurors: George Osbourne, John Tayler, John Seman, John Sander jun., John Aylmer, Robert Kibe, Cuthbert Calloway, William Cooke, John Chacrofte, Thomas Bussby, Clement Bent, William Mansbridge, Thomas Locke, John Bensted, Thomas Wilson. About 10 a.m. on 26 Jan, when 'Jowell' Ayres was in a windmill at Birdham 'grindinge mault', he went out of the mill and was struck on the left side of the head by the sails of the mill which were moving quickly, receiving a wound 1 inch long of which he immediately died. The sails, wheels and upper stone of the mill were moving at the time of his death and belong to Lancelot bishop of Chichester; they were appraised at 30s. KB 9/720, m 257.
[Delivered with **34**. The coroner was summoned to King's Bench to answer for defects in the inquest; process ceased in or after Hilary 1608 when it was found that there was no defect. KB 9/720, mm 257, 277d; KB 29/247, m 5d.]

45   1 Feb 1606. Stedham in Easebourne hundred. Albany Stoughton, gent., Arundel liberty coroner. Jurors: William Mellyshe, Roger Ailwin, 'Bresingham' Ailinge, Robert Chaper, Robert Blackman, Anthony Aylyng, Richard Ayling, Stephen Russell, Nicholas Bridger, Philip Wilson, John Ailing, Robert Richardes, Denis Randoll, Edward Dyer, William Sherfold. About noon on 31 Jan, when William Barkshere of Stedham, 'husbandman', was lopping an oak which was growing in a hedge in the south part of a close in Woolbeding called 'Milland', by misadventure he suddenly fell from the oak whereby his neck was broken and he immediately died. KB 9/720, m 262.
[Delivered with **34**. KB 9/720, m 277d; KB 29/247, m 5d.]

46   1 Mar 1606. 'Broyle Farme'. Henry Peckham, gent., coroner of the bishop of Chichester's liberties. Jurors: John Whatley, Richard Cooke, Richard Trunnell, James Gates, John Colden, William Gubbet, John Sander, John Thorne, Thomas Rumbridger, Robert Gray, William Churchman, Richard Roffe, William Gaven, Jeremy [*Jeremia*] Emerie, Thomas Egley. About 4 p.m. on ?1 Mar [*eiusdem diei*], when Thomas Sole was 'digginge sand' in a pit at Broyle Heath, he was crushed in all parts of his body by the sudden fall of 3 or 4 cartloads of sand whereby he immediately died. KB 9/720, m 258.
[Delivered with **34**. KB 9/720, m 277d; KB 29/247, m 5d.]

47   17 Mar 1606. Horsham. John Aylwin, gent., coroner of the feoffees of Thomas late duke of Norfolk. Jurors: Arthur Woodgate, Edward Burstowe, William Patching, Thomas Davis, Thomas Wheatly, John Pilfold, Thomas Pike, Edward Jupp, Richard Harrison, Roger Undrell, Edward Boker, Bartholomew Saiers. On 17 Mar Margaret King died a natural death in Horsham gaol. No one else was privy to her death to the jurors' knowledge. KB 9/720, m 245.
[Delivered with **34**. At East Grinstead assizes on 13 July 1604 the grand jury had presented an indictment which charged King, Joan Wise, Alice Growte, Margaret Squyer and Mary Baker, all late of St John sub Castro, spinsters, who had been committed to gaol by Walter Covert, kt, JP, (King under the name of King alias Johnson), with burglary in that on 28 May 1604 they feloniously broke and entered the dwelling-house of Edward Hyde, clerk, at Poynings and took and carried away 2 pairs of flaxen sheets worth 20s, 3 hempen sheets worth 10s, 2 tablecloths worth 4s, 3 hats worth 6s 8d, a child's coat worth 12d, 2 bands and gorgets worth 2s 6d and a flaxen shirt worth 2s 6d belonging to Hyde. They all pleaded not guilty but were convicted; they had no chattels. Growte was hanged; Squyer was remanded in gaol after sentence because she was pregnant; and the others were remanded in gaol without sentence. King, Wise, Squyer and Baker were said to be still in gaol at the assizes of 8 Mar and 8 July 1605, although Wise had died a natural death in the gaol on 15 Apr 1605. Squyer was executed on 29 July 1606 and buried at Horsham on the same day. **30**; ASSI 35/46/3, mm 31, 32, 40; ASSI 35/47/6, m 50; ASSI 35/47/7, m 81; KB 9/720, m 277d; KB 29/247, m 6; *CAR*, nos 9, 14, 19, 36, 61; *CAR Introdn*, 171; SRS, XXI, 366.]

48   Same date, place and coroner as **47**. Jurors: Arthur Woodgate, Thomas Davis, William Patching, Edward Burstowe, John Pilfold, Thomas Wheatlie, Edward Jupp, Thomas Pike, Richard Harrison, Edward Jupp jun., Bartholomew Saiers, Roger Undrell, Edward Boker. On 17 Mar William Chauncellor died a natural death in Horsham gaol. No one else was privy to his death to the jurors' knowledge. KB 9/720, m 247.

[Delivered with **34**. KB 9/720, m 277d; KB 29/247, m 6; *CAR Introdn*, 171.]

49   Same date, place and coroner as **47**.   Jurors: Edward Burstowe, Arthur Woodgate, Thomas Davis, William Patching, John Pilfold, Thomas Wheatley, Edward Jupp, Thomas Pyke, Richard Harrison, Edward Boker, Roger Undrell, Humphrey Eaton.   On 17 Mar Edward Hardham died a natural death in Horsham gaol.   No one else was privy to his death to the jurors' knowledge.   KB 9/720, m 246.
[Delivered with **34**. KB 9/720, m 277d; KB 29/247, m 6; *CAR Introdn*, 171.]

50   3 Apr 1606.   Rye.   Thomas Hamon, Rye mayor and coroner, and the jurats.   Jurors: Thomas Standen, William Helliard jun., William Tesdale, John Stronde, Samuel Baker, John Humfrey, Thomas Whithead, John Furmer, William Apprice, Thomas Brooke, David Haswell, John Ryder, Anthony Harris, Nicholas Bennett, Richard Vinall.   On the night of 2 Apr, exact time unknown, when Nicholas Knott of Rye, 'laborer', was 'on the further side of Rye Ferry' coming from Winchelsea and the ferry boat was 'laid upe', he decided 'to wade over the channell to come over unto Rye' and 'was by misfortune drowned'.   [*Verdict in English.*]   RYE 1/7, ff 614v–615.

51   9 Apr 1606.   Mayfield.   John Egles, Loxfield Camden half-hundred coroner.   Jurors of Mayfield: Abraham Edwardes, John Duke, Henry Dray, Robert Moone, Anthony Hilder, Robert Vinson, John Fuller, Richard Burges, Richard Water, John Parris, John Turnis, John Emerye, Thomas Duke.   About 9 a.m. on 7 Apr Joan Maunser late of Mayfield, 'spinster', gave birth prematurely to a male child, and so he came to his death at Mayfield by misadventure.   KB 9/721, m 295.
[Delivered to the Sussex summer assizes and on to King's Bench in Michaelmas. The death was also classified as a misadventure in King's Bench. KB 9/721, mm 295, 302d; KB 29/247, m 60d.]

52   12 June 1606.   Piddinghoe.   John Aylwin, gent., coroner of the feoffees of Thomas late duke of Norfolk.   Jurors: Henry Sone, Richard Crane, John Owton sen., John Owton jun., George Wood, James Hurst, William Lewes, Edward Worton, John Gyles, John Furnfold, Richard Ade, Richard Selme, Edward Copper.   When Agnes wife of James Marshall of Piddinghoe was going from Piddinghoe to Newhaven, a colt belonging to Thomas Ellis of Newhaven threw her to the ground and 'dyd bruse' and wound her in various parts of her body whereby she immediately died.   The colt remains with Ellis and is worth 26s 8d.   KB 9/721, m 293.
[Delivered with **51**. The note *pro bonis* was written on the inquest but there is no record of process for the deodand on the Controlment Roll. KB 9/721, mm 293, 302d; KB 29/247, m 60d.]

53   15 June 1606.   Chichester.   John Exton and Anthony Smyth, gents, Chichester city coroners. Jurors: Richard Buther sen., Thomas Diggens, John Pickering, John Carpenter, John Fleshmonger, George Mighell, Lawrence Sole, William Clapshewe, Edward Bradlie, William Warner, Thomas Hussye, William Whetham, Christopher Sewer, John Wright, Raymond Collick, Clement Smyth, Thomas Maye, John Gouge.   About 4 a.m. on 14 June Richard Fisher late of Chichester, 'husbandman', aged 45 or thereabouts, feloniously 'did drowne himself' in 'a ponde' called 'le dell hole' near Chichester.   He had goods and chattels worth 10d which remain with the city steward for the use of the mayor and citizens, but no lands or tenements.   KB 9/721, m 301.
[Delivered with **51**. KB 9/721, m 302d; KB 29/247, m 60d.]

54   11 July 1606.   East Grinstead.   Thomas Woodgate, gent., duchy of Lancaster coroner in Pevensey rape.   Jurors: John Payne, John Lee, Stephen Dungate, John Drewe, Henry Browne, Robert Bowyer, Isaac Turner, Henry Arlington, Richard Kydder, Nicholas Wyther, Richard Stavely, George Turner, William Jeale, John Weller, Edward Langridge.   On 15 July [*sic*] Joan Homewood sen. late of East Grinstead, 'spynster', murdered her children, Richard, Thomas and Joan jun., at East Grinstead with a knife worth 1d which she held in her right hand and with which she 'did cutt their throates', giving each of them a wound 1 inch long and 1 inch deep of which they immediately died; and afterwards, on the same day, she feloniously killed herself at East Grinstead, cutting her own throat with the same knife and throwing herself into a pond full of water and drowning herself. At that time she had no goods or chattels, lands or tenements in Sussex or elsewhere to the jurors' knowledge. The inquest was on view of all 4 bodies. KB 9/721, m 300.

[Delivered with **51**. The 3 children (called the children of Richard Homewood of the Dean) were buried at East Grinstead on 17 July. KB 9/721, m 302d; KB 29/247, m 60d; SRS, XXIV, 155.]

55   18 July 1606. Singleton. George Sarys, Singleton hundred coroner. Jurors: Daniel Court, Jerome [*Jerominus*] Legate, John Byrcher, Edward Beedinge, Thomas Vaughan, Robert Coote, John Love, Roger Greenwoodd, Richard Cook, Daniel West, Joseph Crane, William Collyck. On 9 July Edmund Bridger loaded his cart with thorns on Charlton Common at Charlton and then stood on the near wheel of the cart which was then violently pulled away by 'a thilther' [*sc.* thill *or* shaft] horse and Bridger fell from the cart onto the ground on his head whereby he broke his neck and immediately died. The horse and cart with its 2 wheels were the cause of his death and were delivered to Richard Mathewe, gent., hundred bailiff; they are worth 13s 4d. KB 9/721, m 294.

[Delivered with **51**. The note *pro bonis* was written on the inquest but there is no record of process for the deodands on the Controlment Roll of 4 James I. It was, however, probably in respect of the deodands that the bailiff had licence to imparl in Hilary 1610 and again in Trinity 1613. KB 9/721, mm 294, 302d; KB 29/247, m 60d; KB 29/251, m 128.]

56   27 July 1606. Hamsey. John Aylwin, gent., coroner of the feoffees of Thomas late duke of Norfolk. Jurors: George Randoll, John Drapier, John Hatche, John Awood, Robert Couelstock, Richard Braye, John Burthinshewe, Richard Joanes, John Awcock. On 27 July, when Joan Hawkines late of Hamsey, widow, was alone in [*blank*]'s wood at Hamsey, she feloniously hanged herself with 'a trace' worth 1d which she held in both hands, tying it round her neck and round the branch of a tree, whereby she immediately died. At that time she had goods and chattels worth 30s which remain with Thomas Hawkines of Hamsey, 'yeoman', viz 'one peticote [worth] x s, one gowne ij s, one russett peticot xij d, one hatt ij s, one savegard vj d, two necke clothes xviij d, two croseclothes [*sc.* cross-cloths, linen cloths worn across the forehead] xij d, one blewe aporn [*sc.* apron] viij d, one other aporn iiij d, one paier of showes, one paier of stockinges vj d, in monie x s vj d'. [*Inventory mainly in English.*] KB 9/1099, mm 455, 456.

[Delivered to East Grinstead assizes on 13 Mar and on to King's Bench in Easter 1607. Thomas Hawkines was summoned to King's Bench to answer for the goods and chattels; he was discharged in Hilary 1610 because the deputy almoner acknowledged satisfaction. KB 9/1099, mm 453d, 455; KB 29/248, m 6.]

57   9 Aug 1606. Rye. Thomas Hamon, Rye mayor and coroner, and the jurats. Jurors: William Bennester, Ralph Wood, Thomas Humfrey, Michael Colgate, Philip Williams, Edward Jones, William Denby, Peter Cooper, Richard Chauntler, John Radley, James Merry, David Howett, Thomas Hendley jun., Thomas Ceeley. On 8 Aug Thomas Bennett of Rye, 'cordiner' [*sc.* cordwainer], was sent 'about certeyne affaires' of Nicholas Cletor of Rye, 'cordiner', his master, to Winchelsea and 'was benighted before he could gett over at' Winchelsea Ferry 'and so comeing to Rye Ferry some what late in the eveninge could not gett over the ferry at Rye and by that meanes he was constreyned to stay untill it grewe towardes lowe water'. The next morning, 'adventuringe to wade over the ferry or channell before it was lowe water, by mysfortune' he was drowned. [*Verdict in English.*] RYE 1/7, ff 623–623v.

58   6 Oct 1606. Ditchling. John Aylwin, gent., coroner of the feoffees of Thomas late duke of Norfolk. Jurors: Thomas Haslegrove, John Yearden, Thomas Amore, William Gune, Henry Butcher, John Giles, Thomas Laker, John Benson, Andrew Coper, Thomas Waterman, Thomas Pritchett, Jasper Maye. On 6 Oct, when John Alchin late of Ditchling was riding on a horse belonging to John Wood of Ditchling, 'yeoman', he suddenly and against his will fell from the horse to the ground with his right foot hanging in 'a stirrup' of a saddle which was on the horse, whereby the horse fell on Alchin while

he was on the ground and struck him on several parts of his head, of which he immediately died. The horse is worth 16s and remains with John Wood. KB 9/1099, m 463.
[Delivered with **56**. Wood was summoned to King's Bench to answer for the horse; he was outlawed at Lewes on 28 Oct 1613. KB 9/1099, mm 453d, 463; KB 29/248, mm 6, 6d.]

59   24 Oct 1606. Graffham. Albany Stoughton, gent., Easebourne liberty coroner. Jurors: John Colden, Richard Hiberden, Richard Wisdom, Richard Woods, Roger Phillps, Richard Austen, Thomas Swaine, Richard Hammonde, Stephen Graffam, Thomas Paine, Thomas Mershe, Richard Saunders, Thomas Hartley, Nicholas Todman, John Upton, John Tribe, Thomas Wilson. About 11 a.m. [*no day given*] John Wisdom late of Graffham went out of his house taking with him a halter which he tied round his shins, ?tied [*dejunxit*] his hands behind his back with both of his 'cadis [*sc.* caddis, worsted] garters', threw himself forward into a pond containing water 2 feet deep or thereabouts and so feloniously drowned himself. He had no lands or tenements, goods or chattels. KB 9/1099, m 454.
[Delivered with **56**. KB 9/1099, m 453d; KB 29/248, m 6.]

60   29 Dec 1606. Pulborough. Albany Stoughton, gent., Arundel liberty coroner. Jurors: Robert Barnard, Henry Myles, John Mylles, Thomas Dunch, Thomas Coward, John Woodes, Richard Booker, William Hammond, William Hollis, Robert Hill, Edward Duke, Henry Ellis, Edward Tallmet, John Kennett, Richard Hill, John Parson, John Brockfeild, John Knowells, Thomas Mellish, Thomas Hall. About 9 p.m. on 27 Dec, when Edward Cooke of Pulborough, gent., was playing with playing cards with Anthony Bright of Pulborough, 'husbondman', Bright feloniously killed him with a dagger worth 2s which he held in his right hand: he 'did thrust' it into Cooke's left side, giving him a wound 7 inches deep and 1 inch wide of which he languished at Pulborough until 10 p.m. and then died. As soon as he had committed the felony Bright fled. At that time he had goods and chattels worth 17s 6d, part of which are in an inventory attached to this inquest [*now missing*]; they were taken by Nicholas Tompson, gent., for the use of Thomas earl of Arundel and Surrey, lord of the liberty. KB 9/723, m 222.
[Delivered to East Grinstead assizes on 13 Mar and on to King's Bench in Michaelmas 1607. King's Bench ordered Bright's arrest; he was outlawed at Chichester on 19 May 1608. The coroner was summoned to King's Bench to answer for defects in the inquest, which is much amended and omits the place where the felony was committed; he was outlawed at Lewes on 6 Oct 1608. KB 9/723, mm 221, 222, 227d; KB 29/248, m 71d.]

61   29 Apr 1607. Herstmonceux. Samuel Playfere, gent., Hastings rape coroner. Jurors: Richard Butcher, Henry Holbeane, Edmund Shether alias Stace, Richard Lattenden, William Hollock, John Gouldinge, John Benjamyn, Richard Bray, John Baker, Samuel Mote, George Beste, John Rychardes, Abel Smyth, Samuel Harper, William Hoode, Stephen Hatche, John Parson, Herbert Stace, Edmund Olyver, William Hendley. About 9 p.m. on 18 Apr, when John Tree late of Herstmonceux, 'yeoman', and John Kelley of Herstmonceux, 'tanner', were together at James Tayler's house in Herstmonceux, Kelley feloniously killed Tree, violently throwing him to the ground and then throwing himself upon him and crushing him with the weight of his body and with great force, whereby the inside of Tree's chest was so severely injured and crushed that he languished thereof seriously ill at Herstmonceux until 26 Apr and then died. Immediately after committing the felony Kelley fled from Herstmonceux to places unknown. At that time he had goods and chattels worth £4, viz a gelding worth 53s 4d which he took with him and clothing worth 36s 8d which remains at Herstmonceux with Thomas Peerson for the use of Thomas Pelham, esq., lord of the liberty; and no other goods or chattels, lands or tenements to the jurors' knowledge. KB 9/724, m 76.
[Delivered to East Grinstead assizes on 13 July 1607 and on to King's Bench in Easter 1608 when Kelley's arrest was ordered; he was outlawed at Chichester on 20 Apr 1609. Thomas Peerson of Herstmonceux was summoned to King's Bench to answer for Kelley's goods and chattels worth 36s 8d; he was outlawed at the same county court. KB 9/724, mm 75, 76, 76d; KB 29/249, mm 10, 10d.]

62   27 May 1607. Storrington. Albany Stoughton, gent., Arundel liberty coroner. Jurors: John Duppa, gent., John Parram, Robert Barnard, Richard Searle, John Humfrye, John Scutt, Henry Calowe,

Thomas Bennett, Robert Feilder, James Slawghter, William Scutt, Richard Dunch, Robert Pligram. Between 4 and 5 a.m. on 19 Apr John Bennett of Storrington, 'yeoman', went to his barn at Storrington and feloniously hanged himself with 'a peece a hempen trace' of no value which he held in both hands, fixing one end round his neck and the other round 'a winbeame' [*sc.* wind-beam, a cross-beam tying the rafters of a roof] of the barn. At that time he had no lands or tenements but he had goods and chattels worth £55 7s 10d which were taken by John Peirse, gent., for the use of Thomas earl of Arundel and Surrey, lord of the liberty. KB 9/724, m 237.

[Delivered with **65** and on to King's Bench in Easter 1608. Peirse was summoned to King's Bench to answer for the goods and chattels; he had licence to imparl in Hilary 1610 and was discharged in Hilary 1618 when letters patent of 27 (*recte* 22) Feb 1554, enrolled in King's Bench in Hilary 1590, showed the liberties granted to Henry earl of Arundel and his heirs. KB 9/724, mm 237, 243d; KB 29/249, mm 5d, 6; KB 29/251, m 128; *CPR 1553–1554*, 69–70.]

63   2 July 1607. Arundel. Albany Stoughton, gent., Arundel hundred [?*recte* borough *or* rape] coroner. Jurors: Nicholas Bell, Henry Hobbes jun., John Aylewyn, Thomas Mothe, Thomas Reddinge, Richard Heasman, John Bridger, William Marchant, William Cooper, Thomas Coles, John Lucas, William Moore, Anthony Bruster, Richard Richardes, John Arnold. On 29 June, when Christopher Bridger was riding on a white horse worth 53s 4d on 'Sutton Hill' in Sutton, he suddenly and by misadventure fell from the horse to the ground whereby his neck 'was broken', of which he immediately died. Because the horse was moving to his death it is deodand. KB 9/724, m 233.

[Delivered with **62**. The coroner was summoned to King's Bench to answer for defects in the inquest, probably including the failure to record the custody of the deodand; he had licence to imparl in Hilary 1610 and was later pardoned. KB 9/724, mm 233, 243d; KB 29/249, m 6; KB 29/251, m 129.]

64   16 July 1607. Hastings. James Lasher, Hastings mayor and coroner, and other jurats. Jurors: Robert Jenkyn, Nicholas Lobdell, Thomas Streat, Thomas King, Robert Sharvall, Edward Foord, Gregory Gregory, Peter Winckfeld, Henry Sennock, James Shusmyth, John Leaver, Benjamin Brooke. Between 9 and 10 a.m. on 16 July Luke, aged about 3, son of Alice Woolcombe of Hastings, widow, went out of Alice's house without her knowledge to play around the water of the Bourne outside the town walls, accidentally fell into the water and was drowned by misadventure before anyone discovered him. Shortly afterwards he was found by Henry Tyers, a small boy, who told his mother and she hastened there with William Chepman's wife and took Luke out of the water but they were unable to restore him to life. HASTINGS C/A(a) 1, f 123.

65   3 Aug 1607. Lodsworth. Albany Stoughton, gent., Easebourne hundred coroner. Jurors: Edward Leggatt, John Bridger, Richard Lynton, Thomas Billinghurst, John Feilder, Roger Hollest, Edward Leare, Edward Morris, Thomas Page, Edward Longe, Stephen Osbarne, Roger Summers, William Marshall, William Skynner, Philip Marshall, John Yealden. On 2 Aug Thomas Sheppard late of Lodsworth, 'husbondman', murdered Dorothy Sheppard, his natural mother, at Lodsworth with 'a staffe with an iron pike in thend thereof' worth 12d which he held in both hands, striking and stabbing her in several parts of the head and body: he gave her various fatal wounds on the head and 'did breake in peces' 'the skull', whereby she immediately died. Immediately afterwards Thomas was arrested and committed to the county gaol. He had no goods or chattels, lands or tenements. ASSI 35/50/9, m 2. [*Calendared in CAR, no 100.*]

[Delivered to East Grinstead assizes on 22 Feb 1608 when Thomas Sheppard, who had been committed to gaol by Henry Gorynge, kt, JP, pleaded not guilty but was convicted and hanged; he had no chattels. ASSI 35/50/9, mm 2, 8, 38; *CAR*, nos 98–100.]

66   18 Aug 1607. Rye. Thomas Higgons, Rye mayor and coroner, and Thomas Colbrand and Richard Cockeram of Rye, jurats. Jurors: Thomas Radford, George Raynoldes, Isaiah [*Ezaius*] Kindgewood, John Coper, John Gillam, Peter Harrison, Thomas Wattes, Thomas Mason, John Ivy, John Boycott, Richard Barker, John Whithead, Nicholas Bennett, Robert Bower, John Puntelborow, Edward Nower, William Dawson, Richard Thorneborow. Between 2 and 3 p.m. on 17 Aug Robert

Burditt of Rye, 'barber', the town 'gonner', 'standinge uppon the mounte' in the Gun Garden of Rye, 'by misfortune of a peece of ordinance, which was shott of in the Gongarden' 'and broke in peeces uppon the discharginge thereof', 'one peece of the said peece of ordinance that so brake and fleow did streeke' 'Burditt upon the breast and did carry away his right arme, by meanes of which forceable stroake he presently died'. [*Verdict in English.*] RYE 1/8, ff 54–54v.
[This misadventure occurred in the presence of the mayor and others. On 29 Aug it was decreed at the Rye assembly that in view of the poverty of Martha Burditt, Robert's widow, and her child they should be paid quarterly the yearly stipend of 40s granted to Robert for his life, but that payment should cease if she remarried. RYE 1/8, f 56v.]

67   11 Sept 1607. Chichester. Anthony Smyth, gent., Chichester city coroner. Jurors of Chichester: Thomas Diggons, John Hilles, William Flode, Michael Nash, Henry Clarke, Humphrey Colbrooke, Richard Bigges, John Pollard, William Roades, Roger Rawlens, George Bennett, Thomas Swaine, Raymond King, George Leeve, George Michell, Philip Wisdome, Thomas Grigg, John Tuckes, Henry Brace. About 7 p.m. on 9 Sept, when Leonard Smyth late of Chichester, 'taylor', aged 60 or thereabouts, was riding on a horse worth 13s 4d at Broyle Heath near Chichester, he fell together with the horse whereby his head and face were crushed, of which he languished at Chichester until the next day and then died. The horse remains with Thomas Brigham of Chichester. KB 9/724, m 235.
[*Endorsement by the coroner*] 'This happened within the liberty of the bishopp of Chichester, but the partye died within the cittie of Chichester and the horse, as I am credible informed by Thomas Brighames of Chichester, the owner thereof, died also within nine daies after'.
[Delivered with **62**. Brigham was summoned to King's Bench to answer for the horse; he was discharged in Easter 1609 because the deputy almoner acknowledged satisfaction. KB 9/724, mm 235, 243d; KB 29/249, m 6.]

68   6 Oct 1607. Storrington in Arundel rape. Albany Stoughton, gent., West [*on the second occurrence erroneously changed to* East] Easwrith hundred coroner. Jurors: William Egerton sen., Thomas Belchamber, William Egerton jun., Henry Egerton, Thomas Bennett, Henry Chance, Edward Tanner, Richard Pilgryme, William Pilgryme, William Hames, Thomas Boneface, Hugh Blincoe, John Higgyns. On 5 Oct, when John Furder was working in 'a well' at Storrington, by misadventure 'a tubb' of wood worth 12d fell into the well onto his head and 'did bruse' 'the scull', of which 'bruse' he immediately died. Because the tub was moving to his death it is deodand. KB 9/724, m 232.
[Delivered with **62**. The coroner was summoned to King's Bench to answer for defects in the inquest, probably including the failure to record the custody of the deodand; he had licence to imparl in Hilary 1610 and was later pardoned. KB 9/724, mm 232, 243d; KB 29/249, m 6; KB 29/251, m 129.]

69   19 Dec 1607. West Preston in Arundel rape. Albany Stoughton, gent., Poling hundred coroner. Jurors: Richard Parker, John Carden, John Younge, Robert Mayster, Robert Marten, John Eade, John Carter, John Smithe, Thomas Summers, Thomas Gratwicke, John Younge, Thomas Capon, Thomas Standford. On 18 Dec Elizabeth Greene late of West Preston, widow, went to 'a well' full of water at West Preston, feloniously threw herself into it and was immediately drowned. At that time she had no lands or tenements but she had goods and chattels worth 40s which were taken by John Peirse, Poling hundred bailiff, for the use of Thomas earl of Arundel and Surrey, lord of the liberty. KB 9/724, m 238.
[Delivered with **62**. The bailiff was summoned to King's Bench to answer for the goods and chattels; he had licence to imparl in Hilary 1610 and was discharged in Hilary 1618 when letters patent of 27 (*recte* 22) Feb 1554, enrolled in King's Bench in Hilary 1590, showed the liberties granted to Henry earl of Arundel and his heirs. KB 9/724, mm 238, 243d; KB 29/249, mm 5d, 6; KB 29/251, m 128; *CPR 1553–1554*, 69–70.]

70   30 Dec 1607. Fittleworth in Manhood hundred. Henry Peckham, gent., coroner of the bishop of Chichester's liberties. Jurors: Richard Hale, Henry Milles, Henry Whitbred, John Brabie, Henry Smithe, Thomas Hobjohn, George Brookfeild, George Bacheler, Henry Piper, Edward Piper, Stephen Essex, Thomas Sander, James Whetley, John Chrusloe, John Brookfeild, John Hudson, Edward Curtis. About 3 p.m. on 28 Dec, when James Weston late of Fittleworth, 'labourer', was alone in 'the Rushie Feild' at Fittleworth, he feloniously hanged himself with 'a line' of no value which he held in both hands, putting one end round his neck and tying the other round a branch of a willow. He had no goods or chattels, lands or tenements. KB 9/724, m 239.

[Delivered with **62**. The result of the inquest was presented at the view of frankpledge at Houghton on 4 Apr 1608 when the deceased was called James West. The jurors did not know what goods he had at the time of his death or where they were. KB 9/724, m 243d; KB 29/249, m 5d; WSRO, MP 76, f 24.]

71 1 Feb 1608. Lamberhurst. John Egles, Loxfield Camden half-hundred coroner. Jurors: Richard Tharpe of Lamberhurst; William Sellen, William Benge, Edward Hosmer, all of Wadhurst; Alexander Lindridge of Lamberhurst; Richard Atkin of Wadhurst; John Sheefe, William Peniall, Thomas Maye, William Maye, Nicholas Weller, Thomas Austen, William Maye, all of Lamberhurst. About 1 p.m. on 13 Jan Rebecca Henberye of Lamberhurst, widow, gave birth prematurely to a male child at Lamberhurst and so he came to his death by misadventure and not otherwise. KB 9/724, m 234.

[Delivered with **62**. This death was also classified as a misadventure in King's Bench. Rebecca Henberye had been committed to Horsham gaol by John Colepeper, esq., JP, on suspicion of murder before the East Grinstead assizes of 22 Feb 1608 but she seems not to have stood trial. ASSI 35/50/9, m 38; KB 9/724, mm 234, 243d; KB 29/249, m 6; *CAR*, no 98.]

72 9 Feb 1608. Folkington. Thomas Woodgate, gent., duchy of Lancaster coroner in Pevensey rape. Jurors: Thomas Peirce, Edmund Wade, William Hogbeane, Lawrence Wade, John Tytland, John Stewarde, John Wensham, William Daniell, Bartholomew Awcock, John Atwood, John Parker, William Skynner, William Potnell, William Dorredge, John Higham, John Gyles. On 2 Feb Isaac Harmer late of Folkington, 'husbandman', feloniously hanged himself at Folkington with a halter worth ¼d, putting it round his neck and tying it to 'a beame'. At that time he had goods and chattels worth £9 16s 2d which remain with Thomas earl of Dorset, Lord Treasurer of England. KB 9/724, m 240.

[Delivered with **62**. The Lord Treasurer was summoned to King's Bench to answer for the goods and chattels, erroneously said to be worth £9 6s 2d; process continued until he was returned as being dead; he had died on 19 Apr 1608. The suicide was presented at the Folkington view of frankpledge some time in 1608. The volume containing the record of the presentment is at present missing, but according to a printed translation the cord with which Harmer hanged himself was worth 1d; his goods and chattels were appraised at the view at £8 15s and were seized for the use of the lord of the manor, Thomas earl of Dorset, but he, having pity on Harmer's relict Elizabeth and his children, granted the goods and chattels to them for 20s. KB 9/724, mm 240, 243d; KB 29/249, m 5d; *SNQ*, I, 190.]

73 19 Feb 1608. Wivelsfield. John Aylewyn, gent., coroner of the feoffees of Thomas late duke of Norfolk. Jurors: Ninian Burrell, John Godley, Richard Godley, Thomas Ileman, John Paine, Thomas Hoder, Thomas Kidd, John Geale, Thomas Ashford, John Fawknor, Thomas Picknoll, Thomas Awcocke. About 3 p.m. on 7 Feb, when Ann Standen late of Wivelsfield, Charity Esterfeild and Joan Tycrofte were eating and drinking together at Wivelsfield in the dwelling-house of Henry Standen of Wivelsfield, Ann's father, John Sponer late of Wivelsfield, 'laborer', came to the house holding 'a gunne' in both hands 'beinge chardged with powder and haile shott'. As Sponer sat with Ann, Charity and Joan, having the gun in both hands, suddenly it 'was dischardged' by misadventure and without Sponer's knowledge and will, and Ann 'was wounded' in the lett arm by the shot, of which she languished at Wivelsfield until 8 p.m. and then died. She was thus killed by misadventure. The gun is worth 2s. ASSI 35/50/9, m 18. [*Calendared in CAR, no 116.*]

[Delivered with **65**. Sponer had been committed to gaol by Edward Culpepper, kt, JP, on suspicion of murder but seems not to have stood trial. ASSI 35/50/9, m 38; *CAR*, no 98.]

74 21 Feb 1608. Horsham. John Aylwin, gent., coroner of the feoffees of Thomas late duke of Norfolk. Jurors: Richard Gates, William Beard, James Edwardes, Edward Bristowe, John Hudson, Gilbert Sayers, 'Marckes' Pledge, Edward Boker, Robert Bonus, William Hilton, Nicholas Pyke. On 21 Feb James Bodle died a natural death in Horsham gaol. No one else was privy to his death to the jurors' knowledge. KB 9/724, m 227.

[Delivered with **62**. Bodle had been committed to gaol by Thomas May, kt, JP, on suspicion of murder but died just before the East Grinstead assizes of 22 Feb. He is recorded as having been buried at Horsham on 30 Jan although the inquest was said to have been taken on view of his body. ASSI 35/50/9, m 38; KB 9/724, m 243d; KB 29/249, m 6; *CAR*, no 98; *CAR Introdn*, 171; SRS, XXI, 367.]

75   9 Mar 1608. Chichester. John Exton and Anthony Smith, gents, Chichester city coroners. Jurors of Chichester: James Coobberley, William Dore, Thomas Jenman, Thomas Smith, Richard Butcher jun., John Binden, Thomas Champion, William Clapshewe, William Stevenson, John Hobson, William Sowton, Richard Penten, Raymond Kinge, Ralph Etherington, John Norris, John Bartilmewe, George Kee, Henry Clarck, John Weight. About 2 p.m. on 8 Mar, when Alice Bridaye late of Chichester, aged 3 or thereabouts, was 'playinge' among other children by the River Lavant in a place called 'Without Eastgate' at Chichester, by misadventure she 'did fall into' the river and was drowned. No one else was privy to her death. KB 9/725, m 446.
[Delivered to East Grinstead summer assizes and on to King's Bench in Michaelmas. KB 9/725, m 456d; KB 29/249, m 75.]

76   26 Mar 1609. Chichester. John Exton and Anthony Smyth, Chichester city coroners. Jurors: Richard Trigges, Henry Chyttie, Richard Chatfeild, Richard Michell, Henry Gracie, Edward Setcap, Richard Cnell, Alan Gardner, William Tolpat, William Bartlet, William Clapshoo, Richard Westwood, Thomas Akeres, Richard Penton, William Penton, Robert Cawley. On the night of 25 Mar, when she was alone, Priscilla Taylor of Chichester, 'spinster', feloniously took poison into her body, so killing herself. She had no goods or chattels, lands or tenements. KB 9/727, m 310.
[Delivered with 77 and on to King's Bench in Michaelmas. KB 9/727, m 313d; KB 29/251, m 73d.]

77   25 Apr 1609. Sompting. John Aylwin, gent., coroner of the feoffees of Thomas late duke of Norfolk. Jurors: Edward Barnard, John Gilbert, Philip Stamer, Thomas Campion, Edward Baker, John Short, William Michilborne, Edward Smithe, John Turneagaine, Thomas Kent, Philip Pollingham, Thomas Turner. On 14 Apr Samuel Eightacre late of Sompting, 'husbandman', feloniously killed Bartholomew Denis alias Ellis at Sompting with a staff worth 1d which he held in both hands, giving him 3 fatal 'bruses' on his head — one on the right side of the head, another on the left and the third 'under the lyst [*sc.* list, the lobe] of the left ear' — of which he languished at Sompting until 24 Apr and then died. At the time of the felony Eightacre had no goods or chattels, lands or tenements in Sussex or elsewhere to the jurors' knowledge. ASSI 35/51/9, m 13. [*Calendared in CAR, no 142.*]
[Delivered to East Grinstead assizes on 17 July when a bill of indictment was preferred which charged Eightacre, called a miller, with murdering Denis on 21 Apr in the road at Sompting with a cudgel worth 2d which he held in his right hand, giving him a wound on the front of the head 2 inches deep of which he immediately died, and then given him 7 other wounds on the head of which he would have immediately died if he had not died of the first blow. The grand jury, to which Robert Humfrey, William Turnagayne and John Gurlyn gave evidence, reduced the charge to manslaughter. Eightacre, who had been committed to gaol by Thomas Leedes, kt, JP, confessed to the inquest verdict. He then successfully pleaded benefit of clergy and was branded and released. ASSI 35/51/9, mm 13, 39, 45, 46d; KB 9/727, m 281; KB 29/251, m 74; *CAR*, nos 125, 142.]

78   30 Apr 1609. Durrington. John Aylwin, gent., coroner of the feoffees of Thomas late duke of Norfolk. Jurors: Henry Rowland, John Munnery, Cyprian Tirrill, Thomas Grey, Henry Streter, Robert Munnery, John Pollord, Henry Herne, Edward Peter, John Wheatley, 'Jeffer' Lucas, John Strete. About 4 a.m. on 30 Apr Thomas Duke feloniously hanged himself on a plot of his land at Durrington with 'a taile roope' worth 4d which he held in both hands, putting one end round his neck and tying the other round a branch of 'an aple tre'. At that time he had goods and chattels worth £10 4s 6d which were 'praised the thirtith daie of Aprell at his house in' Durrington and remain with Robert and John Munnery, viz 'a garden plott of beanes and peace [worth] v s, item a litle feild of peace x s, item one acre of tares viij s, item dim. an acre of barlie viij s, item a grey mare xv s, item a cowe xl s, item a bullock, a sowe and piges xj s, item fower shepe x s, item certen implementes of husbandry xx d, item a table and 3 joyned stoles iiij s, item a fether bed and bolster, j blanckett, j coverlett, 2 paier of shetes and the badstede xvj s, item wooden vessell and other implementes ij s, item j cubbard, brasse and peuter x s, item ij spittes and other fier implementes xij d', total £7 1s 8d. [*Inventory mainly in English.*] KB 9/727, mm 308, 309.

[Delivered with **76**. The Munnerys were summoned to King's Bench to answer for the goods and chattels worth £10 4s 6d; both were outlawed at Chichester on 5 Sept 1610. KB 9/727, mm 309, 313d; KB 29/251, m 73d.]

79 31 May 1609. Mayfield. John Egles, Loxfield Camden half-hundred coroner. Jurors: Thomas Maynard, Hugh Lucke, both of Mayfield; Nicholas Puxtie of Wadhurst; Thomas Lighe, Thomas Duke, both of Mayfield; Abraham Mabb of Wadhurst; John Fuller, Anthony Hilder, Thomas Marten, Henry Marten, John Turnice, Richard Burgis, Robert Kent, all of Mayfield. On 15 May Thomas Moone late of Mayfield, 'laborer', died a natural death at Mayfield. KB 9/727, m 376.

[Delivered to King's Bench by the coroner in Michaelmas. KB 9/727, m 376d; KB 29/251, m 69d.]

80 8 June 1609. Wadhurst. John Egles, gent., Loxfield Camden half-hundred coroner. Jurors of Wadhurst: William Briantt, Thomas Kindgwood, Richard Ford, William Grombridge, William Selen, Thomas Upten, Thomas Russell, Andrew Skiner, Francis Baker, Thomas Norton, Abraham Mabb, Francis Endge, William Cord. About 10 a.m. on 3 June, when Simon Burgis was working in 'a marle pett' at Wadhurst, by misadventure 'a pece of marle or earth' fell onto his body, threw him to the ground and so crushed and wounded his body that he languished thereof at Wadhurst until 7 June and then died. KB 9/727, m 301.

[Delivered with **76**. KB 9/727, m 313d; KB 29/251, m 73d.]

81 30 June 1609. Worth. John Aylwin, gent., coroner of the feoffees of Thomas late duke of Norfolk. Jurors: James Hyde, Alexander Tailor, Stephen Burgis, John Bulton, Walter Kinge, John Tye, William Baker, Richard Blunden, Thomas Tibboll, Giles Netlingham, Richard Harroden, Thomas Bett. On 30 June John Swyft murdered Francis Swyft, aged ½ year, at Worth, taking him in his hands and giving him several '?nipes and bruses' on various parts of his body with his hands of which he immediately died. John Swyft then immediately fled. At that time he had no goods or chattels in Sussex to the jurors' knowledge. KB 9/727, m 311.

[Delivered with **76**. John Swyft's arrest was ordered by King's Bench; he was outlawed at Chichester on 17 May 1610. He had been committed to Horsham gaol by Thomas Churcher, esq., JP, on suspicion of murder before the East Grinstead assizes of 23 Mar 1610 when he was still in gaol but did not stand trial. ASSI 35/52/8, m 51; KB 9/727, m 313d; KB 29/251, m 73d; *CAR*, no 161 (Swift rendered Owist).]

82 28 July 1609. Framfield. John Aylwin, gent., county coroner. Jurors: John Squier, John Chambers, John Martin, Robert Abroke, Daniel Kent, Robert Smithe, John Levitt, Andrew Orgle, Gregory Tailor, William Warnett, John Smither, Richard Hook. On 7 July Cuthbert Browne late of Warbleton, 'yeoman', assaulted William Brokes at Framfield, beating, wounding and illtreating him, and feloniously killed him with 'a pole' worth 1d which he held in both hands, stabbing him in the left eye whereby the eye immediately 'fell out' and giving him a wound 3 inches deep and 1 inch wide of which he languished until 10 July and then died. Immediately after committing the felony Browne fled. At that time he had no goods or chattels, lands or tenements. ASSI 35/52/8, m 35. [*Calendared in CAR, no 178.*]

[Delivered to East Grinstead assizes on 23 Mar 1610 when Browne was still at large. ASSI 35/52/8, m 35; *CAR*, no 178.]

83 27 Aug 1609. Chidham. Thomas Filder, Bosham manor coroner. Jurors: John Tilley, Michael Gase, William Wapham, William Skearle, William Rendall, Edward Amearse, John Trimlet, John Foster, Edmund Lee, Michael Jelley, William Sheparde, Henry Wackeford, James Squier, George Shepard, Henry Copis, John Souter, John Nicolson. On 21 Aug 'Warram' Blushe of Chidham, 'carpenter', murdered Andrew Wolgar at Chidham, giving him many fatal wounds of which he languished at Chidham until 25 Aug and then died. At the time of the murder Blushe had no lands or tenements,

goods or chattels to the jurors' knowledge. ASSI 35/52/8, m 45. [*Calendared in CAR, no 177.*]
[Delivered with **82**. At the assizes a bill of indictment similar to the inquest verdict was preferred which added that
Blushe had thrown Wolgar to the ground and then pressed on him with his knee, giving him a wound with his knee on
the left side of his chest of which he languished from 21 to 25 Aug and then died. The grand jury, to which George
Sheppard, Richard Hoskyn, Dorothy Booker, Ann Harvey and Joan Rofe (*or* Rose) gave evidence, reduced the charge
to manslaughter. Blushe, who had been committed to gaol by the coroner, was not tried at the Lent assizes but was
remanded in gaol. He died before the 1610 summer assizes, having been buried at Horsham on 6 Apr. ASSI 35/52/8,
mm 34, 45, 51; *CAR*, nos 161, 177; SRS, XXI, 372.]

84   11 Jan 1610. Lewes. John Aylwin, gent., coroner of the feoffees of Thomas late duke of
Norfolk. Jurors: John Standen, William James, Thomas Burkin, William Feilder, Edward Bastard,
William Fysher, John Streter, John Hintie, Thomas Thomson, John King, Edward Turle. On 11 Jan
James [*later called* John] Crampe died a natural death in Lewes gaol. No one else was privy to his
death to the jurors' knowledge. KB 9/728, m 167.
[Delivered with **82** and on to King's Bench in Easter. KB 9/728, m 208d; KB 29/252, m 7; *CAR Introdn*, 171.]

85   13 Jan 1610. Lewes. John Aylwin, gent., coroner of the feoffees of Thomas late duke of
Norfolk. Jurors: John Streter, William James, Thomas Hawkines, John Chesman, John Mantle, William
Turle, William Tailor, Edward Waller, Stephen Machin, William Dodson, Thomas Burkin, William Feilder.
On 13 Jan John Morgane died a natural death in Lewes gaol. No one else was privy to his death to the
jurors' knowledge. KB 9/728, m 166.
[Delivered with **84**. KB 9/728, m 208d; KB 29/252, m 7; *CAR Introdn*, 171.]

86   20 Feb 1610. Mayfield. John Egles, Loxfield Camden half-hundred coroner. Jurors of Mayfield:
William Relfe, Thomas Webb, Andrew Moone, Robert Moone, Thomas Relfe, William Moone, Richard
Riche, Richard Somer, William Gillatt, William Marten, Daniel Draye, John Bonicke, Robert Cade.
About 4 p.m. on 10 Feb, when Grace, one of the daughters of Robert Tyhurst of Mayfield,
'husbondman', was alone, she was found dead in her father's pit at Mayfield, having then come to her
death there by misadventure. KB 9/730, m 625.
[Delivered to Sussex summer assizes and on to King's Bench in Michaelmas. KB 9/730, m 645d; KB 29/252, m 65.]

87   8 Apr 1610. Wadhurst. John Egles, Loxfield Camden half-hundred coroner. Jurors of Wadhurst:
Thomas Wenborne, William Baldocke, John Pollye, William Selden, James Vallance, Christopher
Maunser, Isaac Somer, Richard Sharp, Nicholas Barham, Thomas Norton, Amyas *or* Amos [*Amoseus*]
Younge, Ralph Gardener, William Holland, Edward Apce. About 5 a.m. on 8 Apr, when William Kitchenam
late of Wadhurst, 'yoman', was alone near John Barham's pit at Wadhurst, he feloniously threw
himself into the pit and drowned himself. At that time he had no lands or tenements within the liberty,
but he had goods and chattels of his own worth 74s net which were valued on 9 Apr by Thomas
Wenborne, Nicholas Barham, John Pollye and William Baldocke 'with many other', viz 'his purse,
girdell and mony and his apparell [worth] 2s 6d, item one mare, a pack sadle, a wanty [*sc.* a rope for
fastening a pack on a pack-saddle] and a halter 20s, item one grinston [*sc.* grindstone] 12d, item in the
hale one table, a setle and a chayer 6s, item in the drinking chamber scertayne lumber 3s 4d, item in a
litle rome a cubbard 5s, item in the loft chamber 3 chaffe beddes, a chest 5s, item scertayne trenchers
to the number of xx grose 15s, item 3 badd bedstedeles 3s, item scertayne hoopes and other lumber 2s,
item a payer of fetters and a horse locke 2s, item tymber to make trenchers and his working tooles 5s,
item 3 stockes of bees 3s 4d, item wood to the value of two loades 2s, item som faggottes 3s', total £3
18s [*sic*]; and on the said 9 Apr, on the taking of this inquest, they were taken by Robert Horlye, half-
hundred bailiff, for the use of Thomas Maye, kt, lord of the liberty, as forfeit to Maye by reason of the
felony and they are now with Maye. [*Inventory mainly in English.*] KB 9/730, mm 639, 640.
[Delivered with **86**. The bailiff was summoned to King's Bench to answer for the goods and chattels worth £3 14s;
he was outlawed at Chichester on 10 Aug 1611. KB 9/730, mm 639, 645d; KB 29/252, m 65.]

88   13 Apr 1610. Lamberhurst. John Egles, gent., Loxfield Camden half-hundred coroner. Jurors: Thomas Pavis of Lamberhurst; Richard Weston, Robert Sare, John Pollye, all of Wadhurst; Edward Walter of Lamberhurst; John Smyth of Mayfield; John Dyne of Wadhurst; William Peniall, Daniel Baldocke, Richard Langham, all of Lamberhurst; John Grombridge, Stephen Ollye, William Holland, Richard Burgis, William Selden, all of Wadhurst. On 10 Apr John Blackmore of Lamberhurst, 'laborer', drank so much spirits [*aqua vite*] at Richard Fowle's house in Lamberhurst that he died. KB 9/730, m 630.
[Delivered with **86**. This was classified in King's Bench as a death by misadventure. KB 9/730, mm 630, 645d; KB 29/252, m 65.]

89   6 May 1610. Rudgwick. 'Albany' Stoughton, gent., Rotherbridge liberty coroner. Jurors: Walter Champion, John Naldred, Christopher Napper, Richard Napper, John Hobbes, Michael Greenefeild, William Cooper, Richard Ireland, Henry Humfrey, Henry Wacham, Robert Greenefeild, Francis Booker, William Turner. On 6 May, when Edward Clayton, aged 5, was playing round a pit in Rudgwick, he suddenly and by misadventure fell into the pit and was drowned. KB 9/730, m 627.
[Delivered with **86**. KB 9/730, m 645d; KB 29/252, m 65.]

90   1 June 1610. Ditcham in Dumpford hundred. Henry Peckham, gent., county coroner. Jurors: John Mills, Nicholas Hall, Henry Hall, John Pitt sen., John Pitt jun., William Emes, George Hether, Stephen Vengom, James Rickman, Thomas Freland, Richard Wever, Stephen Brishant, Henry Wever. About 8 a.m. on 31 May, when John Moodie of Ditcham, 'labowrer', was alone in a place at Ditcham called 'the stable', he feloniously hanged himself with a piece of leather of no value tied round his neck. He had no goods or chattels, lands or tenements. KB 9/730, m 638.
[Delivered with **86**. Moodie was buried on the day of the inquest by order of the coroner in the highway near Hemner in Harting between two lordships. KB 9/730, m 645d; KB 29/252, m 65; *Sussex Family Historian*, XI, 75.]

91   26 June 1610. Coldwaltham. Henry Peckham, gent., coroner of the bishop of Chichester's liberty. Jurors: John Knoles, William Bacom, Richard Knowles, John Braby, Edward Northe, John Rose, Daniel Braby, Edward Greene, Stephen Hopkins, Henry Piper, Richard Stone, Richard Rooke, Henry Mills, Roger Paise, John Scut, Henry Whitbred, Richard Smithe. About 6 a.m. on 4 June, when Alice Willard was alone in John Willard's dwelling-house in Coldwaltham, she gave herself a wound in the stomach 6 inches long and 1 inch wide with a knife which she held in her right hand, of which she immediately died. She had no goods or chattels. KB 9/730, m 637.
[Delivered with **86**. This was classified in King's Bench as a felonious suicide. KB 9/730, mm 637, 645d; KB 29/252, m 65.]

92   13 July 1610. Wadhurst. John Egles, Loxfield Camden half-hundred coroner. Jurors: John Barham of Wadhurst; Stephen Panckhurst of Mayfield; William Crottoll of Wadhurst; Thomas Maynard, Thomas Lighe, John Ducke, all of Mayfield; William Benge, William Courthopp, William Briant, John Hethfild, George Daw, Alexander Collen, all of Wadhurst. About ?3 a.m. on 12 July, when Joan Maynard, who had recently come from the house of her husband, Richard Maynard of Mayfield, 'yoman', to that of Lancelot Faulkner in Wadhurst, was lying in bed with 2 other women, she rose from the bed and went 'in the higher gallire [*sc.* gallery]', from there crossed into 'a hole or open place' and thence onto 'a gutter between the house and the chimnies'. While walking on 'the topp' of 'the bricke wale' she suddenly fell backwards onto the ground, broke her neck, 'did bruse and breake' the rest of her body and so came to her death. [*Damaged.*] KB 9/1083, m 103.
[Delivered to East Grinstead assizes on 18 Feb and on to King's Bench in Easter 1611. KB 9/1083, m 87d; KB 29/253, m 5d.]

93   20 July 1610. Easebourne. 'Albany' Stoughton, gent., Rotherbridge liberty coroner. Jurors: Anthony Lickfowld, Robert Launder, Thomas Kent, Thomas Lander, Edward Lere, Robert Legatt,

John Bridger, John Kent, Philip Marshall, Stephen Osborne, John Yalden, William Payne, Roger Somner, John Hollis, Robert Briger. On 19 July, when Peter Middleton was riding a gelding of a 'flebitten' colour at Easebourne, he suddenly and by misadventure 'did fall' from the gelding's back onto the ground, whereby his neck was broken and he immediately died. The gelding is deodand and remains with John Peirse, Arundel rape bailiff. KB 9/730, m 629.
[Delivered with **86**. The bailiff was summoned to King's Bench to answer for the gelding worth (*blank*); he was discharged in Hilary 1618 by virtue of letters patent of 28 (*recte* 22) Feb 1554 to Henry earl of Arundel, enrolled in King's Bench in Hilary 1590, which granted him and his heirs, inter alia, all deodands within his lands. The coroner was also summoned to King's Bench to answer for defects in the inquest, almost certainly including the omission of the deodand's value; he was outlawed at Chichester on 10 Aug 1611. KB 9/730, mm 629, 645d; KB 29/252, m 65; *CPR 1553–1554*, 69–70.]

94   27 July 1610. Duncton. 'Albany' Stoughton, gent., Rotherbridge liberty coroner. Jurors: Thomas Sandham sen., John Cotes, Thomas Morris, Thomas Sandham jun., William Blunden, John Blunden, Thomas Markes, William Cover, John Napper, William Phillipps, Robert Ford, Richard Ayling, Valentine Bridger, Jeremy [*Jeremia*] Sheete. On 26 July, when Simon Stoughton of Woolavington was riding on a 'browne' blind gelding at Woolavington, by misadventure the gelding ran under a tree and Stoughton 'did knocke' his head against the tree, receiving 'a bruse' of which he immediately died. The jurors appraised the gelding at 5s and it remains with John Peirse, Arundel rape bailiff, for the use of Thomas earl of Arundel and Surrey, lord of Rotherbridge liberty and of the rape. KB 9/730, m 628.
[Delivered with **86**. The bailiff was summoned to King's Bench to answer for the gelding; he had licence to imparl in Michaelmas 1613. KB 9/730, mm 628, 645d; KB 29/252, m 65.]

95   Same date, place and coroner as **94**. Jurors: Thomas Sandham sen., John Cotes, Thomas Morrys, Thomas Sandham jun., William Blunden, Thomas Markes, William Cover, John Napper, Robert Goble, William Phillipps, Robert Forde, Richard Ayling, Valentine Briger, Henry Sheete. On 26 July Hugh Marshall went to a pit full of water at Duncton, feloniously threw himself into it and drowned himself. At that time he had no goods or chattels, lands or tenements to the jurors' knowledge. KB 9/730, m 641.
[Delivered with **86**. KB 9/730, m 645d; KB 29/252, m 65.]

96   27 July 1610. Slinfold. 'Albany' Stoughton, gent., Rotherbridge liberty coroner. Jurors: Robert Penfowld, John Puttocke, John Songer, Anthony Hayler, John Stringer, Thomas Penfowld, George Hearth, Thomas Puttocke, William Vachan, John Cooper, Anthony Brumefeild, John Edwardes. On 25 July, when Abraham Baytes was riding on 'a stone horse' [*sc.* a stallion] of 'baye' colour in 'a river' at Slinfold, by misadventure he fell from the horse's back into the water and was drowned. The horse is deodand and remains with John Peirse, Arundel rape bailiff. KB 9/730, m 626.
[Delivered with **86**. The bailiff was summoned to King's Bench to answer for the horse worth (*blank*); he had licence to imparl in Michaelmas 1613. The coroner was also summoned to King's Bench to answer for defects in the inquest, almost certainly including the omission of the deodand's value; he was outlawed at Chichester on 10 Aug 1611. KB 9/730, mm 626, 645d; KB 29/252, m 65.]

97   10 Aug 1610. Dallington. Samuel Playfere, gent., Hastings rape coroner. Jurors: Benjamin Edwardes, Stephen Rabbet, William Ponte, Stephen Stace, John Avery, Robert Feild, David ...eman, John Katchloe, Richard Hebden, John Hugget, Robert ?Wood, Richard Lowl?, Alexander Rolfe. On 18 Apr, when Abigail Parsons late of Warbleton was in the house of John Parsons, her husband, at Warbleton, John Howsell late of Warbleton, 'husbondman', and 'Moses' Mott late of Herstmonceux, 'husbondman', feloniously killed her: Howsell violently kicking her on the left side of the abdomen, she being pregnant, and throwing her on her back upon 'a cradle', whereby her abdomen and back were severely injured and 'brused', whereof she languished at Warbleton until 8 Aug when she was delivered prematurely of a foetus and then died; and Mott being feloniously present aiding and abetting Howsell to commit the felony. Immediately after committing the felony Howsell and Mott

fled. They had no goods or chattels, lands or tenements at that time or ever after to the jurors' knowledge. [*Damaged.*] KB 9/1083, m 31.
[Delivered to King's Bench in Easter 1611 by the coroner. King's Bench ordered the arrest of Howsell and Mott; both were outlawed at Chichester on 15 Apr 1613. The township of Warbleton was summoned to King's Bench to answer for their escape; it made fine in Easter 1617. KB 9/1083, mm 31, 31d; KB 29/253, m 2.]

98   3 Dec 1610. Ashington. John Aylwyn, gent., coroner of the feoffees of Thomas late duke of Norfolk. Jurors: William Whitebread, ..., John Lacester, Thomas Horley, Thomas Bennett, Richard Lynfeild, Solomon Barlowe, Thomas Juppe, William Langford, Thomas Scotchford, Richard Langford, Henry Lynfeilde, ... On 3 Oct, when John Gaston late of West Grinstead, 'yeoman', was fishing in a stream which ran through William Parson's field in West Grinstead, Parson found him fishing and struck him on his body with an iron-pointed staff. Gaston fled backwards from Parson as far as a high hedge beyond which he could not flee and Parson furiously pursued him, violently and continuously striking him with the staff and wishing to kill him. Thereupon Gaston, to save his life and because he could in no other way escape death, struck Parson on 'the throate' with an iron-pointed staff which he held in both hands, giving him a wound 1½ inches deep and 1 inch wide of which he immediately died; and so Gaston killed him in self defence and not feloniously or of malice aforethought. [*Damaged.*] C 260/182, no 13.
[Delivered to East Grinstead assizes on 18 Feb 1611 by the coroner and to Chancery by the assize judges on a writ of 7 Feb 1612. Gaston was pardoned for the death by letters patent of 17 Feb 1612 which were accepted at East Grinstead assizes on 24 Feb. C 260/182, no 13; WSRO, SAS Lewes Deeds B625; *SNQ*, VIII, 153.]

99   8 Jan 1611. Wadhurst. John Egles, Loxfield Camden half-hundred coroner. Jurors: Thomas Maynard of Mayfield; Thomas Upten, John Barratt, Robert Sare, Richard Lucke, Richard Weston, William Upten, William Grombridge, James Vallance, Francis Enge, John Hethfild, Thomas Aligh, Christopher Bate, Nicholas Poccocke, John ?Rdrst, Abraham Luck, all of Wadhurst. About 5 p.m. on 6 Jan, when George Longly late of Wadhurst was in Frankham field in Wadhurst walking from Rotherfield to his dwelling-house in Wadhurst, a man thought to be called 'John Above the Wind' came and murdered him with 'a clubbe staffe six foot longe' worth ½d which he held in both hands, giving him a wound on the left side of the ... which penetrated the scalp to the brain whereby he immediately died. [*Damaged.*] KB 9/1083, m 88.
[Delivered with **92**. This was classified in King's Bench as a murder by a man unknown although an order was made for the arrest of John Above the Wind; process seems to have immediately ceased. KB 9/1083, mm 87d, 88; KB 29/253, m 5.]

100   17 Jan 1611. Hastings. Richard Wytheris, Hastings mayor and coroner. Jurors: Thomas Lasher sen., John Crabb, Thomas Palmer, Thomas Lasher jun., Richard Hollybon, John Crashfeild, William Fawtley, John Wood, 'shomaker', George Bradbury, Thomas Stapley, Thomas Thistlethwaites, Christopher Salter, William Lovell, James Gabriell. Between 9 and 11 a.m. on 16 Jan Margery wife of Stephen Tayler of Hastings, 'brewer', climbed 'the staires' and went alone into her small and private bedroom in the highest part of her husband's house in Hastings and feloniously hanged herself with a cord worth 2d which she found there and which she fixed round a cross-beam and tied round her neck. Shortly afterwards she was found by Stephen and his servants. HASTINGS C/A(a) 1, f 149v.

101   12 Mar 1611. Peasmarsh. Samuel Playfere, gent., Hastings rape coroner. Jurors: John Austen, Thomas Davy, Thomas Mathewe, Richard Iden, William Holte, John Sampson, Stephen Beechinge, Thomas Fowle, Thomas Bennett, Richard Fryer, William Davye, Thomas Holman, Herbert Aneston, William Danyell, William Avan, John Walter, William Wympsherst. On 6 Feb John Hobden late of Dallington, 'laborer', who was very weak and ill, died a natural death at Peasmarsh. KB 9/1084, m 155.
[Delivered with **102** and on to King's Bench in Michaelmas. KB 9/1084, m 131d; KB 29/253, m 62d.]

102   26 Mar 1611. West Dean in Singleton hundred. George Sarys, gent., king's coroner in the liberty of Lady Elizabeth Lumley, widow. Jurors: John Strettyn, William Keyse, Richard Crowcher sen., William Collick, John Farr, William Haselere, Henry Rusbridger, Thomas Paye, John Collick, John Love, Robert Coote, Robert Aylwyn. On 25 Mar Jasper Tregose of West Dean, 'yeman', met John Aylwyn at West Dean, insulted him with abusive words and feloniously killed him in the road with 'a armed sword' which he held in both hands, giving him a wound in and through the left thigh 2 inches wide and 5 inches deep of which he immediately died. Tregose's goods and chattels were delivered to Richard Mathewe, gent., bailiff of the hundred. ASSI 35/53/8, m 8. [*Calendared in CAR, no 206.*] [Delivered to East Grinstead assizes on 24 June when the inquest was declared void because it was insufficient (probably because the goods and chattels were not valued) and it was ordered to be drafted afresh. On the same day a writ was issued to the sheriff for Tregose's arrest and production at the next Sussex assizes; at the East Grinstead assizes of 24 Feb 1612 the sheriff, Edward Bellingham, kt, returned that he was not found in his bailiwick. The revised draft of the inquest is generally expressed in more usual form, with some pieces of information in a different order; it omitted the insult with abusive words, valued the sword at 2s, said that Tregose held it in his right hand, and for the delivery of his goods and chattels to the bailiff substituted the statement that at the time of the felony he had no goods or chattels, lands or tenements to the jurors' knowledge. The revised inquest was delivered to the assizes of 24 Feb 1612 and on to King's Bench in Easter. King's Bench ordered Tregose's arrest; he was outlawed at Lewes on 16 Mar 1614. The township of West Dean was summoned to King's Bench to answer for his escape; it had licence to imparl in Trinity 1614. ASSI 35/53/8, m 8; ASSI 35/54/9, m 2; KB 9/734, mm 457, 458, 458d; KB 29/254, m 2; *CAR*, nos 206, 235.]

103   15 May 1611. Hastings. Martin Lyfe, Hastings mayor and coroner. Jurors of Hastings: John Crabb, Anthony Wennell, Thomas Streat, John Crashfeild, John Boddy, James Bacheller, George Bradbury, Robert Wright, Peter Grover, William Lovell, James Furner, Anthony Pretty, James Gabriell, Christopher Fawtley, George Easton. About 8 a.m. on 15 May Thomas Woolf late of Southwark in Surrey, 'petty chapman', murdered John Martin, 'petty chapman', at Hastings with 'a crabtree cudgell picked with yron' worth 3d which he held in his right hand, giving him a wound on the back of the head 1½ inches long and ½ inch deep of which he immediately died. Afterwards Woolf fled. The jurors asked that this inquest be recorded in the common book or register of Hastings. HASTINGS C/A(a) 1, f 152v.
[Woolf was captured by the hue and cry, brought before the mayor and jurats and committed to Hastings gaol without bail until the next gaol delivery, on 22 May, when the grand jury presented an indictment identical to the inquest verdict but omitting the last 2 sentences. Woolf pleaded not guilty to the indictment but was convicted of murder and of fleeing and sentenced to death; he had no goods or chattels. He was executed on 24 May near the hermitage on the road leading to the priory, near the place where the murder was committed. HASTINGS C/A(a) 1, ff 152v–153.]

104   31 July 1611. Old Fishbourne. Richard Jellie, Bosham hundred chamberlain and coroner. Jurors: Thomas Michelborne, Nicholas Penn, William Napcroft, Thomas Feilder, John Feilder, Thomas Barnham, Richard Bawcomb, Thomas Hore, William Styles, William Bone, William Redwell, John Longvill, John Styll, John Foster, William Barnham. On 31 July, when Francis Blighton late of Fareham in Hampshire, 'barber surgion', was riding on the road at Old Fishbourne, he 'was taken with a bleeding at the nose' of which he died a natural death on the road. KB 9/734, m 381.
[Delivered with **107** and on to King's Bench in Easter 1612. KB 9/734, m 403d; KB 29/254, m 5.]

105   5 Oct 1611. Lamberhurst. John Egles, Loxfield Camden half-hundred coroner. Jurors: Thomas Stonard, William Baldocke, William Maynerd, all of Lamberhurst; Peter Marckwicke of Wadhurst; Thomas Lindridg of Lamberhurst; Nicholas Taylor, Richard Burges, John Pollye, William Terrye, all of Wadhurst; Thomas Hatton, William Dyne, John Maye, Richard Crowherst, Robert Wilkin, William Longlye, Richard Sharpe, all of Lamberhurst. On 4 Oct Elizabeth Edmundes late of Lamberhurst died a natural death at Lamberhurst. KB 9/734, m 382.
[Delivered with **104**. KB 9/734, m 403d; KB 29/254, m 5.]

106   3 Jan 1612. Slindon in Aldwick hundred. Henry Peckham, gent., county coroner. Jurors: John Whittington, Lawrence Chace, John May, Edward Harvest, Philip Guppie, John Court, 'Guillam'

Bateman, William Nowell, Joseph Purdue, Bartholomew White, Robert Gruggen, Thomas White, George Deane. About 5 p.m. on 31 July 1611, when Henry Wise, aged 12, was playing in 'Slindeane Streete', by chance he 'did pull downe the tayle of a little cart with strawe theyrin' whereby he was crushed and immediately died. The cart is worth 2s 6d and remains with George Coles for the king's use. KB 9/734, m 396.
[Delivered with **104**. Coles was summoned to King's Bench to answer for the cart; he was discharged in Hilary 1613 because the deputy almoner acknowledged satisfaction. KB 9/734, mm 396, 403d; KB 29/254, mm 4d, 5.]

107   30 Jan 1612. Framfield. John Aylwyn, gent., county coroner. Jurors: William Warnett, George Taylor, John Smyther, Richard Broke, John Packham sen., William Testor, John Wood, John Martyn, John Chamber, John Alcocke, John Gower, John Lambert, Richard Goldsmith. On 19 Jan, when John Levett of Framfield, 'yeoman', Barnabas Cade late of Framfield, 'laborer', and Edward Isted late of Framfield were playing together with several others at Framfield, Levett, who held 'a cudgell' worth ¼d in his right hand, 'did throw' it, intending to hit 'a henn' which was nearby. When he had thrown it, suddenly and without his knowledge Anthony Deane came into the road where he had thrown it, whereby Levett struck him with the cudgel on the head, giving him a wound 2 inches deep and 1 inch wide of which he immediately died; and so Levett killed him by misadventure and not feloniously or of malice aforethought. At that time Levett had no goods or chattels, lands or tenements to the jurors' knowledge. ASSI 35/54/9, m 38. [*Calendared in CAR, no 233.*]
[Delivered to East Grinstead assizes on 24 Feb. There is a note *se defendendo* at the foot of the inquest, a copy of which was sent into Chancery by the assize judges on a writ of 20 June 1612. ASSI 35/54/9, m 38; C 260/182, no 22.]

108   6 Feb 1612. Lamberhurst. John Egles, gent., Loxfield Camden half-hundred coroner. Jurors of the half-hundred: Richard Sharpe, Robert Benge, Thomas Hatton, John Dyne, Daniel Baldocke, Thomas Lyndridge, Richard Carew, John Chiesman, Robert Newill, Henry Leddall, John Mason, Nicholas Dixon, John Longley. On 22 Jan Agnes Pavy late of Lamberhurst, 'spinster', gave birth to a live male child at Lamberhurst and afterwards, on the same day, she murdered him there, taking him in her hands and breaking his neck with both hands of which he immediately died. At that time she had no goods or chattels, lands or tenements to the jurors' knowledge. ASSI 35/54/9, m 17. [*Calendared in CAR, no 227.*]
[Delivered with **107**. Pavy, who had been committed to gaol by John Colepeper, esq., JP, pleaded not guilty at the assizes but was convicted and hanged; she had no chattels. ASSI 35/54/9, mm 17, 19, 43d, 44; *CAR*, nos 222, 227.]

109   17 Feb 1612. Mayfield. John Egles, Loxfield Camden half-hundred coroner. Jurors: John Peckham, Robert Stephens, Thomas Trice, Abraham Gasson, Richard Wyborn, Thomas Whappam, James Crowherst, all of Mayfield; Abraham Langham of Wadhurst; Robert Blatchenden, Thomas Noakes, both of Burwash; John Elliott, William Merser, Lawrence Hilder, John Stephens, all of Mayfield. On 14 Feb, when Abraham Wimble late of Mayfield was alone in Coxdown field in Mayfield, he died a natural death. KB 9/734, m 383.
[Delivered with **104**. KB 9/734, m 403d; KB 29/254, m 5.]

110   19 Mar 1612. Framfield. John Aylwin, gent., county coroner. Jurors: John Button, John Squier, John Smither, John Sickle, John Topsill, John Alfry, William Barneham, William Brackpole, Richard Paige, Robert Edwardes, James Vyne, George Taylor. On 10 Mar Ann Thatcher died a natural death at Framfield. KB 9/736, m 291.
[Delivered with **112** and on to King's Bench in Michaelmas. KB 9/736, m 308d; KB 29/254, m 65d.]

111   7 Apr 1612. Westergate in Aldingbourne. Anthony Smyth, gent., the bishop of Chichester's coroner. Jurors: Walter Godman, Thomas Edwardes, William Trott, Thomas Duke, John Elson jun., William Smyth, George Finch, Roger Savage, John Bennet, Henry Butcher, John Stapler, Thomas Smyth, William Emery, Robert Marner, Richard Clayton. About 3 p.m. on 6 Apr, when John Woolf jun.

of Westergate, aged 15 or thereabouts, was alone in 'a barne' belonging to John Woolf sen. of Westergate, his father, at Westergate, he feloniously 'did hang himselfe' with 'a little rope or cord' worth 1d which he held in both hands: he put one end round his neck and the other he 'did throwe or caste over' 'a hamerbeame' in the barn and 'did winde round' his right arm 'and make faste'. He had no goods or chattels, lands or tenements. KB 9/736, m 304.
[Delivered with 110. KB 9/736, m 308d; KB 29/254, m 65d.]

112   16 Apr 1612. Easebourne. 'Albany' Stoughton, gent., county coroner. Jurors: Nicholas Aylinge jun., William Aylinge, Anthony Aylinge, Nicholas Bridger jun., William Carter, Ralph Chandler, George Smith, John Gosden, John Chandler, 'Cristofer' Chandler, John Challen, Thomas Kempe, Christopher Tydye, Ralph Kempe. On 14 Apr, when Ralph Hollis and John Hollis late of Easebourne, 'laborer', were playing 'trape balle' in friendly fashion with several others at Easebourne, in the course of the game John threw 'a ball' which immediately by misadventure and against his will struck Ralph, his brother, on the left side of the head under the ear, giving him a wound of which he immediately died; and so John killed him by misadventure and not otherwise. At that time he had no goods or chattels, lands or tenements to the jurors' knowledge. ASSI 35/54/10, m 2. [Calendared in CAR, no 245.]
[Delivered to East Grinstead assizes on 13 July.]

113   12 July 1612. Wadhurst. John Egles, gent., Loxfield Camden half-hundred coroner. Jurors: Nicholas Maunser, Abraham Maunser, William Barham, Thomas Maunser, John Younge, Richard Cliften, John Webbe, Paul Gunill, all of Wadhurst; John Page of Mayfield; Nicholas Gunill, Joseph Chapman, George Hasselden, Thomas Coleman, all of Wadhurst. About 10 a.m. on 8 June, when Abraham Wood late of Wadhurst, 'laborer', who was ill, was working in 'a marle pitt' at Wadhurst, by misadventure a piece of soil suddenly fell on his body and 'did bruse' it, of which illness and 'brusing' he languished at Wadhurst until 16 June and then died. KB 9/736, m 294.
[Delivered with 110. The death was classified in King's Bench as a misadventure. KB 9/736, mm 294, 308d; KB 29/254, m 65d.]

114   15 Aug 1612. Cuckfield. Thomas Rickward, county coroner. Jurors: Jewell [Jewelis] Parvis, Nicholas Delve, Stephen Jynner, Thomas Gatland, Hugh Anstie alias Feild, Walter Aptitt, James Eede, Robert Thorneden, Thomas Vynall, Henry West, Thomas Anstie alias Feild, Thomas Aylerd, Henry Symons, Richard Parke. On 22 July 'a certaine nagg', a gelding belonging to John Brooker of Hurstpierpoint, 'yoman', worth 30s by misadventure gave Andrew Payne late of Cuckfield, 'horssryder', a severe wound in the brain with its hoof and shoe at Cuckfield of which he immediately sickened and languished until 26 July and then died at Cuckfield. The gelding remains with Brooker. KB 9/737, m 278.
[Delivered with 122 and on to King's Bench in Easter 1613. Brooker was summoned to King's Bench to answer for the gelding; he was outlawed at Lewes on 17 Mar 1614. 'Old' Andrew Payne was buried at Cuckfield on 30 July 1612 although the inquest is said to have been held on view of his body. KB 9/737, mm 278, 290d; KB 29/255, m 6; SRS, XIII, 141.]

115   20 Sept 1612. Lyminster. Albany Stoughton, gent., Arundel rape coroner. Jurors: Richard Olliver, John Kewill, John ..., Thomas Gawen, John Forde, John Watersfeild, William Jackson, Thomas S..., Richard Ireland, John Hardinge, Peter Colley. On 16 Sept, when John Len of Lyminster was riding on a 'grey' gelding on the road at Lyminster, suddenly and by misadventure he 'did fall' from its back upon ... and 'received' a wound on the left side of ... of which he languished at Lyminster until 18 Sept and then died. The gelding was the cause of his death, is worth £5 and remains with John Peirce, gent., bailiff of Thomas earl of Arundel and Surrey, lord of the rape. [Damaged.] KB 9/739, m 387.
[Delivered with 123 and on to King's Bench in Michaelmas 1613. The bailiff was summoned to King's Bench to answer for the gelding; he had a writ of error in Hilary 1617 and his outlawry was reversed in Trinity 1617 by virtue of letters patent to Henry late earl of Arundel, enrolled in King's Bench in Hilary 1590. KB 9/739, mm 387, 399d;

KB 29/255, m 89; KB 29/261, m 175d; *CPR 1553–1554*, 69–70.]

116   16 Oct 1612. Pagham in Aldwick hundred. Henry Peckham, gent., county coroner. Jurors: John Grinlie, John Smithe, John Lawrence, Richard Haule, John Burrey, Thomas Hammon, Robert Cooke, Thomas Downer, Robert Dashe, Richard West, Henry Henshewe, John Wilcocke, Richard Morle, William Pratt. About 5 a.m. on 15 Oct John Watersfeild late of Pagham, 'husbandman', feloniously threw himself into 'a well' at Pagham and drowned. He had goods and chattels worth £13 6s 8d which were delivered to George Coles for the Lord Almoner's use. KB 9/737, m 280.
[Delivered with **114**. This death was classified in King's Bench as a misadventure, presumably in error. KB 9/737, mm 280, 290d; KB 29/255, m 6.]

117   25 Nov 1612. Westhampnett. John Aylwin, gent., county coroner. Jurors: William Rose, Edward Rose, Jeremy [*Jeremia*] Legatt, Thomas Vahan, Thomas Stere, James Flotte, Thomas Fuller, John Scardevill, Robert Payne, Robert Randoll. On 25 Nov, when John Greye was alone in William Aylmer's field in Westhampnett, he feloniously hanged himself with 'a roope' worth ½d, tying one end round the ?lowest branch [*?carinum*] of a tree which was growing there and putting the other end round his neck. At that time he had no goods or chattels to the jurors' knowledge. KB 9/737, m 286.
[Delivered with **114**. KB 9/737, m 290d; KB 29/255, m 6.]

118   9 Dec 1612. Petworth. Albany Stoughton, [gent.], Arundel rape coroner. Jurors: Thomas Sturt sen., William Bridger, Thomas Pratt, Thomas Humphrie, Nicholas Turgis, John Dey, Edward ...orch, Thomas Goble, John Ducke, Robert Bloxsom, John Pygeon, William Sandham, James Baker. On 7 Dec Nicholas Bisser [*once written* Brisser] suddenly and by misadventure fell into 'a furnace' full of 'scaldinge worte' at Petworth in which he was suffocated and immediately died. [*Damaged.*] KB 9/739, m 391.
[Delivered with **115**. On the Controlment Roll Bisser is called late of West Hoathly, labourer, but that description should almost certainly belong to Richard Johnson (**128**) whose name was omitted from the deaths by misadventure. Bisser, again called Brisser, was buried at Petworth on 20 Dec 1612. KB 9/739, m 399d; KB 29/255, m 89; PAR 442/1/1/1.]

119   4 Jan 1613. Horsham. Thomas Rickward, gent., coroner of Lewes and Bramber rapes. Jurors: William Artridg, Edward Booker, Robert Sharp, Benjamin Winson, John Alesbery, Thomas Person, Christopher Bezer, John Jenden, Henry Newman, William Chamber, Thomas Clark, George Gilbert, John Champion, Richard Weller, Thomas Champion, Alexander Inge, Humphrey Jenoway. On 28 Dec 1612 Thomas Gratwick, a prisoner in Horsham gaol, was ill there with 'an ague' of which he languished until 1 Jan 1613 and then died a natural death there. KB 9/737, m 258.
[Delivered with **114**. Gratwick was buried at Horsham on the day of his death although the inquest is said to have been taken on view of his body. KB 9/737, m 290d; KB 29/255, m 6d; *CAR Introdn*, 171; SRS, XXI, 377.]

120   17 Jan 1613. Fittleworth in Manhood hundred. Henry Peckham, gent., coroner in the bishop of Chichester's liberties. Jurors: Henry Piper jun., Henry Lutter, John Mills, Henry Wade, Thomas Hobjohn, Thomas Piper, Thomas Rodes, Roger Shepherd, James Whetley, John Brookfeild, Henry Smithe, John Brinkwell, Thomas Greenfeild. About 7 p.m. on 3 Feb 1613 [*in the said year*] an unknown man came to Fittleworth and in order to escape arrest for suspicion of burglary, as he thought, he feloniously threw himself into a large river there and drowned himself. At that time he had no goods or chattels to the jurors' knowledge. KB 9/737, m 287.
[Delivered with **114**. KB 9/737, m 290d; KB 29/255, m 6.]

121   15 Feb 1613. Cuckfield. Thomas Rickward, county coroner. Jurors: Nicholas Virrall, Roger Verrall, Drew Cheale, Hugh Affeild, John Burtenshaw, Thomas Vynall, Thomas Aylerd, John Jenner, Edward Bechely, Edward Fawlkner, Edward Jenner, John Peirce, William West, Walter Aptitt, Richard Parkes, Thomas West, John Weller. About 1 p.m. on 12 Feb John Snell of Cuckfield sen., 'husbandman',

aged 88 or thereabouts and almost blind [*captus fere occulis*], by misadventure fell 'into a certaine little watercourse' in the lands of Philip Murton of Cuckfield, 'woodbrooker', and was drowned. KB 9/737, m 279.
[Delivered with **114**. 'Old' John Snell of South Hall was buried at Cuckfield on 13 Feb although the inquest is said to have been taken on view of the body. KB 9/737, m 290d; KB 29/255, m 6; SRS, XIII, 141.]

122   19 Feb 1613. Midhurst. Albany Stoughton, gent., Arundel rape coroner. Jurors: William Stent, John Locke, John Hudson, John Albery, John Vincent, John Figg, John Polinge, Thomas Webb, Nicholas Bisshopp, George Morrys, George Wattles, John Butcher, Godfrey Grevett, Thomas Hodges sen., Thomas Durgate, Thomas Upton, Gifford Young. On 11 Feb Thomas Pittes late of Easebourne, 'yeoman', assaulted Jeremy [*Jeremia*] Flote at Midhurst, striking him violently on the head with 'a staffe' which he held in his right hand and giving him several 'blowes'. Flote retreated from Pittes as far as 'a stone walle' beyond which he could not flee and Pittes pursued him, striking him violently on the head and wishing to kill him. Thereupon Flote, to save his life, struck Pittes on the left side of the head with 'a spitter' [*sc.* a spade] worth 8d which he held in his right hand, giving him a wound which penetrated to the brain and of which he languished until 17 Feb and then died at Easebourne. Thus Flote killed him in self defence and to save his life, not feloniously or of malice aforethought. At the time of the killing he had no goods or chattels, lands or tenements. ASSI 35/55/8, m 1. [*Calendared in CAR, no 246.*]
[Delivered to East Grinstead assizes on 8 Mar. The inquest is subscribed *se defendendo*. ASSI 35/55/8, m 1.]

123   29 Mar 1613. Wivelsfield. Thomas Rickward, gent., coroner of Lewes and Bramber rapes. Jurors: Stephen Jenner, John Fawkner, Richard Perkin, Francis Cooper, George Stone, Richard Pentecost, William Neale, Richard Uden, William Sayer, Thomas Joye, Francis Person, Isaiah [*Esaius*] White, John ..., John Todnorten, Henry Bawcomb. On 4 Mar Agnes Cheesman late of Wivelsfield, 'spinster', gave birth to a live male child at Wivelsfield. On the same day she murdered him at Wivelsfield: she struck and 'did bruse' his head with both hands, giving him 'a bruse' of which he immediately died. At that time she had no goods or chattels, lands or tenements to the jurors' knowledge. [*Damaged.*] ASSI 35/55/7, m 33. [*Calendared in CAR, no 266.*]
[Delivered to East Grinstead assizes on 5 July when Cheesman, who had been committed to gaol by the coroner, pleaded not guilty but was convicted and hanged; she had no chattels. ASSI 35/55/7, mm 33, 36, 41, 41d; *CAR*, nos 253, 265, 266.]

124   7 Apr 1613. Midhurst. Albany Stoughton, gent., Arundel rape coroner. Jurors: Thomas Upton, John Lockier, Thomas Hogges sen., Richard Wysome, William Morye, William Walder, Thomas Osborne, William Hamond, John Atkinson, Godfrey Greene, John Morye, Edward Mearshe, Peter Gates. On 3 Apr, when William [*later called* Thomas] Eapnell late of Bepton was walking alone by a stream in Midhurst, he suddenly and by misadventure fell into it and was drowned. At that time he had no goods or chattels, lands or tenements to the jurors' knowledge. KB 9/739, m 388.
[Delivered with **115**. KB 9/739, m 399d; KB 29/255, m 89.]

125   23 Apr 1613. Kirdford. Albany Stoughton, gent., Arundel rape coroner. Jurors: William Humfrey, John Rogers, Henry Stridocke, Henry Scute, Richard Overington, John Wood, George Studman, Miles Sutor, Robert Holland, Thomas Willson, Hugh Dunnadge, Thomas Stridocke, James Milles, William Stedman, Richard Wood. On 21 Apr Thomas Flote feloniously hanged himself until he was dead at Kirdford with 'a birchen withe' which he took in both hands: he 'did fasten' one end of it round a branch of a tree which was growing nearby and the other end round his neck. At that time he had no goods or chattels, lands or tenements to the jurors' knowledge. KB 9/739, m 395.
[Delivered with **115**. KB 9/739, m 399d; KB 29/255, m 88d.]

126   11 May 1613. Rottingdean. Thomas Rickward, gent., coroner of Lewes and Bramber rapes. Jurors: Thomas Geere, Robert Howell, Henry Cheale, Richard Wickersham, William Boone, Henry

Jeffery, William Fryer, Richard Jenninges, John Baldey, John Beard, Thomas Marten, William Gurr, Richard Bennett, William Boys, Richard Harris. On 7 May Katharine Haddes late of Rottingdean, 'spinster', gave birth to 2 live female children at Rottingdean. On the same day she murdered them both at Rottingdean: with both hands she 'did straightly and cruelly fasten and tye' 'a garter' worth ¼d round the neck of the first-born child and 'did strangle and choke' her, by reason of which 'strangling and chokeinge' she immediately died; and on the same 4 [*in error for* 7] May she thrust the other child into 'a hoole' of a wooden post with both hands, thereby giving her several 'bruses' on her body of which she likewise immediately died. At that time she had no goods or chattels, lands or tenements to the jurors' knowledge. The inquest was on view of both bodies. ASSI 35/55/7, m 35. [*Calendared in CAR, no 268.*]

[Delivered with **123**. At the assizes Haddes, who had been committed to gaol by the coroner, pleaded not guilty but was convicted and hanged; she had no chattels. ASSI 35/55/7, mm 35, 36, 41, 41d; *CAR*, nos 253, 265, 268.]

127   15 May 1613. Rye. Richard Fowtrell, Rye mayor and coroner, and the jurats. Jurors: John Gillam, 'Noah' Radford, Richard Chauntler, Thomas Seeley, John Pindlebury, Thomas Humfrey, 'Moyses' Peadle, William Burishe, John Kempe, Peter Cooper, John Parkes, John Feilde, Thomas West, Edmund Waters, Michael Colgate. About 4 or 5 p.m. on 13 May, when Robert Mullenex, 'yeoman', and William Lamperd, 'gent', both of Fairlight, were in the house of Richard Barker of Rye, 'inholder', 'playinge at cardes at a game called newe cutt', with Edward Skynner of Rye, 'taylor, standinge by them and lookeinge upon them', 'Lamperd, dealinge the cardes, did turne upp' 27 for Mullenex and 28 for himself, whereupon Mullenex said 'The game is myne' and Skynner said it was not his. Then Mullenex said to Skynner that 'he did lie', whereupon Skynner 'suddenlie tooke upp a stone pott standinge before him at the table with beere and did flinge it at' Mullenex's head 'and strooke him on the lefte side of his heade', breaking the skull, so that Mullenex 'did presentlie sincke downe', whereof he lay languishing in Barker's house until the next day and then died at 3 or 4 p.m., 'whereby wee finde the same to be manslaughter'. 'Skynner did fly for the saide facte' and 'at the tyme of his flyinge had the third parte' of 3 tenements and 3 gardens in Rye, 2 of which 'are sett, lyinge and beinge' in Lower Street and the other in Watchbell Street, and 'certaine goodes and cattalles in his handes' worth £5 13s 4d, as more fully appears in an inventory on the file of letters. [*Verdict in English.*] RYE 1/9, ff 382v–383.

[Another copy of the verdict, undated and not mentioning the mayor and jurats but with the signatures and marks of the jurors and identical to the above apart from minor variations, mainly of spelling, is followed by the inventory which was also taken on 15 May, viz 'one joyned table with a frame (worth) v s, item one joyned settle iij s, item two small brandirons vj d, item more three chaires xviij d, item one dagger iiij d, item two stone pottes iij d, item one bryne tub vj d, item one iron chaffingdish ij d, item one candlesticke of wood j d, item one tyne [*sc.* tin, a tin vessel] and a washing blocke vj d, item three hundred of old brickes ij s, item v firr boardes ij s vj d, item one old plancke iiij d, item one garden plot of beanes xij d, item ij tubs and a payle vj d, item a shoppe board ij s vj d, item a paire of sheeres and a pressing iron vj d, item one cage cubhord xvj d, item one joyned bedsteddle iiij s, item one trucke bedsteddle xij d, item two beddes x s, item one joyne stole iiij d, item one long chest ij s, item one basket bed vj d, item one chaire iiij d, item one joyned bedsteddle xx s, item one fether bed xvj s, item one fether boulster ij s, item one covering and a blancket v s, item one chest xij d, item one joyned chaire xviij d, item one courte cubhord iij s, item one small cubhord xviij d, item one stoole vj d, item one box ij d, item ij chestes v s, item iij paire of sheetes vj d, item one great cubhord x s. Some is v li xiij s iiij d' (*recte* £5 12s 4d).

At the inquest William Lamperd of Fairlight, gent., aged 40 or thereabouts, Robert Richardes of Rye, yeoman, and Edward Jervyse of Hastings, gent., all gave evidence to the same effect before the mayor and Richard Cockram, Mark Thomas and Matthew Young, jurats, viz that they were in Barker's house with Mullenex and Skynner on 13 May and there was 'some unkindness of speech used between Skynner and Mullenex', about half an hour before Mullenex was hurt, concerning money lent between them; that Lamperd and Mullenex played cards and disputed the result and Skynner struck Mullenex with the stone pot, all as in the inquest verdict; that after Mullenex had sunk down all the others went up to him and asked him how he was, to which he replied 'Well, I thank God' and then went to his bed and lay down; and that Skynner went out of the chamber immediately after striking the blow, which was between 4 and 5 p.m.

Four surgeons also gave evidence at the inquest: Thomas Gunton of London, aged 87 or thereabouts, and

Edward Jenkinson, Quintin Pye and John Kevell, all of Rye. They all deposed that, having opened Mullenex's skull, they found it to be cracked and broken by being struck by a pot and that, in their judgment, 'the contused or bruised blood' that 'lay in great abundance upon the brain' was the cause of his death.

There is a third and much more formal copy of the inquest in Latin which does not mention the presence of the jurats and describes the jurors as men of Rye. The verdict is that about 4 p.m. on 13 May Skynner feloniously killed Mullenex in Barker's house in Rye, throwing a stone pot worth 4d, which contained beer, at Mullenex's head with his right hand, giving him a wound on the left side of the head to the brain of which he lay languishing in Barker's house until the next day and then died about 3 p.m. On 14 May Skynner feloniously fled from Rye on account of the felony. What goods and chattels, lands and tenements he had at the time of the felony or of the flight or still has the jurors do not know.

The grand jury, to which John Kevell, Quintin Pye and Robert Richardes gave evidence, presented an indictment similar to the last version of the inquest verdict but without the last 2 sentences. Skynner pleaded not guilty to the indictment and was convicted of killing Mullenex by chance medley only, viz by throwing a pot by which Mullenex was struck by chance and misadventure of which he later died. After striking him, Skynner fled from Rye on that account. He had no goods or chattels at the time of his flight or ever after to the trial jurors' knowledge. On his petition he was then released on bail to obtain a pardon. RYE 8/3; RYE 32/2; RYE 47/83, no 4; RYE 47/84, unnumbered document; HMC, XIII, App. IV, 149.]

128   15 May 1613. Bolney. Thomas Rickward, gent., coroner of Lewes and Bramber rapes. Jurors: Thomas Beecher, Thomas Geere, William Styfflyn, Henry Holmewood, Richard Gallupp, Roger Allen, Edward West, Ralph Esson, Edward Haraden, Joseph Harland, John Harland, Thomas Hyder, Thomas Gander. About 5 p.m. on 14 May, when Richard Johnson late of West Hoathly, 'laborer', was working in the wood of Henry Ward of Cuckfield, gent., in Bolney, cutting wood, by misadventure 'an oaken logg' worth 2s 'did rowle and bruse' his body, giving him 'a bruse' on the left side of the head and chest of which he immediately died. The log remains on Ward's lands in Bolney. KB 9/739, m 390.
[Delivered with **115**. Ward was summoned to King's Bench to answer for the log; he had licence to imparl in Michaelmas 1614. Johnson was buried at Bolney on the day of the inquest. KB 9/739, mm 390, 399d; KB 29/255, m 89; SRS, XV, 46.]

129   27 May 1613. Cuckfield. Thomas Rickward, coroner of Lewes and Bramber rapes. Jurors: Thomas Page, Thomas Brockett, John Tully, Thomas Harbert, Richard Bechely, Edward Osborne, John Weller, Richard Myles, Walter Burt, William Ilman, Gerard Poulter, Richard Spurling, Edward Masters. On 26 May Edward Pynyon alias Praye late of Cuckfield, 'laborer', murdered Joan wife of Richard Norman late of Cuckfield, 'hammerman', at Cuckfield with a knife worth 1d which he held in his right hand, giving her a wound in the lower part of the left buttock 1½ inches deep and ½ inch wide of which she immediately died from loss of blood. At that time he had no goods or chattels, lands or tenements to the jurors' knowledge. ASSI 35/55/7, m 34. [*Calendared in CAR, no 267.*]
[Delivered with **123**. At the assizes Pynyon, who had been committed to gaol by John Shurley, kt, JP, pleaded not guilty and was acquitted of murder but convicted of manslaughter; he had no chattels. He then successfully pleaded benefit of clergy and was branded and released. Joan wife of 'Old' Richard Norman, who had been killed by a forgeman, was buried at Cuckfield on 28 May. ASSI 35/55/7, mm 34, 36, 41, 41d; KB 9/739, m 373; KB 29/255, m 89d; *CAR*, nos 253, 265, 267; SRS, XIII, 142.]

130   5 June 1613. Mayfield. John Eagles, gent., county coroner. Jurors: Thomas Maynard, Thomas Peckham, William Younge, Thomas Aligh, Thomas Weston, Ralph Weston, Robert Thawyer, Ralph Acourt, John Duke, Richard Pococke, William Relfe, Thomas Parke, William Wood, Ralph Hylls, Richard Stephenson. About 5 p.m. on 4 June, when Thomas Saunder of Mayfield, 'laborer', was alone in John Weston's stable at Mayfield, he feloniously hanged himself with 'a halter' worth 3d which he held in both hands, putting one end round his neck and tying the other round 'a beame' of the stable. He had no goods or chattels, lands or tenements. KB 9/739, m 396.
[Delivered with **115**. KB 9/739, m 399d; KB 29/255, m 88d.]

131   30 June 1613. Billingshurst. Albany Stoughton, gent., Arundel rape coroner. Jurors: William

Ham..., ... Grenefeild, John Wince, John Bett, Edward Turner, Benjamin Streater, Robert Pag..., John Streate, Anthony Reade. On 1[?8 June], when Henry Wales was walking by 'a windemill' in Billingshurst, 'a saile' of the mill by misadventure struck him on the right side of the head, giving him 'a bruse' of which he immediately died. 'The saile' was the cause of his death and was appraised at 13s 4d. [*Damaged.*] KB 9/739, m 389.

[Delivered with **115**. The coroner was summoned to King's Bench to answer for defects in the inquest, probably including the omission of the custodian of the deodand; he was outlawed at Chichester on 27 Oct 1614 and later pardoned. KB 9/739, mm 389, 399d; KB 29/255, m 89.]

132 13 July 1613. Rye. Richard Fowtrell, Rye mayor and coroner, and the jurats. Jurors: John Frauncys, John Davy, 'Noah' Radford, Francis Daniell, John Pindlebury, John Overington, William Hackelton, Clement Church, John Kempe, Matthew Duglas, Henry Davys, Thomas West, Henry Jeake, Richard Cheverell, Thomas Cruddock. About 2 or 3 a.m. on 10 July John Laynham, 'fisherman', and Richard Dyer, 'cockman', both of Rye, 'were at controversey and fell out in bad speaches and wordes', whereupon Laynham 'did geve a spurne [*sc.* spurn, a kick] at' Dyer 'and did strike and hitt him with his foote on the flancke of the lefte side of the belly neere unto the privie members and did with the saide spurne breake the reme [*sc.* rim, the peritoneum] of the saide Dyer's belly', of which he lay languishing until the night of 12 July and then died about 10 p.m. 'And so wee finde it to be manslaughter'. Laynham had and has goods and chattels in Rye worth 49s 7d, as more fully appears in an inventory on the file of letters. [*Verdict in English.*] Rye 1/9, ff 389–389v.

[Another copy of the verdict, undated (although written under the heading 26 July 1613) and not mentioning the mayor and jurats but with the signatures and marks of all the jurors except Radford and Jeake (Francis Daniell and Henry Davy [*sic*] both described as sen.), is identical to the above. It had originally contained the statement that 'in the tyme of his languishment' Dyer told his master John Ingram, his mistress Ingram's wife, William Turner, Thomas Savy's wife and others who then came to see him that Laynham had given him 'such a blowe which would be his death'; but that was struck through. The verdict is followed by the names of those who were to give evidence, viz Thomas Pett, John Duck, William Turner, John Engram and his wife, Thomas Savy's wife, James Fawlere's wife and William Alexander's wife. After that comes the inventory of Laynham's goods and chattels taken on 26 July, viz 'a joyned table and a forme (worth) vj s, item one cubhord and cubhord cloth viij s, item an old frying pan, an andiron, a paire of pot hangers and a latten dripping pan and a candlesticke xvj d, item two little tables xviij d, item iij tankerdes or cans of wood, ij wooden platters, iij dishes of wood and half a dozen of trenchers vj d, item a paire of bellowes and a ladle ij d, item v earthen dishes, a small pewter dish and a small salt seller xij d, item a chaire and ij stooles iij d, item one kettle, one skillet and one basting ladle of brasse, a paire of iron pot hangers and iij tubs xviij d, item one bedsted, one flock bed, a coverlett, (a blanckett *struck through*) and two paire of sheetes xvj s, item two old chestes xvj d, item a kneding tub and an old sword xij d, item two old tramell nettes (*sc.* trammel nets, fishing nets) x s , Somma ij li ix s vij d' (*recte* £2 8s 7d).

There is a third and much more formal copy of the inquest in Latin. It is dated 13 July (*altered from* 15 May) and does not mention the presence of the jurats but names all 15 jurors. The verdict is that between 2 and 3 a.m. on 10 July Laynham feloniously killed Dyer (*once written above* Robert Mulleneux *struck through*) at Rye: he 'did spurne' him with his right foot on the left side 'of the flanke', giving him a wound by which 'the reme' of the abdomen was broken and of which he lay languishing at Rye until about 10 p.m. on 12 July and then died.

On 1 Sept a recognizance was entered before the mayor and jurats by John Laynham in £40 and by Edward Laynham, Thomas Bylke, Anthony Bradd and Edward Peeterson, all of Rye, fishermen, in £5 each for John Laynham's appearance at the next hundred court to answer for the manslaughter and in the meantime for his good behaviour. The grand jury, to which John Nicholes, Richard Lock, Thomas Pett, Elizabeth Savy, Helen Alexander, William Turner and John Wren gave evidence, presented an indictment in similar terms to the formal version of the inquest verdict. Laynham pleaded not guilty to the indictment and was acquitted.

On 13 July Laynham had been examined before the mayor and Richard Portriffe, Thomas Ensing, William Thorp and Matthew Young and said that between 2 and 3 a.m. on 10 July, having carried nets on the ferry, he returned on the ferry intending to go to bed, but John Nicholes caused him to sit down at the quay right outside Franck's door and then Richard Cornishe came to him from aboard a boat. Laynham accused Cornishe of breaking up the hatches or stealing something from the boat. Cornishe then told Laynham to go home to bed and he would find someone in bed with his wife and called him cuckold. At that, while he was sitting, Laynham struck Cornishe on the ham or side of the leg with his own leg, and that was all he did to him.

On 18 July before the mayor and Richard Portriffe, jurat, John Nicholes of Rye, fisherman, and Richard Locke deposed that Laynham did not strike Cornishe or offer him any violence, Locke adding that Cornishe merely struck Laynham sideways with his leg. RYE 1/9, ff 401v–402; RYE 8/4; RYE 32/1; RYE 47/84, unnumbered documents; RYE 47/86, unnumbered document.]

133   29 July 1613. Bolney. Thomas Rickward, gent., coroner of Lewes and Bramber rapes. Jurors: John Langford, John Haselgrove, Joseph Costedell, William Morley, Humphrey Wales, John Payne, Nicholas Bull, John a Wood, Gerard Winton, Richard Jupp, Robert Shudd, Richard Gallop, Robert a Wood. On 27 July Richard Whiting late of Bolney, 'laborer', went to Henry Dunton's empty dwelling-house at Bolney and feloniously hanged himself with 'a little rope' worth ¼d which he held in both hands and tied on a staff lying on 'the beames' of the house, dying immediately. At that time he had no goods or chattels, lands or tenements to the jurors' knowledge. KB 9/741, m 216.
[Delivered to the Sussex Lent assizes and on to King's Bench in Easter 1614. KB 9/741, m 220d; KB 29/257, m 8d.]

134   15 Sept 1613. Jevington. Thomas Rickward, gent., under-coroner of the duchy of Lancaster in Pevensey rape and of Loxfield Dorset half-hundred. Jurors: Henry Holmewood, Edward Payne, Abraham Sherren, Thomas Earle, John Fonnell, Simon Sherren, Nicholas Roust, Henry Wincett, Simon Woodale, Edward Renn, John Griffin, John Peirce, Richard Earle. About 4 p.m. on 11 Sept, when John Sherren of Jevington, 'husbandman', was making 'a new yex or axile tree' for a wagon belonging to Thomas Bray of Westdean, gent., at Jevington and his daughter, Elizabeth Sherren late of Jevington, 'spinster', was holding the end of the old axle-tree while her father unloosened it from the wagon in order to replace it with the new one, by misadventure the wagon fell on Elizabeth's right side, giving her 'a bruse' of which she immediately died. The wagon is deodand, is worth 6s 8d and remains with Thomas Bray at Westdean. KB 9/741, m 203.
[Delivered with **133**. Bray was summoned to King's Bench to answer for the wagon; he was outlawed at Lewes on 16 Mar 1615 but obtained a writ of error in Hilary 1619. KB 9/741, mm 203, 220d; KB 29/257, m 9.]

135   5 Oct 1613. Horsted Keynes. Thomas Rickward, gent., under-coroner of the duchy of Lancaster in Pevensey rape and of Loxfield Dorset half-hundred. Jurors: John Weller, William Sale, James Chamberlaine, Henry Mylles, Charles Turner, William Brooker, Richard Page, Edward Waters, Richard Ward, John Smyth, Roger Marten, Richard Cooleman, John Lacy. About 9 a.m. on 4 Oct, when Richard Tye late of Horsted Keynes, 'husbandman', intended to clean his well at Horsted Keynes and was looking to see how much water there was in it, by misadventure he suddenly fell into the well and was drowned. KB 9/741, m 201.
[Delivered with **133**. KB 9/741, m 220d; KB 29/257, m 9.]

136   12 Oct 1613. Hurstpierpoint. Thomas Rickward, gent., coroner of Lewes and Bramber rapes. Jurors: John Whitepayne, Robert Whitepayne, Edward Luxford, Richard Burtenshaw, John Chatfeild, Richard Gander, Henry Gander, Richard Virgo, Thomas Blaxton, James Starr, John Savidg, Edward Brooker, John Brooker, Edward Masters, Gerard Burtenshaw. On 18 Sept Edward Smeed late of Hurstpierpoint, 'taylor', went to 'a little pitt' at Hurstpierpoint which was then full of water, feloniously threw himself into it and was drowned, dying immediately. At that time he was seised in his demesne as of fee of a messuage, a barn and 50 acres of land in Hurstpierpoint which are and from time immemorial have been customary tenements of the manor of Hurstpierpoint and are held of George Goring, kt, lord of the manor. At the same time he possessed goods and chattels which were appraised by the coroner and jurors and delivered to the custody of Rose Smeed, late his wife, at Hurstpierpoint on the day of the inquest, viz 'iiij^or keyne [sc. kine, cows], one bull and ij, two yeareinges [worth] xiiij li, item two hogges and v sheates [sc. sheats, pigs under a year old] ij li, item ij geese xx d, item ix loades of haye iiij li, item vj quarters of oates ij li, item one harrow, one wheeleborrow and one ladder iiij s, item in ould woode, one dounge cort and two rackes iij s iiij d, item v oulde sheetes v s, item ij flock beddes with ould coverlettes and blanckettes xx s, item iij chestes x s, item one table with a frame ij s vj d, item

one yron pott iiij s, item ij ould boorded beddstedles iiij s, item other smale implementes of houshould stuffe v s', total £24 19s 6d. [*Inventory mainly in English.*] KB 9/741, mm 214, 215.
[Delivered with **133**. Rose Smeed was summoned to King's Bench to answer for the goods and chattels; she was waived at Lewes on 16 Mar 1615. KB 9/741, mm 214, 220d; KB 29/257, m 8d.]

137   1 Nov 1613. Maresfield. Thomas Rickward, gent., under-coroner of the duchy of Lancaster in Pevensey rape and of Loxfield Dorset half-hundred. Jurors: Thomas Upton, Martin Hoad, John Rymington, Roger Peirce, William Smyth, William Russell, Thomas Mowshurst, Thomas Norman, John Franckwell, John Myller, John Foord, Richard Rose, William Awcock. About 1 p.m. on 30 Oct Robert Smyth late of Maresfield, 'carpenter', assaulted John Morrell of Maresfield, 'laborer', at Maresfield and of his own choice 'did wrestle' with him. 'In his wrestling' Smyth, holding Morrell's body on his back, suddenly and voluntarily threw himself on the ground, giving himself 'a bruse' on the left side of which he languished at Maresfield until 5 p.m. and then died by misadventure and not otherwise. KB 9/741, m 202.
[Delivered with **133**. KB 9/741, m 220d; KB 29/257, m 9.]

138   10 Dec 1613. Hastings. Thomas Young, Hastings mayor and coroner, and the jurats. Jurors: Thomas Wynter, John Leedes, Richard Martyn, Sabb Stevenson, John Harrys, Peter Grover, Christopher Salter, George Easton, William Dighton, Christopher Joye, Nicholas Foster, Edward Palmer, John Chowll, George Hawkyns. About 5 a.m. on 26 Nov William Watkyn late of Hastings, 'shipwright', went alone out of his house in St Clement's parish, Hastings, heading towards the priory where he put 'one slop of his canvas drawmy slops' [*sc.* hose] round his neck and tied the other slop to a large stone and then, with his hands tied, feloniously threw himself into the water in 'le new sluce' or the haven near the priory and drowned himself. At that time he possessed goods and bedding [*or furnishings: supellect'*] worth 40s, some pieces of timber and 'a new keele or frame of a ship' worth 40s and some 'shipbordes' worth 40s, total value £6, as appears in a schedule or inventory of particulars remaining on this year's file. HASTINGS C/A(a) 1, ff 173–173v.

139   18 Dec 1613. Horsham. Thomas Rickward, gent., coroner of Lewes and Bramber rapes. Jurors: Emanuel Brockwell, Henry Fenner, John Davy, Ambrose Heale, William Lawton, James Wright, John Gynn, John Bettser, William Beard, Richard Jenden, Thomas Clarke, Edward Waller, Henry Slater, Edward Booker, James Slater, William Waterton. On 10 Dec John Howell late of Wisborough Green, 'laborer', a prisoner in Horsham gaol, was sick with 'an ague' of which he languished there until 13 Dec and then died a natural death. KB 9/741, m 189.
[Delivered with **133**. Howell was buried at Horsham on the day of his death although the inquest was said to have been taken on view of his body. KB 9/741, m 220d; KB 29/257, m 9; *CAR Introdn*, 171; SRS, XXI, 379.]

140   29 Dec 1613. Hellingly. Thomas Rickward, gent., under-coroner of the duchy of Lancaster in Pevensey rape and of Loxfield Dorset half-hundred. Jurors: Robert Crowherst, Gilbert Beckett, Lawrence Ammett, Richard Gosden, William Acton, Herbert Akcherst, George Crowherst, Robert Acton, William Ferrett, John Fuller, ?Elias [*Eliasius*] Parker, Thomas Sawyer, Richard Burnett, Austin Clark, Walter Tompson. On 6 [*later given as* 7] Dec Elizabeth wife of Robert Carrington of Hellingly, 'tanner', feloniously cut her throat at Hellingly with a knife worth 1d which she held in her right hand, giving herself a wound of which she immediately died. At that time she had no goods or chattels, lands or tenements to the jurors' knowledge. KB 9/741, m 213.
[Delivered with **133**. KB 9/741, m 220d; KB 29/257, m 8d.]

141   27 Jan 1614. Horsham. Thomas Rickward, gent., coroner of Lewes and Bramber rapes. Jurors: Henry Roffye, Hamlet Borer, John Truelove, John Michell, Arthur Waller, John Steere, William Chambers, Christopher Beaser, John Jen, John Davye, William Artredg, James Slater, Andrew Duke. About 5 a.m. on 17 Oct 1613, when Thomas Dalton late of Guildford in Surrey, 'husbandman', was

'hunting a hare' with hunting-dogs in a park belonging to John Carrill, kt, at Warnham by a large fishpond and the dogs were swimming in the pond, Dalton, who was following them, by misadventure fell from a bridge into the pond and was drowned. KB 9/741, m 204.
[Delivered with **133**. Dalton, called Thomas Dalken, bachelor, was buried at Horsham on the day of the inquest. KB 9/741, m 220d; KB 29/257, m 9; SRS, XXI, 379.]

142   7 Feb 1614. Portslade. Thomas Rickward, gent., coroner of Lewes and Bramber rapes. Jurors: Edward Blaker, Richard Pollerd, John Ampleford, Robert Owens, Thomas Ockenden, John Collyer, Henry Holt, Henry Owden, Thomas Barrow, John Owden, Henry Wood, Thomas Lucy, John Holt. On 21 Jan John Honnor late of Portslade, 'butcher', feloniously cut his throat at Portslade with a knife worth ½d which he held in his right hand, giving himself a wound of which he languished at Portslade until 2 Feb and then died. At the time of the felony he had no goods or chattels, lands or tenements to the jurors' knowledge. KB 9/741, m 217.
[Delivered with **133**. KB 9/741, m 220d; KB 29/257, m 8d.]

143   21 Feb 1614. Horsham. Thomas Rickward, gent., coroner of Lewes and Bramber rapes. Jurors: Thomas Holland, John Steere, Gilbert Sayres, William Chambers, Ambrose Cheale, Thomas Person, Richard Weller, John Dennis, Edward Bristo, James Slater, Henry Dungat, Richard Gates. On 27 Jan Thomas Duffild late of Dunsfold, 'laborer', a prisoner in Horsham gaol, was sick with 'an ague' of which he languished there until 5 Feb and then died a natural death about 8 a.m. KB 9/741, m 190.
[Delivered with **133**. Duffild may have been one of the 2 unnamed prisoners who were buried at Horsham on 4 and 5 Feb although the inquest was said to have been taken on view of his body. KB 9/741, m 220d; KB 29/257, m 9; *CAR Introdn*, 171; SRS, XXI, 379.]

144   27 Mar 1614. West Stoke in Bosham hundred. Thomas Holmes, Bosham manor chamberlain and, according to the custom of the manor, coroner in the precinct of the manor and hundred of Bosham. Jurors: John Tilley, Michael Gose, William Jolliffe, Richard Churcher, Edward Lucas, John Cooper, Christopher Mose, Michael Jolliffe, Michael Marchant, Henry Skayne, John Goldock, Richard Lee, Robert Bradbridge, Robert Scardvile, John Chawcroft. On 26 Mar John Durrant late of West Stoke, 'laborer', feloniously 'did drowne himselfe' at West Stoke 'in a certaine well'. At that time he had no lands or tenements, goods or chattels. No one else was privy to his death. KB 9/743, m 414.
[Delivered with **145** and on to King's Bench in Michaelmas. KB 9/743, m 416d; KB 29/257, m 75d.]

145   8 June 1614. Wadhurst. John Butcher, gent., Loxfield Camden half-hundred coroner. Jurors: William Bryan, John Dunmole, Thomas Clarke, Thomas Peckham, John Parris, Hugh Lucke, Thomas Alye, William Younge, Thomas Upton, Gregory Daw, John Wyllard, Richard Lucke, Richard Weston, Thomas Russell, William Holland, Edward Walter, Thomas Duke. On 30 May, when Richard Longly late of Wadhurst, 'butcher', and George Hosmer of Wadhurst 'weare playeng att foot ball' at Wadhurst, Longly feloniously killed Hosmer with a stone worth ¼d which he held in his right hand, giving him a wound on 'the nose' ¼ inch wide and 2 inches deep of which he languished at Wadhurst until the next day and then [died]. Immediately after committing the felony Longly fled to places unknown, wherefore the jurors amerced the inhabitants of Wadhurst at … At the time of the felony he had 3s 6d in money, which remains with Robert Sare of Wadhurst, and no other goods or chattels, lands or tenements to the jurors' knowledge. [*Damaged.*] ASSI 35/56/4, m 14. [*Calendared in CAR, no 294.*]
[Delivered to East Grinstead assizes on 25 July when Longly was not in gaol. He was committed to gaol by Thomas Maye, kt, and Thomas Aynscombe, JPs, before the East Grinstead assizes of 17 July 1615 when he pleaded not guilty to the inquest verdict and was acquitted, the trial jury finding that Hosmer had died a natural death; Longly had not fled and was therefore released. ASSI 35/56/4, mm 14, 33d, 34; ASSI 35/57/7, mm 59, 66, 66d; *CAR*, nos 294, 308, 325.]

146   1 July 1614. Rotherfield. John Luck, gent., Rotherfield hundred coroner. Jurors: Nicholas Taylor, John Allen, Hugh Turnor, Walter Coppinge, Stephen Coppinge, Edward Holland, William

Newman, John Lockier, Thomas Filtnes, John Stapley, Nicholas Maynard of 'Pinders', Adam Farmer, Robert Kent, Nicholas Stapley, Thomas Maynard, George Barber alias Nyn, Richard Stapley, Edmund Latter. On 29 June William Baker late of Rotherfield, 'husbondman', Edward Hothly's servant, treasonably murdered Hothly, then his master, at Rotherfield with 'a sledge' worth 16d which he held in his right hand, giving him 'a bruse' on the chest of which he languished for half an hour and then died at Rotherfield. Immediately after committing the murder Baker fled to places unknown, wherefore the jurors amerced the inhabitants of Rotherfield at 20s. At the time of the murder Baker had no goods or chattels, lands or tenements to the jurors' knowledge. ASSI 35/56/4, m 15. [*Calendared in CAR, no 295.*]

[Delivered with **145**, as was another copy, probably a draft because it is less complete and is unsigned. Apart from minor variations, the jurors are described as being of Rotherfield hundred and the final 2 sentences are omitted. Baker was still at large at the time of the assizes. ASSI 35/56/4, mm 15, 20; *CAR*, no 295.]

147   28 Dec 1614. Rye. Matthew Young, Rye mayor and coroner, and the jurats. Jurors: Thomas Pett, Thomas Cruddock, Henry Davy, Michael Colgate, Robert Wotton, William Rogers, Richard Flynt, Richard Chauntler, Thomas Henly jun., Thomas Seeley, Thomas Whithead, Edward Peterson, John Dickerson, John Skidmore, John Tolkyn. Thomas Fisher jun., 'haveinge bene extreame sick a longe tyme before his imprisonement and so continueing sicke in bede in' Rye gaol 'by the space of a fortnight or thereaboutes', between noon and 1 p.m. on 27 Dec 'by the handy worke and visitation of God died'. The view of the body was in the gaol. [*Verdict in English.*] RYE 1/9, ff 475v–476.

[A subscription notes that the copy of the inquest was on the file of letters of Young's mayoralty.]

148   5 Jan 1615. Lewes. John Teynton, gent., coroner of Lewes and Bramber rapes. Jurors: William Dodson, William Taylor, John White, Robert Stente, John Wales, Peter Keisse, William Stuckle, John Ringe, Joseph Baylye, Nicholas Shelley, Benjamin Hodder, David Sternes, Henry Rose, Walter Crouch, Henry Townsende. On 1 Jan William Fisher late of Lewes, 'barbor', feloniously killed Mark Nursse at Lewes with 'a wooden pale' worth 1d which he held in both hands, giving him a wound on the back of the head ½ inch deep and 1½ inches long of which he languished that day and died at Lewes before dawn of the next day. ASSI 35/57/6, m 2. [*Calendared in CAR, no 301.*]

[Delivered to East Grinstead assizes on 27 Feb when the grand jury, to which Martha Nurse, John Todd, William Crayne and John Spere gave evidence, presented an indictment which charged Fisher and Thomas Salter late of Lewes, barber, with murdering Nursse at Lewes on 1 Jan, Fisher striking him with a wooden pale worth ¼d which he held in both hands and giving him a wound on the back of the head ½ inch deep and 1½ inches wide of which he languished at Lewes for 10 hours and then died, and Salter being feloniously present aiding and abetting him. Fisher and Salter both pleaded not guilty to the indictment. Salter was acquitted; he had not fled and was therefore released. Fisher was acquitted of murder but convicted of manslaughter; he had no chattels. He was remanded in gaol because Nursse's relict brought an appeal against him, but at the next assizes, on 17 July, she failed to prosecute it. Fisher then successfully pleaded benefit of clergy and was branded on the left hand and released. Also on 17 July the grand jury, to which John Langridg gave evidence, presented an indictment which charged John Wildgose of Salehurst, kt, sheriff, with negligently allowing Fisher, who had been committed to Horsham gaol under his custody on 27 Feb, to escape on 20 June and to remain at large at Lewes for 3 days. Wildgose later confessed, before the year 15 James I, and was fined £10. ASSI 35/57/6, m 1; ASSI 35/57/7, mm 12, 59, 66, 66d; KB 9/747, m 204; KB 29/259, m 90; *CAR*, nos 301, 308, 329.]

149   30 May 1615. Brighton in Whalesbone hundred. John Teynton, gent., Lewes rape coroner. Jurors: Henry Robertes, Derek Payne, John Comport, Henry Howell, Henry Killicke, Edward Mihell, Thomas Clarke, Stephen Gonne, Richard Gonne, John Freind, William Gillam, Nicholas Jackett, William Hiscocke. On 27 May, when James Dericke was driving 'an emptie carr' at Brighton drawn by a blind horse which was yoked to the cart, both belonging to Derek Payne, his master, and Dericke was sleeping negligently on the cart, the horse strayed and by misadventure both Dericke and the horse and cart fell together from the high cliffs onto the beach whereby he immediately died. The horse and cart were the cause of his death and the jurors appraised the cart, which was broken into many parts,

at 3s 4d; the parts remain with George Coles, deputy almoner of Sussex. KB 9/747, m 219.
[Delivered with **150** and on to King's Bench in Michaelmas. There was no process for the deodand. KB 9/747, mm 219, 222d; KB 29/259, m 89.]

150   8 June 1615. Thakeham. John Teynton, gent., Bramber rape coroner. Jurors: John Lee, Hugh Tyllye, Toby Farelye, Christopher Soale, George Smyther, John Worger, Roger Smyth, John Pollard, John Pricklowe, William Cooke, Robert Haler, James Waite, ..., Edward Duke, Richard Woode. On 30 May Cuthbert Leighe late of Parham, gent., feloniously killed William Melsham at Thakeham with 'a sword' of iron and steel worth 2s 6d which he held drawn in his right hand, giving him a wound in the right side of the chest 2 inches deep and 1 inch wide of which he languished at Thakeham until 7 June and then died. [*Damaged.*] ASSI 35/57/7, m 20. [*Calendared in CAR, no 320.*]
[Delivered to East Grinstead assizes on 17 July when an indictment was preferred identical to the inquest verdict except that it charged Leighe with murder and valued the sword at 2s. The grand jury, to which 'Incent' Sheffeild, Walter Listeed, John Sheffeild and Edward Bennitt gave evidence, reduced the charge to manslaughter. Leighe, who had not been in gaol before the assizes, pleaded not guilty to the indictment as amended but was convicted; he had no chattels. He then successfully pleaded benefit of clergy and was branded and released. Also on 17 July the coroner was amerced £5 'for nott perfect examinacions touching the death of Melsham' and each of the JPs who bailed Leighe was amerced £10 for bailing him. ASSI 35/57/7, mm 20, 41, 53, 65, 66, 66d; KB 9/747, m 204; KB 29/259, m 90; *CAR*, nos 304, 308, 318, 320.]

151   18 June 1615. Lewes in Swanborough hundred. John Teynton, gent., Lewes rape coroner. Jurors: Samuel Brooke, John Ade, John Howell, Richard Howell, Henry Barrenden, John Towner, Richard Barrenden, William Ade, Thomas Pycombe, Simon Johnson, Richard Sherrye, Nicholas Panckhurst, Andrew Chicell, William Inkersell. On 25 June [*sic*], when Margery Powell, who had ridden from St John's market-place in 'a cart' drawn by 4 horses belonging to Richard Begeler of St Anne's parish in Lewes and had arrived at her dwelling-house, was getting down from the back of the cart which was standing still there, by misadventure she fell from the back of the cart onto the ground on her head whereby she immediately died, all the horses then standing in the cart. KB 9/747, m 216.
[Delivered with **149**. The coroner was summoned to King's Bench to answer for defects in the inquest; he was discharged in Michaelmas 1617 because the inquest was amended. Both mentions of the horses are interlined. KB 9/747, mm 216, 222d; KB 29/259, mm 89, 89d.]

152   19 June 1615. Warnham in Steyning half-hundred. John Teynton, gent., Bramber rape coroner. Jurors: Henry Roffey, William Perkin, Thomas Borer, John Eversed, John Charman, John Buttler, William Knight, Ralph Smyth, Hamlet Borer, John Michell, John Partman, William Charman, James Forster, John Freeman. On 17 June John Boughton, who had intended to wash himself in 'the gardeine ponde' and had washed his body for quite a long time, afterwards, intending to get back out of the water, by misadventure fell to the bottom of the pond and so was drowned. KB 9/747, m 217.
[Delivered with **149**. KB 9/747, m 222d; KB 29/259, m 89.]

153   28 June 1615. Southover. John Teynton, gent., Lewes rape coroner. Jurors: William Adams, Edward Chidwicke, John Androwes, Henry Saunders, John Howell, William Ade, Richard Sherrey, Andrew Chicell, William Lane, John Augur, Richard Kydder, George Kitchiner, Simon Johnson. On 23 June, when Thomas Chambers, who had been driving 'a brewer's carte' drawn by 4 horses which were yoked to it, all belonging to Henry Plommer of Southover, his master, was removing a half-tun of ale lying in the front of the cart which was standing still, one of the horses called 'the thiller' [*sc.* thill-horse, the shaft-horse] twisted to graze on the ground, by reason of which one of the wheels of the cart by misadventure went over Chambers's body which was severely crushed, of which he languished until 25 June and then died. The thill-horse and cart were the cause of his death and the jurors appraised them at 20s; they remain with George Coles, deputy almoner of Sussex. KB 9/747, m 220.
[Delivered with **149**. Coles was summoned to King's Bench to answer for the thill-horse and a wheel, worth 20s,

which were the cause of Chambers's death; he was discharged in Hilary 1616 because William Johnson, esq., the king's deputy almoner, acknowledged satisfaction. The coroner was also summoned to King's Bench to answer for defects in the inquest; he was discharged in Michaelmas 1617 because the inquest was amended, probably by the substitution of 'cart' for 'wheel' in the last sentence, *carra* being written over an erasure on both occurrences. KB 9/747, mm 220, 222d; KB 29/259, m 89.]

154   3 July 1615. Rye. Matthew Younge, Rye mayor and coroner, and the jurats. Jurors: Peter Bennet, Henry Davys, John Whithead, Clement Church, John Pindlebury, John Rider, John Kempe, Thomas Radford, Nathaniel Holmes, Thomas Kyte, Matthew Duglas, Thomas Hart, Robert Wotton, Edward Waters. Between 1 and 2 p.m. on 2 July John Swane, 'goinge into the water to swyme or washe him self in the salt water neare unto' the New Conduit in Rye, 'in the cricke [*sc.* creek] there was by mysfortune drowned'. The view of the body was at 'le Sluce' within the liberties of Rye. [*Verdict in English*.] RYE 1/9, f 501.
[A subscription notes that the signed inquest was on the file of letters of Younge's mayoralty.]

155   4 July 1615. Rotherfield. John Lucke, gent., Rotherfield hundred coroner. Jurors: William Coe, George Barber, Thomas Maynard, John Homsby, John Vincent, James Alchorne, Abraham Aynscombe, Richard Ashdowne, John Lockyer, Richard Longley, Robert Baker, Nicholas Turner sen., Nicholas Turnor jun., John Burgis, John Baker, John Maynard, John Cheeseman, Alexander Cheeseman, Abraham Ashdowne. On 3 July, when Thomas Filtnes was sitting on an empty cart drawn by 2 mares and 2 oxen in Waterdown Forest at Rotherfield, he suddenly and by misadventure fell from the cart upon the ground, breaking his neck and dying immediately. The mares, oxen and cart were the cause of his death and the jurors appraised them at £8, which sum was paid to William Johnson, esq., deputy of Lancelot bishop of Ely, the king's almoner. KB 9/747, m 215.
[Delivered with **149**. KB 9/747, m 222d; KB 29/259, m 89.]

156   11 July 1615. Thakeham in East Easwrith hundred. John Teynton, gent., Bramber rape coroner. Jurors: James Waterman, Michael Slawter, Robert Haler, William Tanner, Thomas Tye, John Bridger, Edward Streater, Richard Streater, William Libscome, George Smyther, Hugh Pollard, John Worger, William Cothe, Nicholas Frenche, John Greene, Richard Kember, John Pollington. At 11 a.m. on 10 July, when Anthony Harrison was driving 'an empty courte' drawn by 2 horses which were yoked to it, all belonging to Thomas Hudson of Thakeham, his master, the horses ran wildly down a hill against Harrison's will, and by misadventure both the horses and the near wheel of the cart went over the body of Elizabeth daughter of William Androws which was severely crushed, whereof she languished until 3 p.m. and then died. The horses and cart were the cause of her death and the jurors appraised them at 53s 4d; they remain with George Coles, deputy almoner of Sussex. KB 9/747, m 218.
[Delivered with **149**. Coles was summoned to King's Bench to answer for a wheel and 2 horses, worth 53s 4d, which were the cause of the death; he was discharged in Hilary 1616 because William Johnson, esq., the king's deputy almoner, acknowledged satisfaction. The coroner was also summoned to King's Bench to answer for defects in the inquest; he was discharged in Michaelmas 1617 because the inquest was amended, probably by the substitution of 'cart' for 'wheel' in the last sentence, *caruca* being written over an erasure on both occurrences. KB 9/747, mm 218, 222d; KB 29/259, m 89.]

157   19 July 1615. West Grinstead in West Grinstead hundred. John Teynton, gent., Bramber rape coroner. Jurors: Richard Browne, Richard Wood sen., William Langforde, Peter Davye, John Haler, John Jupe, Thomas Scotchford, Richard Woode jun., John Wolven, John Agate, William Verrill, Richard Langford, John Spatchurste, John Martyn. On 14 July Henry Miles late of West Grinstead, 'warrener', feloniously killed John Steele at West Grinstead with 'a bearinge bill' of wood, iron and steel worth 8d which he held in both hands, giving him 'a bruse' on the left side of the head of which he languished at West Grinstead until the next day and then died. At the time of the felony Miles had no goods or chattels, lands or tenements. ASSI 35/58/7, m 26. [*Calendared in CAR, no 338.*]
[Delivered to East Grinstead assizes on 26 Feb 1616 when the grand jury, to which John Steele, Richard Leethinge,

Brian Touchener, Richard Owlder, Michael Elmy and George Smyther gave evidence, presented an indictment identical in substance to the inquest verdict except that it charged Miles with murder and omitted the last sentence. Miles pleaded not guilty to the indictment and was acquitted of murder but convicted of manslaughter; he had no chattels. He then successfully pleaded benefit of clergy and was branded on the left hand and released. ASSI 35/58/7, mm 7, 9, 26; KB 9/749, m 74; KB 29/261, m 12d; *CAR*, nos 335, 338.]

158   20 July 1615.   West Tarring in Tarring hundred.   John Teynton, gent., Bramber rape coroner. Jurors: William Chauncye, Richard Peeter, Richard Payne, John Follicke, William Parson, James Lyste, John Hillman, Richard Grinfeild, William Moner, Thomas Leake, Thomas Warne, Robert Bonde, Richard Knighte.   On 10 July Peter Colly late of Rustington feloniously killed Thomas Selden at Bramber with 'a pyke staffe' of wood and iron worth 4d which he held in both hands, giving him a wound on the left side of the head 1 inch deep and ¼ inch wide of which he languished at West Tarring until 18 July and then died.   At the time of the felony Colly had goods and chattels, value unknown to the jurors, which remain with John Peirce, gent., bailiff of Thomas earl of Arundel and Surrey, lord of the rape, who claims to have all felons' goods within the rape.   Immediately after the felony Colly fled.   KB 9/751, m 244.
[Delivered with **157** and on to King's Bench in Michaelmas 1616. Colly's arrest was ordered in King's Bench; he was outlawed at Lewes on 4 June 1618. The coroner was summoned to King's Bench to answer for defects in the inquest; he was discharged in Trinity 1618 because the inquest was amended, although the inquest shows no sign of amendment; perhaps it was completely rewritten. There are notes *defectus versus villatam* and *pro bonis* on the inquest, but no proceedings against West Tarring for Colly's escape or concerning the goods and chattels are recorded on the Controlment Roll. KB 9/751, mm 243, 244; KB 29/261, mm 96, 96d.]

159   31 Aug 1615.   Bolney in Wyndham hundred.   John Teynton, gent., Lewes rape coroner.   Jurors: Peter Martyn, John Gratwyck, John Bull, John Wood, Thomas Gratwyck, Benjamin Gratwycke, John Michell, Philip Clemens, Thomas Bull, Stephen Bull, Ralph Bull, Thomas Dunstall.   On 28 Aug, when Thomas Wycker of Bolney, 'laborer', who was very weak and aged over 80, intended to wash his hands in a pond called 'the Northfeild pitt' in Cowfold, as was his custom, by misadventure he fell into the pond and was drowned.   KB 9/749, m 94.
[Delivered with **157** and on to King's Bench in Easter 1616. Wycker was buried at Bolney on 30 Aug 1615 although the inquest was said to be taken on view of his body. KB 9/749, m 112d; KB 29/261, m 5d; SRS, XV, 47.]

160   2 Sept 1615.   Warnham in Singlecross hundred.   John Teynton, gent., Bramber rape coroner. Jurors: Thomas Sommersall, John Charman sen., James Forster, Arthur Waller, Thomas Martyn, Thomas Pilfolde, Richard Deane, Francis Ede, William Dudley, William Charman, Henry Knight, Thomas Thornden, John Potter, Samuel Edwardes, John Taylor, Thomas Lucas, William Perkin.   On 31 Aug, when Thomas Boorer was driving 'an empty wayne' drawn by 'six oxen and steeres and two horsbeastes' which were yoked to it, all belonging to him, at 'Stones Greene' in Capel, Surrey, and was sitting in the front of the wain, by misadventure he fell from it upon the ground whereby he immediately died.   The jurors appraised the oxen and horses at 20 marks and the wain at 20s and they remain with George Coles, deputy almoner in Sussex.   KB 9/749, m 96.
[Delivered with **159**. KB 9/749, m 112d; KB 29/261, m 5d.]

161   7 Sept 1615.   Lindfield in Streat hundred.   John Teynton, gent., Lewes rape coroner.   Jurors: Richard Barham, John Veroll, Thomas Rushe, Robert Johnson, John Kinge, John Chowne, Thomas Page, Edward Geffrye, Richard Leopard, Simon Warden, John Bexell, Thomas Burtenshaw.   On 5 Sept, when Edward Fawkner, 'husbandman', was working in a marl pit at Lindfield owned by Richard Scryven of Lindfield, 'husbandman', and was filling 'a marle court' by using 'a shovell' which he held in both hands, by misadventure a large heap of marl, 2 tons in amount, fell on his body whereby he immediately died.   KB 9/749, m 95.
[Delivered with **159**. KB 9/749, m 112d; KB 29/261, m 5d.]

162   9 Oct 1615. East Grinstead. John Butcher, gent., duchy of Lancaster coroner in Pevensey rape. Jurors: John Harman, Daniel Owtred, Abraham Lullenden, William Braband, Thomas Venner, Henry Browne, John Budgyn, Nicholas Wythers, Edward Cripps, James Duffeild, Theophilus Duffeild, Thomas Underhill, Nicholas Bushney, William Streate, Richard Stapley. Between 5 and 6 p.m. on 7 Oct Edward Parry late of East Grinstead, 'husbandman', murdered Edward Britton at East Grinstead with 'a wodden stake' worth ¼d which he held in both hands, striking him on the neck and breaking it, of which he languished at East Grinstead until 9 p.m. and then died. Immediately after the felony Parry fled to places unknown. At the time of the felony and flight he had no goods or chattels, lands or tenements to the jurors' knowledge. KB 9/751, m 246.
[Delivered with **158**. Parry's arrest was ordered in King's Bench; he was outlawed at Lewes on 4 June 1618. East Grinstead was summoned to King's Bench to answer for his escape; it made fine in Trinity 1620. Britton was buried at East Grinstead on the day of the inquest. KB 9/751, mm 245, 246; KB 29/261, m 96; SRS, XXIV, 165.]

163   9 Oct 1615. Shipley in West Grinstead hundred. John Teynton, gent., Bramber rape coroner. Jurors: Basil Willard, Thomas Martyn, Richard Michell jun., Richard Worsfold, Richard Hurst, Edward Haler jun., James Hurst, John Penfold, Thomas Grover, William Freeman, Richard Agate, Giles Sherwood, Nicholas Shave. About 8 a.m. on 7 Oct William Daniell feloniously cut his throat at Shipley with 'a shredding kniffe' worth 2d which he held in both hands, giving himself a wound 2 inches deep and 6 inches long of which he immediately died. At that time he had goods and chattels worth £7 as appraised by the jurors, which remain with George Coles, deputy almoner of Sussex, viz 3 bales of hay, 16 measures of meal, 16 measures of oats, 3 pigs and some bedding [*quedam supellectillia*]. KB 9/749, m 101.
[Delivered with **159**. KB 9/749, m 112d; KB 29/261, m 5d.]

164   23 Oct 1615. Rotherfield. John Lucke, gent., Rotherfield hundred coroner. Jurors of the hundred: Alexander Cheasman, Adam Farmor, John Elliott, Anthony Snatt, Christopher Hider, John Vincent, John Cheasman, Stephen Coppinge, James Coppinge, William Hale, Abraham Aynscombe, Richard Ashdowne, Robert Baker, Lawrence Clarke, William Hodly, George Barbor, John Maynord of Hamsell. On 9 Aug, when John Staply was loading 'a wayne' belonging to him with 'sheaves of wheate' at Rotherfield, suddenly and by misadventure he fell from the wain upon the ground, languished for the next 9 hours and then died at Rotherfield. When he fell from 'the wayne' there were 6 oxen and a mare belonging to him in it; they did not move the wain nor was it moved when he fell from it. KB 9/751, m 299.
[Delivered with **170** and on to King's Bench in Michaelmas 1616. The coroner was summoned to King's Bench to answer for defects in the inquest; he was outlawed at Chichester on 27 Aug 1618. KB 9/751, mm 299, 312d; KB 29/261, mm 94, 94d.]

165   8 Nov 1615. Rye. Thomas Ensinge, jurat, deputy of Mark Thomas, Rye mayor and coroner, and the jurats. Jurors: John Bayley, Thomas Kytt, Thomas Radford, 'Noah' Radford, Richard Chauntler, Anthony Coster, John Foulstone, Robert Rogers, John Hilles, Robert Wotton, Clement Church, John Tolkyn, John Pindlebury. Richard Tirrick of Rye, 'carpenter', 'dyed by the handy work of God and by no other means so far as they knowe'. [*Verdict in English*.] RYE 1/9, f 517v; RYE 47/88, unnumbered document.

166   20 Nov 1615. Lewes. John Teynton, gent., Lewes rape coroner. Jurors: William Pearse, John Pimble, Thomas Snatt, John Mathy, Richard Newton, Gershom [*Gershamus*] Baylye, John Godley, Henry Rose, Thomas Gonne, John Todd, John Kinge, William Savidge, Robert Parkes, Peter Pimble, Robert Carter, Richard Martyn. On 16 Nov Henry Colthurst, a lunatic, in his madness stabbed Jane Thomas in the middle of the chest at Lewes with 'a little kniffe' of iron and steel worth 2d which he held in his right hand, giving her a wound ¼ inch deep and ?½ inch wide of which she languished at Lewes until 18 Nov when she died either of the wound or a natural death; the jurors do not know which. At the time of the wounding Colthurst had goods and chattels, but of what value the jurors do not know. ASSI 35/58/7, m 25. [*Calendared in CAR, no 352.*]

[Delivered with **157**. A note at the foot of the inquest calls this a natural death and Colthurst did not stand trial at the assizes. ASSI 35/58/7, m 25.]

167   26 Dec 1615. Nuthurst in Singlecross hundred. John Teynton, gent., Bramber rape coroner. Jurors: Thomas Hill, William Davy, Henry Lyndfeild, William Gates, Edward Brystow, Walter Gagg, William Griffyn, Francis Wynton, John Wood, Robert Harman, William Lyntott, Henry Cooper, Thomas Older. On 23 Dec, when James Harding, servant of John Wood of Nuthurst, 'yoman', was riding on 'a blacke nagg' belonging to his master, intending to wash it in 'the parsonage ponde' near Wood's house in Nuthurst, by misadventure he fell from the horse into the pond and was immediately drowned. The jurors appraised the horse at 10s; it remains with Wood. KB 9/749, m 93.

[Delivered with **159**. Wood was summoned to King's Bench to answer for the horse; he was discharged in Trinity 1618 because the deputy almoner acknowledged satisfaction. KB 9/749, mm 93, 112d; KB 29/261, m 5d.]

168   23 Jan 1616. Binsted. Henry Peckham, gent., Avisford hundred coroner hac vice only. Jurors: Henry Page, Richard Page, Benjamin Blundell, Thomas Leper, Richard Knowles, John Bryant, John May, John Cutfeld, Edward Etherton, James Bryant, John Grigge, Richard Hames, Robert Nash, Robert Whittington. About 3 p.m. on 20 Jan William Haule, 'labourer', feloniously drowned himself in 'a well' at Binsted. At that time he had goods and chattels worth £8 which remain with John Peirce, gent., bailiff of Thomas earl of Arundel and Surrey, lord of the liberty, for the earl's use. KB 9/751, m 306.

[Delivered with **164**. Peirce, called the king's bailiff, was summoned to King's Bench to answer for the goods and chattels; he was discharged in Hilary 1618 by virtue of letters patent of 27 (*recte* 22) Feb 1554 to Henry late earl of Arundel, enrolled in King's Bench in Hilary 1590. KB 9/751, mm 306, 312d; KB 29/261, mm 93d, 94; *CPR 1553–1554*, 69–70.]

169   8 Mar 1616. Itchingfield in East Easwrith hundred. John Teynton, gent., Bramber rape coroner. Jurors: Thomas Streater, John Pilfold, Richard Whyte, Edward Slawter, Henry Parker, Edward Sayres, Thomas Champion, William Booker, Edward Bristow, Henry Michell, George Gilberte, Thomas Davye, James Slawter, Thomas Baker, Robert Honywood, Matthew Woode. On 17 Dec 1615 John Feiste feloniously hanged himself in a room of the dwelling-house of Elizabeth Feiste, widow, his mother, at Itchingfield with 'a wainerope' which he held in both hands, tying one end to a beam of the house and the other round his neck. At that time he had goods and bonds [*credita*] worth £38, of which £30 remains with Thomas Nye of Slinfold, gent., £5 with Walter Nicholles of Itchingfield and £3 with Edward Etheridge of Rustington. KB 9/751, m 474.

[Delivered by the coroner to King's Bench in Michaelmas. Nye, Nicholles and Etheridge were summoned to King's Bench to answer for the goods and chattels (*sic*); Nye had licence to imparl in Easter 1617 and Nicholles and Etheridge were outlawed at Chichester on 25 Sept 1617. KB 9/751, mm 474, 475d; KB 29/261, m 89d.]

170   18 Mar 1616. Felpham. Albany Stoughton, gent., Avisford hundred coroner. Jurors: Anthony Nashe, John Leeche, Edward Sutton, John Hobben, John Gawen, John Gratwick, Richard Knight, … Newington, Thomas Valor, William Dier, Robert Ayles, Roger Ayles, John Flower jun., William Gillam, Thomas Page. On 10 Mar William Reggatt, 'shomaker', John Reggatt, 'shomaker', and Thomas Carde, 'marriner', all of Felpham, feloniously killed Henry Tailor at Felpham: the Reggatts 'did [throw him upon the] ground' whereby he received 'a bruse' of which he languished at Felpham until 16 Mar and then died; and Carde was present aiding and abetting them. [*Damaged.*] ASSI 35/58/8, m 34. [*Calendared in CAR, no 380.*]

[Delivered to East Grinstead assizes on 8 July when the Reggatts and Carde, who had been committed to gaol by the coroner, were remanded on bail to the next assizes, but there is no record of their appearing then or later. ASSI 35/58/8, mm 40, 40d; *CAR*, no 360.]

171 24 Apr 1616. Brighton in Whalesbone hundred. John Teynton, gent., Lewes rape coroner. Jurors: John Gunter, Thomas Jeffrey, John Wales, Adam Waller, Erasmus Surridge, Peter Booker, Robert Scutt, Henry Howell sen., Thomas Humphrey, John Taylor sen., John Taylor jun., Henry Blake, Stephen Gunne, William Gunne, Robert Freinde, Nicholas Jackett, Thomas Champion. On one or more days in March Isabel wife of Robert Woodgat of Denton, gent., feloniously killed Joan Giles, her husband's young servant [*servula*], at Denton with staves, small staves, straps and hot tongs worth 6d which she held in both hands, striking, whipping, pinching and ill-treating her on many parts of her body and giving her very many 'bruses' and other wounds in almost all of her body of which she languished at Denton and Brighton until 21 Apr and then died at Brighton. ASSI 35/58/8, m 36. [*Calendared in CAR, no 381.*]

[Delivered with **170**. At the assizes the inquest was declared void because insufficient, presumably by reason of its vagueness, and the grand jury, to which Ann Newton, Elizabeth Hood, Ann Ballard and John Ashbye gave evidence, presented an indictment which charged Isabel Woodgat of Denton, spinster, wife of Robert Woodgat, with murdering Giles: on 29 Mar she struck her on the head at Denton with a cowl-staff worth ¼d which she held in both hands, giving her several fatal wounds; on 31 Mar she struck her on the back at Denton with a wanty (*sc.* a rope for use with pack-saddles or horses) worth 1d which she held in her right hand, giving her several more fatal wounds; and on 2 Apr she burnt her fingers and legs at Denton with a pair of hot tongs worth 6d which she held in both hands, giving her yet more fatal wounds; of all of which Giles languished at Denton until 21 Apr and then died. Isabel Woodgat was at large at the time of the assizes and so the indictment was sent to King's Bench in Michaelmas when her arrest was ordered; she was waived at Lewes on 4 June 1618. ASSI 35/58/8, m 36; KB 9/751, mm 235, 236; KB 29/261, m 96d; *CAR*, no 381.]

172 28 Apr 1616. Chichester. Thomas Greenefeild and Anthony Smyth, Chichester city coroners. Jurors of Chichester: John Bartholomew, Edward Dallinder, William Crue, William Sandham, Richard Bigges, 'Ryman' Collick, Thomas Armiger, Nicholas Dallinder, John Stowell, George Mekins, Francis Bristoe, William Watson, 'Lancelott' Martenn, Edward Lambold, Edmund Sargeant, Thomas Shancken, James Wild, Thomas Abram, Thomas Tupper. Between 10 and 11 a.m. on 27 Apr, when John Austen late of Chichester, 'taylor', who was very seriously ill and not of sound mind, was lying in his bed in an upper room in the dwelling-house of Agnes Durant, widow, in East Street, Chichester, he suddenly rose from his bed, went to a window of the room which was near the bed, thrust his legs out of the window and, slipping out of it, fell to the ground in East Street, thereby so severely crushing his head that he immediately died. At that time he had no lands or tenements, goods or chattels. KB 9/751, m 300.

[Delivered with **164**. The note *felo de se* was written on the inquest in King's Bench, but the death is recorded among the misadventures on the Controlment Roll. KB 9/751, mm 300, 312d; KB 29/261, m 94.]

173 8 May 1616. Slaugham in Buttinghill hundred. John Teynton, gent., Lewes rape coroner. Jurors: John Garston, William Ashfolde, John Parkes, Richard Vynall, Richard Davye, John Alexander, Philip Barfoote, Walter Barrett, Roger Harrise, Robert Terry, William Ashfold, Henry Jenner, James Sater. On 7 May, when William Greener was walking on a new roof belonging to Walter Coverte, kt, at Slaugham, by misadventure he fell backwards 18 feet upon 'a greate sommer' [*sc.* summer, the main horizontal supporting beam], thereby dying immediately. KB 9/751, m 472.

[Delivered with **169**. KB 9/751, m 475d; KB 29/261, m 89d.]

174 20 May 1616. Aldwick in Aldwick hundred. Henry Peckham, gent., county coroner. Jurors: Robert Lutman, John Lightfoot, Robert Rose, John Ayles, John Stoner, Thomas Stert, Thomas Burry, William Burry, William Davies, John Miles, Richard Wyker, William Challwyn, William Borden, William Monery, John Gonnyn, Robert Gonnyn. About 4 p.m. on 18 May Margaret Cowdry, widow, feloniously hanged herself in her dwelling-house with 'an halter' of no value. She had goods and chattels worth £14 which remain with George Coles of Amberley for the king's use. KB 9/751, m 305.

[Delivered with **164**. Coles was summoned to King's Bench to answer for the goods and chattels; he had licence to imparl in Easter 1617. On a writ of exigent of 14 Apr 1619 Coles was exacted at Lewes on 6 May, Chichester on

3 June, Lewes on 1 July, Chichester on 29 July and Lewes on 26 Aug when he was outlawed by judgment of John Bucher and John (*recte* Richard) Williams, gents, county coroners. In Easter 1620 Coles appeared in King's Bench, surrendered to the marshal and produced a writ of error of 6 May 1620 for the revocation of the outlawry if the court should find error in the record and process. He pleaded that there were 4 errors: it did not appear by the inquest whether or not the jurors were good and lawful men of Aldwick and the 3 neighbouring townships; it did not appear by the inquest whether or not the jurors were empanelled and sworn to inquire how Cowdry came to her death; the inquest did not state in what place and county she killed herself; and Coles was called George Coles of Amberley in the inquest but George Coles of Amberley, deputy almoner of Sussex, in the writ of exigent and therefore the writ was not warranted by the record; all contrary to the law of the land. Coles was delivered on bail to Edmund Freman of Pulborough, yeoman, and William Reynolds of St Margaret's, Westminster, tailor, until later in the term when the court upheld his plea, revoked and annulled his outlawry and restored him to the common law and to all that he had lost by reason of the outlawry, and he went sine die. A writ of 16 May 1620 ordered George bishop of Chichester to deliver to Coles without delay all goods and chattels, lands and tenements which the bishop had seized as forfeit by reason of Coles's outlawry. KB 9/751, mm 305, 312d; KB 27/1463, Rex m 57d; KB 27/1493, Rex mm 25–25d; KB 29/261, mm 93d, 94; KB 29/263, m 42d; KB 29/269, mm 31, 34.]

175   5 *or* 6 June 1616 [*MS* Wednesday 6 June, *but 6 June was a Thursday*].   West Tarring in Brightford hundred.   John Teynton, gent., Bramber rape coroner.   Jurors: Thomas Peeter, Thomas Knight, William Blackman, William Skynner, John Fowler, Thomas Blaker, Stephen Stammer, Thomas Rutland, Thomas Winsson, William Nevell, Richard Jackson, Edward Owen, William Hune. On 4 June Alice Leonard feloniously drowned himself in a well near her dwelling-house at ?Heene [*MS* Lyme, Lyne] in West Tarring. At that time she had no goods or chattels. KB 9/751, m 475.
[Delivered with **169**. KB 9/751, m 475d; KB 29/261, m 89d.]

176   7 June 1616. Warnham. John Teynton, gent., [*blank*: Bramber *omitted*] rape coroner. Jurors: Robert Cooper, John Maye, Hamlet Boorer, John Eversed, Gilbert Man, William Dudley, Thomas Martyn, Richard Deane, Samuel Edwardes, John Sherwyn, Thomas Sommersall, William Wheeler. On 6 June, when Richard Charman was working in 'a marle pitt' belonging to Henry Roffey, his master, in 'Telgat' field in Warnham, a large amount of 'marle' by misadventure fell on the left side of his head, giving him 'a bruse' of which he immediately died. KB 9/751, m 471.
[Delivered with **169**. KB 9/751, m 475d; KB 29/261, m 89d.]

177   16 June 1616. Nuthurst in Steyning hundred. John Teynton, gent., Bramber rape coroner. Jurors: John Seale, Richard Lindfeild, Edward Hill, Ockenden [*Ockendenus*] Robertes, Stephen Pyke, Richard Gates, James Cooper, John Pollington, William Davye, William Griffyn, Walter Gagg, John Wood, Thomas Towner. On 15 June, when John Bridges was riding on his chestnut mare from Nuthurst towards his dwelling-house in Ardingly, by misadventure he fell from the mare onto the ground, dying immediately. The jurors appraised the mare at 20s, which sum remains with George Coles of Amberley, deputy almoner of Sussex. KB 9/751, m 473.
[Delivered with **169**. Coles was summoned to King's Bench to answer for the mare; he had licence to imparl in Easter 1617. He was outlawed, appeared in King's Bench with a writ of error, pleaded the errors, was bailed and had his outlawry revoked and his possessions restored, all as in **174** except that the errors were that it did not appear by the inquest in which county Nuthurst was or whether or not it was in the rape of which Teynton was coroner and that it did not appear on what day and at what place Bridges died. KB 9/751, mm 473, 475d; KB 27/1463, Rex m 57; KB 27/1493, Rex mm 22–22d; KB 29/261, m 89d; KB 29/263, m 42d; KB 29/269, mm 31, 34.]

178   3 Aug 1616. Hastings. Richard Waller, Hastings mayor and coroner. Jurors: Richard Porter, Thomas Wynter, Nicholas Staplus, Thomas Fuller, John Rygat, William Lovell, Thomas Thistlethwaites, John Michell sen., John Bryant, Richard Downe, George Easton, Richard French, Richard Chambers, Richard Peck, George Oliver, John Grevett, Thomas Haynes. On 2 Aug, when Thomas Wincheden, aged about 9, servant of John Wincheden of Pett, 'yom[an]', was driving his master's empty wagon from Hastings towards his master's house at Pett and was sitting in the wagon, he suddenly fell out of it onto the ground on his head near Nordens Cross within the liberty of Hastings and broke his neck, whereby he died by misadventure. HASTINGS C/A(a) 1, f 192v.

179   13 Sept 1616. Worth in Buttinghill hundred. John Teynton, gent., Lewes rape coroner. Jurors: Charles Jude, gent., Nicholas Saxbee, Ambrose Wickham, Richard Gates, John Whyte, George Riche, Thomas Bryan sen., Peter Furrell, Richard Basforde, Thomas Bryan jun., Roger Nele, Richard Willett, Rhys [*Risus*] Morgann. On 10 Sept Henry Hatcher feloniously gave himself a wound on the right side of his abdomen 2 inches deep and almost 1 inch wide at Worth with a knife worth 1d which he held in his right hand, of which he languished until the next day and then died at Worth. At the time of the felony he had movable goods in his house worth 13s 4d, a mare worth 26s 8d and 'rye and otes' worth 15s, all of which remain with George Coles, deputy almoner of Sussex. KB 9/753B, m 144.
[Delivered with **185** and on to King's Bench in Easter 1617. There is no entry on the Controlment Roll about the goods and no note *de bonis* on the inquest. KB 9/753B, mm 140d, 144; KB 29/263, m 4d.]

180   7 Oct 1616. West Hoathly in Streat half-hundred. John Teynton, gent., Lewes rape coroner. Jurors: Thomas Scyssme, Jasper Wheeler, Stephen Dungat, Francis Hamlayre, Nicholas Cripps, George Wheeler, John Bryan, John Gebbe, John Milles, Richard Cleare, John Harbor, James Streater, Edward Pigott, Richard Weller. On 3 Oct, when Richard Gatland was cutting through [*perfodiens*] an oak belonging to Philip Cumber of West Hoathly, his master, at West Hoathly, by misadventure the oak suddenly and without Gatland noticing it fell on his body, so severely crushing it that he immediately died. The oak was the cause of his death and the jurors appraised it at 2s, which sum remains with George Coles, deputy almoner of Sussex. KB 9/753B, m 149.
[Delivered with **179**. Coles was summoned to King's Bench to answer for the oak; he was discharged in Easter 1619 because William Johnson, esq., the king's deputy almoner, acknowledged satisfaction. KB 9/753B, mm 140d, 149; KB 29/263, m 5.]

181   8 Oct 1616. Lurgashall in Rotherbridge hundred. Albany Stoughton, gent., Arundel rape coroner. Jurors: Anthony Kickefould, Thomas Aylen, Robert Yealden, William Eed, John Fullicke, William James, Michael West, John Morrice, William Oulder, William White, John Hackman, Thomas Hogsfleashe, John Man, William Jackson, James Bassage. On 6 Oct William Tompson late of Tillington, 'husbandman', murdered Gervase Phillps in River Park in Lurgashall with a sword of iron and steel worth 12d which he held in his right hand, giving him a wound on the left side of the chest 1 inch wide and 6 inches deep of which he immediately [died]. Tompson immediately fled to places unknown. At that time he had no goods or chattels, lands or tenements to the jurors' knowledge. KB 9/755, m 378.
[Delivered with **188** and on to King's Bench in Michaelmas 1617. Tompson's arrest was ordered in King's Bench; he was outlawed at Chichester on 27 Aug 1618. Lurgashall was summoned to King's Bench to answer for his escape; it made fine in Trinity 1621. KB 9/755, mm 377, 378, 414d; KB 29/263, m 112d.]

182   21 Oct 1616. Steyning. John Teynton, gent., Bramber rape coroner. Jurors: John Turner, John Newman, Richard Bryant, John Weston, Samuel Hatcher, John Slutter, William Danyell, Thomas Worcencrofte, William Vagger, Richard Jupp, Thomas Cogger, Walter Crabbe. On 27 Sept Alan Winson was sick and weak at Steyning and languished until 13 Oct when he died a natural death at Steyning. KB 9/753B, m 164.
[Delivered with **179**. KB 9/753B, m 140d; KB 29/263, m 5d.]

183   29 Oct 1616. West Grinstead in West Grinstead hundred. John Teynton, gent., Bramber rape coroner. Jurors: William Whitebread, John Martyn, William Veroll, Thomas Parson, Roger Tyler, Richard Pannett, Benet Greene, Richard Linefeild, Thomas Veroll, Thomas Parson, John Laceter, Thomas Horley, Thomas Searle, William Vagge, Thomas Parson, John Bennet. About 9 p.m. on 27 Oct, when Richard Coope, who was very drunk, was crossing a stream on a wooden bridge in 'Grinsted mead' in West Grinstead, by misadventure he fell from the bridge into the stream where he was immediately drowned. KB 9/753B, m 151.
[Delivered with **179**. KB 9/753B, m 140d; KB 29/263, m 5.]

184   22 Nov 1616. Worth in Buttinghill hundred. John Teynton, gent., Lewes rape coroner. Jurors: Edward Hatcher, Edward Nicholas, George Weste, Edward Blondell, Thomas Ware, John Harlinge, John Sommer, John Jupp, Roger Harrison, Robert Sellwhyn, John Pellyn, Richard Stanstreete, John Crowcher. On 20 Nov, when James Saunder was working in a stone quarry at Worth, by misadventure 20 tons of marl or earth fell upon his body, so severely crushing it that he immediately died. KB 9/753B, m 150.
[Delivered with **179**. The coroner was summoned to King's Bench to answer for defects in the inquest, presumably for omitting to value and safeguard the marl; he was discharged in Michaelmas 1617 because the inquest was amended, although the omission remains. KB 9/753B, mm 140d, 150; KB 29/263, m 5.]

185   8 Jan 1617. Tillington in Rotherbridge hundred. Albany Stoughton, gent., Arundel rape coroner. Jurors: William Briger, Thomas Humfrie, William Markes, John Mellearshe, Aaron Smyth, Michael Cranly, James Barton, Stephen Aylwin, Matthew Kinge, Thomas Sturt, Thomas Polinge, Lawrence Sturt, John Jackson, James Hamlyn, Edward Haies, John Puttocke, William Alderton. On 6 Jan Henry Hoborow late of Northchapel in Petworth, 'husbandman', feloniously killed Thomas Cufaud in River Park in Tillington with 'a hanger' [*sc.* a short sword] of iron and steel worth 5s which he held in his right hand, giving him a wound on the head which penetrated to the brain and of which he immediately died. At that time Hoborow had no goods or chattels, lands or tenements to the jurors' knowledge. ASSI 35/59/6, m 23. [*Calendared in CAR, no 393.*]
[Delivered to East Grinstead assizes on 3 Mar when the grand jury presented an indictment which charged Henry Hobery alias Hobroughe, yeoman, and William Payne, freemason, both late of Northchapel, with murdering Thomas Cuffaud, gent., at Tillington on 6 Jan: Hobery striking him on the left side of the head with a sword of iron and steel worth 6s 8d which he held in his right hand and giving him a wound 7 inches wide and 3 inches deep of which he immediately died; and Payne being feloniously present aiding and abetting him. At the time of the assizes Payne was at large. Hobery, who had been committed to gaol by Henry Goringe, kt, JP, pleaded not guilty to the indictment but was convicted and hanged; he had no chattels. Also at the March assizes Henry Goringe was amerced £40 because, although he had taken examinations concerning the case, he did not attend the court as required by his office. ASSI 35/59/6, mm 23, 25, 26, 42, 42d, 43; KB 9/755, m 376; *CAR*, nos 387, 391–393.]

186   26 Jan 1617. Hailsham. John Bucher, gent., Pevensey rape coroner. Jurors: Abraham Bodle, Edward Buckhurst, Alexander Vyne, John Underdowne, Thomas Bodle, Robert Symmons, William French, Stephen Mathew, Thomas Scrase, Stephen Underdowne, John Hunt, William Roide, John Clyffe, Thomas Pymme, Ellis Faireway, Edward Hooke. About midnight on 21 Dec 1616 Mary Reynoldes of Hailsham, widow, gave birth to a live male child at Hailsham and then murdered him on the same day at Hailsham, putting her hands on his mouth and neck and suffocating him, whereby he immediately died. At that time she had no goods or chattels, lands or tenements to the jurors' knowledge. Immediately after committing the felony she fled to places unknown. ASSI 35/59/6, m 22. [*Calendared in CAR, no 401.*]
[Delivered with **185**. At the assizes the grand jury presented an indictment almost identical to the inquest verdict but omitting the last 2 sentences. Reynoldes, who had been committed to gaol by Nicholas Parker, kt, JP, pleaded not guilty to the indictment and was acquitted; she had not fled and was therefore released. ASSI 35/59/6, mm 22, 33, 38, 42d, 43; *CAR*, nos 391, 400, 401.]

187   29 Jan 1617. 'Coldwaltham Parke' in Coldwaltham in Manhood hundred. John Addams, gent., coroner of the bishop of Chichester's Sussex liberties. Jurors: John Braby, Thomas Cooke, Henry Mylles, Henry Whitebrett, Jasper Catchelove, Thomas Hobjohn, George Brookfeild, Henry Carver, Henry Smyth, Roger Brookfeild, John Wade, William Bachelor, Richard Head, Anthony Erly, Thomas Scutt, all of Coldwaltham; Richard Rooke of Coates; Thomas Elson of Fittleworth; Thomas Stone of Wisborough Green; John Green, Edward Blundle, William Humfry, all of Pulborough; Henry Warren of Bury. Between 11 a.m. and noon on 28 Jan, when Richard Waters late of Wisborough Green, 'laborer', aged 40 or thereabouts, was working 'in fellinge' 'a beechen tree' which was growing in 'Coldwaltham Parke' and 'felled' it, 'the ground end' of the tree by misadventure fell upon his body, broke 'the righte legg' and struck and broke his abdomen and bowels whereby he immediately died. The tree lies in 'Coldwaltham Parke' in the ownership of Samuel bishop of Chichester and is appraised by the jurors at 10s. KB 9/753B, m 148.

[Delivered with **179**. The bishop was summoned to King's Bench to answer for the tree; process continued until Trinity 1626 but no resolution is recorded. The coroner was also summoned to King's Bench to answer for defects in the inquest, no doubt the omission of the final sentence which was written later in a very small hand over an erasure; process ceased in Hilary 1619 because the inquest was amended. KB 9/753B, mm 140d, 148; KB 29/263, mm 5, 8d.]

188   7 Mar 1617. Eastbourne. John Butcher, gent., county coroner. Jurors: Richard Bartholomewe sen., Richard Edwardes, John Crunden, Robert Dyer, Henry Fennell, John Dyer, Edward Herryott, Richard Bartholomewe jun., John Reeve, Thomas Springatt, Edmund Bennett, John Payn, John Blide, Richard Funell, Thomas Fayreman. About 6 p.m. on 2 Mar James Pierce late of Eastbourne, 'laborer', murdered Ursula Hornden at Eastbourne, offering her 'rattesbane' and giving it to her to eat with the intention of killing her. She took the poison from him and ate it, thereby languishing at Eastbourne for 8 hours after 'eating' it and then dying. At the time of the felony Pierce had no goods or chattels, lands or tenements to the jurors' knowledge. ASSI 35/59/7, m 13. [*Calendared in CAR, no 425.*]

[Delivered to East Grinstead assizes on 21 July when a bill of indictment was preferred almost identical to the inquest verdict, but stating that the poisoning was between 6 and 7 p.m., omitting the last sentence and adding that on 1 Mar Katharine Cowper late of Eastbourne, spinster, wife of Richard Cowper, had feloniously incited and advised Pierce at Eastbourne to commit the murder. The grand jury affirmed the charge against Pierce but rejected that against Cowper. Pierce, who had been committed to gaol by Nicholas Parker, kt, JP, pleaded not guilt to the indictment but was convicted and hanged; he had no chattels. ASSI 35/59/7, mm 13, 20 , 23, 39; *CAR*, nos 420, 424, 425.]

189   12 Apr 1617. Horsham. John Teynton, gent., Bramber rape coroner. Jurors: Thomas Rowlande, Henry Voyce, Edward Bristowe, Edward Seares, John Poe, Stephen Russell, Richard Waller, John Awoode, Thomas Baker, William Griffyn, Richard Lyndfeilde, William Martyn. On 7 Apr John Booker late of Horsham feloniously killed Robert Tolpett at Horsham, striking and kicking him on his face, head and loins with his hands and feet and giving him many 'brewses' of which he languished at Horsham until 10 Apr and then died. At the time of the felony Booker had no goods or chattels, lands or tenements. ASSI 35/59/7, m 12. [*Calendared in CAR, no 434.*]

[Delivered with **188**. At the assizes an indictment was preferred almost identical to the inquest verdict, but calling Booker a yeoman, saying that the bruises were on Tolpett's head and back and charging Booker with murder; the last sentence is omitted. The grand jury, to which Ann Tolpett, Richard Waise and John Strode and probably Thomas Forman, Joseph Turner and Charles Miller gave evidence, reduced the charge to manslaughter. Booker was at large at the time of the assizes. Tolpett, called a young man, was buried at Horsham on the day of the inquest. ASSI 35/59/7, mm 9, 12; *CAR*, no 434; SRS, XXI, 385.]

190   25 Aug 1617. Hurstpierpoint in Buttinghill hundred. John Teynton, gent., Lewes rape coroner. Jurors: Richard Beach, Edward Heath, Richard Awcocke, Richard Parson, John Wheeler, Thomas Rendfcild, Thomas Anstye, Edward Davy, Thomas Cowlstocke, Francis Alexander, John Russell, Thomas Whyte, Richard Feiste, John Parker. On 23 Aug Thomasin Robertes, widow, feloniously drowned herself in 'the wasᵢ ₁g ponde' near William Lashmere's dwelling-house at Hurstpierpoint. At that time she had goods and clothing at Hurstpierpoint worth 35s which remain with William Lashmere; and other goods, property [*jura*] and credits at Brighton, value unknown to the jurors, but which are appraised in the attached inventory and remain with Ockenden Robertes of Brighton, 'yoman'.

26 Aug. Brighton. Inventory of Thomasin Robertes's goods, chattels and credits taken by Edward Myhell, constable, William Guyllam, George Randall, Henry Blaker, Richard Gonne and William Prinsopp. 'In the hall: inprimis one table with a frame, a forme, a syde table with a frame, six joyned stooles, three chayres [worth] xv s vj d; item a presse cubbord and twoe brusshes xij s iiij d; item ij° brandyrons, ij° gridyrons, ij° fyre shovelles, a slyce, one payre of tounges, three spittes, ij° payre of potthangers, a cleaver, a slyce, a jacke and furniture, a payre of bellowes xix s. In the butiry: item one

yron pott, iij brasse kettelles, iiij^or brasse possnettes [*sc.* posnets, small metal pots for boiling], j brasse pott, iij^e pewter dishes, iiij^or sawcers, two skymmers, one chaffing dish and a basting ladle xxiij s vj d; item three earthen pottes ix d; item twoe dripping panns, ij° fryinge pannes, iij^e crockes, two wooden platters and a trugge iiij s viij d; item an iron pestell and morter, a pewter saulte, a breadgrate, a pewter platter xvj d. In the roome over the buttry: item two lynnen spynninge wheeles, a musterd querne, a flaskett ij s iiij d; item j skeyne of yarne and xij bottoms of lynnen yarne ij s viij d; item two buckettes and skeyne wynders vj d. In the chamber over the hall: item one table with a frame, a lyverye cubbord, a bedsteddle with curteyns and vallence, ij° newe fetherbedes, iij blankettes, a coverlett, ij° fetherboulsters, a pillocote [*sc.* pillow-case], a wicker chayre and a little greene chayre v li; item a bason, ewre and cubbord and a lokinge glasse iij s x d; item a joyne boxe and in it ij° ruff-bandes, j smocke, iiij^or aperins, iij kerchers, iiij^or stomachers, a payre of cuffes, a payre of gloves and other wearinge lynnen xv s; item a joyne chest v s; item in yt ij° cloth gownes, viij payre of sheetes, ij° payre of course sheetes, vij pillocotes, j kercher, vij tableclothes, xvij tablenapkins, viij towelles, j hatt, purse and gyrdle vj li xviij s; item one other joyne cheste iiij s; item in the same xxvij napkins, ix table clothes, vij towelles, xiij kerchers, ix pere of sheetes and j tableclothe v li x s. In the little closett: item liij peeces of pewter, a ladle, a chafingdishe, a warmingpann, iij saultes, ij° chamberpottes, ij° brasse candlestickes, iiij^or pewter candlestickes, ij° pewter pottes, ij° cawdell cupps [*sc.* caudle cups, cups for warm drinks], j bottle, viij spoones, trenchers, wodden vesselles and glasses, j baskett xliij s vj d. In the garrett: item j high bedsteddle, j trondle bedsteddle [*sc.* a trundle-bed or truckle-bed, a low bed running on truckles or castors, probably kept under the high bed], a mattress, matt and tester, j fetherbed, j bolster, ij° pillows, j paire of sheetes, a pillocote, ij° blanquettes, j coverlett and a little brasse candlesticke l s; item j greate chest and iij other chestes vij s; item in the great chest sheetes xiij payre xliij s iiij d; item xj tableclothes, vj towelles, v trugges, j payre of sheetes and a peece of lether xv s ij d; item in an other chest xlvj li of flaxe xxx s. Item in the presse in the hall ij° carpettes, j coverlett, vj cusshions and a tablecloth xxiij s; item a bible and ix small bookes v s. In an owthouse: item a brasse kettle, an iron grate, a peele [*sc.* peel, a baker's shovel], a flaskett, vj tubbes, an old salting troughe, a chopping blocke, xj tubbes more and a kneadinge troughe x s. In the owtchamber: item a bedsteddle, a fetherbed, twoe bousters [*sc.* bolsters], a flockbed, a coverlette, a blanquett and a pillow xl s; item a joyne cheste an in yt a wastecote, a peticoat, a carpett, j crocke, ij° chestes and ij° blanquettes xxxij s iiij d. In a lofte over that chamber: item two ould bedsteddles iij s iiij d. In the wellhouse: item v tubbes xx d. In a little deske: item the same deske ij s vj d; item therin xiij old groates and xxxix sengle peece vij s vij d; item a silver cupp xl s; item vj silver spoones xxx s'. Total £42 2s 10d [*recte* £39 12s 10d].

'Goodes gyven her by her late husbandes last will and testament besydes this inventary above mentioned as appeareth by the sayd will: item in ready mony to be payd within one quarter of a yeare after his deceasse cc li; item after certeyne lyves not yet expired lxvj li xiij s iiij d; item a desperat debte of l li from Sir Thomas Leedes, knight, l li; item an ould mare xx s'. Total of the whole inventory £359 16s 2d [*recte* £357 6s 2d]. [*Inventory mostly in English.*] KB 9/123, mm 1, 2. [Delivered by the coroner to King's Bench in Michaelmas. The note *pro bonis* was written on the inquest but there were no proceedings in King's Bench for the goods and chattels. KB 9/123, mm 1, 1d; KB 29/263, m 136d.]

191   3 Dec 1617. Waldron. John Bucher, Pevensey rape coroner. Jurors: Richard Tompsett, Richard Brithredge, John Willard, John Pulman, Thomas Daniell, Abraham Watson, Stephen Moore, John Barton, Richard Horscrofte, Francis Fipps, German [*Jarmanus*] Mitten, William Rainsford, Robert Kenward. On 20 Oct John Medherst by misadventure fell into 'a ditche' full of water at Waldron and John Cowper of Waldron, 'ripyer' [*sc.* rippier, one who carries fish in land to sell], then came there and feloniously killed him with 'a horshalter' worth 2d which held in both hands, throwing it round his neck and strangling him whereby he immediately died. On 21 Oct Elizabeth Hardes, widow, and Mary [*blank*]man, 'spinster', both of Waldron, knowing that Cowper had committed the felony, feloniously harboured and comforted Medherst [*recte* Cowper] at Waldron. At the time of the felony Medherst [*recte* Cowper] had no goods or chattels, lands or tenements to the jurors' knowledge. ASSI 35/60/5, m 7. [*Calendared in CAR, no 462.*]

[Delivered to East Grinstead assizes on 23 Feb 1618. Cowper, Hardes and Mary Inman had been committed to gaol by Thomas Aynscombe, esq., JP, but Cowper, who had been ill at Waldron before his committal on 19 Dec 1617, had died in gaol on 9 Jan and been buried at Horsham on 18 Jan. At the assizes Hardes and Inman were remanded on bail to appear at the following assizes but no record of that assizes survives. **192**; ASSI 35/60/5, mm 7, 33, 33d; *CAR*, nos 445, 462.]

192   10 Jan 1618. Horsham. John Teynton, gent., Bramber rape coroner. Jurors: John Lea, James Gratwicke, Joshua Alleyne, John Davy, William Artridge, William Sommersall, Thomas Horley, Richard Weller, John Dennys, Thomas Baker, John Robinson, Edward Seares, Emanuel Brockwell. On 19 Dec 1617, before he was brought into Horsham gaol, John Cooper was very weak from ill health at Waldron, and he languished at Horsham from 19 Dec until 9 Jan 1618 and then died a natural death in the gaol where he was detained. KB 9/754, m 324.

[Delivered with **191** and on to King's Bench in Easter. At an inquest at Waldron on 3 Dec 1617 Cooper had been charged with the manslaughter of John Medherst on 20 Oct at Waldron and he had been committed to gaol by Thomas Aynscombe, esq., JP. A rippier of Waldron, he was buried at Horsham on 18 Jan 1618. **191**; KB 9/754, m 333d; KB 29/265, m 4; SRS, XXI, 386.]

193   21 Jan 1618. Crimsham in Pagham. Richard Willyams, gent., county coroner. Jurors: Thomas Awcock, John Goble, Henry Chatfeild, John Bridger, Robert Cooke, John Chatfeild, John Hillard, William Meeres, John Fayres, Thomas Downer, John Elmes, William Eyles, William Gaston. About 10 p.m. on 20 Jan, when Thomas Wilson of Crimsham, Ann his wife and his whole household were sleeping in their beds in his dwelling-house at Crimsham, Anthony Melsam, a common felon and thief, came with several other evildoers unknown, 'attemptinge' to break, enter and burgle the house with the intention of murdering Thomas Wilson or at least 'to robb' him of his goods and money in the house. Then Wilson killed Melsam with a gun worth 3s 4d which was loaded 'with gunpowder and haileshott', taking it in both hands, striking Melsam with the lead shot on the left side of the head and giving him several wounds of which he immediately died. Thus Wilson killed him in self defence and in defence of his wife and household and of his goods and money and not otherwise, and so he should be acquitted and discharged by virtue of the statute of 24 Henry [VIII, c 5]. ASSI 35/60/5, m 5. [*Calendared in CAR, no 459.*]

[Delivered with **191**. At the assizes the grand jury affirmed the inquest verdict and Wilson confessed to it. ASSI 35/60/5, m 5; *CAR*, no 459.]

194   10 Feb 1618. Lancing in Burbeach [*recte* Brightford] hundred. John Teynton, gent., Bramber rape coroner. Jurors: Nicholas Page, gent., Thomas Peeter, Henry Chatfeild, Thomas Hall, Stephen Jenner, Thomas Campyon, William Peckham, John Fowler, John Turnegen, Denis Novell, Stephen Stammer, Richard Wolvyn, William Turnegen, John Parson, Richard Stapeler. About 9 p.m. on 1 Feb Agnes Allyn feloniously drowned herself in the well known harbour called 'Shoram Haven' in New Shoreham. At that time she had movable goods and household articles in her house at Shoreham worth 40s which remain with George Coles, deputy of the High Almoner of England, a yearly rent of 26s 8d in Horsham and another yearly rent of 30s for her life at Horley in Surrey. KB 9/756, m 75.

[Delivered to King's Bench by the coroner in Trinity. Coles was summoned to King's Bench to answer for the goods and chattels worth 40s; he was discharged in Hilary 1620 by virtue of letters patent of James I to Lancelot late bishop of Chichester, then High Almoner of England, enrolled in King's Bench in Michaelmas 1605. KB 9/756, mm 75, 75d; KB 29/265, m 61d.]

195   30 Apr 1618. Horsham. John Teynton, gent., Bramber rape coroner. Jurors: Thomas Clarke, John Jenne, John Steere, Abraham Bladen, Thomas Wheatly, Edward Bristowe, Thomas Baker, William Sommersall, Thomas Champyon, James Slaughter, Richard Champyon, William Wright, Matthew Wood. On 11 Mar, before she was brought into Horsham gaol, Mary Ducke was very weak from ill health at Mayfield, of which she languished from 11 Mar until 29 Apr and then died a natural death in the gaol. KB 9/1087, m 93.

[Delivered to the Sussex summer assizes and on to King's Bench in Michaelmas. Ducke was buried at Horsham on the day of the inquest. KB 9/1087, m 81d; KB 29/265, m 100d; SRS, XXI 387.]

196   4 May 1618. Horsham. John Teynton, gent., Bramber rape coroner. Jurors: Thomas Wood, Thomas Grombridge, Thomas Baker, Richard Niblett, John Jenn, Joshua Allen, Thomas Wheatly, Thomas Champyon, William Waterton, Matthew Wood, Daniel Hall, Edward Jupp, William Champyon, William Chambers. On 27 Apr John Kewell was very weak from ill health at Horsham, of which she languished until 4 May and then died a natural death in Horsham gaol. KB 9/1087, m 94.
[Delivered with **195**. Kewell was buried at Horsham on the day of the inquest. KB 9/1087, m 81d; KB 29/265, m 100d; SRS, XXI, 387.]

197   21 May 1618. Littlehampton. John Eagle, gent., Arundel rape coroner. Jurors: Thomas Oliver sen., John Arnolde, Thomas Oliver jun., John Edmondes, Thomas Greene, John Lenn, Thomas Oliver, John Kewell jun., Thomas Cuckney, John Grevett, Thomas Stronge, John Dudman, Thomas Kewell, John Woode, Thomas Brookeman, John Smyth, Thomas Kerle, William Oliver, William Lenn, William Streater, William Berrisson, William Jupe, Silas [*Sylvanus*] Horscrofte, Robert Budd. On 20 May Thomas Bayley late of Littlehampton, architect, died a natural death at Littlehampton. KB 9/1087, m 95.
[Delivered with **195**. KB 9/1087, m 81d; KB 29/265, m 100d.]

198   25 May 1618. Chichester. Thomas Greenefeild and Anthony Smyth, Chichester city coroners. Jurors of Chichester: John Cowper, Henry Colbrooke, Thomas Clarck, Thomas Diggons, Walter Dickenson, John Hobson, Thomas Calloway, William Fludd, Richard Manning, Henry Allen, Robert Napper, William Baverstock, Henry Roades, Thomas Bray, Roger Bradfold, John Butcher, Ralph Allen, William Crewe. About 1 p.m. on 22 May a 'gray' horse belonging to Edward Lawrence, citizen and alderman of Chichester, 'did strike with his heeles' the abdomen of George Sommer late of Chichester, 'husbandman', aged 22 or thereabouts, so violently at Broyle Heath near Chichester, within the bishop of Chichester's liberty, that his abdomen was very severely injured and crushed, of which he languished at Chichester until the next day and then died. The horse with 'his harnes' was taken into the hands of Samuel bishop of Chichester and they are appraised at 33s 4d. KB 9/1087, m 85.
[Delivered with **195**. The bishop was summoned to King's Bench to answer for the horse and harness; he was discharged in Hilary 1624 because the deputy almoner acknowledged satisfaction. KB 9/1087, m 81d; KB 29/265, m 100d.]

199   17 Feb 1619. Arundel. John Eagle, gent., Arundel rape coroner. Jurors: Clement Dryland, gent., Anthony Goughe, John Midleton, William Bennett, John Bryant, Richard Scardvill, John Staper, Richard Cobden, Nicholas Rickman, George Payne, Thomas Deane, John Strong, Edward Browning, Thomas Edwardes, Henry Sheppard, John Knowles, Edward Ludgater. About 1 p.m. on 12 Jan 'Enoch' son of John Rowse sen. of Arundel, 'victualer', 'being alone in a certeine cockboate swymming uppon the comon river of Arrundell aforsaide', by misadventure and against his will fell into the river and was suddenly drowned by its surges. KB 9/757, m 282.
[Delivered to the Sussex Lent assizes and on to King's Bench in Easter. The coroner was summoned to King's Bench to answer for defects in the inquest, presumably for not having the boat appraised and safeguarded; he was said to have been outlawed in the Essex county court at Chelmsford on 28 Aug 1621, 'Essex' being also written in the margin of the Controlment Roll against the entry. He was later pardoned. KB 9/757, mm 282, 293d; KB 29/266, mm 4, 4d.]

200   22 Mar 1619. Chichester. Thomas Greenefeild and Anthony Smyth, Chichester city coroners. Jurors of Chichester: William Wickman, John Fleshmonger sen., Stephen Humfry, Robert Diggons, Henry Wynes, Austin Willerton, John Coward, Edward Bragg, William Barber, John Binckes, Thomas Lethey, Thomas Hush, John Stapler, Henry Roades, William Bartlett, Robert Tupper, John Ward, Richard Greenefeild. About 5 p.m. on 20 Mar, when John Gounter late of Chichester, esq., was riding on 'a nagg' of 'grey' colour belonging to John Young of St Pancras's parish in the east suburbs of

Chichester, 'horsebreaker', in 'Broyle Lane' near Chichester and within the liberties of the city, he 'did fall' from the horse whereby his head was injured and crushed of which he died at Chichester about 10 p.m. The horse with 'the sadle and brydle' which it then 'was sadled and bridled with' is worth 46s 8d and remains with Young. KB 9/1089, m 75.

[Delivered to the Sussex summer assizes and on to King's Bench in Michaelmas. Young was summoned to King's Bench to answer for the harnessed horse; he was outlawed at Chichester on 30 May 1622. Process resumed under Charles I. KB 9/1089, mm 64d, 75; KB 29/266, mm 119d, 120.]

201   4 May 1619. Sedlescombe. John Aynscombe, gent., Battle liberty coroner. Jurors: Alexander Leonard, Thomas Tailor, Thomas Sharpe, Richard Brende, Thomas Sagett, Ninian Hedd, James Watson, Leonard Aylard, James Saggett, Nicholas Goodman, Goddard Foster, John Farnecombe. On 2 May John Hilles died a natural death at Sedlescombe and not by reason of any force inflicted upon him by any other person. KB 9/1089, m 81.

[Delivered with **200**. KB 9/1089, m 64d; KB 29/266, m 120.]

202   31 May 1619. Southover. John Teynton, gent., Lewes rape coroner. Jurors: John Knowles, William Leane, Henry Sparkes, John Auger, Thomas Virgo, John Crampe, John Bexlie, Lawrence Townsende, Simon Michell, William Dodson, John Cobby, Walter Crowch, William Browne, Goddard Broade. On 29 May, when Stephen Reames, 'carpenter', and John Musgrave, 'yoman', both of Southover, and Nicholas Chauntlor of Barcombe, 'yoman', were about to unload 'a timber logg' from a cart belonging to John Dapp of Barcombe, 'yoman', at Southover, as they 'did lifte up from the carte the timber logg' the cart 'was dryven awaye' and the logg fell upon 'a falling bancke' and rolled down the bank, the end of the log, which was crooked, by misadventure rolling over Elizabeth Holford's body and giving her 'a bruse' on the right side of the head of which she immediately died. The log was the cause of her death and was appraised by the jurors at 8s, which sum remains with William Parker, constable of Southover, on behalf of the whole parish. KB 9/758, m 270.

[Delivered to King's Bench by the coroner in Easter 1620. The constable was summoned to King's Bench to answer for the log; he was discharged in Hilary 1622 because the deputy almoner acknowledged satisfaction. KB 9/758, mm 270, 271d; KB 29/269, m 2d.]

203   19 June 1619. Rotherfield. John Luck, gent., Rotherfield hundred coroner. Jurors: John Maynard, Edward Willson, James Coppinge, Stephen Coppinge, William Maye, William Hale, John Baker of Brownings, John Cheseman, William Ovenden, John Maynard of Hamsell, Robert Baker, James Alchorne, William Coe, George Barbor, Herbert Fermor, William Chowne. On 11 June, when John Pickett was driving 'a marle court' loaded with 'marle' and drawn by 4 oxen, one of the oxen, of black colour, kicked him on his body, greatly crushing it, whereby he immediately died. The black ox was the cause of his death, was appraised by the jurors at 53s 4d and remains with Leonard Morley of Rotherfield. KB 9/1089, m 76.

[Delivered with **200**. Morley was summoned to King's Bench to answer for the ox; he was outlawed at Lewes on 21 Sept 1620. Process resumed under Charles I. KB 9/1089, mm 64d, 76; KB 29/266, mm 119d, 120.]

204   6 July 1619. Cliffe. John Bucher, gent., Loxfield Dorset half-hundred coroner. Jurors: John Page, Richard Luxford, John Parker, John Adams, Robert Palmer, Daniel Prier, Thomas Cheale, John Bennett, William Woodd, Thomas Smallfield, John Edwardes, Robert Beale. About 4 p.m. on 26 May, when William and Abel Rossam were both riding at South Malling on a 'baye' gelding which belonged to William to 'a marlepitt' full of water situated in John Page's bottoms in South Malling, the gelding went to the pit to drink with William and Abel on it and suddenly and by misadventure it 'did slide' into the water, which was about 7 feet deep, whereby William and Abel fell into the water and were drowned. The jurors appraised the gelding at 5s, which sum remains with John Bucher of Wadhurst, gent., for the use of Richard earl of Dorset, lord of the liberty, who etc. The inquest was held on view of both bodies. KB 9/758, m 225.

[Delivered to the Sussex Lent assizes and on to King's Bench in Easter 1620. John Bucher of Wadhurst was summoned

to King's Bench to answer for the gelding; he was outlawed at Chichester on 30 May 1622. Process resumed under
Charles I. KB 9/758, mm 225, 236d; KB 29/269, m 4d.]

205   3 Sept 1619. Trotton. Richard Willyams, gent., county coroner. Jurors: John Apsley, gent.,
Robert Aylwyn, John Fullocke, John Morris, Thomas Snowe, Thomas Beale, Thomas Bridger, John
White sen., William Tate, Richard Bridger, Richard White, John Randoll, John White. On 1 Sept, when
'an empty waine' was being drawn by 2 oxen at Trotton, by misadventure the wain 'did overthrowe'
suddenly and fell on the body of Henry Gregory, aged 16 or thereabouts, so crushing it that he
immediately died. The oxen with the wain and its wheels moved to his death, are appraised at £3 and
remain with Anthony Foster, esq. KB 9/759, m 131.
[Delivered to King's Bench by the coroner in Trinity 1620. Foster was summoned to King's Bench to answer for the
deodands; he was discharged in Trinity 1621 because the deputy almoner acknowledged satisfaction. KB 9/759,
mm 131, 131d; KB 29/269, m 56d.]

206   25 Sept 1619. Graffham in Easebourne hundred. John Addams, gent., coroner of the liberties
of Thomas earl of Arundel and Surrey. Jurors: John Marten, Richard Hiberden, William Norris sen.,
William Norris jun., Edward Ward sen., Edward Ward jun., Henry Ewen sen., Richard Wakeford,
George Hill, 'Emery' Aylinge, John Richardson, John Jay, Robert Champion, all of Graffham; Richard
Austen, Anthony Neal, Tobias Farnedell, John Austen, Daniel Austen, Stephen Graffam, John Gosden,
John Goldock, Thomas Elmes, Thomas Wakeford, all of Heyshott. Between 2 and 3 p.m. on 24 Sept,
when Richard Weppam late of Lodsworth, 'laborer', aged 40 or thereabouts, was digging 'chalke' in
Graffham, he 'undermyned the earth' so carelessly that 'three cart-loads of the same chalk and earth'
fell upon the whole of his body, completely burying and shattering him whereby he immediately died
by misadventure. The chalk and earth are not committed to anyone's keeping because they are of no
value. KB 9/758, m 224.
[Delivered with **204**. KB 9/758, m 236d; KB 29/269, m 4d.]

207   30 Sept 1619. Oving in Manhood hundred. John Addams, gent., coroner of the bishop of
Chichester's liberties. Jurors of Oving: Thomas Ameers, John Barnes, William Coode, Robert Grey,
Henry Russe, Thomas Nash, William Sander, Richard Goble, John Sparckes, Robert Horscroft, William
Blaker, William Higgens, John Dean, Richard Goar, William Moory. Between 2 and 3 p.m. on 29 Sept,
when John Smyth, aged 20 or thereabouts, lately household apprentice to Robert Ameers of Oving,
'yeoman', was driving 'an empty carte' belonging to Ameers with 5 horses from Stedham towards
Ameers's dwelling-house in Oving and was sitting on one of the horses commonly called 'the body
horse' [*sc.* shaft-horse], by misadventure he fell from the horse onto the ground at Cocking Causeway
in Easebourne hundred and within the liberties of Thomas earl of Arundel and Surrey and the 5 horses
dragged the left wheel of the cart over 'the smale of the belly' of Smyth, from which cause alone he
died about 4 p.m. at Singleton between Stedham and Oving. The 5 horses with 'their harnes which
they had on' and the cart with its wheels were then worth £12 in all and were delivered for safe
custody to John Peers, gent., one of the earl's bailiffs. KB 9/758, m 222.
[Delivered with **204**. The bailiff was summoned to King's Bench to answer for the deodands; he was discharged by
letters patent of Easter 1617. KB 9/758, mm 222, 236d; KB 29/269, m 4d.]

208   7 Oct 1619. Ifield in Brightford [*recte* Burbeach] hundred. John Teynton, gent., Bramber rape
coroner. Jurors: Thomas Milles jun., Thomas Milles sen., Robert Hill, William Comber, Samuel Wright,
William Stevens, Edward Woodman, John Wonam, Thomas Heythorne, Benjamin Woodman, William
Delves, William Aleighe. About 5 a.m. on 30 Sept, when Eleanor Wood, maidservant of Giles Thorp of
Ewhurst in Ifield, gent., intended to carry a bucket full of water 'from the fishing pond' at Ewhurst, by
misadventure she fell into 'the fyshponde' where she was immediately drowned. KB 9/758, m 269.
[Delivered with **202**. KB 9/758, m 271d; KB 29/269, m 2d.]

209   9 Oct 1619. Clapham in Burbeach [*recte* Brightford] hundred. John Teynton, gent., Bramber rape coroner. Jurors: John Hide, Edward Gray, John Calforde, Thomas Wyett, John Pannett, Edward Sowten, Thomas Hollingall, Robert Oulder, Thomas Glocester, Richard Greveth, John French, Richard Peeter, Henry Rowland, John Streete. On 7 Oct, when Thomas Payne was driving a cart loaded with 'ocken [*sc.* oak] wood', with 5 horses yoked to it, and going down from the top of Patching Hill in Patching, the rear mare called 'the thiller' [*sc.* thill-horse, the shaft-horse] so strayed that, although Payne restrained her with all his strength, the further wheel of the cart went up upon 'a stony little bancke' whereby the cart and its load fell upon his body giving him 'fowr mortall bruses' on the head, both arms and the chest of which he immediately died. Thus the rear mare and the cart with the wood were the cause of his death, the other 4 horses not moving to his death. The jurors appraised the mare, which was black, at 33s 4d, the cart at 20s and the wood at 2s 6d; they remain with Robert Brooke, constable, on behalf of the whole parish of Clapham. KB 9/758, m 271.
[Delivered with **202**. The constable was summoned to King's Bench to answer for the mare, cart and wood, said to be worth 55s; he was discharged in Michaelmas 1620 because the deputy almoner acknowledged satisfaction. KB 9/758, mm 271, 271d; KB 29/269, m 2d.]

210   7 Dec 1619. Shopham Bridge in Sutton in Rotherbridge hundred. John Addams, gent., coroner in the liberties of Thomas earl of Arundel and Surrey. Jurors: Thomas Sturt sen., Thomas Sturt jun., William Bridger, Nicholas Warner sen., John Edsall jun., Robert Allen, all of Tillington; Edward Quayse, Nicholas Turgis, Richard Browninge, John Satcher, Thomas Smyther, Richard Satcher, James Foord, William Wisdome, all of Petworth; Richard Hale of Coldwaltham. About 9 a.m. on 5 Dec Robert Ward late of Petworth, 'laborer', aged 40 or thereabouts, went to 'a ware [*sc.* weir] for fish' which was in the river at Shopham Bridge and in the tenure of James Coote of Sutton, 'yeoman', and saw 2 'fish potts' in the weir. Being alone, he tried to drag the pots from the river with 'a payer of garters' worth ½d which he held in both hands, tying one end of them round the pots and keeping the other end in his hands, to inspect the pots to see how many fish had been caught in them. By reason of Ward's violent pulling of the garters and the weight of the pots the garters 'wear broken asunder', one part being left in his hands and the other tied to the pots, whereby Ward by misadventure fell backwards into the river and was drowned, dying immediately. KB 9/758, m 223.
[Delivered with **204**. KB 9/758, m 236d; KB 29/269, m 4d.]

211   12 Jan 1620. Lewes. John Teynton, gent., Lewes rape coroner. Jurors: Richard Sterne, Benjamin Hoder, John Wales, Richard Pigott, John Mattheu jun., Lawrence Allfrey, Richard Blomer, William Goldum, Thomas Burkin, John Lane, Francis Gouldsmyth, John Todd, Shem [*Shemus*] Michell. On 8 Jan Nicholas Newton was born 10 or 11 weeks prematurely at Lewes, as fully appeared to the jurors by the testimony of various women, by reason of which prematurity only he languished until the next day and then died a natural death at Lewes between 10 and 11 p.m. KB 9/758, m 267.
[Delivered with **202**. KB 9/758, m 271d; KB 29/269, m 2d.]

212   17 Jan 1620. Broyle Heath in Manhood hundred and in the parish of St Peter the Great, Chichester. John Addams, gent., coroner of the bishop of Chichester's liberties in Sussex. Jurors: Henry Edwardes, William Hartly, John Sommer, John Chase, Thomas Clement, Richard Rolfe, John Edwardes, Thomas Woolridge, William Cole, Richard Wilson, Thomas Sommer, William Grange, Richard Emery, all of Mid Lavant; John Vallor, Henry [Standen, Thomas Steevens *struck through*] Ragles, Stephen Ragles, all of West Lavant; Roger Greentree, Henry Standen, Thomas Steevens, all of East Lavant. Between 3 and 4 p.m. on 10 Jan Thomas Binsteed, aged 10 or thereabouts, lately household apprentice to John Deanford of Mid Lavant, 'brickmaker', went out of Deanford's dwelling-house in Mid Lavant to Broyle Heath on Deanford's order to watch Deanford's sheep which were grazing there and, having entered Broyle Heath, he 'layd downe upon the ground' and slept in the cold until he became so cold and frozen that, being alone, he could not raise his body from the ground but, lying frozen on the ground, he died there of the cold only. KB 9/758, m 210.

[Delivered with **204**. This was classified as a natural death in King's Bench. KB 9/758, mm 210, 236d; KB 29/269, m 5.]

213   18 Jan 1620. Tillington in Rotherbridge hundred. John Addams, gent., coroner of the liberties of Thomas earl of Arundel and Surrey. Jurors: William Bridger of Tillington; John Page, Robert Holmwood, Edward Quaise, all of Petworth; John Kinge, James Hardam, both of Dean; John Sadler, John Puttock, Stephen Aylwin, all of Tillington; Thomas Polinge of 'Brooke'; Henry Kinge of Greatham; John Edsall, Francis Hardam, both of Upperton; John Aylwin of Petworth; Robert Keys of Upperton; Thomas Smyth of Tillington; Thomas Holloway, John Puttocke jun., both of Upperton. Between 6 and 7 a.m. on 16 Jan, when Jane Humfry, aged 24 or thereabouts, late wife of Thomas Humfry jun. of Tillington, 'yeoman', was ill in the dwelling-house of Thomas Humfry sen. in Tillington, she got out of the bed in which she was lying while her husband was lying asleep in it and, being alone, threw herself into 'the well' of Thomas Humfry sen. which was next to and belonged to his house and feloniously drowned herself in its water, dying immediately. At that time she had no goods or chattels, lands or tenements. KB 9/758, m 231.
[Delivered with **204**. KB 9/758, m 236d; KB 29/269, m 4.]

214   19 Jan 1620. Warnham in Singlecross hundred. John Teynton, gent., Bramber rape coroner. Jurors: John Maye, John Pilfould, Edward Willett, John Charman, Thomas Martyn, Thomas Lucas, Arthur Waller, James Fuller, John Michell, Thomas Baker, William Sommersall, Richard Jupp, William Wheeler. About 10 p.m. on 16 Jan, when Robert Sayres [*once later called* Sawyer], who was very drunk, intended to travel to his house from Master Cottham's dwelling-house in Warnham, the ground being covered with snow and ice, he strayed from his route onto Warnham Pond which was frozen and by misadventure the ice broke and he was immediately drowned. KB 9/758, m 268.
[Delivered with **202**. Sayres was buried at Warnham on the day of the inquest. KB 9/758, m 271d; KB 29/269, m 2d; PAR 203/1/1/1.]

215   15 Mar 1620. Lyminster in Poling hundred. John Addams, gent., coroner of the liberties of Thomas earl of Arundel and Surrey. Jurors: Richard Talmey, Edward Greenfeild, both of Lyminster; John Pannett, Ralph Collin, James Hilles, Richard Irlland, Thomas Olliver jun., all of Toddington; John Edmans, John Knell jun., John Golldes, John Knell sen., Thomas Edman, all of Littlehampton; Joseph Richardes, Benjamin Oliver, Robert Franklin, Robert Budd, all of Lyminster. About 8 a.m. on 14 Mar a river near the sea in Lyminster, which ebbed and flowed into the sea, threw a man, unknown to the jurors, who was wearing only 'a shirt' of linen of no value, onto the bank of the river dead. When, where or how he came to his death the jurors do not know. KB 9/760, m 464.
[Delivered to East Grinstead assizes on 17 July and on to King's Bench in Michaelmas. This was classified as a misadventure in King's Bench. KB 9/760, m 464; KB 29/269, m 89.]

216   22 Mar 1620. Chichester. Thomas Greenefeild and Anthony Smyth, gents, Chichester city coroners. Jurors of Chichester: Thomas Wright, Samuel Major, Thomas Woodison, William Barber, Richard Ward, Henry Wines, John Ward, Henry Allen, James Smyth, Thomas Hush, Edward Napper, Edward Lighttlote, 'Randall' Tutty, Edward Gill, John Standen, Richard Maning, John Hardham, Nicholas Teeling. About 5 p.m. on 21 Mar, when Thomas Callowaye late of Chichester, aged ½ year or thereabouts, son of Thomas Callowaye of Chichester, 'cordyner' [*sc.* cordwainer, shoemaker], was in the hands or arms of Elizabeth Maning, aged 6 or thereabouts, because of her weakness and against her will he fell by misadventure from her hands or arms 'into a tubb of scalding wort' and 'was scalded' and from 'the same scalding' he died about 1 a.m. that night. The tub, which is wooden, is worth 12d and remains with the coroners. KB 9/760, m 466.
[Delivered with **215**. The coroners were summoned to King's Bench to answer for defects in the inquest, possibly the omission of the custody of the tub which is interlined; they were later pardoned. KB 9/760, m 466; KB 29/269, mm 89, 89d.]

217 23 Mar 1620. Iping in the liberties of Thomas earl of Arundel and Surrey. Anthony Smyth, gent., county coroner. Jurors: Roger Heather, Thomas Caplin, Thomas Heather, John Swayne, Thomas Ayling, Richard Heather, Thomas Betzer, John Billet, John Good, Anthony Ayling, Thomas Hayward, Richard Chaper, Robert Chawcroft, John Bridger, William Grenetre, William Barckshire, Thomas Bolsom. Between 7 and 9 a.m. on 19 Mar Katharine, aged 30 or thereabouts, late wife of Richard Duffeild of Iping, 'yron fyner', tried to draw water from 'the fludgate river' in Iping with 'a buckett' worth 12d which she held in both hands and, as she was raising the bucket from the river, by misadventure she fell from the bank and was drowned in the river. The bucket remains with Thomas Smythe. KB 9/760, m 465.
[Delivered with **215**. The coroner was summoned to King's Bench to answer for defects in the inquest, possibly the omission of the last sentence which is interlined; he was later pardoned. The note *pro bonis* was written on the inquest but there were no proceedings in King's Bench for the bucket. KB 9/760, m 465; KB 29/269, mm 89, 89d.]

218 18 Apr 1620 [*MS* Tuesday 17 Apr, *but 17 Apr was a Monday*]. Horsham. John Teynton, gent., Bramber rape coroner. Jurors: Ralph Heath, Edward Slawter, Richard Horly, Richard Boker, Richard Clarke, Edward Jupp, Henry Parker, James Waller, John Itchurst, Thomas Hatton, Matthew Wood, Richard Daws, William Sommersall. On 12 Apr William Barnard was very weak through ill health in Horsham gaol and languished there until 17 Apr when he died a natural death. KB 9/760, m 244.
[Delivered into King's Bench in Michaelmas, probably by the coroner. Barnard, called of Goring, was buried at Horsham on the day of the inquest (18 Apr). KB 29/269, m 95d; SRS, XXI, 389.]

219 30 July 1620. Piddinghoe in Fishersgate [*recte* Holmestrow] hundred. John Teynton, gent., Lewes rape coroner. Jurors: Richard Crane, Richard Tompsett, John Tompsett, William Bennett, John Crane, Richard Earsey, William Locke, Thomas Easton, John Easton, John Proberbes, Stephen Simons, John Hudson, Thomas Griffyn, Felix Reade, Thomas Diblocke, Robert Maynarde, John Gyles, Richard Gyles. About 11 p.m. on 23 July, when John Nicholles was coming from Newhaven to Piddinghoe and intending to cross 'a shallow ryver', he climbed up the bank of the river at Tarring Neville, in which parish he lived, and, being very drunk, by misadventure fell backwards into the river where he was immediately drowned. KB 9/764, m 192.
[Delivered by the coroner into King's Bench in Michaelmas 1621. KB 9/764, mm 192d, 193d; KB 29/270, m 60.]

220 16 Oct 1620. Hastings. Richard Waller, Hastings mayor and coroner. Jurors: Nicholas Staplus, John Baylif, Thomas Palmer, Thomas Streat, William Chepman, Mark Lucket sen., William Gawen, George Easton, George Chambers, Francis Wenam, Edmund Webb, John Pretty, William Dighton, John Bryand, Richard Downe, Richard Amyatt, John Boys, Robert Lawen. About [*blank*] p.m. on 15 Oct, when Edward Sargent of Hastings, 'fisherman', aged about 24, son of Mark Sargent sen. of Hastings, 'fisherman', was among other seamen on the seashore at Stonebeach in St Clement's parish, Hastings, striving to draw his father's boat [*navicula*] called 'le Blessing' of Hastings, weighing about 20 tons, out of the sea onto the land with 'a capston' (as the fishermen of the town have always done whenever a ship is brought to land) and was intent upon that business, the boat suddenly and unexpectedly overturned and fell on one side upon Edward, crushing him with its weight, breaking his chest and neck and pressing his body upon the ground whereby he was killed by misadventure. The boat therefore accrues to the town as deodand. HASTINGS C/A(a) 1, f 220v.

221 6 Jan 1621. Horsham. John Teynton, gent., Bramber rape coroner. Jurors: Edward Sares, Ralph Hall, Thomas Wheatly, Gilbert Sayres, Richard Clarke, Peter Chambers, Thomas Baker, Francis Bushnell, James Slawter, Robert Dalton, John Denise, Abraham Bladen, Edward Jupp. On 5 Jan Roger Short feloniously hanged himself in the dwelling-house at Horsham in which he lived 'with the leather of a stirrop fastned to a rafter that went crosse the house aforesayd', the other part of it being tied round his neck. At that time he had no goods or chattels, lands or tenements. KB 9/764, m 193.
[Delivered with **219**. KB 9/764, m 193d; KB 29/270, m 60.]

222   2 Apr 1621. Northiam. John Bucher, gent., county coroner. Jurors: John Davy, William Sharpe, John Glidd, Richard Glidd, George Piper, Roger Tree, Richard Tree, Henry Sheath alias Stace, William Wenborne sen., Edward Brigden, Richard Robinson, Richard Wimble, John Sheather, David Collins, John Dawe, Thomas Perkins, John Snowe, Edward Evans.   On 29 Mar Mary Delve of Northiam, 'spinster', gave birth to a male child at Northiam and on 2 Apr she murdered him at Northiam, taking him in her right hand by the legs and throwing him into a pit full of water with both hands whereby he was drowned, dying immediately.   At the time of the felony she had no goods or chattels, lands or tenements to the jurors' knowledge. ASSI 35/63/6, m 32. [*Calendared in CAR, no 511.*]
[Delivered to Horsham assizes on 2 July when the grand jury, to which John Iden, Elizabeth Austen, Joan Evenden and Mary Love and probably William White and John Fruen, gents, gave evidence, presented an indictment virtually identical to the inquest verdict except that the murder was given as on 29 Mar and the last sentence was omitted. Delve pleaded not guilty to the indictment but was convicted and hanged; she had no chattels. ASSI 35/63/6, mm 32, 45, 45d, 51, 55d; *CAR*, nos 500, 509, 511.]

223   3 May 1621. West Ashling [in] Funtington. Thomas Filder, Lady Berkeley's coroner. Jurors: Edward Woodnot, Edward Tococke, John Merie, Robert Kennet, John Souter, Jordan Temes, Richard Boune, George Sheperd, William Jellife, John Coldine, William Kimber, John Chalcroft, Thomas Langridge, John Nicollsone, Edward Lucas, Bartholomew Till, William Marshe, Christopher Worthington, Roger Martine, Richard Bartholomewe, Richard Swaine.   On 2 May, when Agnes Paufoot was drawing water from a well near her house in West Ashling, by misadventure she fell into the well and was drowned.   There was no other cause of her death to the jurors' knowledge. KB 9/764, m 312.
[Delivered with **222** and on to King's Bench in Michaelmas. KB 9/764, m 319Bd; KB 29/270, m 56.]

224   8 May 1621. Thakeham in East Easwrith hundred. John Teynton, gent., Bramber rape coroner. Jurors: Ambrose Buttler, gent., John Gratwycke, John Hayne, Hugh Tully, John Pollarde, William Bysshopp, Richard Wood, John Hayward, John Philpe, Edward Holland, William Wase, Nicholas Trull, John Wady.   On 29 Apr William Jupp late of Wiston, 'husbandman', and Philip Parson, 'husbandman', and Edward Surery, 'husbandman', both of Wiston, feloniously killed Richard Lee at Washington: all 3 or one of them striking him on the top of the head with 'a cudgell' worth ¼d [which] they or he held in one hand and giving him a wound 1 inch long; all 3 or one of them throwing a stone which they or he held in one hand, hitting him on the front of the head and giving him another wound 1 inch long and ½ inch deep; and all 3 or one of them '[did] spurne and kycke' him on the chest and sides giving him several 'mortall bruses'; of all which wounds and 'bruses' he languished at Thakeham until 4 May and then died.   At the time of the felony Jupp, Parson and Surery had no goods or chattels, lands or tenements.   On that day Jupp and Surery fled. [*Damaged.*] ASSI 35/63/6, m 29. [*Calendared in CAR, no 510.*]
[Delivered with **222**. At the assizes the grand jury presented two indictments. One charged Parson, Jupp and Surery, all called late of Washington, with feloniously killing Lee at Washington on 29 Apr: Parson violently throwing him to the ground and, as he lay there, kicking him with both feet on the chest and sides and giving him several bruises of which he languished at Thakeham until 4 May and then died; and Jupp and Surery being feloniously present aiding and abetting him. Jupp and Surery were at large at the time of the assizes, but Parson pleaded not guilty to this indictment and was acquitted; he had not fled but was remanded on bail to appear at the next assizes. The second indictment was identical to the first except for stating that the felony was committed in daytime and adding that afterwards, on 29 Apr, Jupp and Surery fled on account of the felony through the negligence of the inhabitants of Washington and escaped through lack of good custody and organization by its constables. On 4 Mar 1623 the assize judges issued a capias for the appearance of Jupp and Surery at the following assizes, at East Grinstead on 14 July, when the sheriff returned that they had not been found. A writ of exigent was therefore issued on that day to try to secure their appearance at the next Lent assizes, but they were both outlawed at Chichester on 6 Mar 1624. Also on 14 July 1623 a distringas was issued for the appearance of the inhabitants of Washington at the next Lent assizes to answer for the escape of Jupp and Surery. A further similar distringas was issued on 8 Mar 1624. Washington was later pardoned by the general pardon of 21 James I c 35. ASSI 35/63/6, mm 28, 29, 44, 51, 55d; ASSI 35/65/7, m 47; ASSI 35/66/5, mm 103, 106; ASSI 35/66/6, m 81; *CAR*, nos 500, 509, 510, 656, 718, 719, 754.]

225 19 May 1621. Willingdon. Edward Raines, gent., deputy of Richard earl of Dorset, duchy of Lancaster coroner in Pevensey rape. Jurors: Robert Levet, William Martin, William Nicholas, Edward Howell, Edward Bodle, William Cradle, Henry Winset, Thomas Whate, Richard Andrewes, Joseph Glidde, William Adamson, John Griffin, Nicholas Thorpe. Between 1 and 2 p.m. on 5 May, immediately or shortly after Mary Hemsley of Willingdon, 'spinster', had given birth to a male child, she murdered him in 'the hall' of Nicholas Reynoldes's house at Willingdon. At that time she had no goods or chattels, lands or tenements in Sussex to the jurors' knowledge. ASSI 35/63/6, m 31. [*Calendared in CAR, no 506.*]

[Delivered with **222**. At the assizes a bill of indictment was preferred which charged Hemsley with murdering the child in the house of Nicholas Reynoldes of Willingdon, yeoman, on 5 May, after giving birth there, by wrapping him in an apron and smothering him whereby he immediately died; Reynoldes with feloniously inciting Hemsley at Willingdon on 24 Apr to commit the felony; and his wife, Katharine Reynoldes late of Willingdon, spinster, with feloniously comforting and aiding her at Willingdon on 6 May, knowing that she had committed the felony. The grand jury, to which Matthew Terry and Richard Saxpes gave evidence, affirmed the charge against Hemsley but rejected those against the Reynoldeses. Hemsley pleaded not guilty to the indictment and was acquitted; she had not fled and was therefore released. The Reynoldeses were committed on bail to appear at the next assizes, held at East Grinstead on 4 Mar 1622, when Nicholas Reynoldes was delivered by proclamation. There is no further record of Katharine. ASSI 35/63/6, mm 31, 38, 42, 55d; ASSI 35/64/6, m 48d; *CAR*, nos 500, 505, 506, 554.]

226 9 June 1621. Woolbeding in Easebourne hundred in the liberties of Thomas earl of Arundel and Surrey. Anthony Smyth, gent., county coroner. Jurors: Roger Heather, Nicholas Ayling, William Ayling, John Hudson, John Billet, Robert Chaper, Thomas Griste, John Swayne, John Hopkin, William Hogsfleshe, William Hobb, Nicholas Bridger, George Smyth, Daniel Knight, Thomas Ayling, John Betsworth, Thomas Heather, Robert Taylor, Nicholas Ayling, Richard Bridger. About 10 a.m. on 8 June, when William Levet late of Woolbeding, 'joyner', aged 24 or thereabouts, and Thomas Fachin of Woolbeding, 'yeoman', were amicably and happily playing together at Woolbeding with 'one prong staffe with yron speans [*sc.* prongs]' worth 4d which Fachin held in both hands and with a small piece of wood called 'wainscot' which Levet held in both hands, 'le speans' by reason of Fachin's violent movement 'did suddenlie flye out' of 'the said prong staffe' [and against] his will and intention gave Levet 2 wounds, one on the out[side] of the left eye about 2 inches deep and the other on the forehead penetrating to the scalp, of which he died about 4 p.m. Thus Fachin killed him by mischance, against his will and intention. He had no lands or tenements, goods or chattels to the jurors' knowledge. 'The said prongstaffe and yron speans' were committed to the keeping of the earl's bailiff of Easebourne hundred. [*Damaged.*] ASSI 35/63/6, m 30. [*Calendared in CAR, no 522.*]

[Delivered with **222**. At the assizes Fachin was committed on bail to appear at the following assizes when he was to sue for a pardon, but at the East Grinstead assizes of 4 Mar 1622 he was again bailed to appear at the next assizes. There is no record of his appearance at East Grinstead on 22 July. ASSI 35/63/6, m 55d; ASSI 35/64/6, m 48d; *CAR*, nos 522, 553.]

227 11 June 1621. Rye. John Palmer, gent., Rye mayor and coroner, and the jurats. Jurors: Thomas Starkey, Richard Chauntler, Abraham Kennett, Thomas West, Thomas Radford, Henry Davies sen., Robert Fremly, William Smeede, Richard Moose, Thomas Maxwell, Richard Henly, John Starkey, Thomas Keete, William Malpace, Thomas Seely. On 17 May George Whales of Rye, 'bricklayer', 'was overthrowne and trampled on by a sorrell nagge of Thomas Peene's' of Rye, 'rippier', outside the Landgate of Rye 'and there was taken upp, being allmost dead, and carried to his house, who suddainely thereuppon fell sicke and so languished untill he died'. The jurors, 'further searching and enviewing the dead body', 'found a greate bruise under his left side near unto his hart of a swart blackish colour, so that the overthrowing and trampling' by the horse were the cause of his death. [*Verdict in English.*] RYE 1/10, f 222v.

[At the Rye assembly of 28 Jan 1622 it was resolved that Peene should pay the corporation £3 for the horse which was deodand. RYE 1/10, f 256.]

228　15 June 1621. Rodmell in Holmestrow hundred. John Teynton, gent., Lewes rape coroner. Jurors: Richard Marshall, gent., John Marshall, John Dumbrill, John Tester, Henry Goodwyn, Robert Maynard, John Holland, Richard Longly, John Longley, John Whyte, John Evans, William Everest, Thomas Snelling, Richard Alcherne, Richard Gyles. On 13 June, when William Copperd was standing carelessly by the funnel [*infundibulum*] of a windmill in Rodmell, by misadventure 'the trendle of the cogwheele of the sayd wyndemill' immediately twisted his left arm and so the whole of the left side of his chest in the cogwheel whereby the arm and left side of the chest were severely wounded, torn and crushed, of which he languished until about 2 a.m. on 14 June and then died. 'The round poste, the sayles or sweepes, the trendle, the cogwheele and the upper stone or rimer' of the mill were the cause of his death; the jurors appraised them at 13s 4d and they remain with Henry Lucas, Holmestrow hundred constable, and the other parishioners of Rodmell. KB 9/764, m 322.
[Delivered by the coroner into King's Bench in Michaelmas, on a different date from that of **219** and **221**. The constable was summoned to King's Bench to answer for the deodands; he was discharged in Michaelmas 1621 because the deputy almoner acknowledged satisfaction on 10 Aug, but the constable was to pay the fees due in the Crown Office. KB 9/764, mm 322, 322d; KB 29/270, m 56.]

229　22 June 1621. Easebourne in the liberty of Thomas earl of Arundel and Surrey. Anthony Smyth, gent., county coroner. Jurors: Edward Legate, William Shotter, Richard Lock, John Ide, Richard Hibberden, Thomas Payne, Clement Lutter, Nicholas Carter, Richard Tamen, John Chandler, Nicholas Kemp, John Ottye, Thomas Redman, John Noble, Richard Bridger sen., Richard Bridger jun., Richard Bridger of 'Tye Howse', John Challen, William Cotes, Ralph Kemp, William Trybe, Nicholas Ayling, Christopher Bridger, Richard Borrye. On 22 June Katharine Gosden late of Easebourne, 'spinster', aged 45 or thereabouts, was found dead in 'the ryver' near 'Easeborne meade' in Easebourne where she was drowned by misadventure only. KB 9/764, m 313.
[Delivered with **223**. KB 9/764, m 319Bd; KB 29/270, m 56.]

230　26 June 1621. Keymer in Buttinghill hundred. John Teynton, gent., Lewes rape coroner. Jurors: Edmund de Tree, Thomas Button, Thomas Esterfeild, Edward Brooker, John Brooker, John Fe...st, Nicholas Jenner, Roger Virgoe, Richard Burtenshawe, John Johnson, John Pollington, John Newman, Stephen Valleyre, Thomas Gere. On 25 June, when John Spatchurst was 'ridinge from St John's fayre' in Keymer towards his house in Nuthurst, he 'did constrayne his horse to runne a very swyfte gallopp' and by misadventure the horse 'did stumble', causing Spatchurst to fall violently to the ground from the horse whereby the back of his head 'was greatly and mortally broken and brused' of which he immediately died. The horse was the cause of his death. The jurors appraised the horse, 'of a reddish bay color', 'with the brydle and saddle' at 60s and they remain with Mary Spatchurst, widow, late John's wife. KB 9/764, m 321.
[Delivered with **228**. Mary Spatchurst was summoned to King's Bench to answer for the deodands; she was discharged in Michaelmas 1621 because the deputy almoner acknowledged receiving 50s for the horse, but she was to pay the fees due in the Crown Office. KB 9/764, mm 321, 321d, 322d; KB 29/270, m 56.]

231　16 July 1621. Lewes. John Teynton, gent., Lewes rape coroner. Jurors: William Browne, John Streater, Matthew Hunter, Thomas Giles, Henry Wales, Anthony Beecher, Timothy Browne, Thomas Whiskett, Stephen Machyn, Nicholas Spicer, Thomas Lasson, Peter Roy, Lawrence Alfrey, William Stuckle, Richard Pigott. On 14 July, when Walter Crowch was climbing a wall near the garden of Thomas Pelham, kt and bt, in Lewes, intending to get down to call the wife of Richard Savidge of Lewes, 'victualler', he took hold of a branch of a plum tree of no value by one hand, intending with its help to get down from the wall into the garden, but by misadventure the branch unexpectedly broke whereby Crowch fell from the top of the wall onto 'paved stones' in the garden and thereby broke his neck and immediately died. KB 9/764, m 320.
[Delivered with **228**. KB 9/764, m 322d; KB 29/270, m 56.]

232　14 Jan 1622. Mayfield. John Butcher, gent., county coroner. Jurors: Thomas Wickersham,

Robert Martyn, Solomon Wenborne, John Burges, John Parrys, Richard Pocock, John Duplack, Nicholas Page, Thomas Relf, John Care, Thomas Trice, Thomas Duplack, John Burwill. On 12 Sept 1621, when Robert [*written over* William *erased: on some occurrences* William *is uncorrected*] Daniell and Edward [*throughout written over an erasure*] Goldsmith late of Rotherfield, 'miller', were playing with several other of the king's subjects a game called 'the pitchinge of the barr' in William Holland's close in Rotherfield and Goldsmith was throwing 'an axelltree or barr' with both hands and with the full force of his body, Daniell rashly thrust himself in front of the others who were standing around within the compass of the throw, whereby the axle-tree, having been thrown by Goldsmith so violently, by misadventure fell on the right side of Daniell's head, giving him 'a bruse' of which he languished for 4 hours and then died at Rotherfield. Thus Daniell was killed not through any felony but solely through his own rashness and by misadventure. At that time Daniell [*in error for* Goldsmith] possessed goods and chattels worth £5 which remain with him. ASSI 35/65/6, m 8. [*Calendared in CAR, no 621.*]
[Delivered to East Grinstead assizes on 3 Mar 1623. At the East Grinstead assizes of 14 July Goldsmith was bailed to appear at the following assizes, held on 8 Mar 1624 at East Grinstead, when he was again remanded on bail until the next assizes, but there is no further record concerning him. ASSI 35/65/7, m 57d; ASSI 35/66/5, m 112d; *CAR*, no 722.]

233   9 Feb 1622. Horsham. John Teynton, gent., Bramber rape coroner. Jurors: Thomas Awood, Thomas Champyon, Edward Sares, Edward Trigge, Joshua Allen, Robert Playsted, John Hatton, Edward Jupp, Ralph Hall, Thomas Clarke, Richard Clarke, William Weller, John Denyce. On 8 Feb Ann Coker late of Horsham gaol, to which she had earlier been committed by Thomas Bysshopp, kt and bt, and Walter Barthlott and William Mill, esqs, JPs, on suspicion of felony, died a natural death there and not otherwise to the jurors' knowledge. KB 9/766, m 224.
[Delivered to East Grinstead assizes on 4 Mar and on to King's Bench in Easter. On 4 Mar the grand jury presented an indictment which charged Matthew Arnold, William Coker and Ann Coker, all late of Graffham, labourers, with burglary, viz breaking and entering Nicholas Ide's dwelling-house at Graffham on the night of 1 July 1621 and stealing and carrying away a gown worth 40s, a petticoat worth 40s, 2 doublets worth 20s, 2 pairs of hose worth 30s, 3 yards of fustian worth 8s, a coverlet worth 10s and 2 blankets worth 8s belonging to Ide, who gave evidence to the grand jury. All 3 were said to be at large and the assize judges therefore issued a capias (which called Ann Coker spinster) for their appearance at the next assizes, on 22 July, when the sheriff returned that they had not been found. Similar writs, with similar returns, were issued on 2 Aug 1622 and 4 Mar 1623. Finally a writ of exigent was issued by the assize judges at East Grinstead on 14 July 1623, as a result of which William Coker and Arnold were outlawed and Ann Coker was waived at Chichester on 6 Mar 1624. Ann Coker was, of course, long since dead and had been buried at Horsham, described as Goodwife Cocok, a prisoner, on the day of the inquest. ASSI 35/64/6, m 28; ASSI 35/64/7, m 37; ASSI 35/65/6, m 50; ASSI 35/65/7, m 52; ASSI 35/66/5, m 104; KB 9/766, m 231d; KB 29/271, m 5; *CAR*, nos 550, 586, 622, 661, 718; *CAR Introdn*, 171; SRS, XXI, 391.]

234   5 Apr 1622. Rye. John Palmer, gent., Rye mayor and coroner. Jurors: Edward Meller, John Fowlestone, Abraham Kennett, John Whithead, Henry Jeake, John Royall, William Smeede, Thomas Bromely, Thomas Radford, John Humersome, Robert Page, Thomas Keete. On 4 Apr John Hubard of New Romney in Kent, clerk, Marmaduke Watson, John Gibbs, Richard Jacob, John Richardes and an unknown man were 'by extreame fowle weather, the wind being alofte and the sea raginge, cast away nere unto the Gungarden within the liberties of the towne of Rye'. 'The boate beinge about to sincke', 'Hubard, being in the water, was seene swimming unto the rockes neere unto the Gungarden and, looking backe, saw a fisherboate unto which he made, who, being sudainely environed with barrell boardes which then flooted upon the water and were before in the ferrie boate, could not come to the said fisherboate so that they [*sc.* the jurors] thinke the said barrell boardes were partly the cause of' Hubard's drowning. Afterwards the jurors appraised the barrel boards at 13s 4d. Hubard and the unknown man had been found ?floating [*natantes*] on the water, and other 4 on the shore within the liberties of Rye after the ebb-tide. The inquest was held on view of all 6 bodies. [*Verdict in English.*] RYE 1/10, f 266v.

235   19 Apr 1622. Selmeston. Edward Raines, gent., duchy of Lancaster coroner in Pevensey rape. Jurors: Stephen Pentecost, John Barnden, John Hilles, Edward Austen, Thomas Wright, John Catt, Nicholas Acton, Richard Torle, Thomas Wade, John Selwin, Edward Hooke, John Martin, John Taylor. About 6 a.m. on 18 Apr Eleanor Warwicke of Selmeston, 'spinster', murdered a male child to which she had recently given birth: she 'chooked, smothered and strangled' him, whereby he immediately died at Selmeston. At that time she had no goods, lands or tenements in Sussex to the jurors' knowledge. ASSI 35/64/7, m 29. [*Calendared in CAR, no 563.*]

[Delivered to East Grinstead assizes on 22 July when the grand jury, to which Margery Curle, Joan Clarke and Susan Clever gave evidence, presented an indictment similar to the inquest verdict but specifying that the birth was at Selmeston on the day of the murder and that Warwicke strangled the child with both hands and omitting the last sentence. Warwicke, who had been committed to gaol by the coroner, pleaded not guilty to the indictment but was convicted and hanged; she had no chattels. ASSI 35/64/7, mm 6, 12, 29, 42; *CAR*, nos 561–563.]

236   17 May 1622. Sedlescombe. George Cole, Battle liberty coroner. Jurors of the liberty: Christopher Stunt, Ninian Hedd, Goddard Foster sen., Alan Gibon, Joseph Parker, Edmund Pullen, Thomas Eagles, Thomas Sagett, Richard Farnecombe, John Carter, Goddard Foster jun., Giles Burton. On 15 May Robert Dale of Sedlescombe, 'butcher', came on behalf of Richard Dale, his father, before Arnold Edwards, gent., deputy steward of the king's court held at Battle, and sought process to be served against Richard Bran, 'carpenter', according to the custom of the town; and Robert Dale and Daniel Luffe, in the absence of the bailiff of the liberty, were named and appointed bailiffs jointly and severally pro hac vice to serve the process upon Bran. Thereupon, at Robert Dale's request, Arnold Edwards then made the following process according to the custom of the town: capias of 30 Apr 1622 from John Clerk, esq., chief steward of George Moore and John Walter, kts, and of Thomas Spencer, esq., of their liberty of Battle, to the liberty bailiff and to Luffe and Dale, bailiffs pro hac vice, to arrest Bran and to have him before Clerk or his deputy at the next court on 21 May at Battle to answer Richard Dale in a plea of trespass on the case. Later, about 8 p.m. on 15 May, Robert Dale came to George Bourne's house in Sedlescombe where Bran was sitting with others at a table in the hall, went up to Bran and said: 'I arest you in God's name and the king's at the suite of Richard Dale'. At that time Robert Dale had 'a littell paper' in his hands, but had no 'weapon', and immediately after speaking those words he went away from Bran to the door of the hall. After the arrest had thus been made, Bran got up from the table, drew 'a pricker' of iron and went towards the hall door saying: 'Whosoever layeth handes upon me or offereth to staye me, I will kill him'. Thereupon Richard Dale, who was also there, seized 'a corde batt of wood' worth ¼d from a room of the hall and rushed against Bran with it. Then Robert Dale took the bat out of Richard's hands in the hall and killed Bran with it, raising it with both hands, striking him on the right side of the head and giving him a wound by which he immediately fell to the ground and of which he languished for about an hour and then died there. Before Robert gave Bran the wound, Richard Dale helped Robert to strike Bran and at the time of the killing was present aiding Robert. Robert Dale fled and had no goods or chattels, lands or tenements to the jurors' knowledge. Richard Dale did not flee, but what goods and chattels, lands and tenements he had the jurors do not know. ASSI 35/64/7, m 28. [*Calendared in CAR, no 570.*]

[Delivered with **235**. At the assizes the grand jury, to which Alice Bran, Thomas Harrie (*or* Harris), Charles Cox, Edward Williams, Henry Grymshere, Richard Boune, William Pynnion, John Bran, Thomas Brecher, George Borne, George Coole and possibly Richard … gave evidence, presented an indictment which charged the Dales with feloniously killing Bran at Sedlescombe on 15 May: Robert striking him on the right side of the head with a wooden billet worth ¼d which he held in both hands and giving him a wound of which he languished at Sedlescombe for an hour and then died; and Richard (called late of Sedlescombe, carpenter) being feloniously present aiding and abetting him. Robert Dale was at large at the time of the assizes, but Richard Dale, who had been committed to gaol by John Wildegos, kt, and Anthony Apsley, esq., JPs, pleaded not guilty to the indictment and was acquitted; he had not fled and was presumably released. ASSI 35/64/7, mm 13, 18, 28, 42; *CAR*, nos 561, 569, 570.]

237   7 June 1622. Willingdon. Edward Raines, gent., duchy of Lancaster coroner in Pevensey rape. Jurors: Thomas Cooke, William Nicholas, William Cradle, William Martin, John Steddall, Matthew

Terry, Thomas Pemmell, John Mabbe, Edward Akeherst, William Wood, John Reade, Robert Wood, William Skinner, James Alchorne. About 2 p.m. on 23 May William Reinoldes, now or late of Willingdon, 'warrenner', murdered Henry Robinson late of Willingdon, 'husbandman', in 'le Parke' of Willingdon with 'an iron shodden spadestaffe' worth 6d which he held in both hands, giving him a wound on the right side of the head 1 inch long and ½ inch deep of which he languished until 30 May and then died at Willingdon. Reinoldes fled on account of the felony. At the time of the felony and flight he had no goods, lands or tenements in Sussex to the jurors' knowledge. ASSI 35/64/7, m 27. [*Calendared in CAR, no 580.*]

[Delivered with **235**. At the assizes the grand jury, to which John Dapp, John Iten, Richard Saxbee, Henry Mere and John Gwynn gave evidence, presented an indictment similar to the inquest verdict except that it omitted the hour and exact place of the murder and the last 2 sentences. Reinoldes was at large and on 22 July the assize judges therefore issued a capias for his appearance at the following assizes when the sheriff returned that he had not been found. The indictment was sent into King's Bench in Easter 1623 when another capias was issued; Reinoldes was outlawed at Lewes on 16 Oct 1623. ASSI 35/64/7, m 27; ASSI 35/65/6, m 55; KB 9/1113, unnumbered membranes; KB 29/272, m 4; *CAR*, nos 580, 627.]

238   28 June 1622. Rye. John Palmer, gent., Rye mayor and coroner. Jurors: Peter Cooper, John Fowlstone, George Tuggett, Thomas Starkey, Edward Meller, Thomas Bromely, Nicholas Bowyer, John Whitthead, Walter Bayly, Thomas Grove, John Stevens, John Kempe. William Marsh, who was in Rye gaol, 'breakinge open a doore that went up to the uppermost part of the said prison, havinge taken of his fetters, endeavouringe to escape by breakinge of prison, and havinge gott up to the place where he intended his escape', which was the highest part of his part of the gaol, fell from it to the ground and received 3 fatal wounds, one in the head, another in the back and the third in the arm. [*Verdict in English.*] RYE 1/10, f 269.

[All the jurors signed the inquest or made their marks — in the order in which they are named above but for Thomas Grove being before Walter Bayly — except for Peter Cooper. The first place, presumably that of foreman, is taken by Walter Baker who made his mark.]

239   28 June 1622. Kirdford in Rotherbridge hundred. John Teynton, gent., Arundel rape deputy coroner [*but he signed the inquest as coroner*]. Jurors: William Smart, Richard Bristow, John Segrow, Thomas Bennett, William Grevett, William Humphrey, John Bryant, Thomas Wilson, John Serjeante, John Gibson, John Parkman, … Poore, Nicholas Alderton, John Edsall. On 25 June, when James Cooter, 'carpenter', and John Herring, 'taylor', both late of Madehurst, were bringing Roland Buckland to Horsham gaol, they feloniously killed him at Kirdford with 'a bearinge staffe' worth 1d which one or both of them held in one hand, giving him several 'mortall bruses' on the head and loins of which he immediately died. At that time Cooter and Herring had goods and chattels worth 40s which are with W… Grenfeild and Samuel Butcher, constables of Madehurst. [*Damaged.*] ASSI 35/64/7, m 30. [*Calendared in CAR, no 564.*]

[Delivered with **235**. At the assizes the grand jury, to which William Hollas and Thomas Greenefeild gave evidence, presented an indictment which charged Cooter and Herring, both called late of Kirdford, with feloniously killing Buckland at Kirdford on 25 June: Cooter striking him on the head with a bearing staff worth 1d which he held in both hands and giving him several bruises of which he immediately died; and Herring being feloniously present aiding and abetting him. Cooter and Herring, who had been committed to gaol by the coroner (called Bramber rape coroner), pleaded not guilty to the indictment and were acquitted; they had not fled and were therefore presumably released. ASSI 35/64/7, mm 7, 12, 30, 42; *CAR*, nos 561, 562. 564.]

240   17 Aug 1622. Seaford. Samuel Hide, Seaford bailiff and coroner. Jurors: John Beane, John Fastin, John Browne, Edmund Pain, William Cooper, Philip Baker, John Start, John Tester, Francis Cheesman, William Longley, Andrew Beck, Stephen Beane, John French, John Callard, Thomas Mersall. On 16 Aug, when Arthur Pollard, gent., and Thomas Castreat were together in Chyngton Lane within the liberties of Seaford, Pollard having in his hands 'a gun' worth 5s loaded 'with powder and shott', suddenly and by mischance the gun 'did discharge and goe of' and the shot struck Castreat on the right side of the neck, giving him a wound 1 inch deep and 1 inch wide of which he immediately died. Thus Pollard killed Castreat by misadventure without any malice. Pollard then had no goods or chattels, lands or tenements to the jurors' knowledge. The jurors appraised the gun at 5s; it remains with William Giles. SEA 6, p 148.

241   28 Oct 1622. Isfield in Isfield hundred. John Teynton, gent., deputy of Edward Raynes, gent., Pevensey rape coroner, [*but Teynton signed the inquest as coroner*]. Jurors: Thomas Chattfeilde, John Isted, Ralph Allen, George Parris, Arthur Button, John Parris, Roger More, Reynold Burges, Abraham Peckham, William Watson, Richard Swann, James Collman, Ralph Heath, Richard Topsell, Thomas Brightridge, Denis Hode. On 25 Oct, when Samuel Cowchman was walking by the edge of 'Isfeild Ryver' [*sc.* the Ouse] to search for suitable places for placing fish-nets and fish-hooks in the river and for baiting the hooks to catch fish, as was his daily custom, by misadventure he fell into the river and was immediately drowned. KB 9/1113, unnumbered membrane.
[Delivered with **232** and on to King's Bench in Easter 1623. KB 9/1113, dorse of unnumbered membrane.]

242   5 *or* 6 Nov 1622 [*MS* Tuesday 6 Nov, *but 6 Nov was a Wednesday*]. West Tarring in Tarring hundred. John Teynton, gent., Bramber rape coroner. Jurors: Nicholas Page, gent., James Graves, gent., Thomas Botting, James Lyste, Richard Peeter, Richard Grenfeild, John Barnarde, Robert Wright, John Fowler, Richard Cook, Thomas Campyon, Richard Grevethe, John Harward, Philip Stammer. On 1 Nov John Lydbitur of West Tarring, 'husbandman', feloniously killed Edward Duke at West Tarring with 'a hedginge bill' of wood, iron and steel worth 6d which he held in both hands, giving him a wound on the left side of the head 2 inches long and 1 inch deep of which he languished at West Tarring until 4 Nov and then died. Lydbitur did not flee after committing the felony. At the time of the felony he had a tenement, a barn and certain lands in West Tarring held by copy of court roll and worth £5 yearly, £5 in money in the keeping of Richard Grinfeild of West Tarring, 20 sheep worth £4, a cow worth 30s, and wheat, barley and vetch in his barn at West Tarring worth £5 10s; which goods and chattels, lands and tenements remain in the keeping of Walter Weston, constable there, James Graves, John Barnard and Richard Grinfeild on behalf of the whole parish of West Tarring for the king's use. ASSI 35/65/6, m 10. [*Calendared in CAR, no 597.*]
[Delivered with **232**. At the assizes the grand jury presented an indictment identical to the inquest verdict but which omitted the last 2 sentences. Lydbitur pleaded not guilty to the indictment but was convicted; he had no chattels. He then pleaded benefit of clergy but failed to read and was hanged. ASSI 35/65/6, mm 10, 30, 33, 60d; *CAR*, nos 596, 597.]

243   12 Nov 1622. Battle. George Cole, Battle liberty coroner. Jurors of the liberty: Alexander Leonard, John Farnecombe, Giles Burton, William Hull, John Griffin, Thomas Sharpe, Thomas Hamon, Thomas Ahurst, Lawrence Smyth, Abraham Mathew, John Winterborne, Edward Joanes. On 11 Nov 'Nehemiah' Maynard of Heathfield, 'blacksmyth', feloniously killed Thomas Brett of Battle, 'husbandman', at Battle with a piece of tin [*stannum*] worth 2s, giving him 2 wounds on the front of the head of which he languished there for 2 hours and then died. At the time of the felony Maynard had a white mare worth 30s and no other goods or chattels to the jurors' knowledge. ASSI 35/65/6, m 9. [*Calendared in CAR, no 601.*]
[Delivered with **232**. At the assizes a bill of indictment was preferred which charged Maynard with murdering Brett about 5 p.m. on 11 Nov at Battle with a piece of steel (*calybis*) worth 2s which he held in his right hand, giving him a wound on the front of the head ½ inch wide and 2 inches long of which he immediately died. The grand jury, to which Abraham Thomas gave evidence, reduced the charge to manslaughter. Maynard pleaded not guilty to the indictment as amended but was convicted; he had no chattels. He then successfully pleaded benefit of clergy and was branded and released. ASSI 35/65/6, mm 9, 34, 36, 60d; KB 9/1113, unnumbered membrane; KB 29/272, m 10; *CAR*, nos 600, 601.]

244   22 Dec 1622. New Fishbourne. George Mathew, gent., Stockbridge hundred coroner. Jurors: Edward Jennynges, Nicholas Aylinge, Thomas Hudson, John Hooker, John Collowaye, John Turnor,

Edward Hooker, John Wingham, Richard Martyn, Henry ?Brann, John Wright, John Turnor, William Wright, Thomas Lynn. On 10 Dec Ann [*later called* Agnes] Hebberden late of New Fishbourne, 'spinster', gave birth to a live female child at New Fishbourne and immediately afterwards the child became ill and languished at New Fishbourne for 8 hours and then died a natural death on the said 29 Dec [*sic*]. KB 9/1113, unnumbered membrane.
[Delivered with **241**. New Fishbourne is written above Framfield, which is struck through, on 2 occasions. KB 9/1113, dorse of unnumbered membrane; KB 29/272, m 4.]

245 14 Feb 1623. Hurstpierpoint in Twineham [*recte* Buttinghill] hundred. John Teynton, gent., Lewes rape coroner. Jurors: Richard Butcher sen., Thomas Chatfeild, Francis Langford, Richard Parson, Thomas Awood, Thomas Agate, Francis Wolger, Thomas Fawkner, John Rickwarde, Edward Harland, Richard Lashmer, Edward Masters, William Lashmer, William Bowell, Nicholas West. On 11 Feb, when John Peckham was walking on the lands and pastures of Richard Butcher jun. of Hurstpierpoint, his master, to watch Butcher's cattle [*pecora*], he passed near the edge of 'a marlpitt' where many small thorn-bushes [*vepres*] were growing and stumbled among the bushes whereby by misadventure he fell into the pit and was immediately drowned in its water. KB 9/1113, unnumbered membrane.
[Delivered with **241**. KB 9/1113, dorse of unnumbered membrane.]

246 11 Mar 1623. Rye. Richard Fowtrell, Rye mayor and coroner. Jurors: William Cooker, John Fowlkestone, Abraham Kennett, Thomas Frencham, William Smeede, Thomas Babb, Thomas Adkins, Thomas Alley, James Meller, Walter Baylie, Thomas Beale, John Stevens. Alice Cloake [*altered from* Alice wife of John Scragge of Rye, ?'cutler', *on the first occurrence*] 'died not of any blowe or stroke that Robert Thril's man did give her, but of her naturall death'. [*Verdict in English.*] RYE 1/10, f 311.

247 11 Apr 1623. Horsham. John Teynton, gent., Bramber rape coroner. Jurors: Henry Sater, Thomas Clarke, … [?W]aterton, Thomas Champion, Richard Clarke, Edward Feilder, Robert Budd, Nicholas Brett, John Denyce, Robert …, [Edw]ard Jupe, Richard Gatton, Matthew Wood. On 11 Apr Henry Millard, who had previously been committed to Horsham gaol by Thomas [Sa]ckevill, esq., JP, on suspicion of felony, died a natural death there and not otherwise to the jurors' knowledge. [*Damaged.*] KB 9/769, m 173.
[Delivered into King's Bench in Michaelmas, probably by the coroner. Millard had been committed to gaol on suspicion of burglary before the East Grinstead assizes of 3 Mar 1623 when he was remanded in gaol until the following assizes. He was buried at Horsham on the day of the inquest. ASSI 35/65/6, mm 60d, 61; KB 29/272, m 90d; *CAR*, no 595; SRS, XXI, 392.]

248 23 Apr 1623. Hastings. Richard Boys, gent., Hastings mayor and coroner. Jurors: James Bacheller, William Dighton, Richard Downe, Nicholas Foster, Thomas Tayler sen., Thomas Stevenson sen., Richard Chambers, Richard Amyat, Christopher Watts, Edmund Webbe, Thomas Tayler jun., John Staplus, Robert Mills. On 11 Apr William Gawen of Hastings, 'fisherman', feloniously killed Richard Geerey, 'butcher', at Hastings with 'a hand gunne' worth 6s 8d 'charged with powder and birding shott' which he held in both hands: he 'did discharge' it, giving Geerey a wound with the lead shot on the outside of the right thigh 3 inches wide and 2 inches deep of which he languished until 22 Apr and then died at Hastings. The jurors requested that this inquest be entered and enrolled of record in the common register of the town by the common clerk according to the custom of the town from time immemorial. HASTINGS C/A(a) 2, f 10v.
[At Hastings sessions of the peace and gaol delivery before Richard Boys, mayor, and certain jurats, JPs, on 10 June the grand jury, having read a bill of indictment identical to the inquest verdict, found Gawen not guilty as charged but that Geerey had struck him many times with a staff about 7 feet long and by chance had touched the lock of the hand gun with the staff whereby the lock fell and ignited the powder in the gun by reason of which the gun was discharged upon him, giving him the fatal wound, and so Geerey killed himself by misadventure. Gawen was thereupon discharged by proclamation and went quit from court. HASTINGS C/A(a) 2, ff 12–12v.]

249 23 Apr 1623. Mayfield. John Butcher, gent., county coroner, and Thomas Houghton, gent., Loxfield Camden half-hundred coroner. Jurors: Thomas Maynard, Thomas Sawyer, John James, Robert Martyn, Abraham Relfe, John Parris, Josiah Birche, Henry Robyns, Hugh Lucke, John Modle, Andrew Moone, Geoffrey Moone, John Maye, Thomas Moone, Robert Moone, Thomas Peckham, John Longeley. On 14 Apr Richard Larkins, who was sick with both 'the joynct gowte' and fever, died a natural death at Mayfield. KB 9/769, m 190.
[Delivered to East Grinstead assizes on 14 July and on to King's Bench in Michaelmas. KB 9/769, mm 188, 210d; KB 29/272, m 90d.]

250 10 June 1623. Horsham. John Teynton, gent., Bramber rape coroner. Jurors: Edward Brystowe, Edward Sayres, Joshua Allen, Ralph Hall, Thomas Champyon, Richard Clarke, Robert Best, John Holdyn, William Henn, James Slawter, John Grombridge, Thomas Galpyn. On 4 June Robert Randall, who had previously been committed to Horsham gaol by Richard Lewkner and Thomas Bowyer, esqs, JPs, on suspicion of felony, died a natural death there and not otherwise to the jurors' knowledge. KB 9/769, m 191.
[Delivered with **249**. Randall was buried at Horsham on the day of his death although the inquest was said to have been held on view of his body. KB 9/769, mm 188, 210d; KB 29/272, m 90d; *CAR Introdn*, 171; SRS, XXI, 392.]

251 2 Aug 1623. 'Le Beachwood' in the parish of St John sub Castro, Lewes, in Barcombe hundred. John Teynton, gent., Lewes rape coroner. Jurors: Thomas Valentyne, William Markes, Nicholas Aleighe, Richard Joanes, Thomas Sponer, Edward Dowglas, John Morris, John Cowlstock, William Gibbs, Henry Wood, Samuel Smasser, Edward Valentyne, John Sponer, John Dyne. On 1 Aug William Reggatt feloniously hanged himself at 'le Beachwood' with 'a horsetrace' worth 2d which he held, placing one end round his neck and tying the other round 'a joyste'. At that time he had 5s in his purse, 2 'little chestes or coffers' and his clothing which the jurors appraised at 20s, and 20s with his lady, Katharine wife of William Markwicke, all of which remain with the said William Markwicke, constable of Barcombe hundred; 40s with John Baylye of Falmer, 'laborer'; and no other goods, rights or chattels to the jurors' knowledge. KB 9/769, m 112.
[Delivered into King's Bench in Michaelmas, almost certainly by the coroner. A settlement concerning the goods and chattels was made with the almoner. KB 9/769, m 112; KB 29/272, m 91d.]

252 25 Sept 1623. Hastings. Richard Boys, Hastings mayor and coroner. Jurors: James Bacheller, Silvester Guylham, [Richard Denne *struck through*], Joseph Moore, Richard Amyat, Emanuel Browne, John Staplus, Richard Cristofer, Henry Lasher, Peter Yelding, Nicholas Foster, Thomas Tayler, Edmund Webb, John Coosens, Thomas Stevenson sen. On 22 Sept John Lopdell rode on his 'sorrell' gelding worth 40s on the sea-shore from his dwelling-house in Hastings to Eastbourne to transact business there. About 7 or 8 p.m. on the same day, a little after full tide, having completed his business, he was returning on the sea-shore towards his house and trying to cross the harbour of Pevensey called Pevensey Haven, which is within the liberty and jurisdiction of the town and port of Hastings, on the gelding when by misadventure he was thrown from its back into the water by the force of the water running out of the harbour and was drowned. The gelding was therefore forfeit as deodand to the mayor, jurats and community of Hastings, and the Hastings chamberlain was ordered to seize it, keep it for the use and profit of the town and answer for it. HASTINGS C/A(a) 2, ff 13–13v.

253 8 Nov 1623. Lancing in Brightford hundred. John Teynton, gent., Bramber rape coroner. Jurors: Richard Norton, gent., Henry Chatfeild, William Deane, William Blackman, George Alchyn, John Turningan, John Gibbs, John Capon, Stephen Stammer, Richard Stapeler, William Wassher, James Horly, Thomas Hunter, Thomas Rutland. On 6 Nov William Swyft, servant of John Thomas, took 'a gun' in both hands, it 'being charged with gunpowder and hailshott' of lead, in the fire-place [*caminus*] of Thomas's dwelling-house in Lancing, not knowing that it was loaded and not intending any malice or injury or having any anger towards Ann Martyn or anyone else there. While he was holding it in both hands, the gun suddenly, by misadventure and not of his felonious intent but against his will 'was dischardged and shott of' and the 'haylshot' struck Ann Martyn on the chest, giving her a wound 5 inches deep of which she immediately died. So she came to her death by misadventure and not otherwise. The gun is worth 8s and remains with John Thomas of Lancing, 'yoman'. On the day of the death Swyft had no goods or chattels to the jurors' knowledge. ASSI 35/66/5, m 51. [*Calendared in CAR, no 704.*]

[Delivered to East Grinstead assizes on 8 Mar 1624 when Swyft, who had been committed to gaol by Henry Goringe, esq., JP, was remanded on bail to appear at the following assizes, but there is no record of his appearance then. ASSI 35/66/5, mm 112, 112d; *CAR*, nos 671, 722.]

254 25 Feb 1624. Rye. Mark Thomas, gent., Rye mayor and coroner. Jurors: John Carew, William Starkey, Stephen Mason, Henry Dann, John Whithead, John Folkestone, George Tuggett, Walter Bayly, Thomas Radford, Francis Chesheire, 'Morris' Steward, 'Moses' Cradocke. Joan Barnett alias Doughton gave birth to a female child in the house of Katharine Chiston, widow, and 'by the willfull negligence of the said Joane the child died'. Her body was found among rocks [*intra petras*] near Katharine Chiston's cliff in Rye. [*Verdict in English.*] RYE 1/11, f 21v.

[There are signs and signatures of all the jurors except Tuggett. On the day of the inquest, and probably at it, John Earle, Philip Moore and Henry Man, all of Rye, fishermen, gave evidence before the mayor and Richard Fowtrell, Thomas Ensing, John Palmer, Joseph Benbricke, John Cooper, Christopher Marshall and Alan Gribell, jurats, that about 9 a.m. on 25 Feb they found a dead female child among the rocks under the cliff right against Widow Chiston's house, lying on her left side with her right hand on her head. On the same day Joan Barnett alias Doughton of Rye, spinster, was examined before the same and said that Thomas Frencham late of Rye, innholder, lay with her in the cellar of his house called the Chequer in the previous May, and again in another house on the hill outside the Landgate but within the liberties of Rye where he lived after he moved from the Chequer. On both occasions she asked him what she should do if she proved to be pregnant and he replied: 'Take something to make it away with'. Asked if she had told him since he lay with her that she was pregnant, she said that she had not because she had not seen him since; and she did not take anything during her pregnancy to terminate it. To further questions she said that about 1 or 2 a.m. on Tuesday 23 (*recte* 24) Feb she gave birth alone to a female child and, after it was born, laid it on the bed. Half an hour later it gasped and died. She let it lie on the bed until the morning and then wrapped a cloth around it and laid it under the bed. A good while later she took it from there and carried it to her 'dame's shop' where she let it lie until 8 p.m. and then took it out of the shop, carried it to the cliff and threw it down on the rocks into the sea. Asked why she had thrown it over the cliff, she replied that it might not be known and that the devil had put it in her mind.

Barnett was tried on an indictment which charged her with giving birth to a live female child at Rye about 2 a.m. on 24 Feb and immediately afterwards murdering her by throwing her naked on a bed when it was very cold and allowing her to lie there for half an hour, whereby she died from the cold and the throwing down naked between 2 and 3 a.m. Barnett was convicted; she had no goods or chattels. RYE 1/11, f 21v; RYE 47/99, unnumbered documents.]

255 16 Mar 1624. East Preston. John Eagle, gent., county coroner. Jurors of East Preston and 3 neighbouring townships, viz Rustington, Littlehampton and Toddington: Thomas Oliver, John Breadon, Thomas Upperton, John Finche, John Cnell, John Hammon, John Brooke sen., John Br[ook]e jun., John Arnold, William Cnell, Thomas Selden, John Hibberden, John Whitington, William Perley, Thomas Cnell, John Hooper. About 4 p.m. on 14 Mar, when John Allen, aged 4, the natural son of Matthew Allen of Arundel, merchant, was playing near a ditch in an orchard belonging to Henry Stradling of East Preston, gent., by misadventure he suddenly fell into it and was drowned. KB 9/772, m 106.

[Delivered into King's Bench by the coroner in Easter. KB 9/772, m 106d; KB 29/273, m 4d.]

256 13 May 1624. Eastbourne. Edward Raynes, gent., Pevensey rape coroner. Jurors: James Hutchins, John Rickardes, John Hollandes, Nicholas Lucas, William Hollandes, John Elficke, James Torle, Abraham Bodle, Robert Salter, John Payne, John Fowler, Christopher Sennocke, John Hersley. Between 9 a.m. and 1 p.m. on 8 May, when John Crunden jun. late of Eastbourne, 'yeoman', was alone at Eastbourne, he feloniously threw himself into a well near the messuage of Thomas Parker, gent., called 'Erchinghams' and drowned himself. At that time he had goods and chattels worth £55 18s 8d, as appears in the attached inventory.

13 May. Inventory of Crunden's 'goodes, chattels, housholdstuffe and readie money' taken and appraised by the coroner, Richard Bartholmew and Thomas Crunden, Eastbourne hundred constables, and James Hutchins, John Rickardes 'and divers other good and lawfull men of the said hundred'. 'His purse and readye money therein [worth] ij s. In the hall: item one old cupboord, an old table, forme and chaire iij s iiij d; item one dozen of pewter there vjs viij d; item foure brasen kettles, one copper posnet and a brasen chafingdish x s; item two iron pottes iiij s; item in old lumber and other small triviall thinges there iij s iiij d; summa xxix s iiij d. In the low roome next the hall or the parlour: item one old fetherbed, one old coverlet and blancket, an old plaine bedsted, two pillowes and a boulster, one plaine boorded chest, one table, a little forme, six cushions and one joyned stole xxx s. In the buttry: item old lumber there vj s viij d. In the seller: item barrels, tubs and lumber there xj s. In the chamber over the parlour: item two old steddles for bedds, one little chaffe bed, two old coverlettes, two old chestes, eight paire of sheetes and two table clothes xlij s. In the chamber over the hall: item two old flockbedcs, two linnen trendles and other small lumber xiij s iiij d. Item six swine xxvj s viij d; item two bushels of wheate vj s; item eight bushels of oaten malt viij s; item wood and faggotes about the house xxvj s viij d; item two waines, two dungcourtes, two plowes, two harrowes, twenty wattles and other implementes of husbandry xlvj s viij d; item three acres and an halfe of wheate on the ground iij li x s; item nineteene acres of barley on the ground in the landes hee used of Mr Parker xxv li vj s viij d; item nine acres of pease and tares on the ground in the landes hee used of Mr Parker vij li xj s; item fyve acres of barley on the landes hee used belonging to the mannor of Radmell [sc. Rodmill] vj li xiij s iiij d; item dung and compost about the barnes and house x s; item thinges omitted and forgotten iij s iiij d'. Total £55 18s 8d [recte £56 0s 8d]. [Inventory mostly in English.] KB 9/776, mm 69, 70.

[Delivered by the coroner into King's Bench in Easter 1625. A settlement concerning the goods and chattels was made with the High Almoner. KB 9/776, mm 69, 69d; KB 29/274, m 6.]

257 21 July 1624. Slaugham in Buttinghill hundred. John Teynton, gent., Lewes rape coroner. Jurors: Richard Hall, William Gattford, John Gattforde, Walter Barrett, Richard Snashal, Walter Staly, Richard Aylewyn, John Ketch, Henry Post, Daniel Hall, Robert Archpole, Thomas George, Andrew Wright. Between 9 and 10 p.m. on 20 July, when Henry Fenner and William Puttock intended to wash themselves in 'the furnace pond' in Slaugham, they were drowned together by misadventure. The inquest was held on view of both bodies. KB 9/777, m 22.

[Delivered to King's Bench in Trinity 1625, probably by the coroner. KB 29/274, m 26d.]

258 10 Sept 1624. South Harting. John Eagle, gent., county coroner. Jurors of South Harting and 3 neighbouring townships, viz East Harting, West Harting and South Holt: Francis Shallett, gent., Mark Pytt sen., Edward Ameeres, John Mill, Richard Silver, John Treddle, Anthony Todd, Richard Lypscomb, Nicholas Randall, Thomas Pitt, William Randall, John Wilde sen., John Wilde jun., John Hargrave, William Russell, John Ayling, Edmund Wilde, John Pitt, John Kent. About 9 p.m. on 5 Sept John Gamlin of South Harting, 'laborer', murdered Richard Coles late of South Harting, 'husbandman', in 'the lyme meade' in South Harting with 'a holme [sc. holm-oak] cudgell' worth ½d which he held in his right hand, giving him 'one mortall wounde' on the right side of the head and the right ear 1 inch wide, 3 inches long and 1 inch deep of which he immediately died. He had no goods or chattels, lands or tenements in Sussex or elsewhere at that time or ever after to the jurors' knowledge. ASSI 35/67/8, m 63. [Calendared in CAR, no 792.]

[Delivered to East Grinstead assizes on 7 Mar 1625, when Gamlin, who had been committed to gaol by William Ford, kt, Nicholas Jordan and another, JPs, pleaded not guilty but was convicted and hanged; he had no chattels. ASSI 35/67/8, mm 63, 64, 85, 87d; CAR, nos 780, 791, 792.]

259 12 Sept 1624. West Hoathly. Edward Raynes, gent., duchy of Lancaster coroner in Pevensey rape. Jurors: Charles Turner, John Trepe, Thomas Tye, John Luxford, Francis Gasson, Edward Payne, Thomas Gasson, Lawrence Langridge, John Herryott, Matthew Martyn, Richard Balcombe, Robert

Jenner. On 28 Aug, when Jasper Vinall late of West Hoathly, 'husbandman', aged 34 or thereabouts, and Edward Tye of West Hoathly, 'husbandman', were playing with several other of the king's lieges at a customary game called 'crickett' at Horsted Green in Horsted Keynes and Vinall and Tye were playing together, Tye, bearing no malice and not intending to cause injury to Vinall or anyone else there, in his turn hit a ball [*quadam pila palmaria*] high into the air and, for his greater advantage in the game, intended to hit it again as it was dropping to the ground. Vinall, for his greater advantage intending to catch the ball as it fell, suddenly came running quickly behind Tye's back whereby Tye, not seeing him, by misadventure and against his will struck Vinall on the forehead with a small staff called 'a crickett batt' worth ½d which he held in his right hand, giving him 'a bruise' of which he languished at West Hoathly until 10 Sept and then died. Thus Vinall was killed not by any felony but solely through his own rashness and negligence and by misadventure. Tye had no goods or chattels, lands or tenements on 28 Aug or at any time since to the jurors' knowledge. ASSI 35/67/8, m 68. [*Calendared in CAR, no 810 and, with comment, in SNQ, XVI, 217–221, 319–320.*] [Delivered with **258**.]

260   4 Oct 1624. Rye. Richard Gibbridge, gent., deputy of Mark Thomas, gent., Rye coroner. Jurors: Benjamin Martyn, Nicholas Bowyer, Peter Cooper, Thomas Starkey, John Hummersome, Thomas Radford, John Ryoll, James Meller, John Kempe, John Stevens, Edward Jones sen., William Smeede. About 5 a.m. on 3 Oct, when Bridget Earle, 'spinster', servant of Anthony Norton, was 'lying in her bed asleepe, a chimney in the house with the rage and extreame violence of the wind that blew' that morning 'fell downe uppon her and killed her'. [*Verdict in English.*] RYE 1/11, f 51v.

261   22 Oct 1624. Shipley in East Easwrith [*recte* West Grinstead] hundred, Bramber rape. John Teynton, gent., coroner of Thomas earl of Arundel and Surrey, earl marshal. Jurors: Richard Agate, George Dendye, Nicholas Marlott, John Hurst, Robert Tyckner, Richard Stedman, Richard Cupp, 'Moysis' Cooper, James Short, Charles Pavy, Richard Syndall, Arnold Shepperde. About 6 a.m. on 20 Oct, when George Ansty was alone in a field at Shipley, he feloniously hanged himself with 'a corde' worth 1d which he held in both hands, putting one end of it round his neck and tying the other round a branch of an oak. At that time he had no goods or chattels in Sussex to the jurors' knowledge. KB 9/777, m 32. [Delivered with **257**. KB 29/274, m 26.]

262   3 Nov 1624. Mayfield. Thomas Houghton, gent., Loxfield Camden half-hundred coroner. Jurors: Thomas Modle, John Kerwyn, Thomas Westgate, Thomas Sawyer, John Modle, John James, John Burges of Clayton, Henry Robyns, Andrew Moone, Henry Boreman, Robert Moone, Robert Martyn, Richard Wilmisherst, John Duke, John Parfitt, John Peeke, Thomas Moone. On 16 Oct, when Thomas Dawe and other of the king's subjects were in 'a marlepitt' in a parcel of land called 'le tenne acres' in Mayfield, which was then in the occupation of William Dawe of Mayfield, 'husbondman', then Thomas Dawe's master, 'for digginge and fillinge of marle' and Thomas Dawe held 'a shovell' in both hands and filled it with marl, intending to throw the marl into 'the carriage', by misadventure a large amount of earth and marl which was overhanging the pit suddenly fell on his body, threw him to the ground, broke his left arm and crushed his abdomen and other parts of his body of which he languished at Mayfield until 1 Nov and then died. KB 9/776, m 190. [Delivered with **258** and on to King's Bench in Easter 1625. KB 9/776, m 195d; KB 29/274, m 3d.]

263   2 Dec 1624. Wadhurst. Thomas Houghton, gent., Loxfield Camden half-hundred coroner. Jurors: William Bryan, gent., Thomas Lucke, Andrew Skynner, Peter Trice, David Pennyall, Richard Forde, Henry Warde, John Hawkyns, Christopher Wedd, James Vallance, Thomas Baker, Thomas Bate, John Gilbert, Edward Cruttall, Peter Markewick. About 4 p.m. on 26 Nov William Kitchenham of Wadhurst, 'collyer', feloniously killed Richard Longley late of Wadhurst, 'husbondman', at Wadhurst with 'a hedginge bill' worth 6d which he held in both hands, giving him a wound on the right side of the head 4 inches long and 1 inch deep of which he languished at Wadhurst until 28 Nov and then died. At the time of the felony Kitchenham had no goods or chattels, lands or tenements to the jurors' knowledge. ASSI 35/67/8, m 75. [*Calendared in CAR, no 794.*]

[Delivered with **258**. At the assizes a bill of indictment was preferred identical to the inquest verdict except that it charged Kitchenham with murder and omitted the last sentence. The grand jury reduced the charge to manslaughter. Kitchenham, who had been committed to gaol by Anthony Fowle, esq., JP, pleaded not guilty to the indictment as amended but was convicted; he had no chattels. He then pleaded benefit of clergy but failed to read and was hanged. ASSI 35/67/8, mm 61, 64, 75, 85, 87d; *CAR*, nos 780, 791, 794.]

264   13 Dec 1624. Steyning. John Teynton, gent., Bramber rape coroner. Jurors: William Smyth, John Gromes, William Pellatt, John Bacom, William Alsee, John Spencer, James Owden, James Tharpe, Thomas Johnson, Roger Barnes, Thomas Wood, William Pearle, John Washer. About 6 p.m. on 12 Dec James Crowdson late of Steyning, 'laborer', murdered Richard Gregory at Steyning with 'a little kniefe' worth 1d which he held in his right hand, giving him a wound on the left side of the abdomen 1 inch wide and 3 inches deep of which he immediately died. At that time Crowdson had no goods or chattels, lands or tenements in Sussex to the jurors' knowledge. ASSI 35/67/8, m 74. [*Calendared in CAR, no 793.*]

[Delivered with **258**. At the assizes the grand jury presented an indictment identical to the inquest verdict but omitting the last sentence. Crowdson, who had been committed to gaol by the coroner, pleaded not guilty to the indictment. He was acquitted of murder but convicted of manslaughter; he had no chattels. He then pleaded benefit of clergy but failed to read and was hanged. ASSI 35/67/8, mm 62, 64, 74, 85, 87d; *CAR*, nos 780, 791, 793.]

265   31 Dec 1624. Hurstpierpoint in Buttinghill hundred. John Teynton, gent., Lewes rape coroner. Jurors: Thomas Luxford, William Jordan, Richard Lashmere, Alan Savidge, William Pryor, John Chatfeild, Richard Gander, Richard Burtenshaw, John Cowlstocke, John Wickham, John Russell, Thomas Wakefeild, Thomas Herriott, Henry Gallop, Edward Burt, Thomas Cowlstocke. About 3 p.m. on 28 Dec Thomas Starr was brought by Edward Goring of Lewes, kt, to ride on his horse in certain rivers and on 'Dannardes Bridge' in Hurstpierpoint, which bridge was then almost under water, to test, prove and discover whether or not Goring might ride across the bridge without danger; and while Starr was riding on the bridge one of its planks was detached whereby the horse stopped and by misadventure fell into the water with Starr who was immediately drowned. The horse was the cause of his death and the jurors appraised it at 5 marks. They believe it to be with Goring. KB 9/777, m 21.

[Delivered with **257**. Goring was summoned to King's Bench to answer for the horse; he was outlawed at Chichester on 12 Oct 1626. KB 9/777, m 21; KB 29/274, m 26d.]

266   25 Apr 1625. Hastings. John Barley, Hastings mayor and coroner. Jurors: James Bacheller, George Fletcher, John Staplus, Richard Basden, John Jenkins, John Perigo, Thomas Walls, Emanuel Browne, Mark White, Robert Wright, George Oliver, Robert White, John Howlett, John Michell, Ralph Mylls. About 10 p.m. on 24 Apr, when Thomas Butcher of Hastings, 'fisherman', aged about 14, the servant of John Fawteley of Hastings, 'fisherman', was on the sea-shore called Stonebeach in St Clement's parish, Hastings, in the company of other young 'fisher boys' watching the tide, as was the custom there among fishermen, the youths negligently lay on the ground to sleep under the side of 'a small hookeman boate' [*sc.* a boat from which men fished with lines and hooks] belonging to James Wright called 'le Joan' of Hastings, weight 6 tons and worth 20s, which was on Stonebeach. While they were sleeping the boat was suddenly overturned by the force of the wind and thrown onto one side upon the youths, among whom Butcher was crushed by the weight of the boat and his head and body were destroyed on the ground, whereby he was immediately killed by misadventure. The jurors requested that this inquest be recorded in the common book of Hastings according to ancient custom. HASTINGS C/A(a) 2, f 21.

267   21 Sept 1625. Horsham. John Teynton, gent., Bramber rape coroner. Jurors: Edward Bristow, Henry Foyce, Richard Cox, Thomas Lamb, John Holden, Richard Jenner, Thomas Lyncolne, John

Hatton, Ralph Hall, Benjamin Meekes, Edward Feilder, Thomas Champion. On 20 Sept John Fuller late of Chiddingly, 'husbandman', who had previously been committed to Horsham gaol on suspicion of felony by John Shurley, kt, JP, died a natural death there and not otherwise to the jurors' knowledge. KB 9/780, m 160.
[Delivered to the Sussex Lent assizes and on to King's Bench in Easter 1626. Fuller was buried at Horsham on the day of the inquest. KB 9/780, m 196d; KB 29/275, m 3; SRS, XXI, 394.]

268   12 ?Oct 1625. Lamberhurst. Thomas Houghton, gent., Loxfield Camden [half-hundred] coroner. Jurors of the half-hundred: Edward ..., John ..., John Grombridge, William Barham, William Upton, Thomas Longley, Edward Cruttall, Stephen Ollive, Thomas Shosmyth, Thomas Juden, John Gilbert, ..., Edward Selden, Daniel Baldicke. On 27 Aug Thomas Darrell, gent., John Roseblade alias Hickley, 'mason', and Mary Roseblade alias Hickley, 'spinster', his wife, all late of Lamberhurst, feloniously killed Edward Harvye late of Lamberhurst, 'mason', at Lamberhurst: they '[did] bruise' him by striking, beating, kicking and crushing him on the shoulders, back and abdomen with their feet of which he languished at Lamberhurst until 30 Aug and then died. [What goods or] chattels, lands or tenements Darrell and John Roseblade [had] at the time of the felony [or] after [or] still have the jurors do not know. [*Damaged*.] ASSI 35/68/8, m 15.
[Delivered to Horsham assizes on 10 July 1626.]

269   2 Feb 1626. Hastings. William Byshop, jurat, deputy of John Barley, Hastings mayor and coroner. Jurors: James Bacheller, William Dighton, Emanuel Browne, Thomas Tayler, 'sadler', Richard Springett, Edmund Webb, John Jenkyns, Robert Mylls, Richard Cristofer, Richard Amyatt, Nicholas Foster, Peter Yeilding, Robert Marshall. On 30 Jan Agnes Joye of Hastings, 'spinster', feloniously killed herself in the house of Henry Palmer, her master, at Hastings by drinking a quantity of mercury mixed in a drink and eating a quantity of 'rattesbane', a poison, mixed in soup with the intention of poisoning and killing herself. She languished from the action of the poisons in her body until 1 Feb and then died. At the time of her death she possessed 'her wearing apparrell' worth 40s. HASTINGS C/A(a) 2, f 26v.
[The Hastings chamberlain was made answerable for the 40s. HASTINGS C/A(a) 2, f 26v.]

270   9 Feb 1626. Horsham. John Teynton, gent., Bramber rape coroner. Jurors: Thomas Smyth, William Waterton, Richard White, John Lea, Joshua Allen, Thomas Grombridge, Thomas Wheatly, Richard Hunt, Richard Clarke, William Chambers, Thomas Lyncolne, Philip Jenden, Ralph Hall. On 8 Feb Thomas Muckford, servant of Henry Worsfold of Horsham, 'brewer', was driving a cart with 3 horses harnessed to it and 'laden with sixe little vesselles of beare' [*sc.* beer] from Horsham towards Nuthurst and Robert Hudnall was riding in the cart. As it was going very slowly down 'Birchingbridg Hill' with Muckford holding back the rear horse called 'the thiller' [*sc.* thill-horse, the shaft-horse] with all his strength, by misadventure the cart with its load fell to the ground whereby Hudnall immediately died. 'The thiller', the cart and the 6 vessels of beer moved to his death, but the other horses did not. The jurors appraised 'the thiller', which had defective sight [*qui captus est occulis*], at 3s 4d, the cart at 10s and the beer which was not lost at 10s; they remain with Worsfold. KB 9/781, m 99.
[Delivered into King's Bench by the coroner in Trinity. A settlement concerning the deodands was made with the High Almoner. Hudnall, called 'a poore fellow, killed with a carte', was buried at Horsham on the day after the inquest. KB 9/781, mm 99, 101d; KB 29/275, m 27; SRS, XXI, 395.]

271   24 Mar 1626. Eastbourne. Edward Raynes, gent., duchy of Lancaster coroner in Pevensey rape. Jurors: Thomas Crunden, Edmund Renne, Edward Austen, James Hutchins, John Breadon, John Holland, John Harris, John Eeles, John Turle, William Martin, John Elficke, William Browne, Henry Fennell. About 7 p.m. on 20 Mar Alexander Whate of Eastbourne, 'husbandman', feloniously killed Thomas Baker with a knife worth 2d which he held in right hand, giving him a wound on the left ear 1 inch wide or thereabouts and 2 inches deep or thereabouts of which he died at Eastbourne within 4 hours. At the time of the felony Whate had no goods or chattels, lands or tenements in Sussex or

elsewhere to the jurors' knowledge. After committing the felony he fled. ASSI 35/68/8, m 13.
[Delivered with **268**. At the assizes the grand jury, to which John Rickward gave evidence, presented an indictment which charged Whate with murdering Baker at Eastbourne on 20 Mar with a knife of iron and steel worth 2d which he held in his right hand by giving him a wound in the left side of the head, a little under the ear, 1 inch wide and 2 inches deep of which he immediately died. Whate was at large at the time of the assizes. The indictment was sent into King's Bench in Easter 1627 and Whate was summoned to that court to answer for the murder; he was outlawed at Lewes on 11 Oct. ASSI 35/68/8, m 13; KB 9/1094, mm 86, 87; KB 29/276, m 3.]

272   1 Apr 1626 [*MS* 1 Charles I, AD 1626, *but 1 Apr 1 Charles I was 1625*]. Ringmer. Edward Raynes, gent., duchy of Lancaster coroner in Pevensey rape. Jurors: Thomas Aptot, Thomas Dorridge, John Edwardes, Edward Davie, Richard White, John Winberry, Edward Foster, Henry Grantum, John Harman, John Lidlowe, Thomas Smalfeild, Thomas Floud. On 27 Mar Joan Blackman late of Ringmer, 'spinster', murdered a female child, to which she had recently given birth, at Ringmer by suffocating her whereby she immediately died. At that time Blackman had no goods or chattels, lands or tenements in Sussex to the jurors' knowledge. ASSI 35/68/8, m 11.
[Delivered with **268**. At the assizes the grand jury, to which Richard Howell and his wife gave evidence, presented an indictment which charged Blackman, who had been committed to gaol, with giving birth to the child at Ringmer on 27 Mar 1626 (*2 Charles I*) and on the same day murdering her by taking her, while alive, in both hands and strangling her whereby she immediately died. Blackman pleaded not guilty to the indictment and was acquitted; she had not fled. ASSI 35/68/8, mm 11, 33, 40, 54.]

273   22 Apr 1626. South Mundham. John Eagle, gent., county coroner. Jurors: John Harvey, Henry Chatfeilde, John Smyth, William Eyles sen., Richard Eiles, Robert C..., William Rigsbey, John Dunton, John Goble, Alexander Shave, Thomas Weston, Clement Keene, William Watler, John Bridger, William Eiles jun., Richard Napcrofte, Alan Tupper. On 5 Apr Joan Power late of South Mundham, 'spinster', gave birth to a live male child at South Mundham and later on the same day murdered him at South Mundham, taking him in ?both [hands], violently throwing him onto a mound of earth [*tumulus*] and suffocating him whereby he ... [died]. Power had no goods or chattels, lands or tenements at the time of the felony or ever after to the jurors' knowledge. [*Damaged.*] ASSI 35/68/8, m 34.
[Delivered with **268**. At the assizes Power pleaded not guilty and was acquitted; she had not fled. The trial jury found that the child had died a natural death. ASSI 35/68/8, mm 34, 40.]

274   24 Apr 1626. Aldingbourne. Eusebius Hayes, gent., coroner of the bishop of Chichester's liberty. Jurors: Richard Knight, John Peachey, Thomas Nash, John Truslowe, Edward Gibbons, Ellis Amias, Henry Roffe, Thomas Goble, Robert Liliatt, Thomas Hale, Henry Deacon, Nicholas Violett, John Ward, Thomas Aylmer, William Farr, Thomas Hartley, Richard Bigges, Thomas Gray. On 14 Apr Thomas Martin of Aldingbourne, 'husb[andman]', died a natural death at Aldingbourne and not otherwise to the jurors' knowledge. KB 9/782, m 211.
[Delivered with **268** and on to King's Bench in Michaelmas. KB 9/782, m 231d; KB 29/275, m 59d.]

275   15 May 1626. Thakeham in East Easwrith hundred. John Teynton, Bramber rape coroner. Jurors: John Gratwicke, John Hayne, John Butcher, John Bridger, James Waterman, Edward Harrowden, Thomas Archall, George Willeson, John Wodyer, John Greene, John Myles, Ambrose Booker, John Haywarde, Richard Tye, Benjamin Belchamber. On 24 Apr, when George Smyther was at Guildford in Surrey, William Brinckwell of Guildford, 'butcher', Alice his wife, Edward his son and Alice Monday his daughter came and assaulted him. William feloniously killed him with 'a cleaver' of iron and steel worth 18d which he held in both hands, giving him several 'bruises' on the head, back and loins of which he languished at Thakeham from 24 Apr until 7 May and then died; and Alice and Edward Brinckwell and Alice Monday were present on 24 Apr aiding and abetting William. ASSI 35/68/8, m 12.
[Delivered with **268**. At the assizes the grand jury, to which Elizabeth Smyther, John Wood and John Groves gave evidence, presented an indictment which charged all 4 with murdering Smyther at Guildford on 24 Apr: William

Brinckwell giving him a wound on the kidneys with a cleaver of iron and steel worth 18d which he held in both hands of which he languished at Thakeham from 24 Apr until 7 May and then died; and Alice Brinckwell late of Guildford, spinster, alias Alice wife of William Brinckwell, Edward Brinckwell late of Guildford, butcher, and Alice Brinckwell late of Guildford, spinster, being feloniously present aiding and abetting him. At the time of the assizes Alice the daughter was at large, but the 3 others pleaded not guilty to the indictment. Edward and Alice wife of William were acquitted; they had not fled. William was acquitted of murder but convicted of manslaughter; he had no chattels. He then successfully pleaded benefit of clergy and was branded. ASSI 35/68/8, mm 12, 37, 40.]

276 29 May 1626. Frant. John Lucke, gent., Rotherfield hundred coroner. Jurors of the hundred: John Pocoke, Lawrence Clarke, William Hugget, Thomas May, John Newman, John Lockyer sen., Thomas Crips, John Maynord sen., John Lockyer jun., John Russell, Thomas Kayly, Robert Johnson, Thomas Hosmer, Thomas Marckwike, George Barbor, Arthur Maynord, William Allen. On 9 May James Coppinge of Frant, 'husbandman', feloniously hanged himself on a beam of his barn at Frant with 'a halter' worth 2d which he held in both hands, tying one end round his neck and the other round the beam, whereby he died immediately. At that time he possessed goods and chattels which remain with John Weller of Rotherfield, bailiff of the hundred, viz 'all his houshould stufe in his house [worth] vj li, item eighteene bushells of wheate iij li iij s, item thirty bushells of otes xxxij s vj d, item eight load of hay liij s iiij d, item six hogges iij li, item fower oxen xv li iij s iiij d, item fower kyne and a bull xij li, item three horsbeastes vij li, item thirty toe sheep and seaventeen [*changed from* eighteene] lambs xij li, item the wheat upon the ground xiij li iij s, item the otes upon the ground v li, item the pease upon the ground xiij s iiij d, item the powlterii ij s vj d'. [*Inventory in English.*] KB 9/782, mm 226, 227.
[Delivered with **274**. The bailiff was summoned to King's Bench to answer for the goods and chattels worth £81 10s 6d (*recte* £81 11s); he had licence to imparl in Trinity 1627. KB 9/782, mm 227, 231d; KB 29/275, m 59.]

277 27 June 1626. Hastings. John Brett, Hastings mayor and coroner. Jurors: Nicholas Staplus, Nicholas Foster, Robert Sargent sen., John Fawtley, Peter Yeilding, Emanuel Browne, Robert Marshall, Richard Amyatt, Peter Winckfeild, William Gawen, James Wright, Thomas Moore, George Clapham, Thomas Tayler sen. About 11 a.m. on 22 June, when Simon Boys late of Hastings, 'fisherman', was returning from fishing in the sea towards Stonebeach near 'le pere' of Hastings in a fishing boat called 'le Anne' of Hastings, weight 12 tons, belonging to Thomas Luckett, Mark White and Robert White, in the company of several other fishermen, he got out of the boat onto the land. While he was working with the other fishermen in drawing the boat out of the sea onto Stonebeach, as they were accustomed to do, the boat unexpectedly overturned and fell on one side upon Boys, crushing his head and body, of which he languished for 5 days and then died about 1 a.m. on 27 June at Hastings by misadventure. The boat is worth 100s. The jurors requested that this inquest be entered of record in the common register of Hastings in the customary manner. HASTINGS C/A(a) 2, f 32.

278 6 July 1626. Wadhurst. Thomas Houghton, gent., Loxfield Camden half-hundred coroner. Jurors of the half-hundred: Richard Markewicke, Thomas Boreman, William Watson, Richard Collyns, John Curde, Francis Enge sen., Nicholas Puxtie, Richard Reade, Nicholas Burges, Edward Chapman, William Beecher, John Polley, Richard Denman, John Reynoldes, David Penyall. On 30 June Edward Eaton late of Wadhurst, 'carpenter', feloniously killed Richard Maye late of Frant, 'butcher', at Wadhurst with 'the edge' of '[a] peele' [*sc.* peel, a spade] worth 1d which he held in both hands, giving him a wound on the middle of the head 4¾ inches long, ¾ inch wide and ½ inch deep of which he languished at Wadhurst until 2 July and then died. What goods and chattels, lands or tenements Eaton had at or ever after the time of the felony or still has the jurors do not know. [*Damaged.*] ASSI 35/68/8, m 10.
[Delivered with **268**. At the assizes an indictment was preferred which charged Eaton with murder, the details being as in the inquest verdict except that the peel was valued at 2d, the wound was said to be on the front of the head and 4 inches wide and ½ inch deep, and the last sentence was omitted. The grand jury, to which William Barham, William Thomas and John R...es gave evidence, reduced the charge to manslaughter. Eaton pleaded not guilty to the

indictment as amended but was convicted and hanged; he had no chattels. ASSI 35/68/8, m 20.]

279   7 Aug 1626. Horsham. John Teynton, gent., [Bramber] rape coroner. Jurors: William Chambers, John Davy, John Morecocke, Robert Lintot, John Chapman, Benjamin Meekes, Richard Hunt, Edward Booker, Edmund Dearinge, Matthew Napper, Thomas Wheatly, Thomas Clarke, Ralph Hall. On 1 Aug, when Thomas Holliday was working in a lofty room, which was unfinished, in the new house of Richard Ny, gent., in Horsham, by misadventure he fell headlong between 2 beams of the room to the ground whereby his head and body were so greatly crushed that he languished at Horsham until 5 Aug and then died. KB 9/1094, m 97.
[Delivered to East Grinstead assizes on 5 Mar and on to King's Bench in Easter 1627. Holliday, described as 'a batchelour, killed by a fall in the building of a house of Mr Richard Nyes at Tanbridge', was buried at Horsham on the day of the inquest. KB 9/1094, m 107d; KB 29/276, m 3; SRS, XXI, 395.]

280   9 Nov 1626. Washington. John Teynton, gent., Bramber rape coroner. Jurors: John Pollard, Benjamin Bellchamber, William Andrew, John Elizander, Walter Henly, David Dudgion, Richard Piper alias Butcher, John Caplyn, William Scutt, Thomas Etheridge, Ferdinand Grantham, Alexander Roch, John Mansell. On 7 Nov Mary wife of John Peeter of Washington, 'husbandman', being non compos mentis, voluntarily threw herself into 'Duckly Ponde' in Washington and so died. KB 9/1094, m 105.
[Delivered with **279**. It is enrolled on the Controlment Roll as a felonious suicide. KB 9/1094, m 107d; KB 29/276, m 3.]

281   26 Dec 1626. Horsham. John Teynton, gent., Bramber rape coroner. Jurors: Francis Booker, Abraham Bladen, John Morecocke, John Bennett, Robert Lyntott, Robert Sharpe, William Colefox, John Holden, Richard Clarke, Alexander Inge, Edward Hobbs, Richard Waller, Thomas Berwick. On 24 Dec Repentance [*Repententianus*] Right late of Henfield, 'husbandman', who had previously been committed to Horsham gaol for felony by Nicholas Ersfeild, esq., JP, died a natural death there and not otherwise to the jurors' knowledge. KB 9/1094, m 95.
[Delivered with **279**. A Repentance Champion, a poor prisoner, was buried at Horsham on 25 Dec. KB 9/1094, m 107d; KB 29/276, m 3; SRS, XXI, 396.]

282   12 June 1627 [*3 Charles I*]. Frant. John Lucke, gent., Rotherfield hundred coroner. Jurors: John Maynard sen., William Chowne, John Baker, Abraham Ashdowne, Robert Baker, Stephen Baker, George Turnor, John Gyles, Thomas Maye, Peter Crowhurst, Thomas Hosmer, John Harte, Peter Crowherst. On 10 June 1626 [*2 Charles I aforesaid*] Edmund Turnor of Frant feloniously hanged himself at Frant with 'a halter' worth 2d which he held in both hands, tying one end round the branch of a [tree *omitted*] and the other round his neck and dying immediately. At that time he possessed certain [goods and chattels *omitted*] worth 13s 4d which remain with John Weller of Rotherfield, Rotherfield hundred bailiff. KB 9/1096, m 120.
[Delivered to the Sussex summer assizes and on to King's Bench in Michaelmas. The bailiff was summoned to King's Bench to answer for the goods and chattels; he was discharged in Easter 1640 when the deputy almoner acknowledged satisfaction. The coroner was also summoned to King's Bench to answer for defects in the inquest, perhaps including the omissions noted; no further process is recorded. KB 9/1096, mm 115d, 120; KB 29/276, mm 54d, 55.]

283   5 July 1627. Nuthurst. John Teynton, gent., Bramber rape coroner. Jurors: John Bartlet, John Davy, Richard Michell, Richard Booker, Richard Bourne, Ravenscroft Foyce, John Feist, William Stone, Michael Burton, William Gate, Roland Pollington, George Mower, John Hewes, John Tincker, Thomas Gromebridge. On 27 June, when John Steyninge was crossing 'a wooden footbridge' over a small stream called 'Cobsall Brook' in Nuthurst, being then and having for the previous 6 days been weakened by ill health, by misadventure he fell from the bridge into the water running under it and was immediately drowned. KB 9/783, m 167B.
[Delivered to the Sussex Lent assizes and on to King's Bench in Easter 1628. KB 9/783, m 171d; KB 29/277, m 3d.]

284   14 Aug 1627. Bosham. William Kymber, Bosham hundred coroner. Jurors of Bosham and 3 neighbouring townships, viz Hook, Southwood and Broadbridge: Henry Grigg, Thomas Langrish, William Kelly, Andrew Colpes, Henry Colpes, Robert Grigg, William Cooper, Adam Dallington, William Cockwell, William Wheeler, Humphrey Penbrook, Bartholomew Till, John Bigges, John Rickman. About 2 p.m. on 13 Aug, when Mary, aged 3, daughter of William Lealand of Bosham, clerk, was playing alone around or near a stream which ran through Bosham churchyard, by misadventure she suddenly fell into the water and was drowned. KB 9/783, m 114.
[Delivered by the coroner into King's Bench in Easter 1628. KB 9/783, m 114d; KB 29/277, m 4d.]

285   22 Feb 1628. Horsham. John Teynton, gent., Bramber rape coroner. Jurors: John Mardeson, Richard Clarke, Thomas Galpyn, Thomas Baker, William Gromebridge, William Deane, Thomas Longhurst, Emanuel Lyntot, Thomas Clarke, Robert Honnywood, Ralph Hall, William Willperforce, John Genn. On 21 Feb John Constable late of Steyning, 'husbandman', who had previously been committed to Horsham gaol on suspicion of felony by Henry Goringe, esq., JP, died a natural death there and not otherwise to the jurors' knowledge. KB 9/783, m 162.
[Delivered with **283**. Constable was buried at Horsham on the day of the inquest. KB 9/783, m 171d; KB 29/277, m 3d; SRS, XXI, 398.]

286   ... Mar [1628. Chichester.] R[ichard] Williams and John ?Pannett, gents, [Chichester city] coroners. Jurors: Thomas Ball, Thomas C..., ...er jun., Francis Longe, Thomas ...tes, Richard Gore, Thomas Comber, William Copperthwaite, ... ?Nunn, ..., William Beverstocke, Anthony Somes, John Budd, Henry Lillyott, Ralph Allen, John Rogers, Thomas Hart, Edward C..., ... Madgwicke. [Between] 5 and 6 a.m. on 8 Mar William Hamblen late of Chichester, gent., [feloniously killed] William Fowkes alias Foux in 'Kingston Farm Landes' [in the parish] of St Pancras outside the liberties of Chichester with 'a rapier' of iron and steel worth 12d which he held ..., giving him a fatal wound on the left side of his body between the ribs ... wide ... of which ... at Chichester ... At the time of the felony ... to the jurors' knowledge. [*Damaged.*] ASSI 35/70/8, m 42.
[Delivered to East Grinstead assizes on 14 July 1628 when the grand jury presented an indictment which charged Hamblen with murdering Fowkes in the parish of St Pancras about 6 a.m. on 8 Mar with a rapier of iron and steel worth 12d which he held in his right hand, giving him a wound in the left side of the chest between the ribs ½ inch wide and 12 inches deep which penetrated through and across his body and of which he languished at Chichester until 4 p.m. on the same day and then died. Hamblen, who had been committed to gaol by the sheriff, pleaded not guilty to the indictment and was acquitted of murder but convicted of manslaughter; he had no chattels. He then successfully pleaded benefit of clergy and was released on bail to appear at the next assizes until his branding was respited. ASSI 35/70/8, mm 42, 45, 59d, 60.]

287   1 Apr 1628. ... Eusebius Hayes, gent., the bishop of Chichester's coroner. Jurors: ... Watersfeild, John Snellinge, Richard ...?nutt, Richard ..., John Scardvile, John Kewell, John Francklin, Thomas ... On ?7 Mar, when ... was in the garden of William Watersfeild of Ferring, ... Rose ... Margaret Phisens coming into the garden ... dead there. The child ... by reason of the departure of Rose its mother ... said manner ... to the jurors' knowledge. [*Damaged.*] ASSI 35/70/8, m 55.
[Delivered with **286**. At the assizes the grand jury, to which Margaret Phison, ?George ...ish and ?Brian Phis[on?] gave evidence, presented an indictment which charged Rose Higgons with giving birth to a live female bastard child on 7 Mar in William Watersfeild's garden in Ferring and then murdering her there by secretly throwing her down, intending that she should die, and leaving her naked and deprived of any human assistance and with no nourishment, whereby she immediately died. Higgons, who had been committed to gaol by the coroner for 'homicide and murder', pleaded not guilty to the indictment but was convicted and hanged. ASSI 35/70/8, mm 49, 54, 59d. 60.]

288   14 May 1628. Rye. Richard Mills, deputy of John Sharpe, Rye mayor and coroner. Jurors: Peter Bennett, Thomas Grible, John Kempe, Thomas Grove, John Nicolson, William Smeede, Henry Walter, John Hummersome, Thomas Kytt, John Andersonne, Maurice Steward, 'Nathan' Lord. 'Thomas Iden was stroke in his body nere unto his groine by a bay geldinge with a bald face of Mr Thirl's standing in the traves of William Bucke's without the Landgate of Rye, which was the cause of his death. [*Verdict in English.*] RYE 1/11, ff 199v–200.

289   18 May 1628. Rye. Richard Mills, deputy of John Sharpe, Rye mayor and coroner. Jurors: John Anderson, John Wren, John Carter, Thomas Grove, Henry Walter, Maurice Steward, 'Nathan' Lord, John Dickingson, John Pedle, Thomas Waters, Richard Dod, William Gates. John Pike, 'cordwainer', 'lyinge a sleepe uppon a sheere and steepe bancke' in the Gungarden within the liberties of Rye 'right against the courthowse there, as they [*sc.* the jurors] conceive by misfortune fell uppon the rockes' below, breaking his neck and skull of which he died. [*Verdict in English.*] RYE 1/11, ff 200–200v.

290   29 May 1628. Frant. John Lucke, gent., Rotherfield hundred coroner. Jurors: Thomas Maynard, John Maynard, Stephen Baker, Thomas Crippes, John Saxby, Richard Taylor, William Huggett, Stephen Coppinge, ?William Hall, John Cripps, John Vincent, Arthur Maynard, Matthew Hider, William Coe, Simon Vincent, William Allen, Henry Boorne, Christopher Hider, John Harte. On 26 May George Thompson [late] of Frant, 'laborer', [feloniously killed] Thomas Wright at Frant with a ... which he held in his right hand, giving him several fatal 'bruses' ... of which ... at Frant ... At the time of the felony Thompson had no goods or chattels, lands or tenements to the jurors' knowledge. [*Damaged.*] ASSI 35/70/8, m 41.
[Delivered with **286**. At the assizes the grand jury, to which William Thomas, gent., Richard Shoobridge and Peter Benyeare gave evidence, presented an indictment which charged Thompson with feloniously killing Wright about 9 p.m. on 26 May at Frant with a crabtree cudgel worth ½d which he held in his right hand, giving him several wounds on the head and face of which he languished at Frant until 5 a.m. on the next day and then died. Thompson, who had been committed to gaol by the coroner for 'homicide and murder', pleaded not guilty to the indictment but the verdict is illegible. ASSI 35/70/8, mm 41, 46, 60.]

291   2 June 1628. Hastings. Thomas Brian, Hastings mayor and coroner. Jurors: Humphrey Blinkarne, Richard Wheiler, John Isted, Richard Downe, John Hick, Thomas Mannington, John Fyssenden, William Furner, Thomas Stevenson, Richard Springett, James Byrchett, Peter Yeilding, John Wylson, Owen Freeman, Walwin [*Walwinus*] Hollandes. On 31 May John Gynner, aged 18, the elder son of 'Rachel' Gynner of Hastings, widow, and his brother Thomas, aged 14, were playing and jesting together in friendly fashion in their mother's house called 'le West Mill House' in Hastings and a little later John so provoked Thomas with more serious words and blows that Thomas, after various sharp altercations thereby occurring between them, without forethought took in his right hand a pair of scissors which was lying there, thrust it at John and struck him with it, giving him by chance a wound in the left side of the neck between the head and the shoulder about 2 inches deep and 3 inches wide of which he languished for 12 hours and then died between 11 p.m. and midnight of 31 May accidentally and by misadventure. The jurors requested that this inquest be enrolled of record in the common register of Hastings according to the ancient custom of the town. HASTINGS C/A(a) 2, f 41v.
[A marginal note calls the deceased John Jennings.]

292   9 July 1628. Shermanbury. John Teynton, gent., [Bramber] rape coroner. Jurors: Thomas Beard, John Vincent, Owen Gratwicke, Richard Jupp, William Shelley, William Greentree, Roger Hollis, John Buffer, Richard Berry, William Wakeham, Isaac Denman, Robert Jupp, Henry Greene, Thomas Parson. Between 3 and 4 p.m. on 8 June, when William Gratwicke and Richard Vincent of Shermanbury were light-heartedly wrestling together at Shermanbury, they fell together to the ground and by misadventure Gratwicke fell on the point of a knife [which] Vincent had in his garter [*subligaculum*] whereby he received a mortal wound on the outside of the right shin ... inches ... of which [he languished] until 8 July and then [died] ... [*Damaged.*] ASSI 35/70/8, m 44.
[Delivered with **286**.]

293   28 July 1628. Lindfield in Burleigh Arches hundred. John Teynton, gent., Lewes rape coroner. Jurors: Richard Vynall, Francis Weste, Francis West jun., William Symondes, Robert Cooper, William

West, Christopher Neale, Thomas Comber, Simon Musall, Nicholas Marchaunt, Matthew Comber, Jonathan Batcheler, William Tubbe, John Wheeler. On 26 July, when Robert Beldham [*once* Bedham], aged barely 2, was alone at Lindfield near the dwelling-house of his father, Nicholas Beldham of Lindfield, by misadventure he fell into a pit of water and was immediately drowned. KB 9/1098, m 234. [Delivered with **302** and on to King's Bench in Michaelmas 1629. KB 9/1098, mm 228d, 237; KB 29/278, m 74.]

294 30 July 1628. Arundel. Richard Williams, gent., Arundel rape coroner. Jurors: James Huggett, William Owlder, John Arnold, Thomas Kewell, Henry Ac..., Anthony Gough, Nicholas Rickman, Richard Stamper, John Masters, George Payne, William Rice, 'Bowett' Rice, Michael Ball, Jeremy Gough, George Thorne. On 20 July Henry Stradling late of East Preston, 'yoman', feloniously killed John Selden at Angmering [with a staff] worth ½d which he held in his right hand, giving him a wound on [the front of the head] 1½ inches long of which he languished at Arundel until 29 July and then died. Stradling has no goods or chattels to the jurors' knowledge. [*Damaged.*] ASSI 35/71/9, m 26. [Delivered to East Grinstead assizes on 9 Mar 1629 when the grand jury, to which James Bun, Edward Scarvill, Henry Pledge and Thomas Selden gave evidence, presented an indictment similar to the inquest verdict except that the charge was murder, the wound was said to be on the back of Selden's head and the final sentence was omitted. Stradling pleaded not guilty to the indictment and was acquitted of murder but convicted of manslaughter; he had no chattels. He then successfully pleaded benefit of clergy and was branded. ASSI 35/71/9, mm 26, 29, 36.]

295 31 July 1628. Arundel. Richard Williams, gent., Arundel rape coroner. Jurors: Thomas Dunch, Thomas Brigger, John Dyer, William Wells, Richard Knight, John Hambleden, John Knight, Robert Pellatt, Thomas Edmondes, John Wells, Richard Wellson, Thomas Wepham, John Pellatt, William Studman, Henry Begley, John Blayse, Thomas Mersh, Thomas Cutfold. About 6 a.m. on 19 Jan John Beyond the Moon [*ultra lunam*] murdered William Warner at Climping with a knife worth 1d which he held in his right hand and with which he 'did cutt his throate', giving him a wound of which he immediately died. He then tied a halter worth 1d round Warner's neck with both hands and to a beam in a barn at Climping, thus hanging him there after his death. After that he fled. He had no goods or chattels, land or tenements to the jurors' knowledge. KB 9/785, m 74.
[Delivered by the coroner into King's Bench in Michaelmas. John Beyond the Moon was summoned to King's Bench to answer for the murder but process against him then ceased. Climping was also summoned to answer for his escape; process continued until Hilary 1649. A writ of non omittas issued on 27 Nov 1628 to the sheriff of Sussex ordering him to inquire whether or not Warner had committed suicide and, if he had, to appraise all the goods in his possession and in that of others to his use at the time of his death. The sheriff returned the following inquisition and inventory into King's Bench in Hilary 1629:

22 Jan 1629. Arundel. Stephen Boord, kt, sheriff. Jurors: Thomas Edmondes, gent., Henry Staker, Anthony Nashe, Henry Standen, John Staker, Thomas Sumer sen., William Lawrence, Adam Bredham, Richard Haynes, Thomas Sowton, Thomas Rickman, John Watersfeild, Henry Eyles, John Eyles, Henry Gratwicke. About 6 a.m. on 19 Jan 1628, when Warner was alone in his barn next to his dwelling-house at Climping in Arundel rape, he feloniously hanged himself with a rope worth 1d which he held in both hands, putting one end of it round his neck and tying the other round a rafter of the barn. At that time he had goods and chattels worth £102 (*sic*) which are detailed in the schedule annexed and which remain with Alice Warner, widow, his relict, and Richard Knight, her father; and no other goods or chattels to the jurors' knowledge.

21 Jan 1628. Inventory of the goods and chattels of William Warner late of Climping taken by John Peers of Arundel, bailiff of Thomas earl of Arundel and Surrey, appraised by Mr Robert Standen, John Paye, Avisford hundred constable, John Staker and John Harding, and seized for the earl's use. In the hall of his dwelling-house at Ilsham in Climping, 'one joyned cuppbord, one cuppbord cloth, one joyned chayre, one other little joyned chaire, twoe joyned stooles, one old beeched table, one forme, one bedd pann, one little paire of potthangers, about twenty old little bookes, some old ?couzins (*or* courins) and nyne cheeses (worth) xviij s iiij d. Item in the kytchin, twoe brasse caldrons, three brasse kettells, one iron pott, one brasse pott, one other brasse pott with a handle, one litle brasse kettle, one chafyndysh, six old pewter dishes, one paire of bellowes, twoe tuns, one paire of litle andirons, one fire pann, one old fire pann, one ladle, one skymmer, one paire of potthangers xxxiij s iiij d. Item in the buttery, one keeler, fowre small vessells for beere, eight old hoockes; and in the wellhowse, one old little ?morquerne (*or* mozquerne, ?mustard-quern), one cheesepresse, one silting (?*recte* salting) trough, one cherne, one old powdring tubb, twoe keevers, one buckingtubb (*sc.* bucking-tub, a washing- or bleaching-tub), one yoting vate (*sc.* yoting-vat, a

soaking-vat), twoe firkyns, fowre cheesehoopes, one vallor (*sc.* voller, part of a cheese-press) and other lumberment xxx s. Item in the loft over the kitchin and over the wellhowse, one joyned chest, one playne lowe bedsted, twoe very old flockbeddes, twoe old flock bolsters, twoe old blanckettes, one old coverlett, three old sheetes, one lynnen wheele, one halfe bushell, one woollen wheele, twoe old tubbes and old lumber; and in the loft over the wellhowse, about fowre quarters of grey pease, fowre old tubbes, one old plonck table, six cheeses and about twoe bushalls of malt iij li xv s. Item in the lowe beddchamber, one joyned beddstedle with a tester, one fetherbed, twoe bolsters, one paire of sheetes, one blankett, one coverlett, one great joynd chest, three little plaine chestes, one table with a beechen frame, one little round table, one chaire, one course tablecoth, three sheetes putt into one of the small chestes there, one old flaskett (*sc.* flasket, a basket or small flask), twoe old brasse candlestickes and one old carpett iij li. Item in the lofte over the hall, one joynd bedstedle with a tester, one fetherbedd, twoe fether bolsters, one payre of old sheetes, one coverlett, twoe blankettes, one little joynd table, one baskett chaire, twoe lytle playne chestes in one of which is twoe payre of little old sheetes and one short tablecloth xxx s. Item in the loft over the chamber, one bedstedle, one old flock bedd, one old hamper, about three nayle (*sc.* nails, a nail being 2¼ inches) of hempe, some old lumber, one old corslett (*sc.* corslet, body armour) and a pike xvj s. Item in the milkehowse (*or* nuwehowse), one powdring tubb, twoe trugges, five bowles, one little old tubb, one breadgrate, sixe shelves, one boltinghuch (*sc.* bolting-hutch, a sifting-box); under the stares, one old flock bolster iij s iiij d. Item in the copyhold howse wherein Widowe Stone dwelleth, in sackes in a fate (*sc.* vat) and in a loft, about five quarters of barly wynoed, about nyne quarters of wheate, about syxteene bushells of gray pease the threshing and winowing to pay for x li v s. Item one newe bushell and sixe sackes xiij s iiij d. Item in the barne there, about fowre quarters of barlye in a heape lying in the barnes flower, one mowe of barly unthreshd, one mowe of wheate unthreshd, one old wymsheete (*sc.* wimsheet, a winnowing-sheet) xxij li xv s. Item sixe kyne xvj li. Item in the farme barne, one mowe of wheate, one mowe of barlye, about three quarters of pease unthreshd with a parcell of oates unthreshd xxix li xij s viij d. Item in the gates by the dwellyng howse, three fatting hogges and tenne gate hogges (*sc.* ?goat-hogs, year-old goats); and at Clymping, one sowe hogg and one shoote (*sc.* shoat, a young weaned pig) vj li viij s. Item in twoe closes of ground belonging to West Cudlowes, late in thoccupacion of the said William Warner, thirty fower ewes, nyne lambes; at John Bloyses, twenty ewes putt to halfes; and at Robert Pellettes, thirty ewes put to halfes xxiiij li. Item in the gates by the howse, one bull, one steere, twoe cowes, one heyfer heyfer (*sic*); and in land called sommer leazed, nyne ?weynier calves and one young ?waynier mare colt xxij li x s. Item in the barne by the howse, one litle mowe of wheate, two litle mowes of barly and about a quarter of pease unthreshd xxj li. Item in the stable by the howse, twoe working nagges, one old mare, twoe paire of shutt (*sc.* ?shoats) harnest, one paire of thill (*sc.* thill-horses, shaft-horses) harnest; in the gates, twoe old broken cartes, twoe old dung courtes, fowre payre of old shodd iron wheeles, one old broken fyrrlather (*sc.* fir ladder), some old peeces of tymber, three harrowes, three payre of harrowing harnest xiiij li. Item at Houghton Downes goeing upon the lande of one Richard Lee of Houghton, as is supposed, certein wethers supposed to be one hundred whereof one Zowch is the sheppard xxxv li. Item one dublett, one payre of breeches which was his wedding suit, one cloake which is said his brother, John Warner, had out of the howse on Sunday the twentieth of January 1627 (*i.e.* 1628) without leave'.

Alice Warner and Richard Knight were summoned to King's Bench to answer for the goods and chattels worth £102; Warner was waived at Lewes on 25 ... 1629 or 1630 and Knight was outlawed at Chichester on 23 Mar 1631. KB 9/785, mm 74, 74d; KB 9/786, mm 90–92; KB 29/277, mm 72d, 119.]

296   15 Sept 1628. Cuckfield. John Teynton, gent., Lewes rape coroner. Jurors: Walter Burte, John Falkoner, Stephen Jupp, Edward Wyckham, Edward Beachley, John Stone, Thomas Peckham, Thomas Abbotte, Richard Tomsett, Thomas Blundell, William Falkner, Robert Standbridge, Edmund Davye, John Peake, Thomas Bett, Richard Snashall. On 30 Aug Robert Androwes late of Slaugham, 'collier', feloniously killed John Higgins at Slaugham with a staff worth 1d which he held in both hands, giving him 'a bruise' on the left side of the head of which he languished at Cuckfield until 7 Sept and then died. Androwes fled. At the time of the felony he had goods and chattels worth £3. ASSI 35/71/9, m 24.
[Delivered with **294**. At the time of the assizes Androwes was still at large. Higgins, called a pedlar, was buried at Cuckfield on 8 Sept although the inquest was said to be taken on view of his body. ASSI 35/71/9, m 24; SRS, XIII, 157.]

297   30 Sept 1628. Catsfield. Thomas Butcher, gent., Hastings rape coroner. Jurors: Joseph Snipp, Edward Carter, Richard Davy, Thomas Coleman, Richard Compar, John Morrell, Robert Bray, William Coleman, John Cooper, Thomas Honysed, Richard Parker, Robert Harden, Simon Jarvays, William

Colston, John Hode, John Forde, John Haywood. On 26 Sept George Trice late of Battle, 'laborer', murdered John Humfrey late of Catsfield, 'husband[man]', at Catsfield with a staff 10 feet long or thereabouts worth 6d which he held in both hands, giving him 'a bruse' on the left side of the head of which he languished until 28 Sept and then died at Catsfield. After committing the felony Trice fled to places unknown to the jurors. What goods and chattels, lands or tenements he had then or ever after they do not know. KB 9/790, m 268.

[Delivered with **294** and on to King's Bench in Easter 1630, as was an indictment identical to the inquest verdict (but omitting the last 2 sentences) which had been presented at the same assizes by the grand jury to which Thomas Iden, Katharine Hoad, Margaret Humfrey, Elizabeth Pilcher and Mary Danyell had given evidence. Trice was at large at the time of the assizes. King's Bench ordered his arrest on both the inquest and the indictment; he was outlawed at Chichester on 7 Oct 1630 in respect of both. KB 9/790, mm 265–267; KB 29/279, m 5d.]

298 1 Oct 1628. Brede. Anthony Tuttesham, gent., Brede manor coroner. Jurors of Brede: Robert Yealding, Matthew Wood, Richard ..., ...leman, Stephen Peirson, Stephen Mannings, Michael Bromeley, John Cogger, Thomas Copping, Thomas Piper, Richard Sheapard, ..., Richard Fuller. On 13 July Richard son of John Batter of Brede, 'husband[man]', came to the house of Drew Cartwright of Brede, 'husband[man]', in Brede with a hen and remained around the house for a short time. Thomas son of Drew Cartwright, seeing Richard Batter there ready to go away, went to him and told him that he had a new staff and other things which he had recently made to play a game called 'fukes' and that he would bring them and show him if he would stay there a short while. Thomas Cartwright then brought the staff and other things relating to the game while Richard Batter was standing in Drew Cartwright's close in Brede near Drew's dwelling-house. Richard Batter then took the staff, which was 2 feet long or thereabouts, from Thomas Cartwright 'that he might trye' how great a blow he could give with it and, extending his left hand, in which he held the staff, behind him, by misadventure and against his will he struck Thomas Cartwright, who was carelessly standing behind his back, with the staff on the left side of the head, giving him 'a bruse' of which he languished at Brede until 16 July and then died. Thus Cartwright was killed not [feloniously] but merely by his own default and by misadventure. [*Damaged.*] ASSI 35/71/9, m 25.

[Delivered with **294**.]

299 5 Nov 1628. Hastings. Thomas Brian, Hastings mayor and coroner. Jurors: William Goldham, Nicholas Foster, Thomas Wyng, John Jenkin, Peter Grover, John Shaw, Stephen Waters, Richard Springet, John Coosens, Thomas Mannington, Ralph Oliver, Robert Marshall, Richard Staplus jun., Robert Mills, Peter Yeilding. On 4 Nov John Cruttenden late of Eastbourne, 'husbandman', carried malt and wheat on his horses from Eastbourne to Hastings where he delivered it to Sackville [*Sackvillus*] Franck and Widow Gynner. The next day, intending to return to Eastbourne on his horse, he rode along the sea-shore until he came to a place under Gensing cliffs called 'Bulverhide Haven', within the jurisdiction of Hastings, where, trying to cross 'le Haven', [his horse] was violently upended by the current and was thrown into the sea with Cruttenden who was thereby drowned by misadventure. His body was later cast on the foreshore [*super medo littore*] near Hastings by the tide. The jurors requested that this inquest be enrolled of record in the common register of Hastings according to the ancient custom of the town. HASTINGS C/A(a) 2, f 44v.

300 14 Nov 1628. Battle. Henry Cole, Battle liberty [coroner]. Jurors: William Jordan, gent., Thomas Sharpe, William Foster, John Gaunt, John Sharpe, ?William Leonard, Thomas Sheather, Thomas French, John Foster, Thomas Sagott, William Easton, Thomas B..., John Jones, John Cowper, John Roffey. On 12 Nov Thomas Bugges of Battle, 'laborer', murdered John Fuller at Battle with a long staff worth 2d which he held in both hands, giving him 'a bruse' on the left side of the head of which he languished at Battle for 6 hours and then died. At the time of the felony Bugges had no goods or chattels, lands or tenements to the jurors' knowledge. [*Damaged.*] ASSI 35/71/9, m 27.

[Delivered with **294**. At the assizes a bill of indictment was preferred which charged Bugges and William Reynolds, labourer, John Sergeant, tailor, and John Burges, labourer, all late of Battle, with murdering Fuller: Bugges giving him a wound on the left side of the head about 3 p.m. on 12 Nov at Battle with a staff worth 2d which he held in both hands, of which wound Fuller languished at Battle for 3 hours and then died; and the 3 others being feloniously present aiding and abetting him. The grand jury, to which Jane and John Fuller, Thomas Colevile, Edward Yalding, John Hull, Matthew Chittenden and William Reynolds gave evidence, affirmed the charge against Bugges but rejected those against the 3 others. Bugges, who had been committed to gaol by Thomas Sackvill, esq., JP, pleaded not guilty to the indictment but was convicted and hanged; he had no chattels. ASSI 35/71/9, mm 27, 30, 36, 75.]

301   10 Feb 1629. Iping. Richard Williams, gent., Easebourne hundred coroner. Jurors: Nicholas Bettisworth, Thomas Heather, Robert Chawcrofte, Henry Bennyfold, Thomas Ireland, Richard Bound, Richard Smyth, Thomas Aylwyn, Henry Spurrier, Robert Blackman, John Barksheire, William Heather, Daniel Knight. About 8 a.m. on 7 Feb, when Richard Heather late of Iping, 'husbondman', was riding on a gelding on the road recently constructed in the lower part of the common called Iping Marsh in Iping between 'le fornace pond' and the newly built furnace of Peter Bettisworth, kt, the gelding, frightened by the noise of the blast produced by the bellows of the furnace and by the water of the pond running over the wheels of the furnace, suddenly threw itself and Heather from the edge of the pond into the water whereupon they were both immediately drowned by reason of the closeness of the furnace to the road and the depth of the water in the pond. KB 9/795, m 71.
[Delivered into King's Bench in Trinity 1631, probably by the coroner. KB 29/280, m 53d.]

302   15 May 1629. Upper Beeding in Burbeach hundred. John Teynton, gent., Bramber rape coroner. Jurors: Richard Hearte, Richard Snellinge, James Savidge, Thomas Snellinge, Richard Baker, Thomas Hilles, John Lutman, William Crowch, John Pellett, John Robertes, John Pollarde, Ralph Wase, Alexander Roche, John Bisshopp, John Taverner, John Caplyn, James Smyth, Thomas Etheridge, Thomas Juden, Robert Tullie. Between 9 and 10 p.m. on 10 May an unknown man assaulted John Cooper on the road at Bramber and afterwards murdered him, breaking his neck with both hands and then throwing him in the great tidal river [*sc.* the Adur] flowing under Bramber bridge in Bramber. After committing the felony he fled. ASSI 35/71/10, m 27.
[Delivered to East Grinstead assizes on 6 July.]

303   27 May 1629. Lewes. John Teynton, gent., Lewes rape coroner. Jurors: John Bayly, Moses Everiste, Thomas Gouldsmyth, William Duffeilde, Thomas Norton, Edward Collman, Joseph Bayly, Richard Blowmer, John Foorde, Richard Burdett, William Stuckle, Simon Michell, Edward Mullett. On 26 May William Read, aged 5 or 6, by misadventure fell into 'a glovers' pitt' at Lewes and was immediately drowned in the water. KB 9/790, m 286.
[Delivered to the Sussex Lent assizes and on to King's Bench in Easter 1630. KB 9/790, m 290d; KB 29/279, m 5.]

304   7 Sept 1629. Rye. John Nowell, gent., Rye mayor and coroner. Jurors: John Nicolson, Richard Henly, Thomas Grove, Thomas Ally, Henry Tully, John Holland, John Feild, Walter Bayly, 'Nathan' Lord, Nicholas Board, John Humersome, William Malpace. 'Uppon the Sabboth day last, beinge the sixth day of this instant August' [*recte* 6 Sept, *which was a Sunday; 6 Aug was a Thursday*], John son of John Hownsell of Rye, 'mason', 'goinge into the sewer against' St Mary's Marshes to wash himself, 'by some mischaunce, as they [*sc.* the jurors] conceive, was drowned'. [*Verdict in English.*] RYE 1/11, f 263.

305   13 Sept 1629. Hastings. William Barker, Hastings mayor and coroner. Jurors: William Goldham, John Harrys, John Hick, Nicholas Foster, Peter Yeilding, George Oliver, Walwin [*Walwinus*] Holland, 'Abel' Shingleton, Thomas Stedman, Thomas Stevenson jun., George Clapham, Robert Marshall. Between 2 and 3 p.m. on 12 Sept, when her father and mother were out, Agnes Wynkfeild, 'spinster', aged about 18, daughter of Thomas Wynkfeild of Hastings, fisherman, climbed the stairs to a bedroom of her father's dwelling-house in St Clement's parish, Hastings, tied a cord, which was attached around a fishing net worth 2s and hanging from 'a lath', round her neck and feloniously hanged herself. She remained hanging there until found dead shortly afterwards by a maidservant and her mother. The jurors requested that this inquest be enrolled of record in the common register of Hastings according to custom. The net accrues to the town as deodand. HASTINGS C/A(a) 2, f 49v. [A marginal note calls the deceased a maidservant.]

306 21 Sept 1629. Mayfield. Thomas Houghton, gent., Loxfield Camden half-hundred coroner. Jurors: John Muddle, Francis Panckhurst, John Parris, Solomon Wenborne, Thomas Flote, John Turnis, William Foster, Timothy Winter, Richard Peacocke, John Gallett, Isaac Langham, John Peake, Thomas Paine, Simon Willmesthurst, Thomas Moone, Thomas Dupelock, Thomas Bathurst. On 28 Apr [*later* 25 Apr] William Duke of Mayfield feloniously threw himself into 'a well' in Katharine Aynscombe's close at Mayfield and was drowned. At that time he had goods, chattels and money which were appraised by the jury and remain with Katharine Aynscombe of Mayfield, widow, viz 'in his purse vij s vj d, item due unto him by Mrs Katherin Aynscombe for one half yeare's wages xl s, item one bible [worth] iiij s, item twoe paire of breeches, one dublett, one jerkyn, one cloath coate and one hatt xx s, item one box, iij handkerchers, one paire of gloves and one dusson of poyntes [*sc.* points: cords or straps] ij s vj d', total £3 14s. [*Inventory in English.*] KB 9/790, mm 287, 288.
[Delivered with **303**. Katharine Aynscombe was summoned to King's Bench to answer for the goods and chattels; she had licence to imparl in Easter 1631 but was waived at Lewes on 4 Sept 1634. Under 28 Apr 1629 the Mayfield parish register records the fact that Duke, servant of John Aynscombe, drowned himself and did not have a Christian burial. KB 9/790, mm 287, 290d; KB 29/279, m 5; KB 29/280, m 37d; *SAC*, IV, 257.]

307 4 Feb 1630. Horsham. John Teynton, gent., Bramber rape coroner. Jurors: John Lea, William Whitinge, Peter Waterton, Henry Waller, Robert Honnywood, William Wilborforce, John Grombridge, Thomas Wheatley, William Coe, Henry Feiste, Edward Gray, Richard Savage, John Holden, Henry Champion. On 3 Feb George Seargent, a prisoner in the county gaol at Horsham, died a natural death there and not otherwise to the jurors' knowledge. KB 9/790, m 276.
[Delivered with **303**. KB 9/790, m 290d; KB 29/279, m 5d.]

308 8 Mar 1630. [Rye.] John Nowell, gent., Rye mayor and coroner. Jurors: Robert Fremlyn, William Malpace, 'Nathan' Lord, Stephen Dad, William Bucke, Richard Smyth, William Shawe, Jeremy Cox, Robert Overington, Edmund Waters, Richard Leiston, John Reames. On 7 Mar, when Jeremy Davye was 'goinge over the ferrie of Rye in a skippe [*sc.* skiff], the said skippe through the race of the floud was forced against a cable lyinge alongst the channell of Rye Ferry above the ferry way'. Davye, abandoning the skiff, took hold of the cable, but the tide was running so fast that it made him release his hold and so he was drowned in the channel. His body was found in Rye Channel by Leasam Farm. [*Verdict in English.*] RYE 1/11, f 287v.

309 25 June 1630. Brighton in Whalesbone hundred. John Teynton, gent., Lewes rape coroner. Jurors: Thomas Kitchener, John Freind, Robert Freind, John Hayne, James Surredge, Nicholas Jacket, John Slutter, Robert Co..., ... Mihill, John Brooker, Ninian Masters, Henry Killicke, Richard Buckold, John Eston, Adam Weller, Thomas Rose, Robert ..., William Brapley. About 10 a.m. on 24 June, when Joan late the wife of William Gillam of Brighton, who had for a long time been weak from old age and had recently been in ill health, went from a house on the market-place in Brighton, by misadventure 'tw[o] browne steares', which were 3 years old and yoked together but which had broken away from the others, ran into the market-place and immediately and violently trampled on Joan's body, giving her 2 'brewses' with their hoofs — one on the right side of the head and the other on the right side of the chest — of which she languished at Brighton until 4 p.m. and then died. Thus the 2 steers were the cause of her death. The jurors appraised them at £6 and the yoke attached to their necks at 18d; the steers and yoke remain with Thomas Sherley of Preston, gent. [*Damaged.*] KB 9/794, m 379.
[Delivered into King's Bench by the coroner in Easter 1631. Joan, called the wife of William Gillam sen. and said to have been killed by 2 oxen, was buried at Brighton on the day of the inquest. Sherley was summoned to King's Bench to answer for the steers and yoke; he was discharged in Easter 1631 because the deputy almoner acknowledged

satisfaction. KB 9/794, mm 379, 380d; KB 29/280, mm 7, 7d; *Par. reg. of Brighton*, 189.]

310   12 July 1630. Hastings. William Barker, Hastings mayor and coroner. Jurors: William Goldham, John Harrys, Michael Lasher, John Hick, Nicholas Foster, John Wynter, Thomas Stevenson, Thomas Mannington, Roger Martyn, John Shaw, Emanuel Browne, Robert Marshall, Robert Hall, Thomas Love. Between 4 and 5 p.m. on 11 July Thomas Stedwell, son of Robert Stedwell late of Hastings, deceased, aged about 9 and the servant of Henry Barham of Hastings, 'miller', went alone into the pond of Barham's water-mill in the parish of the priory of Holy Trinity, Hastings, and while washing himself there was drowned by misadventure within the sight of [*blank*] Stapley, a small boy. The jurors requested that this inquest be enrolled of record in the common register of Hastings according to custom. HASTINGS C/A(a) 2, f 54v.

311   10 Sept 1630. Winchelsea. John Pettit, Winchelsea mayor and coroner, Paul Wymond, jurat, associated with him. Jurors: George Fremblyn, Ralph Copper, Thomas Rockley, Richard Martyn, 'Havemercie' Cryer, Thomas Willerd, William Neve, Barnabas Burden, John Byshop, John Westborne, Matthew Carter, Thomas Perryn, John Wood, Richard Yeilding, William Pelham, Humphrey Peckham, Christopher Hickmott, William Rockley. On 9 Sept, when Richard Andrewes, aged about 16, the servant of Michael Holmewood of Icklesham, 'yeoman', was driving his master's cart loaded with stones from Winchelsea towards Icklesham, suddenly and by misadventure he fell to the ground near Gallows Hill within the liberty of Winchelsea and the cart by its weight and that of the stones crushed his head, broke his chest and neck and mangled his body on the ground, killing him immediately. The cart with 8 oxen, a horse and the stones, worth £5, accrue to the town as deodand. The jurors request that this inquest be entered of record in the common register of the town according to custom. WIN 58, f 12.
[On 11 Sept it was granted by the coroner and Messrs Wymond and Fray, jurats, and Mr Tompson, John Westborne, John Botting, Thomas Willerd and Thomas Rainoldes, freemen, that Holmewood should have his cart and animals on the payment of 6s 8d to John Botting, Winchelsea chamberlain. WIN 58, f 12; WIN 64, p 9.]

312   16 Nov 1630. Horsham. John Teynton, gent., Bramber rape coroner. Jurors: Thomas Wood, John Allen, Henry Waller, Robert Beste, Ralph Hall, Thomas Champion, Nicholas Barbor, Robert Lintott, Richard Savidge, Thomas Clarke, William Wilberforce, Thomas Galpyn, Richard Gatton, Matthew Niblet, Henry Champion, John Champion, Edmund Jupp. On 16 Nov Thomas Squire, who had previously been committed to the county gaol at Horsham by virtue of 'a capias' returnable on the morrow of All Souls at the suit of Juliana Tye, widow, died a natural death there and not otherwise to the jurors' knowledge. KB 9/794, m 227.
[Delivered to the Sussex Lent assizes and on to King's Bench in Easter 1631. Squire was buried at Horsham on 17 Nov 1630. KB 9/794, m 266d; KB 29/280, m 10; SRS, XXI, 402.]

313   7 Dec 1630. Southwick. John Teynton, gent., Bramber rape coroner. Jurors: Stephen Gouldsmith, Richard Pollard, Bartholomew Smyth, John Mockforde, John Wilkins, John Patchinge, John Newington, Thomas Woode, Richard Farncombe, Thomas Hawkins, John Reforde, John Ayres. Between 4 and 5 p.m. on 5 Dec, when William Warwicke was alone in 'a stall' for oxen at Southwick, he feloniously hanged himself with a halter worth 1d which he held in both hands, putting one end round his neck and tying the other round a beam of the stall. At that time he had no goods or chattels, lands or tenements in Sussex to the jurors' knowledge. KB 9/794, m 380.
[Delivered with **309**. KB 9/794, m 380d; KB 29/280, m 7.]

314   13 Dec 1630. Horsham. John Teynton, gent., Bramber rape coroner. Jurors: Edward Slater, Robert Playsted, Alexander Luxford, Thomas Longhurst, Thomas Bonus, Peter Holydaye, Thomas Wheatlye, John Chambers, John Genn, William Wilbearforce, John Ansell, Arthur Foreman, Robert Lyntot, Nicholas Gardener, Thomas Champion. On 12 Dec William Webb, who had previously been

committed to the county gaol at Horsham by John Leedes, kt, JP, on suspicion of felony, died a natural death there and not otherwise to the jurors' knowledge. KB 9/794, m 226.
[Delivered with **312**. Webb was buried at Horsham on 14 Dec. KB 9/794, m 266d; KB 29/280, m 10; SRS, XXI, 402.]

315   5 Jan 1631. Rye. Alan Gribell, deputy of John Nowell, gent., Rye mayor and coroner. Jurors: Walter Baily, Thomas Waters, Richard Willford, John Burditt, Richard Allen, Stephen Dod, Edmund Waters, John Brad, Anthony Brad, John Harry, Nicholas Fowler, William Malpace. On 5 Jan John Bett of Rye, 'fisherman', hanged himself in 'the washe howse' of the house of 'Phillis' Tuggid, widow, in Rye with 'a haire line fastened to a joyce'. The jurors 'cannot finde that he had any goodes, chattels or debtes at the tyme of his death'. [*Verdict in English.*] RYE 1/11, f 316.

316   5 Jan 1631. Horsham. John Teynton, gent., Bramber rape coroner. Jurors: William Chambers, John Hatton, William Browne, John Dungatt, Ralph Hall, John Harman, John Ellis, Thomas Galpyn, Matthew Niblett, John Gyn, Thomas Renolles, James Pellett, Edward Juppe, Edward Brooker, John Chapman. On 5 Jan John Hill late of Ewhurst in Surrey, 'yoman', who had previously been committed to the county gaol at Horsham by virtue of 'a capias ad satisfaciendum' for £40 at the suit of George Otway and of another for £200 at the suit of John Diddlesfold, died a natural death there and not otherwise to the jurors' knowledge. KB 9/794, m 228.
[Delivered with **312**. KB 9/794, m 266d; KB 29/280, m 10.]

317   Same date, place, coroner and jurors (in the same order) as **316**. On 4 Jan Thomas Brookeman, who had previously been committed to the county gaol at Horsham by virtue of 'a latitat' and 'a capias ad satisfaciendum' for £3, both returnable into King's Bench on Tuesday after the morrow of the Purification next, at the suit of Agnes Napper, widow, died a natural death there and not otherwise to the jurors' knowledge. KB 9/794, m 229.
[Delivered with **312**. KB 9/794, m 266d; KB 29/280, m 10.]

318   25 Feb 1631. Horsham. John Teynton, gent., Bramber rape coroner. Jurors: Richard White, John Satcher, Nicholas Barber, John Dalton, Richard Weller, Edward Feilder, Henry Gromebridge, John Holden, Benjamin Meekes, Thomas Cockinge, Ralph Hall, Edmund Jupp, Robert Beste. On 24 Feb John Little, who had previously been committed to the county gaol at Horsham by Thomas Graye, esq., JP, on suspicion of felony, died a natural death there and not otherwise to the jurors' knowledge. KB 9/794, m 225.
[Delivered with **312**. KB 9/794, m 266d; KB 29/280, m 10.]

319   Same date, place and coroner as **318**. Jurors: Richard White, Thomas Cockinge, Benjamin Meekes, Robert Beste, Nicholas Barbor, Henry Grombridge, Edward Jupp, Ralph Hall, John Holden, Edward Feilder, John Sotcher, Richard Weller, Robert Dalton. On 24 Feb William Tylly, who had previously been committed to the county gaol at Horsham by Henry Goringe, esq., JP, on suspicion of felony, died a natural death there and not otherwise to the jurors' knowledge. KB 9/794, m 230.
[Delivered with **312**. KB 9/794, m 266d; KB 29/280, m 10.]

320   26 Apr 1631. Fernhurst in Rotherbridge [*recte* Easebourne] hundred. Richard Williams, gent., Rotherbridge hundred coroner. Jurors: John Osborne, Thomas Collyer, James Osborne, Thomas Glide, Thomas Skidmore, Walter Slade, Richard Saunder, Siward [*Sewardus*] Collyns, John Hoggesflesh, Thomas Feilder, John Yalden jun., John Tribe, John Shotter, John Page, Thomas Chawcroft, John Biggs sen. Between 6 and 7 p.m. on 24 Apr, when Thomas Wheeler late of Fernhurst, 'husbondman', John Cover of Fernhurst, 'husbondman', and various others were playing with a 'footeball' at Fernhurst, Cover, not intending any ill or harm and not having any malice in his mind towards Wheeler or anyone else there, by misadventure and not feloniously 'did throwe downe' Wheeler upon the ground, from which 'throwing downe' Wheeler received a wound on the neck of which he immediately died. At that

time Cover had no goods or chattels, lands or tenements to the jurors' knowledge. ASSI 35/73/7, m 19.
[Delivered to East Grinstead assizes on 18 July.]

321   25 Aug 1631. Hastings. John Dunck, Hastings mayor and coroner. Jurors: Nicholas Staplus, William Goldham, Thomas Stevenson sen., Joseph Moore, Edward Webbe, Emanuel Browne, John Hayte, Thomas Bradway, Peter Grover, Thomas Roberts, Christopher Watts, James Boycatt. Anthony Fisher of [*blank*], 'taylor', aged 28 or thereabouts, died in 'le hay lofte' at the sign of the Star from sickness and weakness. He entered the loft when sick about 3 days earlier, as is supposed, and was found there by chance by Stephen Pylcher of Hastings, 'labourer', as was testified in evidence to the jurors. HASTINGS C/A(a) 2, f 59v.

322   11 Jan 1632. Horsham. John Teynton, gent., coroner of Thomas earl of Arundel and Surrey, earl marshal. Jurors: William Chambers, John Pyke, Edward Jupp, John Lewer, Richard Gatton, Robert Nye, James Pyke, Ralph Hall, William Champyon, Benjamin Meekes, Thomas Bonus, Richard Pillfolde, Stephen Parson. On 10 Jan William Richardson, who had previously been committed to the county gaol at Horsham by Anthony Fowle, esq., JP, on suspicion of felony, died a natural death there and not otherwise to the jurors' knowledge. KB 9/798, m 199.
[Delivered to the Sussex Lent assizes and on to King's Bench in Easter. KB 9/798, m 214d; KB 29/281, m 6d.]

323   27 Feb 1632. Horsham. John Teynton, gent., coroner of Thomas earl of Arundel and Surrey, earl marshal. Jurors: William Whitinge, William Hunte, Edward Juppe, Henry Feiste, Thomas Wheatlye, John Mose, Robert Beste, Robert Lyntott, James Pyke, Richard Garton, Benjamin Meekes, Humphrey Forman, John Satcher. On 26 Feb Francis Day, who had previously been committed to the county gaol at Horsham by Thomas Sackevill, kt, JP, on suspicion of felony, died a natural death there and not otherwise to the jurors' knowledge. KB 9/798, m 198.
[Delivered with **322**. KB 9/798, m 214d; KB 29/281, m 6d.]

324   4 Mar 1632. Hastings. John Dunck, Hastings mayor and coroner. Jurors: William Goldham, John Harrys, John Hick, Thomas Kitchin, Robert White, Robert Phillip, Richard Sargent, Edward Palmer, Peter Yeilding, Thomas Mannington, Owen Freeman, Thomas Byddenden, Thomas Walls jun., Robert Marshall, John Jenkyn. Between 3 and 4 p.m. on 3 Mar, when his wife and children were out, Edward Reignold, fisherman, aged about 33, climbed the stairs to a bedroom of his dwelling-house in St Clement's parish, Hastings, tied 'a towell' with a cord worth 4d, which was hanging on 'a purloin beame' [*sc.* a purlin or main horizontal beam] there, round his neck and feloniously hanged himself. He remained hanging there until found dead shortly afterwards by Katharine Rolfe, his maidservant. At the time of the felony Reignold had goods and chattels worth £18 15s 4d, as appears in an inventory taken by the jurors which remains of record on the file of the present year. The jurors requested that this inquest be enrolled of record in the common register of Hastings according to custom. 4d for the towel accrues to the town as deodand, as do the goods and chattels according to law and custom. HASTINGS C/A(a) 2, f 60v.

325   25 Mar 1633. Withyham. John Spillet, duchy of Lancaster coroner in Pevensey rape pro hac vice. Jurors: Robert Turner, Robert Quoife, Robert Wick[in]g, Joseph Jesop, Richard Barker, John Medherst, Matthew Everest, Thomas Huntly, John Hilles, Robert Lattenden, Richard Burges, John Burges sen. On 16 Mar, when John Ewridge late of 'Harpington' in Kent, 'miller', was alone at Withyham, he feloniously struck himself on the chest with a knife of iron and steel which he held in his right hand, giving himself a wound 1½ inches long, 1 inch wide and 2 inches deep of which he languished at Withyham until 22 Mar and then died. At the time of the felony he had no goods or chattels in Sussex to the jurors' knowledge. KB 9/807, m 101.
[Delivered by the coroner into King's Bench in Trinity 1635. KB 9/807, m 101d; KB 29/284, m 67d.]

326 11 July 1633. Charlton. Eusebius Hayes, coroner of the Sussex liberty of Richard, Viscount Lumley. Jurors of the liberty: John ?Wood..., William Hale, John Love, Edward Beedinge, John Betsworth, Daniel West, William Tregose, John Thomas, Richard Aylwin, Henry Rusbridger, William Leese, Richard West, John Sandham, John Tignoll, Andrew Molland, John Cobden. About 5 p.m. on 9 July, as John Butcher with 'a sticke' of no value which he held in his right hand and Andrew Aylwin of Charlton, 'laborer', with 'a pronge' [*sc.* fork] worth 2d which he held in both hands 'did jeast' amicably together at Charlton and 'did fence' and each 'did thrust' at the other, Aylwin killed Butcher by chance and misadventure, without any evil intent and not otherwise to the jurors' knowledge, giving him a wound in the left eye with one prong of the fork 2½ inches deep of which he immediately died. [*Damaged.*] ASSI 35/75/9, m 1.
[Delivered to East Grinstead assizes on 29 July. A bill for manslaughter was preferred at the following assizes but neither it nor any verdict survives. ASSI 35/75/9, m 1.]

327 23 Aug 1633. Hartfield. Edward Raynes, gent., county coroner. Jurors: Robert Saxbie, John Sampson, John Goaty, Francis Saxbie, Alexander Alchorne, John Wallis, Thomas Bridger, Nicholas Orgles, John Gasson, Richard Farmer jun., William Pulman, Henry Hep. About 1 p.m. on 13 Aug Rachel Burtenshawe of Hartfield, 'spinster', murdered a female bastard child, to which she had recently given birth, at Hartfield with a knife worth 1d which she held in her right hand, striking her on 'the throat', completely cutting it and giving her a wound 1½ inches long, 1 inch wide and 2 inches deep or thereabouts of which she immediately died. At that time Burtenshawe had no goods or chattels, lands or tenements in Sussex to the jurors' knowledge. ASSI 35/76/9, m 45.
[Delivered to East Grinstead assizes on 6 Mar 1634 when the grand jury, to which John Avery gave evidence, presented an indictment substantially the same as the inquest verdict except that it expressly stated that Burtenshawe had given birth at Hartfield on the day of the felony, said that the knife was of iron and steel and omitted the measurements of the wound and the final sentence. Burtenshawe, who had been committed to gaol by the coroner, pleaded not guilty to the indictment but was convicted and hanged; she had no chattels. ASSI 35/76/9, mm 20, 25, 45, 77, 77d.]

328 23 Oct 1633. Ardingly. John Teynton, gent., Lewes rape coroner. Jurors: Thomas Holforde, Thomas Chapman, Richard Br..., John Gibbe, John Wheeler, Richard Weeker, James Warnett, Alexander Bridges, John Weller, Thomas Page, Walter ?Pouney..., George Tasker, Thomas Pelling. About 6 p.m. on 21 Oct William Cooper of Plumpton, 'husbandman', feloniously killed Richard Hayward at Ardingly with 'a stake' worth ¼d which he held in both hands, giving him 'a bruise' on the right side of the head of which he languished at Ardingly until midnight and then died. The jurors believe that Cooper had goods and chattels at the time of the felony but do not know their value. Cooper did not flee. [*Damaged.*] ASSI 35/76/9, m 44.
[Delivered with **327**. At the assizes a bill of indictment was preferred similar to the inquest verdict but charging Cooper with murder and omitting the last 2 sentences. The grand jury, to which John Norton, Anthony Marchant and Elizabeth Hayward gave evidence, reduced the charge to manslaughter. Cooper pleaded not guilty to the indictment as amended and was acquitted; he had not fled. Hayward, 'an ancient man', was buried at Ardingly on the day of the inquest. ASSI 35/76/9, mm 28, 43, 44; SRS, XVII, 151.]

329 5 Nov 1633. Cuckfield. John Teynton, gent., Lewes rape coroner. Jurors: Thomas Vincente, John Burtenshawe, Thomas Burtenshawe, Edward Kinge, Robert Ansty alias Feild, Richard Brisher, William Norman, Edward Streete, Anthony Ellis, Henry Michell, George Dawes, Francis Scrace, George Jenkyn, Richard Tomsett alias Carver, Thomas Tomson. About 5 p.m. on 1 Nov, when Richard Carden was riding across 'Woodleford Bridge Ryver' in Hurstpierpoint towards his master's house in Cuckfield, by misadventure he and the mare on which he was riding fell into the river and he was immediately drowned. The mare and the water of the river were the cause of his death. The jurors appraised the mare, which was 'baye' coloured, at 16s; it remains with Henry Burt of Cuckfield. KB 9/804, m 166.
[Delivered into King's Bench by the coroner in Trinity 1634. Burt was summoned to King's Bench to answer for the mare; he was outlawed at Lewes on 11 June 1635. Carden, called 'John Carding, drowned', was buried at Cuckfield on

the day of the inquest. KB 9/804, mm 166, 166d; KB 29/283, m 52; PAR 301/1/1/1; SRS, XIII, 161.]

330   24 Mar 1634. Rye. Mark Thomas, gent., Rye mayor and coroner. Jurors: Thomas Maxwell, Stephen Mason, John Kemp, George Blaunch, Edward Greenaway, William Kent, John Whithead, Richard Dad, Richard Henly, Henry Walter, John Pedle, William Gates, John Cooper. On the night of 22 Mar, when Thomas Isack and William Frye of Rye, 'ship carpenters', were 'towinge certaine tymber from' Scots Float to Rye 'at a cockes sterne' and were near the Gun Garden Rocks, with the tide 'cominge verie forceably', and were 'labouringe to save a peice of tymber and to hav it to the cock, the tyde and tymber oversett the cock' and Isack and Frye were 'forced to leave the cock to save themselves', but 'by the greate force of the tide both drowned'. The inquest was held on view of both bodies which were found near the Gun Garden Rocks. [*Verdict in English.*] RYE 1/12, f 103v.

331   28 Mar 1634 [*MS* 10 Charles 1]. Rotherfield. John Luck, gent., Rotherfield hundred coroner. Jurors of the hundred and county: John Weston, John Maynard jun., John Elliott, Thomas Maye, John Wood, Nicholas Clarke, Walter Hall, William Coe, Nicholas Marchant, Alan Catt, John Vincent, William Ovenden, Henry Relfe, Thomas Moone. On 26 Mar [*MS* 10 Charles I, *i.e. 1635, in error for* 9 Charles I], when Richard Vinten was cutting 'corde wood' [*sc.* cord-wood, wood for fuel] with 'an axe' at Rotherfield, by misadventure he struck his right foot with the axe, giving himself a wound 2 inches long and ½ inch deep of which he languished at Rotherfield for 4 hours and then died. The axe was the cause of his death; the jurors appraised it at 12d and it remains with Thomas Middlemore of Rotherfield, gent., for the use of Henry, Lord Abergavenny, lord of the hundred, who claims to have all deodands befalling within the liberty. KB 9/806, m 165.
[Delivered with **339** and on to King's Bench in Easter 1635. Middlemore was summoned to King's Bench to answer for the axe; he was outlawed at Chichester on 18 Feb 1636. KB 9/806, mm 165, 181d; KB 29/284, mm 8d, 9.]

332   1 Apr 1634. Rotherfield. John Luck, gent., Rotherfield hundred coroner. Jurors of the hundred and county: Arthur Maynard, Thomas Markewicke, Thomas Bennett, William Burgis, Herbert Farmer, Edmund Homesbye, William Coe, John Latter, John Maynard jun., William Ovenden, Nicholas Allchorne, John Ashdowne, Thomas Picke, Edward Crowhurst, John Ellis, Richard Petter, John Gyles. On 1 Apr William Turnor jun. died a natural death at Rotherfield. KB 9/806, m 154.
[Delivered with **331**. KB 9/806, m 181d; KB 29/284, m 9.]

333   17 May 1634. Wivelsfield. John Teynton, gent., Lewes rape coroner. Jurors: Nicholas Challoner, gent., Walter Lucas, gent., John Sawyer, John Godley, John Pilbeame, John Woode, William Perkins, Richard Dumbrell, Anthony Alexander, Philip Jenner, Edward Crawley, John Auforde, John Warden, James Warnett, Richard Barham, Alexander Bridges, Richard Cripps, George Poulter, Richard Potter. On 8 May Francis Tompsett late of Wivelsfield died a natural death at Wivelsfield and not otherwise to the jurors' knowledge. KB 9/804, m 165.
[Delivered with **329**. KB 9/804, m 166d; KB 29/283, m 52.]

334   24 June 1634. Hurstpierpoint. John Teynton, gent., Lewes rape coroner. Jurors: John Chatfeild, Thomas Howcombe, Henry Matthew, William Jorden, Thomas Matthew, Bartholomew Dymond, William Bowell, Richard Braker, Robert Swale, Thomas Blackstone, Thomas Fakener, Thomas Brasier, Henry Hansdall. Between 1 and 2 p.m. on 23 June, when Ninian Norton and 2 of his neighbours intended to wash themselves in a pond in a small oak-grove [*roborarium*] in Hurstpierpoint, by misadventure he was suddenly drowned in the pond. KB 9/806, m 310.
[Delivered by the coroner into King's Bench in Easter 1635. KB 9/806, m 312d; KB 29/284, m 4d.]

335   11 Aug 1634. Berwick. Edward Raynes, gent., duchy of Lancaster coroner in Pevensey rape. Jurors: Nicholas Dobson, William Walker, John Cane, John Jefferay, Thomas Ranger, William Earle, John Renne, William Morris, Thomas Brooke, William Teelinge, Robert Dobson, Thomas Harwood.

On 5 Aug, when John Pike late of Berwick, 'laborer', was riding in a wagon [*auriga*] loaded with tree-trunks and wood and drawn by 4 oxen at Laughton, by misadventure the wagon was suddenly overturned whereby the trunks and wood fell on Pike's nose and face, giving him a wound 2 inches long and wide but of very little depth of which he languished at Berwick until 9 Aug and then died. The wagon with its wheels, the trunks and wood and the oxen all moved to the death; they are worth £13 6s 8d and are now with David Foster of Berwick, 'yeoman'. KB 9/806, m 80.

[Delivered by the coroner into King's Bench in Easter 1635. Foster was summoned to King's Bench to answer for the deodands; he was discharged in Trinity 1636 when the High Almoner acknowledged satisfaction. The coroner was also summoned to King's Bench to answer for defects in the inquest; he was discharged in Trinity 1635 because the inquest was amended, although the only sign of amendment is the interlineation of 'of Berwick, yeoman', which appears to have been made not much later than the writing of the inquest. The same words are interlined in the Controlment Roll. KB 9/806, mm 80, 80d; KB 29/284, m 19.]

336 15 Aug 1634. East Ashling. John Edsawe, chamberlain and coroner of the manor and hundred of Bosham. Jurors: Thomas Bridger, William Kember, Thomas Langrish, gent., Edward Scardvile, Thomas Combes, Adam Dallington, Henry Colden, Robert Chaper, Richard Churcher, Richard Bonny, Bartholomew Tyll, Michael Gray, Bartholomew Baylie, William Mersher, Ralph Collins, Richard Harding, William Pocock, Robert Fisher, Aaron Gosden, Thomas Clemens, John White. About 10 a.m. on 14 Aug, when John Jonas alias Chestle and William Bennett were working in 'a marllpitt' on 'the comon heath' at East Ashling, digging 'marll stones', by misadventure about 'fourscore loades' of 'le upper earth or greete' of the pit worth 2d, which was hanging over them, suddenly 'did fall' on them and crushed their bodies of which they immediately died. No one else was privy to either death. The inquest was held on view of both bodies. KB 9/805, m 277.

[Delivered by the coroner into King's Bench in Hilary 1635. KB 9/805, m 277d; KB 29/283, m 135.]

337 26 Aug 1634. Frant. John Lucke, gent., Rotherfield hundred coroner. Jurors of the hundred and county: John Lockyer, Robert Tendalle, gent., John Tree, Walter Cheeseman, Richard Petter, William Maye, Edward Crowhurst, Thomas Tharpe, Alexander Pocock, John Gasson, Richard Cheeseman, Stephen Baker, John Stapely, John Russell, William Chowne, William Allen, Peter Crowhurst. On 20 Aug, when John Gyles, 'shomaker', and Abraham Hosmer, 'husbondman', both of Frant, were riding on the road at Frant and their geldings were running quickly, suddenly and without their knowledge Nicholas Reade came into the road and the 'graye' gelding on which Gyles was riding by misadventure and against his will struck Reade and threw him to the ground, crushing his chest and abdomen of which he languished at Frant until 22 Aug and then died. The grey gelding was the cause of his death; the jurors appraised it at 50s and it remains with Thomas Middlemore of Rotherfield, gent., for the use of Henry, Lord Abergavenny, lord of the hundred, who claims to have all deodands befalling within the liberty. KB 9/806, m 166.

[Delivered with **331**. Middlemore was summoned to King's Bench to answer for the gelding; he was outlawed at Chichester on 18 Feb 1636. KB 9/806, mm 166, 181d; KB 29/284, m 8d.]

338 22 Sept 1634. Steyning. John Teynton, gent., Bramber rape coroner. Jurors: William Smith, James Turner, John Gromes, Thomas Cowlstocke, Benjamin Nework, William Pellett jun., Philip Bennett, John Foster, William Pellett sen., Richard Longmer, William Longmer, William Parke, John Hamans, John Kester, Thomas Wood, William Wilson, John Bawcombe. About 7 p.m. on 20 Sept John Blackman mounted his horse at Steyning and rode towards Lancing where he lived. About 8 p.m. he was found lying on the ground on the road towards Lancing before he had ridden 'two furlonges' from Steyning. He lay there until 3 a.m. on 21 Sept and then was carried from the road to the house of Thomas Bawcumbe of Steyning where he died within an hour. The jurors therefore returned that he fell from the horse, which fall and his lying on the ground for 6 or 7 hours and wine were the causes of his death. They appraised the horse at 26s 8d in case it should happen to be forfeit to the king or to Thomas earl of Arundel and Surrey, earl marshal, lord of the liberty; it remains with Margaret Blackman of Lancing, widow. KB 9/806, m 311.

[Delivered with **334**. Margaret Blackman was summoned to King's Bench to answer for the horse which was said to be worth 36s 8d; she was waived at Chichester on 18 Feb 1636. KB 9/806, mm 311, 312d; KB 29/284, m 4d.]

339   21 Oct 1634. Buxted. Edward Raynes, gent., county coroner. Jurors: Nicholas Whitehead, John Payne, Thomas Collyns, Thomas Burtenshawe, Edward Glosseter, Richard Sampson, James Gasson, John Dicker, Thomas Wickershawe, John Kennard, John Alchorne, John Pettitt. On 11 Aug, when Richard Page late of Buxted, 'husbandman', was standing near 'Howborne Pond' in Buxted, holding 'a fowlinge peece charged with powder and hayleshott' in both hands, he suddenly saw some 'wild duckes' near and on the banks of the pond and 'did discharge' the gun in the direction of the ducks intending to kill them. It so happened that William Blackamore late of Buxted, 'laborer', was then lying asleep on 'the hassockes' which were growing near the bank and near the place where Page saw the ducks. Not knowing that Blackamore was there, Page suddenly and by misadventure 'did hitt' him with the lead shot discharged from the gun at the ducks, giving him several wounds in and on the left shoulder, left arm and left side ½ inch deep of which he languished at Buxted until 16 Oct and then died. Thus Page killed him by misadventure, against his will and not feloniously or from malice prepense. ASSI 35/77/6, m 6.
[Delivered to East Grinstead assizes on 2 Mar 1635. The assize judges returned a copy of the inquest into Chancery on a writ of ?9 June, for the granting of a pardon, the writ stating that Page had been remanded in gaol. C 260/185, nos 1–2.]

340   24 Oct 1634. Jevington. Edward Raynes, gent., duchy of Lancaster coroner in Pevensey rape. Jurors: William Lewes, William Cradle, William Wood sen., William Wood jun., John Howell sen., John Howell jun., John Earle sen., John Earle jun., James Store, John Cooper, Thomas Sherwin, George Eridge. On 15 Oct, when Nicholas Wheateley late of Hellingly, 'husbandman', was going as the servant of Lawrence Ashborneham of Jevington, esq., and by his orders with Ashborneham's cart from Jevington to Hailsham by the road linking those two places, by misadventure he suddenly fell to the ground at Jevington and one of the wheels of the cart ran over his neck, so crushing it that he immediately died. The cart with its 2 wheels moved to his death; they are worth 40s and are now with Ashborneham. KB 9/806, m 79.
[Delivered with **335**. Ashborneham was summoned to King's Bench to answer for the cart and wheels; he was discharged in Easter 1636 because the deputy almoner acknowledged satisfaction. The coroner was also summoned to King's Bench to answer for defects in the inquest; he was discharged in Trinity 1635 because the inquest was amended, although the only sign of amendment is the interlineation of 'of Jevington' which appears to have been made not much later than the writing of the inquest. The same words are interlined in the Controlment Roll. KB 9/806, mm 79, 80d; KB 29/284, m 19.]

341   19 Dec 1634. Cliffe. Edward Raynes, gent., county coroner. Jurors: Richard Meade, Joseph West, Robert Hanson, Thomas Parson, John Cheale, 'Curteous' Goodwin, Nicholas Hall, John Page, 'Foster' Whitebread, John Beldam, Richard Prior, William Waters. Witnesses: Joan Pemell, Joan Gates. On 15 Dec Joan Alce alias Willis late of Cliffe, 'spinster', gave birth to a live male bastard child at Cliffe and later on the same day murdered him, strangling him with both hands whereby he immediately died. At that time she had no goods or chattels, lands or tenements in Sussex to the jurors' knowledge. ASSI 35/77/6, mm 7, 7d.
[Delivered with **339**. At the assizes the grand jury, to which the same 2 witnesses gave evidence, presented an indictment identical to the inquest verdict but without the last sentence. Alce, who had been committed to gaol by the coroner, pleaded not guilty to the indictment but was convicted and hanged; she had no chattels. ASSI 35/77/6, mm 7, 25, 30, 58, 58d.]

342   20 Dec 1634. Brede. Nathaniel Powell, gent., Brede hundred coroner. Jurors of the hundred: Simon Coleman, Richard Borne, Thomas Snepp, John Merriall, Henry Baker, Giles Burton, Thomas Chrisford, Nicholas Guise, Henry Thatcher, Stephen Sampson, Adrian Soane, Stephen Mott, John Chittenham, Joseph Mitten, Richard Lennard, Peter Rushell. On 23 May John Barden late of Brede, 'laborer', murdered Henry Garrett late of Brede, 'laborer', at Brede with 'an iron hammer' worth 12d which he held in his right hand, giving him a wound on the back of the head and breaking 'the scull' of which he immediately died. At that time Barden had no goods or chattels, lands or tenements to the jurors' knowledge. He immediately fled to places unknown. ASSI 35/77/6, m 8.

[Delivered with **339**. At the assizes an indictment was preferred which charged Barden with murder in similar terms to those of the inquest verdict except that it stated that the blow completely broke Garrett's skull and that the wound was 5 inches wide and in depth to the brain and omitted the last 2 sentences; and charged Francis Leonard late of Brede, labourer, with feloniously receiving, harbouring and supporting Barden at Brede on 25 Dec, and Joan Barden late of Etchingham, spinster, with the same at Etchingham on 26 Dec, both knowing that he had committed the murder. The grand jury, to which Richard Leonard, William ?Bonnyface, Thomas Rolfe, Richard Word, (*blank*) Jarrett, widow, and Anthony Dowse gave evidence, affirmed the charge against John Barden but rejected those against the other 2. John Barden, who had been committed to gaol by John Leedes, kt, JP, pleaded not guilty to the indictment but was convicted and hanged; he had no chattels. Joan Barden, who had been committed by Robert Foster, esq., JP, for 'releeving' John Barden, and Leonard, who had been committed by Sir Thomas Sackvill, JP, on suspicion of murder, were delivered from gaol by proclamation. ASSI 35/77/6, mm 8, 24, 30, 58, 58d.]

343   23 Apr 1635. Ifield. John Teynton, gent., Bramber rape coroner. Jurors: John Thorpe, gent., Edward Saridge, Thomas Patchinge, Robert Tylt, Thomas Tugwell, Lawrence Norton, Thomas Olyve, George Bonnick, William Symons, Robert Hamson, William Walker, William Blake, Hugh Nash, Pardon [*Pardonus*] Tillinghurst, Barnabas Browne. On 22 Apr, when George Parker late of Southwark, London, butcher, was riding on the road between Ifield and Horsham, by misadventure the horse staggered and Parker fell to the ground whereby he immediately died and not otherwise to the jurors' knowledge. The jurors appraised the horse, which is 'redd roane' in colour, with its attachments at 40s; it remains with Benjamin Browne, vicar of Ifield. KB 9/806, m 312.

[Delivered with **334**. The vicar was summoned to King's Bench to answer for the horse and attachments; he was outlawed at Chichester on 18 Feb 1636. KB 9/806, mm 312, 312d; KB 29/284, m 4d.]

344   21 May 1635. Waldron. Edward Raynes, gent., county coroner. Jurors: John Chilley, John Tyherst, James Roodes, Richard Osborne, Thomas Roodes, John Bexley, Richard Maynard, John Durrant, Thomas Heathfeild, Thomas Morris, Richard Wood, Nathaniel [*Nathan*'] Taylor, John Longly. On 28 Oct 1634 Robert Appes of Framfield, 'husbandman', murdered Constance Swane late of Framfield, 'spinster', in 'Tilsmere Wood' in Waldron, taking and gripping her by the neck and throat with both hands and strangling her whereby she immediately died. At that time he had no goods or chattels, lands or tenements in Sussex to the jurors' knowledge. ASSI 35/77/7, m 3.

[Delivered to East Grinstead assizes on 6 July 1635 when the grand jury presented an indictment identical to the inquest verdict except that it omitted the last sentence. Appes, who had been committed to gaol by the coroner, pleaded not guilty to the indictment but was convicted and hanged; he had no chattels. ASSI 35/77/7, mm 3, 9, 12, 37.]

345   20 July 1635. Brighton. Edward Raynes, gent., county coroner. Jurors: John Freind, Robert Freind, Thomas Harfcy, Edward Freind, John Gardiner, 'Jacob' Serridge, Richard Moore, Peter Bookes, Roger Carver, Benjamin Browne, John Worger, William Feilder, Robert Bradfold. On 19 July Thomas Bellingham of Southover, esq., murdered John Harris late of Steyning, 'habadasher', at Brighton with a sword of iron and steel worth 6s 8d which he held in his right hand, giving him a wound on the left side of the body a little below the ribs 1 inch long, ½ inch wide and 5 inches deep of which he immediately died. Bellingham immediately fled to Aldrington near Brighton. At that time he had no goods or chattels, lands or tenements in Sussex to the jurors' knowledge. ASSI 35/78/8, m 18.

[Delivered to East Grinstead assizes on 29 Feb 1636. Bellingham, who had been committed to gaol by the coroner, pleaded not guilty and was acquitted of murder but convicted of manslaughter at common law and not by statute; he had no chattels. He then successfully claimed benefit of clergy and was branded and released. Harris was buried at Brighton on the day of the inquest. ASSI 35/78/8, mm 18, 19, 52, 52d; KB 29/285, m 25; *Par. reg. of Brighton*, 193.]

346   3 Nov 1635. Rotherfield. John Luck, gent., Rotherfield hundred coroner. Jurors of the hundred and county: John Maynard jun., Robert Tyndale, gent., Stephen Baker, Alexander Pocock, Thomas Sharpe, Thomas Maye, Thomas Bennett, Nicholas Marchant, Thomas Moone, Thomas Snatt, Edward Hider, Simon Vincent, Arthur Maynard, John Latter, John Wood jun., John Stapely, William Ovenden jun. On 29 Oct Richard Carden late of Rotherfield, 'husbondman', murdered Elizabeth Cheeseman late of Rotherfield, 'spinster', at Rotherfield with a knife of iron and steel worth 1d which he held in his right hand, giving her a wound on the right side of the throat ½ inch wide and 3 inches deep of which she immediately died. At that time Carden had no lands or tenements to the jurors' knowledge, but he had 15s in money which remains with John Mayfeild of Rotherfield, 'yeom[an]', for the use of Henry, Lord Abergavenny, lord of the liberty, who claims to have the goods of felons within the liberty. ASSI 35/78/8, m 24.
[Delivered with **345**. At the assizes the grand jury, to which John and Thomas Maynard, Ann Ashby and Elizabeth Clarke gave evidence, presented an indictment identical to the inquest verdict but without the last sentence. Carden, who had been committed to gaol by the coroner, pleaded not guilty to the indictment but was convicted and hanged; he had no chattels. ASSI 35/78/8, mm 11, 17, 24, 52, 52d.]

347   21 Jan 1636. Rye. Mark Thomas, gent., deputy of Richard Mills, Rye mayor and coroner. Jurors: John Rason jun., William Dallett, John Cooper sen., Thomas Phipps, Richard Wilford, Thomas Grove, William Kent, Thomas Haffenden, Stephen Bruffe, James Newton, Thomas Waters, Henry Edwardes. On 20 Jan Christopher Jennison, servant of Thomas Oke of Rye, fisherman, went from Oke's 'hoigh' [*sc.* hoy, a small vessel] 'unto Nicholas ?Shriner's barke which lay neere togither, where he staid about a quarter of an howre'. Returning, to go back into the hoy about 8 p.m. when it was very dark, he 'step short, as wee conceive, of the said hoighe', fell into the water and was drowned. His body was found in the Puddle against Watchbell Cliff. [*Verdict in English.*] RYE 1/12, f 174.

348   Monday, ... Feb 1636. South Harting. [John E]agle, gent., county coroner. Jurors: John Pytt, Edward Drewe, John Jenman, Robert Sherrier, Thomas Pytt, Richard Silver, Richard Stent, William Smyth, ... Adams, William Smyth jun., Anthony White, Roger Hall, William Trigges, John Wakeforde, John Stoner, Roger Baker, ..., Anthony Colpes. On 1 Feb Elizabeth wife of Henry Sparshall late of South Harting, 'labo[rer]', gave birth to a live male child at West Harting in South Harting and later on the same day murdered him at West Harting, [taking] him in both hands and secretly and [viol]ently throwing him into a well and drowning him, whereby he immediately died. She immediately fled to places unknown to the jurors. She had [no] goods or chattels, lands or tenements at that time or ever [after] to the jurors' knowledge. [*Damaged.*] ASSI 35/78/8, m 23.
[Delivered with **345**. At the East Grinstead assizes of 18 July the grand jury, to which John Irish gave evidence, presented an indictment identical to the inquest verdict except that it called the accused Elizabeth Sparshall late of South Harting, spinster, alias Elizabeth wife of Henry Sparshall of South Harting, labourer, and omitted the last 2 sentences. Sparshall, who had been sent to the Sussex county gaol from the Hampshire county gaol between the assizes of 29 Feb and 18 July, pleaded not guilty to the indictment and was acquitted; she had not fled and was released. ASSI 35/78/8, m 23; ASSI 35/78/9, mm 19, 20, 41, 41d.]

349   30 May 1636. Winchelsea. George Sampson, Winchelsea mayor and coroner. Jurors: John Millward, Thomas Perin, John Sha, John Byshop, Peter Harmer, Richard Philpot, William Brodman, John Ashdowne, Edward Harnett, Thomas Budgin, Edward Dier, John Savage. On 28 May, when George Pynner, 'sailer', servant of John Holden, master of a 'hoy' called 'The Fisherman' of London which was loaded at Winchelsea with timber for the repair of the port of Dover and was leaving Winchelsea for the sea, was hurrying from the Strand of Winchelsea by way of the nearby salt-marshes towards the hoy in order to board her and cross with his colleagues to Dover, before he could reach the hoy he tried to cross a wide and deep ditch containing salt water near Camber castle within the jurisdiction of Winchelsea but could not jump over it, as it seems, and, falling in the salt water in the ditch, was drowned by misadventure. The jurors requested that this inquest be entered in the common register of the town according to custom. WIN 58, f 35v.

350 15 Sept 1636. Worth. Francis Comber, gent., Lewes rape coroner. Jurors: Benet Marten, Abraham Edwards, John Ellphick, John Nicholas, Nicholas Brooker, John Whitston, John Butcher, James Salter, Thomas Tudham, John Younge, John Wood, John Feild, Andrew Venner. About 9 a.m. on 14 Aug, when John Whitfeild of Worth, esq., aged 54, his son Robert and daughters Ann, Elizabeth and Mary were going together from his dwelling-house in Worth to Worth parish church to hear divine service and were sitting in 'a coach' drawn by 4 horses which were attached to it, all belonging to John Whitfeild, in the road, 'the coachman' got down from the coach and, before he could climb back onto it or restrain the horses, the horses suddenly and unprovoked by the coachman ran towards the church with the coach. John Whitfeild, fearing that the coach 'would be overthrowne', ordered Robert to open 'the boote' of the coach in order that all five of them might get out. Robert opened the boot and he and the three daughters jumped out of the coach, landing safely on their feet. John also jumped out, but, being broken with age and sick, could not land on his feet when he reached the ground. Instead, through the force of 'his leapinge' from the coach, by misadventure he 'fell' with the whole of his body upon the ground, whereby his body was crushed and afterwards he vomited blood, of which crushing he languished at Worth until 18 Aug and then died. The coach was not then or ever after overturned and no part of it or of any of it wheels and none of the horses struck, touched or crushed any part of John Whitfeild's body or any of his limbs at the time of his leaping from the coach. ASSI 35/79/9, m 2.
[Delivered to Horsham assizes on 17 July 1637.]

351 7 Oct 1636. Framfield. Edward Raynes, gent., county coroner. Jurors: John Delve, Thomas Wickersham, Samuel Watson, William Smith, Edward Isted, Zacchaeus Skinner, Robert Drowst, John Tiler, Henry Hesman, John Weller, Lawrence Weston, John Awcocke. About 11 a.m. on 6 Oct, when John Smith late of Framfield, 'yeoman', was 'going to take up water' out of 'a marle pitt' on the common or waste land called 'Framfeild Common' near his house in Framfield, he suddenly fell into the pit, which was full of water, and was drowned by misadventure and not otherwise to the jurors' knowledge. KB 9/809, m 122.
[Delivered by the coroner into King's Bench in Trinity 1637. KB 9/809, m 122d; KB 29/286, m 74.]

352 26 Oct 1636. Uckfield. Same coroner and jurors (in the same order) as **351**. About 10 a.m. on 22 Oct, when George White late of Arlington, 'laborer', was felling an oak which was growing on the land of John earl of Thanet in his manor and farm of Claverham in Arlington, now in the tenure of William Reade of Arlington, 'yeoman', with 'an axe' which he held in both hands, by misadventure the oak suddenly fell on 'the breast and stomacke' of White, crushing and wounding them whereof he immediately died. The oak is worth 6s 8d and remains on the earl's lands in his manor or farm of Claverham in the keeping of William Reade. KB 9/809, m 128.
[Delivered by the coroner into King's Bench in Trinity 1637, a week earlier than **351**. Reade was summoned to King's Bench to answer for the oak; he was discharged in Hilary 1638 when the deputy almoner acknowledged satisfaction. KB 9/809, mm 128, 128d; KB 29/286, m 74.]

353 21 Dec 1636. Lindfield. Francis Comber, gent., Lewes rape coroner. Jurors: Richard Crips, Richard Fayrehall, John Newneham, George Poulter, Ninian Cresie, Thomas Basset, John Geale, Walter Dennet, William Simons, James Streater, John Fayrehall, Thomas Joy, Richard Delve, Alexander Bridges, Thomas Cheeseman, Henry Hurst. About 8 p.m. on 17 Dec Jane Evans of Lindfield, 'spinster', murdered an illegitimate female child, to which she had given birth, at Lindfield with 'a knife' worth 1d which she held in her right hand, giving her a wound on the neck 1½ inches long and 1 inch deep and completely cutting through 'the bone of the neck of the said child', of which she immediately died. At that time Evans had no goods or chattels, lands or tenements in Sussex to the jurors' knowledge. ASSI 35/79/8, m 36.
[Delivered to East Grinstead assizes on 27 Feb 1637 when the grand jury, to which Elizabeth Wynn, widow, gave evidence, presented an indictment similar to the inquest verdict except that it expressly stated that Evans had given

birth to the child at Lindfield earlier on the day of the murder and that the blow was on the back of the neck and it omitted the cutting through of the bone and the last sentence. Evans, who had been committed to gaol by Sir Richard Michelborne, JP, pleaded not guilty to the indictment but was convicted and hanged; she had no chattels. ASSI 35/79/8, mm 29, 32, 36, 59, 59d.]

354   [*Undated.*] Frant. John Luck, gent., Rotherfield hundred coroner. Jurors of the hundred and county: Richard Tailor, John Russell, Thomas Tarpe, Walter Coppinge, Thomas Maye, Richard Gambold, Walter Hale, John Lockier, Thomas Pike, John Hilder, Nicholas Fillnes, Simon Vincent, Arthur Maynard, Edmund Homesby, Edward Russell, 'Abedindus' Breach, William Maye, Andrew Skynner. On 7 Dec 1636 Mary Crowhurst late of Frant, 'spinster', alias Mary wife of Edward Crowhurst late of Frant, 'yeoman', murdered Ann Walcott late of Frant, 'spinster', at Frant with a small wooden staff of no value which she held in her right hand, giving her several 'bruses' on the right arm, right buttock, back and chest of which she languished at Frant until 17 Jan 1637 and then died. At the time of the felony Crowhurst had no goods or chattels, lands or tenements to the jurors' knowledge. ASSI 35/79/8, m 33.
[Delivered with **353**. At the assizes the grand jury, to which William Wallcott, John and Mary Lellam and Elizabeth Taylor gave evidence, presented an indictment identical to the inquest verdict but without the last sentence. Crowhurst, who had been committed to gaol by Thomas Butcher, Hastings rape coroner, for killing her maidservant, pleaded not guilty to the indictment and was acquitted; she had not fled and was released. ASSI 35/79/8, mm 22, 23, 33, 59, 59d.]

355   20 Feb 1637. Lewes. Francis Comber, gent., Lewes rape coroner. Jurors: Anthony Beecher, Henry Snelling, William Newton, Joseph Picknoll, John Greene, Robert Bodle, John Henly, Henry ?Samond, Edward Hemsley, William Stuckle, Thomas Burkin, Henry Townsend, John Harris, Thomas Beale, Edmund Taylor. About noon on 11 Feb Mary wife of William Jones of Lewes, 'laborer', murdered William Ginner, 'laborer', at Lewes by giving him 'a buttered-poysoned loafe of bread readie to be eaten'. Eating it, he immediately became ill and languished until 17 Feb when he died at Lewes from the poisoning. [*Damaged.*] ASSI 35/79/8, m 35.
[Delivered with **353**. At the assizes the grand jury, to which Roger Godman, Thomas Fisenden, George Mathewe, Dorothy and Constance Gynner, Dorothy Wellfarre and probably William Jones gave evidence, presented an indictment similar to the inquest verdict but more detailed: it called Jones 'Mary Jones late of St Michael's parish, Lewes, spinster, alias Mary wife of William Jones of St Michael's, labourer', emphasised that she plotted to poison and murder Ginner, said that she took some arsenic, a strong poison, in her right hand, mixed it with butter, put the mixture in a loaf and gave it to Ginner to eat in St Michael's parish and that he took it and ate it, believing it to be wholesome, and languished in St Michael's parish where he died. Jones, who had been committed to gaol by the coroner, pleaded not guilty to the indictment and was acquitted; she had not fled but was required to find 'subsidy men' as sureties for her appearance at the next assizes and was remanded in gaol. She was still in gaol at the Horsham assizes of 17 July when she had not found such sureties. ASSI 35/79/8, mm 30, 32, 35, 59, 59d; ASSI 35/79/9, m 44.]

356   20 Feb 1637. Wadhurst. Thomas Bucher, gent., Hastings rape coroner. Jurors of the rape and county: Nicholas Manser sen., David Barham, John Barham, William Cruttall, Isaac Langham, Nicholas Manser jun., John Kitchenham jun., Edward Jenner, John Sharpe, Nicholas Enfield, John Avery, Richard Farrington, Thomas Foster, Thomas Hickes, Henry Goldsmyth, Edward Morfee, John Goodman, Goddard Foster. On 30 Jan John Merryweather late of Wadhurst, 'laborer', murdered his mother, Alice wife of Nicholas Merryweather of Wadhurst, 'husbond[man]', at Wadhurst, taking her in both hands, throwing her into a stream and holding her mouth and face under the water with both hands whereby she was drowned, dying immediately. At that time he had 'an ewe sheepe' worth 7s and also, in co-ownership with William Merryweather, his brother, 9 sheep worth £1 2s 6d which remain with the coroner. He had no other goods or chattels, lands or tenements at that time or ever after to the jurors' knowledge. ASSI 35/79/8, m 34.
[Delivered with **353**. At the assizes the grand jury, to which Nicholas Merryweather jun., Elizabeth Merryweather, Emblena Winder, widow, and Alice Jarrett gave evidence, presented an indictment identical to the inquest verdict but without the last 2 sentences. John Merryweather, who had been committed to gaol by Anthony Apsley, esq., JP, and the coroner after confessing to the murder on examination, pleaded not guilty to the indictment and was acquitted;

he had not fled and was released. ASSI 35/79/8, mm 28, 32, 34, 59, 59d.]

357   7 Apr 1637. Maresfield. Edward Raynes, gent., county coroner. Jurors: William Smith, John Mowsherst, Nicholas Jeames, John Humfry, John Awcocke, John Foord, Edward Nicholas, Richard Norman, William Crouchester, William Russell jun., Henry Knell, John Page. Witnesses: William Soane, Joan Stocker, Elizabeth Pynion, Adrian Messance. On 13 Feb John Duffeild of Hartfield, 'laborer', feloniously killed Elizabeth Martin late of Maresfield, 'spinster', at Cansiron in Hartfield with a staff worth ¼d which he held in his right hand, giving her several wounds on 'the armes and back' of which she languished at Maresfield until 20 Mar and then died. After committing the felony Duffeild fled. At that time he had no goods or chattels, lands or tenements to the jurors' knowledge. ASSI 35/79/9, mm 1, 1d.
[Delivered with **350**. At the assizes the grand jury, to which the same 4 witnesses gave evidence, presented an indictment identical to the inquest verdict except that the charge was murder and the last 2 sentences were omitted. Duffeild, who had been brought to the Sussex county gaol from the Surrey county gaol, pleaded not guilty to the indictment and was acquitted; he had not fled and was released. ASSI 35/79/9, mm 1, 8, 15, 44.]

358   3 July 1637. Rye. Mark Thomas, gent., deputy of Richard Cockram, gent., Rye mayor and coroner. Jurors: Nicholas Bowyer, William Starkey, Stephen Carpinter, William Gates, Thomas Haffenden, John Feild, Mark Woodford, James Newton, John Diginson, Richard Allen, John Porter, William Wooton. Joan wife of Thomas Danyell of Rye, 'butcher', 'was a deseased woman' and 'she brought her water on Holie Thursday last [*sc.* 6 Apr] to John Kevill to have his advise concerninge her desease, who cast her water and told her his opinion'. On the same day she went to the New Conduit and was hanging her clothes on the cock of the conduit when Thomas Pecock, chamberlain, came and took the clothes and threw them into a ditch there. Then he took hold of one side of her pail and she of the other side and 'the bale [*sc.* bail, hoop-handle] of her payle slipt and she fell to the ground, which did her some hurt; but wee cannot finde it any cause of her death. But lyinge long sick of the dropsey, on Satterday last [*sc.* 1 July] in the night she died, which was the dropsy as two phisicians of our towne who did see her in the tyme of her sicknes and after her death testified uppon theire othes'. [*Verdict in English.*] RYE 1/12, f 229.

359   23 Aug [1637]. Fernhurst. ..., Easebourne hundred [coroner]. Jurors of the hundred and county: ..., John Challen, Nicholas Kempe, Thomas Aylewyn, John Carter, Richard Carter, William Redman, Ralph Cootes, Thomas Skidmore, Th..., Richard Luffe, John Collins, John Ede, John Skidmore, John Coops. On 20 Aug Phyllis Wallis late of Easebourne, ['spinster', alias Phyllis] wife of Henry Wallis late of Easebourne, 'husbondman', [feloniously killed] Joan Floyde of Fernhurst, widow, [at Fernhurst, kicking] her with both feet on the lower part of the abdomen [and giving her a wound of which] she languished [at Fernhurst until the next day and then died]. ... [*Damaged.*] ASSI 35/80/8, m 5.
[Delivered to Horsham assizes on 26 Feb 1638 when the grand jury, to which William Lan..., Elizabeth ... and Robert S... gave evidence, presented an indictment identical to the inquest verdict. Wallis, who had been committed to gaol by Walter Bartlett, esq., JP, pleaded not guilty to the indictment but was convicted and hanged; she had no chattels. ASSI 35/80/8, mm 5, 18, 22, 54.]

360   [*Date missing.*] Arundel. Richard Williams, gent., [Arundel liberty] coroner. Jurors of the liberty and county: ?..., John Pellett, Thomas Coles, 'Jerman' Hills, Benjamin Pennycodd, John Smyth, John ..., John ?More, Anthony Yalton, Francis Older, William Turner, Robert Wilson, Thomas Emery, Matthew Herryng, Henry Wolridge, Robert Pellatt, Henry Stoner. On ... Aug 1637 John Sawnders of Arundel, 'blacksmyth', feloniously killed his wife Joan with 'a woodden shovell' worth 1d ... she languished ... at Arundel ... At the time of the felony he had no goods or chattels, [lands or] tenements to the jurors' knowledge. [*Damaged.*] ASSI 35/80/8, m 1.
[Delivered with **359**. At the time of assizes Sawnders was at large. ASSI 35/80/8, m 1.]

361   [*Date missing.*]   Horsted Keynes.   ...   Jurors: ... Killingbecke, John Turner, John Wood, Thomas Durkin, David Lucas, Thomas ... Lacy, Henry Pellinge, John Cheesman, John Carter.   On [27 Nov] 1637 John Aburne [late of Ardingly], 'carpenter', murdered Thomas Weller late of Horsted Keynes, ..., at Lindfield, kicking him with his right foot on the lower part of the abdomen and giving him 'a bruise' [of which he languished] at Horsted Keynes [until] 2 Dec [and then died].   ... at Ardingly ... At the time of the felony ... knowledge. [*Damaged.*] ASSI 35/80/8, m 7.

[Delivered with 359. At the assizes an indictment was preferred which charged Aburne with murder in terms identical to those of the inquest verdict, but omitting the last sentence, and Anthony Mathewes and Thomas Venner late of Lindfield, labourer, with being feloniously present aiding and abetting him. The grand jury, which heard evidence from 5 witnesses whose names are illegible, reduced the charge against Aburne to manslaughter and rejected that against Mathewes and Venner. Aburne was at large. ASSI 35/80/8, mm 6, 7.]

362   16 Jan 1638.   Stedham.   R. Williams, gent., coroner of the liberty of [Thomas] earl [of Arundel] and of [Easebourne] hundred.   Jurors of the hundred and county: Nicholas Aylinge, John Hudson, Richard Heberden, John ?Sury..., ... ?Wynnarde, Richard Aylinge, Thomas Grist, William Spurrier, Thomas Aylinge, Richard ..., Thomas Ayling.   On 3 Jan, when Richard Smith jun. of Stedham, 'husbondman', was alone in the hall of the dwelling-house of Richard Smith sen., his father, at Stedham, ... 'peece' belonging to his father ... 'and haileshott' and without any ... intending any harm ... on Joan Taylor's throat ... she languished [until 12 Jan] and then died at ...   Thus ... malice or hatred but solely by misadventure ...   At the time of the killing Smith jun. had no goods or chattels ... [*Damaged.*] ASSI 35/80/8, m 4.

[Delivered with 359. At the assizes Smith was given bail. At the Lent 1639 assizes he produced letters patent and went sine die. ASSI 35/80/8, m 4.]

363   18 Apr 1638.   Uckfield.   Edward Raynes, gent., county coroner.   Jurors: 'Walsingham' Wickersham, gent., Robert Drowst, George Hunter, Thomas Vyne, Robert Topsaile, William Peckham jun., Stephen Lintot, John Wood, John Levet, Henry Hoadley, John Paine, Robert Wooddy.   On 16 Apr, when John Carey, aged 15 or thereabouts, the elder son of John Carey of Mayfield, 'gardiner', was 'washing himselfe' in 'a marle pitt' full of water on the common or waste land of Framfield called 'Framfeild Common', he suddenly fell into the pit and was drowned by misadventure and not otherwise to the jurors' knowledge. The pit was dug by William Holman of Framfield, 'yeoman', through whose default it is very dangerous to the king's subjects. KB 9/812, m 78.

[Delivered by the coroner into King's Bench in Hilary 1639. Holman was summoned to King's Bench to answer for the trespass and nuisance of which he was indicted; he had licence to imparl in Hilary 1640. There is a note on the inquest that the pit was near the king's highway. KB 9/812, mm 78, 78d; KB 29/287, m 186d.]

364   17 June 1638.   Itchingfield.   Francis Comber, gent., Bramber rape coroner.   Jurors of the rape: John Shelly, gent., George Dendie, John Nye, John Francis, Francis Stringer, Edward Barber, Thomas Grinfild, Richard Stidman, John Patching, Robert Holland, Richard Marlet, William Duffild.   About 4 p.m. on 13 June, when John Pelling jun. of Shipley, 'yeoman', was mowing in a meadow in Shipley with 'a sith' worth 10d which he held in both hands, by misadventure he killed William Randoll late of Itchingfield, 'husbandman', who was standing nearby, giving him a wound with the scythe on the back of the left shin 3 inches long and 1 inch deep of which he died within 4 hours. At the time of the killing Pelling had no goods or chattels, lands or tenements to the jurors' knowledge. ASSI 35/80/9, m 11.

[Delivered to East Grinstead assizes on 5 July.]

365   12 July 1638.   Petworth.   Richard Williams, gent., Rotherbridge hundred coroner.   Jurors of the hundred: George Johnson, William Morris, Edward Longe, Thomas Pricher, Richard Chapman, James Chapman, ?Bartholomew ..., Richard N..., John Smyth, Paul B...ns, Peter ?Cozoun, William Weanwright, Robert Hillman, Nicholas Brishe, Richard Stanes, Edward Story, John Pucknoll, Thomas Osborne, Hugh Dundagh..., John Tompson.   ... p.m. on ?5 July, when John Harwood of Petworth, 'husbondman',

Nicholas Moone late of Petworth, 'blacksmyth', Daniel ..., Richard Brushe, Richard B...nde, Edward Story, John ..., John ..., Hugh ... and John Tompson were assembled in the barn of Algernon earl of Northumberland, High Admiral of England, in Petworth to discharge and ... and Harwood was coming down from 'the topp of a hay mowe' in the barn on 'a ladder' which was standing there [with] 'a pronge' [*sc.* prong, a fork] worth 2d which belonged to him in his left hand, not having any malice or ... towards anyone then in the barn, he let the fork fall from his hand upon 'the said hay mowe' [and it] 'did hitt' a beam of the barn and fell on the hay mow and then 'did slide downe' from it ... 'the spleene' ... Moone by misadventure on the left shoulder, giving him a wound 1 inch ... and 4 inches deep of which he immediately [died]. Thus Harwood killed him by misadventure and not otherwise. At that time he had no goods or chattels to the jurors' knowledge. [*Damaged.*] ASSI 35/81/5, m 7.
[Delivered to East Grinstead assizes on 4 Mar 1639 when Harwood confessed to the killing. ASSI 35/81/5, m 7.]

366   29 Oct 1638.   Winchelsea.   Daniel White, esq., Winchelsea mayor and coroner.   Jurors: John Botting, William Jones, Edward Harnet, John Ashdowne, George Rockley, Thomas Lane, John Richardson, John Savage, William Hickmott, John Byshop, William Mathew, Roger Greene.   On 27 Oct, when an unknown maidservant was going towards Winchelsea on a footpath in the marshes between Winchelsea and Rye, she stumbled from the force of the violent wind which was then blowing there and, by reason of the large amount of rain which had recently fallen, by misadventure she fell into a ditch full of rain-water and was drowned.   The coroner ordered and the jurors requested that the inquest be entered of record in the common register of the town according to custom. WIN 58, f 44.

367   29 Dec 1638.   Barcombe.   Francis Comber, gent., Lewes rape coroner.   Jurors of the rape: Thomas Burgis, Richard Marckwicke, Martin Earle, Thomas Whiteman, John Whiteman, William Rootes, Junius Rootes, John Clarke, John Bland, Richard Mare, William Nappe, Thomas Marckwicke, Thomas Chauntler, Richard Browne.   About midnight on 24 Dec, when Joan Chesle of Barcombe, 'spinster', was alone in bed in the house of ... [in] Barcombe, she gave birth to an illegitimate male child and afterwards ... of the same night carried him out of the house, threw him [on] the ground in a field at Barcombe near the [dwelling]-house [of William Claygate] and left him there.   He died by reason of the cold and for lack of nourishment ... Joan had no goods or chattels, lands or tenements to the jurors' knowledge. [*Damaged.*] ASSI 35/81/5, m 8.
[Delivered with **365**. At the assizes the grand jury, to which William and Mary Claygate gave evidence, presented an indictment, also damaged, which charged Chesle with murdering the child; the details are similar to those of the inquest verdict with the addition that she secretly threw and left him in the field naked and deprived of all human assistance with the intention of causing his death and that he immediately died, and the omission of the last sentence. Chesle pleaded not guilty to the indictment but was convicted, hanged on 7 Mar 1639 and buried at East Grinstead under the name of Joan Chelsey. ASSI 35/81/5, mm 8, 25; SRS, XXIV, 186.]

368   4 Jan 1639.   Lindfield.   Edward Raynes, gent., county coroner.   Jurors: Andrew Pie, Philip Jenner, Thomas Sayers, Thomas Fairehall, Thomas Gillam, Samuel Blu[?nd], James Longe, Francis Parson, Thomas Woodnutt, Matthew Comber, Stephen Ma...n, ..., Thomas Bury.   About 4 a.m. on 29 Dec 1638 Mary Hocombe of Lindfield, 'spinster', gave birth to a live bastard female child at Lindfield and later on the same day she murdered her at Lindfield, strangling her with both hands whereby she immediately died.   At [that] time she [had no goods] or chattels, lands or tenements in Sussex to the jurors' knowledge. [*Damaged.*] ASSI 35/81/5, m 28.
[Delivered with **365**. At the assizes Hocombe pleaded not guilty but was convicted, hanged on 7 Mar and buried at East Grinstead. ASSI 35/81/5, mm 28, 67d; SRS, XXIV, 186.]

369   28 May 1639.   West Tarring.   Edward Raynes, gent., county coroner.   Jurors: John Hamper, Thomas Bottinge, Thomas Southe, John Barnard, John Chapman, Richard Hamper, Edward Graves, Thomas Farncombe, Thomas Taylor, Richard Carden, Thomas Warrell, ?Richard Porchester, Richard Weston.   On 24 May, when John Barnard late of West Tarring, 'laborer', was 'rideing in a dung courte'

belonging to William Turneagaine of Broadwater, 'yeoman', and drawn by 'foure horse beasts' belonging to Turneagaine at West Tarring, by misadventure the cart suddenly 'was overthrowne' whereby Barnard fell onto the ground and his body was so crushed that he languished at West Tarring for 12 hours and then died. The cart and 4 geldings moved to his death; they are worth £4 6s 8d and are now with Turneagaine. Henry Garway, esq., citizen and alderman of London, claims and should have all deodands within the hundred and manor of West Tarring by virtue of letters patent of 22 May 1609. KB 9/815, m 230.
[Delivered by the coroner into King's Bench in Michaelmas. Turneagaine was summoned to King's Bench to answer for the cart and geldings; he had licence to imparl in Easter 1640. The coroner was also summoned to King's Bench to answer for defects in the inquest; process against him continued until at least Hilary 1641. KB 9/815, mm 230, 231d; KB 29/288, m 111d.]

370   29 Sept 1639. East Grinstead. Edward Raynes, gent., county coroner. Jurors: Robert Bowyer sen., William Freeman, Philip Humber, William Kidder, Stephen Head, Edward Harman, George Harris, Thomas Mathew sen., Thomas Mathew jun., Arthur Underhill, John Underhill jun., Anthony Rice, John Butchinge jun., Robert Milles. About 7 p.m. on 28 Sept, when Judith Kippinge late of East Grinstead, 'spinster', was alone at East Grinstead, she feloniously threw herself into 'a pitt' full of water near the messuage of Edward Paine sen. and was drowned. At that time she had no goods or chattels, lands or tenements in Sussex to the jurors' knowledge. KB 9/815, m 231.
[Delivered with **369**. KB 9/815, m 231d; KB 29/288, m 111d.]

371   20 Jan 1640. Horsham. Francis Comber, gent., coroner of Thomas earl of Arundel and Surrey, earl marshal of England. Jurors of Horsham: Henry Whitell, William Watterton, James Picke, Robert Artridge, William Burridge, Henry Underwood, Thomas Gallpinne, Thomas Peters, Thomas Este, Matthew Bennet, Benjamin Meates, John Lewers, Stephen Batner, Edward Filders, John Haynes. On 19 Jan John Barkham, a prisoner, who had been committed to Horsham gaol by the assize judges at Horsham assizes on 13 July 1639 for speaking scandalous words against William archbishop of Canterbury, primate of all England and metropolitan, died a natural death there and not otherwise to the jurors' knowledge. KB 9/817, m 339.
[Delivered to East Grinstead assizes on 2 Mar and on to King's Bench in Easter. KB 9/817, m 350d; KB 29/289, m 4.]

372   3 Apr 1640. Horsham. Francis Comber, gent., Bramber rape coroner. Jurors of the rape: Henry Whithall, Robert Honiwood, William Browne, Thomas Patching, Edward Hobbs, Henry Patching, Richard Luckins, John Leawer, Robert Beast, John Picke, Ralph Dunstall, William Deane, Peter Waterton, James Harman, John Carpenter. About 6 p.m. on 9 Jan [*MS* 16 *in error for* 15 Charles I] William Scott of Horsham, 'laborer', murdered his wife Agnes at Horsham with 'an axe' worth 1d which he held in both hands, giving her a wound on the right side of the head 1½ inches long and ½ inch deep of which she languished at Horsham until 25 Mar and then died. At the time of the felony he had no goods or chattels, lands or tenements to the jurors' knowledge. ASSI 35/82/5, m 5.
[Delivered to East Grinstead assizes on 11 July when process ceased on the inquest verdict which was found to be insufficient and uncertain, possibly among other things because of the dating error, and the grand jury, to which Joan Jener, John Parsons, Elizabeth Mutton, John Picke, John Holden and possibly Jane Humfrye and Jane Niblett gave evidence, presented an indictment identical to the inquest verdict except that the regnal years were correct, the wound was said to be 1 inch long and the last sentence was omitted. Scott, who had been committed to gaol by Walter Bartlott and Thomas Middleton, esqs, JPs, pleaded not guilty but was convicted and hanged; he had no chattels. ASSI 35/82/5, mm 5, 6, 14, 36, 36d.]

373   18 May 1640. Folkington. Edward Raynes, gent., county coroner. Jurors: John Store, John Parker, John Fuller, Thomas Lashmer, William Hobeame, William Daniel, Robert Stretton, James Fennell, Edward Peirse, John Lewes, William Stapeley, John French. On 30 Apr Philip Renne of Folkington, 'shepheard', murdered Frances Wood late of Folkington, 'spinster', at Folkington with a stone of no

value which he held in his right hand, giving her 3 fatal wounds on the left side of the head 3 inches long and ¼ inch deep of which she immediately died. At that time he had no goods or chattels, lands or tenements in Sussex to the jurors' knowledge. ASSI 35/82/5, m 4.
[Delivered with **372**. At the time of the assizes Renne was at large. ASSI 35/82/5, m 4.]

374   27 Jan 1641. Rodmell. Edward Raynes, gent., county coroner. Jurors: William Hollicke, Francis Brian, John Yeomans, Thomas Elficke, John White, John Elven, James Harman, Thomas Heenes, Thomas Ade, David Selme, Edward Barnden, Richard Ade, John Ballard. On 26 Jan, when Thomas Martin late of Rodmell, 'husbandman', was 'driving a certaine wagon with foure wheeles drawen by foure oxen and laden with a small quantity of hay' at Rodmell, he suddenly and by misadventure fell onto the ground and the oxen pulled the wagon and 'two wheeles of the said wagon did goe over the head' of Martin, so crushing it that he immediately died. The wagon with its wheels, the hay and the 4 oxen moved to his death. The wagon and wheels are worth 30s, the hay 12d and the oxen £13 6s 8d, total £14 17s 8d. The wagon and wheels are with Richard Collar and Francis Shoulder of Rodmell, 'husbandmen', the hay with Thomas Brooke of Rodmell, husbandman, and the oxen with Thomas Collar of Rodmell, husbandman. KB 9/823, m 305.
[Delivered by the coroner into King's Bench in Michaelmas. The Collars, Shoulder and Brooke were summoned to King's Bench to answer for the deodands which were in their hands; they all had licence to imparl in Easter 1642 but were all outlawed at Lewes in May 1647. KB 9/823, mm 305, 305d; KB 29/290, m 71d; KB 29/291, m 35.]

375   9 Feb 1641. Horsham. Francis Comber, gent., Bramber rape coroner. Jurors of Horsham: William Chambers sen., Robert Hurst, Ralph Dunstall, Stephen Batner, Robert Gates, Richard Clark, Richard Savage, William Waterton, John Chapman, Richard Gatton, Edward Filder, Thomas Peeter, George Hodges, John Queene. On 8 Feb Elizabeth Jobe, a prisoner in Horsham gaol, died a natural death there and not otherwise to the jurors' knowledge. ASSI 35/83/6, m 1.
[Delivered to East Grinstead assizes on 6 Mar. At the East Grinstead assizes of 2 Mar 1640 the grand jury, to which Richard and Ann Carpenter and Joan Killicke gave evidence, had presented an indictment which charged Elizabeth Jobe late of East Grinstead, spinster, with stealing and carrying away at East Grinstead on 20 Aug 1639 a petticoat worth 14s and an apron worth 2s 6d belonging to Richard Carpenter and a petticoat worth 10s, a waistcoat worth 9s, 3 aprons worth 15s, a black cap (*galirum*) worth 7s, 6 coifs worth 2s 6d, 6 cross-cloths worth 7s, 4 handkerchiefs worth 3s and 5 neckcloths worth 18d belonging to Joan Killicke. Jobe, who had been committed to gaol by Thomas Middleton, esq., JP, for breaking Richard Carpenter's house in Surrey and stealing goods and money there, to which she had confessed, pleaded not guilty but was convicted and sentenced to be hanged; she had no chattels. She was remanded in gaol after sentence and was still there at the assizes of 11 July 1640. ASSI 35/82/4, mm 6, 9, 37, 37d; ASSI 35/82/5, m 36.]

376   4 Mar 1641. Rye. Robert Urwinn, gent., Rye mayor and coroner, and the jurats. Jurors of Rye: Henry Jeake, Thomas Kyte, William Malpace, James Reinoldes, George Blanch, John Peadle, James Newton, Nicholas Boarde, Angel [*Angelus*] Shawe, William Kent, John Porter, Stephen Braffe. About 2 or 3 a.m. on 4 Mar John Sloman murdered John Smyth late of Rye, 'inkeper', in the 'palor' [*sc.* parlour] of Smyth's house with a rapier of iron and steel which he held in both hands, running violently at him and giving him a wound 'in his breast under the left pap' 3 or 4 inches deep of which he died. Sloman did not flee for the murder and he had no goods or chattels in Rye or its liberties except the rapier which was appraised at 5s. [*Verdict in English.*] RYE 1/13, f 18.
[On 5 Mar 4 men were examined on oath before the mayor and coroner and Richard Cockram, Joseph Benbrigge, Alan Gribell and John Spie. James Freake of Rye, vintner, said that before midnight on 3 Mar Sloman came to Smyth's house where he drank with John Thomas, Richard Jefferie, John Waight and a man named Charles and afterwards they called for the bill which came to 6s, of which Jefferie paid 2s 6d and Thomas 2s and the remaining 18d they left for Sloman to pay; but Sloman not only refused but took up the 2s 6d laid down by Jefferie and the 2s laid down by Thomas and put the money in his pocket. Freake, seeing that, demanded his 6s, but Sloman refused to pay him and abused him, saying that if he wanted his payment he should go to Dover castle for it, and challenged him to fight him for 40s. Freake replied that he did not wish to fight, but wanted him to pay his bill which was his due, whereupon Sloman drew his sword and said to Freake 'Now I'le see what mettle thou art made of' and ran at him with

the rapier, with one hand on the hilt and the other on the blade. To save his life Freake ran from him into the hall, which was the next room, where Smyth, Freake's father-in-law, was sitting by the fire 'taking' a pipe of tobacco in the company of others, and said to them: 'I shall ben like to be kylled by John Sloman who run at me with his rapiere for demandinge of my reckoninge'. A little later, about 2 or 3 a.m. on 4 Mar, Smyth got up and went to Sloman, who had come into the middle of the room with his hat in his hand, and asked him to pay the bill. Sloman immediately took his rapier, which was lying on the table unsheathed, and ran at him and killed him.

John Thomas of Rye said that about midnight on 3 Mar he came to Smyth's house with Sloman, marshal of Dover castle, and went into the parlour and called for Freake to fill them a pint of wine, which Freake brought in to them, and for a dish of fish, which Sloman and a man called Charles, the Lord Warden's man, ate. Afterwards Jefferie came into the room and drank with them. Charles, who was leaving, offered to pay the bill, but Jefferie said he should pay nothing and that the others should pay between them. Jefferie paid 2s 6d and Thomas 2s, leaving 18d for Sloman to pay. Thomas then went from the room into the hall to the fire where he 'drank' a pipe of tobacco with Smyth. After about half an hour Freake ran out of the parlour and told Smyth that Sloman had drawn his rapier at him. Smyth said that he would go to Sloman and make peace, and left Thomas, but immediately returned, sat down in a chair by the fire beside Thomas and said to him: 'I pray, master, pray for me for I have my deathes wound'. He then opened his clothing and showed Thomas his chest where the wound was and died, saying nothing more, about 2 or 3 a.m. on 4 Mar.

Joseph Church, aged 16, said that about 2 or 3 a.m. on 4 Mar Freake came to ask Sloman for 6s in payment of his bill, but Sloman said that he would pay only 4s 6d and if he wanted more he should come to Dover castle for it, although he would fight him for 40s. Freake replied that he did not want to fight. Sloman then put his purse in his pocket, drew his sword, saying that he would try what Freake was made of, shook it at him and ran at him. About a quarter of an hour later Smyth, Church's master, came into Sloman's room and, when he was half way in and about to take off his hat to him, Sloman took up the rapier, which was lying on the table unsheathed, and with one hand on the hilt and the other on the blade thrust at Smyth and killed him.

Francis Kevill of Rye, surgeon, said that about 2 or 3 a.m. on 4 Mar he was sent for to come to Smyth whom he found mortally wounded in the chest under the left nipple. The wound was 4 inches deep and ½ inch wide.

An indictment of John Sloman late of Rye, gent., for murder was sent into King's Bench in Michaelmas and his arrest was therefore ordered. In the same term Sloman was produced in King's Bench by the mayor and 2 jurats on a habeas corpus cum causa, the 'cause' testifying that on 4 Mar Sloman had been committed to gaol by the mayor as coroner because on that day he had murdered Smyth with a sword of iron and steel worth 5s which he held in both hands, giving him a wound in the chest under the left nipple 1 inch long and 3 inches deep of which he immediately died. A trial jury was summoned from Rye for Hilary 1642 until when Sloman was committed to the custody of the marshal of King's Bench. The jury had a charter allowed in Michaelmas 1643. A further capias had been issued for Sloman by King's Bench in Hilary 1642 for manslaughter of which he was indicted and to which he later pleaded not guilty. KB 29/290, mm 68, 110d, 116d, 124; RYE 47/133, unnumbered document.]

377   10 July 1641. Wadhurst. Thomas Bucher, gent., coroner of Loxfield Camden half-hundred in Pevensey rape. Jurors: John Dinmoll, William Cruttoll, Anthony Bucher, Nicholas Puxtie, David Holland, Richard Weston, Alexander Weston, John Weston, Thomas Peckham, John Wells, Thomas Pritchard, Thomas Longley, Abraham Bassett, William Skynner, William Feild. About 1 p.m. on 29 June, when Abraham Symonds, 'the coachman' of George Courthoppe of Ticehurst, kt, was sitting on 'the coach boxe' driving 4 horses which were drawing 'a coach' belonging to Courthoppe in the road at Wadhurst, 'one of the wheele horses' which was 'unrulye' violently kicked Symonds with its back hoofs and threw him from the box to the ground and the horses pulled 'the neare wheeles' of the coach over his right shin as he lay there, from which kicking, throwing and crushing he was injured and crushed on the right shin and various other parts of the body of which he languished at Wadhurst until 3 July and then died. The horses and coach were the cause of and moved to his death; they are worth £50 and remain with Courthoppe. KB 9/823, m 306.
[Delivered by the coroner into King's Bench in Michaelmas. Courthoppe was summoned to King's Bench to answer for the deodands; he had licence to imparl in Hilary 1646. KB 9/823, mm 306, 306d; KB 29/290, m 71d.]

378   18 Sept 1641. Ewhurst. Thomas Bucher, gent., Hastings rape coroner. Jurors: Thomas Jordayne, Matthew Chittenden, Leonard Fryman, John Banckes, John Champen, John Sheather, Thomas Henly, 'Thankefull' Kinge, Henry Sheather, Richard Curd, Joseph Darbye, Thomas Darby, John Carrier, John

Snowe. On 14 Aug Henry Crisford late of Ewhurst, 'laborer', feloniously killed Temperance wife of Richard Dickenson of Ewhurst, 'laborer', at Ewhurst: he 'did throwe downe' Temperance upon the ground with both hands and while she lay there kicked her on the right side of the body on the short ribs with his right foot, giving her 'a mortall bruise' of which she languished at Ewhurst until 12 Sept and then died. At the time of the felony Crisford had no goods or chattels, lands or tenements to the jurors' knowledge. ASSI 35/84/7, m 19.

[Delivered to East Grinstead assizes on 17 Mar 1642 when an indictment was preferred similar to the inquest verdict except that the charge was murder, Crisford was styled husbandman and the last sentence was omitted. The grand jury, to which 2 men and 4 women, whose surnames are missing, gave evidence, reduced the charge to manslaughter. Crisford pleaded not guilty to the indictment as amended and was acquitted; he had not fled. ASSI 35/84/7, mm 14, 15, 19.]

379 8 Apr 1642. Rye. Robert Urwinn, gent., Rye mayor and coroner. Jurors of Rye: Henry Walter, 'Solmon' Boxer, Edward Beale, Edward Borne, Richard Henly, Robert Wood, John Porter, Thomas Cobbe, Richard Downer, Thomas Stonestreate, Richard Flintstone, Joseph Starkey, James Newton, Thomas Grove. Between 8 and 9 p.m. on 2 Apr, when Robert Brad was sitting in the kitchen of William Kent's house, 'beinge in drinke', he got up and went to the back door in the kitchen to go out, but 'the sell of the doore beinge high and the doore openinge outward, it did of a suddaine flinge from him yat he fell over the said sell upon the pavinge stones in the yard, whereby he received divers bruses upon his face and side that his water course was thereby stopped so that he could not voide any water till' 7 Apr; 'which fall we conceive to be the cause of his death'. [*Verdict in English.*] RYE 1/13, f 52.

380 29 June 1642. Lewes. Francis Comber, gent., Lewes rape coroner. Jurors of the rape: John Henley, William Newton, Edward Colman, George Moth, William Dodson jun., John Rennols, Thomas Burken, Roger Fillery, Thomas Brad, Richard Woodoar, John Ford, James Benton, William Stuckell, Samuel Cruttenden. On 30 May, when Thomas Harrison of Lewes, 'grocer', was at Lewes with many more of the king's faithful subjects of Lewes 'trayninge' with 'muskettes' and 'pikes' in quiet and peaceful manner according to ancient and approved custom there, all carrying their muskets which were loaded only with 'gunpowder' to be discharged in the usual way, Harrison and the others discharged them and the gunpowder discharged from Harrison's musket suddenly, by misadventure and against his will drove 'the muskett sticke' made of wood, which was attached 'to the stocke' of the musket, from the stock and onto 'the left thigh' of John Ray who was walking nearby whereby he was fatally wounded. He languished until 20 June and then died of the wound at Lewes. Thus he came to his death by misadventure only and against Harrison's will. The musket is worth 5s and remains with Richard Newton of Lewes. ASSI 35/84/8, m 3.

[Delivered to East Grinstead assizes on 29 July.]

381 16 July 1642. Lewes. Francis Comber, gent., Lewes rape coroner. Jurors of the rape: William Hollick, John Elven, John Marten, John Junnins, Thomas Coller, Thomas Elphick, Thomas Ade, John Ade, John White, Francis Briant, John Baker, Thomas Eves, 'Isaack' Baldy, Abel Parson, Ralph Cooke. On 28 June Richard Overy late of Telscombe, gent., feloniously killed Thomas Elphick late of Telscombe, 'husbandman', at Telscombe with 'a batt' worth ¼d which he held in his right hand, giving him 'one mortall bruise' on the right side of the head of which he languished at Telscombe until 4 July and then died. At the time of the felony Overy had no goods or chattels, lands or tenements in Sussex or elsewhere to the jurors' knowledge. ASSI 35/84/8, m 4.

[Delivered with **380**.]

382 19 July 1642. Rye. Robert Urwinn, gent., Rye mayor and coroner. Jurors of Rye: John Porter, Thomas Seere, Richard Henly, James Newton, Mark Woodford, Philip Scriven, John Feild, Henry Whitwood, Edmund Waters, Robert Clarke, Richard Allan, Bartholomew Breades. Thomas Cooper, the infant son of John Cooper jun. of Rye, merchant, crawled from his father's house along the wall to

John Browne's close and from there to a cellar under part of Browne's house into which he fell and was drowned. [*Verdict in English.*] RYE 1/13, f 54.

383 15 Oct 1642. Rye. John Fagg, esq., Rye mayor and coroner. Jurors of Rye: Benjamin Marten, John Porter, George Blanch, Samuel Callice, Richard Leiston, Joseph Starkey, Richard Downer, James Newton, John Harris, George Cary, John Rason sen., Miles Wildinge, Miles James, Robert Swaine, Robert Church. Between 1 and 2 p.m. on 15 Oct John Skinner of Rye feloniously hanged himself with a small cord fastened to a beam in the garret of his dwelling-house. At that time he had goods and chattels, real and personal, worth £58 2s 8d and £10 7s 6d in money. [*Verdict in English.*] RYE 1/13, f 84v.

384 11 Feb 1643. Rye. John Fagge, esq., Rye [mayor] and coroner. Jurors of Rye: Stephen Carpinter, John Porter, Stephen Bruffe, Richard Allen, Philip Scriven, Stephen Dad, Robert Wood, Angel [*Angelus*] Shaw, Arthur Dier, Benjamin Blist, Nicholas Kennard, Miles James, Thomas Hunmersone, [Henry Whitwo(od) *excluded from the first list of jurors but included among their signatures*]. After 10 p.m. on 10 Feb 'Moses' Peadle of Rye hanged himself with a leather stirrup put round a hook which was fastened to a wall in a chamber over the shop in his dwelling-house. He had goods and chattels worth £3 11s 4d. [*Verdict in English.*] RYE 1/13, f 93.

385 1 June 1644. Winchelsea. Hugh Berisford, gent., Winchelsea mayor and coroner, William Thorpe and George Sampson, jurats, being present. Jurors: William Hickmott, Richard Philpott, John Fordred, Robert Bunce, George Rockley, Arthur Ecklesden, Thomas Baldocke, John Tuffen, John Kinge, John Richardsone, John Ashdowne, Edward Harnett, Thomas Baylie, George Hedge. On 30 May 'John Farneham, beinge at worke within side of' Winchelsea church 'and uppon ye rathers [*sc.* rafters] of ye said church standinge at worke, casually did fall downe of the said rathers unto the flower of ye said church', receiving a fatal wound in the head and other parts of his body of which he immediately died. The jurors requested that the inquest be recorded and that was granted. [*English.*] WIN 58, f 69v.

386 ... Leonard Crooke, gent., deputy ... Jurors: ..., Robert Honywood, John Pike, Henry Grumbridge, William Ryde, John ..., William Heriot, Richard Savadge, Thomas Pyke, Paul Hanwell, Nicholas Barber, James Harman jun., ... Chapman jun., John Tickeridge, William Gratwicke. On 2 Dec ... Edward Bridger, a prisoner in ... gaol, who had earlier been committed there by warrant of Ralph Cooper, esq., JP, trying to break ... and to go at large, Edward Mitchell ..., keeper of the gaol, ... hearing ... and his servants ... finding ... held the prisoner ... intending to kill ... resistance ... in danger ... worth 3s which ... the said prisoner in ... for the space of 24 [*or* 25] ... Bridger ... jurors' knowledge. [*Damaged.*] ASSI 35/86/6, m 32.
[Delivered to East Grinstead assizes on 12 Aug 1645. Bridger was buried at Horsham on 4 Dec 1644, the parish register recording that, while a prisoner, he had been killed in Horsham gaol with a pistol by Mitchell, the tapster there. *Horsham millenium*, 325.]

387 16 Mar 1646. Rye. Alan Gribell, gent., Rye mayor and coroner. Jurors of Rye: John Porter, Stephen Dad, Henry Whitwood, Stephen Bruffe, Thomas Hintie, Miles Wildinge, Angel [*Angelus*] Shaw, William Kent, John Feild, Robert Swaine, Edward London, Mark Hownsell. John son of Francis Kevill, who went to drink, as the jurors supposed, at the little well at Brickwell in the washing place, which was broken and needed mending, fell into the well and was drowned. [*Verdict in English.*] RYE 1/13, f 166.

388 15 May 1646. Brightling. George Courthope, gent., Hastings rape coroner. Jurors: Anthony Medhurst, Walter Sivyer, John Keynard, James Vigor, Thomas Vigor, Richard Basden sen., Richard Basden jun., Thomas Thayer, Thomas Cruttenden, John Wimble, John James, William Gouldsmyth,

Silas [*Silvanus*] Snepp, George Alcock. About 8 p.m. on 3 May John Davis feloniously hanged himself in a bedroom in Thomas Price's dwelling-house at Brightling with 'a small coard' worth 1d which he held in both hands, putting one end round his neck and tying the other round 'a beame' of the house. At that time he had no goods or chattels to the jurors' knowledge. KB 9/834, m 30.
[Delivered to the Sussex summer assizes and on to King's Bench in Michaelmas. KB 9/834, m 30d; KB 29/295, m 62d.]

389 11 Aug 1646. Uckfield. Edward Raynes, gent., county coroner. Jurors: William Smith, John Everest, James Bawcombe, John Weller, Thomas Vine, Philip Deane, Richard Dine, Robert Topsell, 'Faintnot' Bacheler, Nicholas Brackpoole, William Kent, Richard Lewes. On 22 July Thomas Ward, 'laborer', and Robert Wheatley, 'laborer', both late of Framfield, murdered James Russell late of Framfield, 'carpenter', at Framfield: Ward striking him on the left side of the head with a sword of iron and steel worth 2s which he held in his right hand and giving him a wound 2 inches long and ½ inch deep of which he languished at Framfield until the next day and then died; and Wheatley being feloniously present aiding and abetting him. At the time of the felony Ward and Wheatley had no goods or chattels, lands or tenements in Sussex to the jurors' knowledge. ASSI 35/88/1, m 27.
[Delivered to East Grinstead assizes on 16 Mar 1647 when Ward and Wheatley were at large. ASSI 35/88/1, m 27.]

390 1 Sept 1646. Worth. Edward Raynes, gent., county coroner. Jurors: Walter Pawly, gent., Giles Cuddington, Henry Tidie, Ralph Patricke, Thomas Brooker, 'Sidrach' Baldwin, Edward Goldsmith, John Jenner, 'Ninian' Cresie, William Wright, Robert Perrior, William Leach, John Wood. On 24 Aug, when William Egell late of Worth, aged 13½ or thereabouts, was on 'a wayne' loaded with oats at Worth, Richard White of Worth, 'husbandman', killed him by misadventure and against his will and not otherwise with 'a hasell goad' of no value which he 'did throwe' at him, not intending to hurt him in any way, and struck him on the left side of the head above the ear, giving him a wound ½ inch wide and 1 inch deep of which he languished at Worth until 30 Aug and then died. ASSI 35/88/1, m 23.
[Delivered with **389**. At the assizes the grand jury presented an indictment which charged White with feloniously killing Egell at Worth on 24 Aug with a goad worth ½d which he held in his right hand and threw at him, giving him a wound on the left ear ½ inch wide and 1 inch deep of which he languished at Worth until 30 Aug and then died. White pleaded not guilty to the indictment but was convicted; he had no chattels. He then successfully pleaded benefit of clergy and was branded on the hand and released. ASSI 35/88/1, mm 38, 40, 45d; KB 9/836, m 26; KB 29/296, m 18.]

391 3 Sept 1646. Rogate. Richard Smyth, gent., county coroner. Jurors: John Steere, Nicholas Godwin, Nicholas Blackman, Richard White, Richard Triggs, William Eames, John Hamon, Roger Packe, William Hitchcocke, Richard Greenetree, Henry Strudwick, Richard Stent, Richard Signe, William Poleing, John Upsdale, Richard Vallor, John Gary, John Grist, Richard Colpis. About 7 p.m. on 1 Sept Richard Strudwicke late of Wisborough Green, 'yeoman', murdered John March at Rogate with 'a knife' or iron and steel worth 6d which he held in his right hand: he 'did strike and thrust' him on the left side of 'the throate', giving him a wound 1 inch wide and 2 inches deep of which he immediately died. Strudwicke had no goods or chattels, lands or tenements at that time or ever after to the jurors' knowledge. ASSI 35/88/1, m 26.
[Delivered with **389**. Strudwicke, called a blacksmith, had been committed to gaol by George Churcher, esq., JP, at Slinfold on 12 Sept 1646, the day of his arrest, on suspicion of murdering John March late of Itchingfield. He was produced in King's Bench by Thomas Henley, sheriff, in Michaelmas on a writ of habeas corpus, but was recommitted to the county gaol. At the assizes of 16 Mar 1647 he was remanded in custody for further examination of the indictment. At the assizes of 2 Aug 1647 he pleaded not guilty but was convicted and hanged; he had no chattels. ASSI 35/88/1, mm 26, 45d; ASSI 35/88/3, mm 3, 36, 36d; KB 29/295, m 86d.]

392 15 Oct 1646. Framfield. Edward Raynes, gent., county coroner. Jurors: William Peckham, John Smith, Robert Smith, John Squire, John Delve, Robert Lattenden, William Weller, Robert Wooddy, Edward Jarvis, Abraham Hodgkins, Thomas Vyne, Ezra [*Esdra*] Harper, William Foord. On 9 Oct an unknown man murdered John Doble late of Framfield, 'yeoman', at Ringmer with a staff worth ½d which he held in both hands, giving him a wound on the right side of the head 2 inches long but of little depth of which he immediately died. The unknown man immediately fled. KB 9/841, m 72.

[Delivered to King's Bench by the coroner in Trinity 1648 when a capias was issued for the unknown man but it was followed by no further process. Ringmer was summoned to King's Bench to answer for his escape; process continued until Easter 1649. At East Grinstead assizes on 13 Mar 1648 an indictment was preferred which charged John Pickett late of East Hoathly, bricklayer, and John Puxty late of Buxted, husbandman, with murdering Doble at Ringmer on 14 Oct 1647, Pickett breaking his neck with both hands whereby he immediately died and Puxty being feloniously present aiding and abetting him. The grand jury, to which Walter Doble, Edward Bridger, Adam and Ann Eson, Widow Foxe, Nathaniel Enscombe and Thomas Knight gave evidence, rejected the indictment. ASSI 35/89/1, m 121; KB 9/841, mm 72, 72d; KB 29/297, m 36d.]

393   22 Dec 1646. Shermanbury. Edward Raynes, gent., county coroner. Jurors: Thomas Mitchel, gent., Thomas Dunstall, gent., Robert Vincent, Thomas Parson, 'Ockenden' Roberts, Thomas Cripps, John Jupe, John Gratwicke, John Bull, Thomas Bull, John Vincent jun., Thomas Goffe, Robert Mower. On 18 Dec Elizabeth White late of Shermanbury, 'spinster', gave birth at Shermanbury to a live male child which by the laws of England 'was a bastard' and immediately murdered him, taking him in both hands, secretly throwing him completely naked into 'a celler' in the house of John Langford, then her master, at Shermanbury and leaving him there in extreme cold without giving him any nourishment and with the intention that he should die from the cold and lack of sustenance, and he thereby immediately died. At that time she had no goods or chattels, lands or tenements to the jurors' knowledge. ASSI 35/88/1, m 39.

[Delivered with **389**. At the assizes White pleaded not guilty but was convicted and hanged; she had no chattels. ASSI 35/88/1, mm 39, 40, 45d.]

394   3 Mar 1647. Brighton. Edward Raynes, gent., county coroner. Jurors: Thomas Mighell, Henry Mighell, John Peirsy, John Howell, Thomas Fryland, John Humfrey, Stephen Attree, James Piper, Henry Beach, Thomas Kitchener, Thomas Humfrey, Thomas Scutt, John Barnes. On 19 Feb, when John Snoke of Brighton, 'fisherman', was holding in both hands 'a fowling peece' worth 3s 4d which was 'charged with powder and haileshott' in order 'to shoote and kill seamewes [*sc.* sea-mews, sea-gulls] which were flying over 'the seacost' at Brighton and Richard Hammes late of Brighton, 'bricklayer', his closest friend, was in his company and near him, 'the flint' of the gun suddenly and without Snoke's knowledge and wish fell and struck 'the steele' of the gun whereby the gun 'did shoote of and discharge' and shot the lead pellets, by the force of the powder, into the left side of Hammes's head and neck, giving him a wound 5 inches wide and ½ inch deep of which he languished at Brighton until 1 Mar and then died. Thus he came to his death by misadventure and against Snoke's will and not otherwise. The gun remains with Richard Payne of Brighton, 'shipcarpenter'. ASSI 35/88/1, m 24.

[Delivered with **389**. Hammes was buried at Brighton on 15 Mar. *Par. reg. of Brighton*, 155.]

395   22 Apr 1647. Mayfield. George Courthope, gent., Loxfield Camden half-hundred coroner. Jurors: Robert Parris, Solomon Wenborne, Solomon Foster, John Foster, John Ollive sen., John Smyth, John Parris, William Sawyer, Richard Brookes, William Pocock, John Turnis, William Winter, David Maunser, Anthony Foster, Robert Collin, Robert Marshall, John Ollive jun. On 21 Apr, when Sarah late wife of Thomas Pocock of Rotherfield, 'laborer', was riding at Mayfield from Mayfield to Rotherfield on the road between those 2 places, by misadventure she fell from the horse and thereby crushed the left [side] of her body and her neck whereof she immediately died. The horse moved to her death, is worth 30s and remains with Samuel Watkins of Mayfield, 'blacksmyth', one of the borsholders of the half-hundred. KB 9/838, m 369.

[Delivered with **397** and on to King's Bench in Michaelmas. Watkins was summoned to King's Bench to answer for the horse; he had licence to imparl in Michaelmas 1648. KB 9/838, mm 369, 383d; KB 29/296, m 75; KB 29/297, m 85.]

396 11 June 1647. Heathfield. George Courthope, gent., Hastings rape coroner. Jurors: Richard Fuller, Alexander Elliott, George Checksell, William Penckhurst, Thomas Tayler, William Weston, Solomon Heffeld, William Johnson, John Hobbeame, Nicholas Wood, Thomas Dupleck, John Ellis. Between 7 and 8 a.m. on 8 June, when John Mudle was riding from Mayfield to Heathfield by the road between those 2 places, near 'Scotfordsbridge Bridge' in Heathfield by misadventure he fell from the mare and thereby broke his ankle and other bones of his neck of which he languished until between 9 and 10 a.m. on 10 June and then died. The mare moved to his death, is worth 100s and is with Edward Mudle of Mayfield, 'laborer'. KB 9/838, m 370.
[Delivered with **395**. Edward Mudle was summoned to King's Bench to answer for the mare; he had licence to imparl in Michaelmas 1648. KB 9/838, mm 370, 383d; KB 29/296, m 75; KB 29/297, m 85d.]

397 29 June 1647. Maresfield. Edward Raynes, gent., county coroner. Jurors: William Hesman, Thomas Durkin, John Tie, Thomas Kitchenham, Willam Russell, John Cooke, Anthony Smith, John Humfry, Edward Grayborne, William Burges, Thomas Berry, William Attree. On 7 June John Crofts late of Maresfield, 'sawyer', feloniously killed Francis Rabbett late of Maresfield, 'laborer', at Maresfield with a staff worth 1d which he held in both hands, giving him a wound on the left side of the head 1½ inches long and ½ inch deep of which he languished at Maresfield until the next day and then died. Crofts had no goods or chattels, lands or tenements in Sussex at the time of the felony or ever after to the jurors' knowledge. ASSI 35/88/3, m 24.
[Delivered to Horsham assizes on 2 Aug when an indictment was preferred identical to the inquest verdict except that the charge was murder and the last sentence was omitted. The grand jury, to which Margaret Jillam, Elizabeth Mulford, Richard Cheale, John Rolfe, Elizabeth Cooper, Margaret Turner, Katharine Rabbett, Thomas Bray, Ann Mulford and possibly Thomas Cooper gave evidence, reduced the charge to manslaughter. Crofts, who had been committed to gaol by the coroner, pleaded not guilty to the indictment as amended but was convicted; he had no chattels. He then successfully pleaded benefit of clergy and was branded on the hand and released. ASSI 35/88/3, mm 13, 23, 24, 36, 36d; KB 29/296, m 93.]

398 22 Dec 1647. Shipley. Edward Reynes, gent., county coroner. Jurors: John Ward, John Fords, Thomas Lancaster, Thomas Badmering, John Slater, Owen Botting, John Gratwicke, Thomas Parson sen., Thomas Parson jun., Thomas Mitchell, Richard Worsfoald, John Parson. Witnesses: Jane Snashall, Mary Baker, John Piper, Sarah Edwardes, William French, John Dunstall, Robert Hurst, Richard Dunce, Susan Henly, Ann Shawe, Elizabeth Blincoe, Mary Wood, Mary Hurst, Ann Capp, Henry Agate, Richard Pannett, John Haler, Ralph Thorne, Mary Harris, Mary Dyer, Thomas Skynner, Thomas Gates, John Worsfold, Hugh Blincoe, Thomas Edwardes. On 10 Oct Edward Prior, 'yeoman', John Prior, 'yeoman', Abraham Pryor, 'yeoman', all late of Shipley, and Elizabeth Hurst late of Shipley, 'spinster', alias Elizabeth wife of Richard Hurst of Shipley, 'yeoman', feloniously killed Elizabeth Quinten alias Sherwood, widow, at Shipley: Edward Prior violently kicking her on the 'reynes' [*sc.* reins, the region of the kidneys] of her back with his right foot and giving her 'a mortall bruise' of which she languished at Shipley until 10 Dec and then died; and the other 3 being feloniously present aiding and abetting him. None of the 4 had any goods or chattels, lands or tenements at the time of the felony or ever after to the jurors' knowledge. ASSI 35/89/9, mm 10, 10d.
[Delivered to East Grinstead assizes on 13 Mar 1648 when all 4 suspects pleaded not guilty and were acquitted; they had not fled and were released on the payment of their fees. ASSI 35/89/9, mm 2, 10, 37d.]

399 21 Feb 1648. Slaugham. Edward Raynes, gent., county coroner. Jurors: Edward Wickham sen., Arthur Woodgate, Robert Burgate, William Hesman, Richard Hall, John Ashfold, Walter Burt, John Hamper, William Ashfold, Edward Wickham jun., John Garston, Richard Hilles, Robert Feild. Witnesses: William Wilson, Mary George, Elizabeth Towne, Edward Towne. On 13 Feb Robert Archpoole of Slaugham, 'freemason', murdered his wife Mary at Slaugham with 'a woodden mallett' worth 1d which he held in his right hand, violently striking her on the right side of the head and giving her a wound 2 inches wide and 2 inches deep of which she immediately died. He had no goods or chattels, lands or tenements at that time or ever after to the jurors' knowledge. ASSI 35/89/9, mm 9, 9d.

[Delivered with **398**. At the assizes Archpoole, who had been committed to gaol under the name of Robert Archpoole sen. by the coroner on the day of the inquest, pleaded not guilty but was convicted and hanged; he had no chattels. ASSI 35/89/9, mm 2, 9, 37, 37d.]

400   4 Mar 1648. Easebourne. Richard Smyth, gent., county coroner. Jurors: Thomas Upperton, William Booker, John Challen, Richard Combs, Thomas Locke, John Sanders, William Andrews, Richard Locke, Philip Richardson, Thomas Kempe, Christopher Gosden, Richard Taborne, Richard Ayllmer, Thomas Cooke, Henry Oty, Ralph Kempe. On 3 Mar, when Mary Allison late of Easebourne, 'spinster', aged 12, was playing on and near a common footpath in 'Eastborne Parke' with John Luffe, aged 12, Mary Broughton, aged 12, and Mary Clare, aged 7, and William Tidey late of Easebourne, 'laborer', aged 13, was joking and playing among the 'children aforesaid' with 'a birding peece' belonging to Anthony Lickfold of Tillington, gent., which he was carrying from Tillington to Anthony Walbancke of Easebourne, ironsmith, 'to bee amended', the gun, which was loaded with 'gunpowder' and 'hayleshott', suddenly, by mischance and without the knowledge and against the will of Tidey 'did discharge and shoote of', Tidey being completely unaware that it was loaded, and Allison was struck in the lower part of the abdomen by the lead shot and received a wound 2 inches wide and 3 inches deep of which she immediately died by misadventure and against Tidey's will and not otherwise. The gun is worth 6s 8d and remains with Thomas Tydey of Easebourne, 'yeoman'. ASSI 35/89/2, m 7.
[Delivered to East Grinstead assizes on 1 Sept.]

401   17 Mar 1648. Steyning. Edward Raynes, gent., county coroner. Jurors: Philip Seale, Richard Hill, Thomas Strudwicke, Joseph Costidell, Richard Dibbes, William Tyler, Henry Skinner, Thomas Streeter, Thomas Lisle, John Parson, John Lasseter, William Marner, Thomas Tamson. About 3 p.m. on 6 Mar Thomas Juppe late of Steyning, 'yeoman', feloniously killed William Dunstall late of Steyning, 'laborer', aged 11, at Ashurst with 'a hasell driveing goad' worth ¼d which he held in both hands, violently striking and beating him on the back and 'hippes' of which he languished at Ashurst until 11 p.m. on that day and then died. Juppe had no goods or chattels, lands or tenements in Sussex at the time of the felony or ever after to the jurors' knowledge. ASSI 35/89/2, m 11.
[Delivered with **400**. At the assizes an indictment was preferred which charged Juppe and Richard White late of Steyning, yeoman, with murder: Juppe killing Dunstall as in the inquest verdict except for the omission of the last sentence; and White being feloniously present aiding and abetting him. The grand jury, to which Thomas Horley, James Meade and (*blank*) Wolrich gave evidence, rejected the charge against White and reduced that against Juppe to manslaughter. Juppe pleaded not guilty to the inquest verdict but was convicted; he had no chattels. He then successfully pleaded benefit of clergy and was bailed to appear at the next assizes; in the meantime he was to procure a pardon for branding on the hand. ASSI 35/89/2, mm 9–11, 32d.]

402   15 Apr 1648. Rye. Thomas Palmer, gent., Rye mayor and coroner. Jurors of Rye: John Benbrigge, John Feild, William Gates, Robert Cadman, Angel [*Angelus*] Shaw, John Bab, Henry Whitwoode, 'Benjamin' Blist, Nicholas Kennard, Robert Martin, Richard Flinstone, Edward Blaker. Nathaniel son of John Holcum of Rye 'fell from a bridge, which is not fenced, into the river which comes from the Wish and there found dead and taken up by' his father. [*Verdict in English.*] RYE 1/13, f 237v.

403   17 Apr 1648. Boxgrove. Richard Smyth, gent., county coroner. Jurors: John Hobson, Richard Trimnell, Samuel Hull, Ralph West, William Deereling, Thomas Forbench, William Reader, Thomas Gibbens, Thomas Hamon, William Hamon, Henry Hasted, Thomas Hartly, John Newnam, Thomas Hamonds, John Bryant. On 13 Apr Thomas Symonds died a natural death at Boxgrove. ASSI 35/89/2, m 6.
[Delivered with **400**.]

404   24 Apr 1648. East Chiltington. Edward Raynes, gent., county coroner. Jurors: Nicholas Challoner, gent., William Paine, Richard White, Henry Barnden, Henry Cane, Thomas Skinner, Richard Cheale, Richard Hider, Thomas Hider, John Jenner, Hugh Rickward, Thomas Stedwell. On 21 Apr

Elizabeth Launder late of Keymer, 'spinster', gave birth at East Chiltington to a live male child which by the laws of England 'was a bastard' and later on that day she murdered him by taking him in both hands, throwing him naked into 'a brooke' full of water at East Chiltington and drowning him, whereby he immediately died. At that time she had no goods or chattels, lands or tenements in Sussex to the jurors' knowledge. ASSI 35/89/2, m 18.

[Delivered with **400**. At the assizes Launder, who had been committed to gaol by the coroner, pleaded not guilty but was convicted and sentenced to be hanged; she had no chattels. She then pleaded pregnancy but a jury of matrons found her not to be pregnant. ASSI 35/89/2, mm 13, 14, 18, 32d, 33.]

405   30 June 1648. Warbleton in Hastings rape. George Courthop, gent., county and Hastings rape coroner. Jurors of Sussex and Hastings rape: Thomas Roberts, gent., Thomas Jenner, gent., Thomas Lade, gent., Ellis [*Elizias*] Ellis, Thomas Fry, William Gouldsmyth, ... Lovekinge, Stephen Wilmsett, John Bray, William Crooch, Thomas Tayler, Nicholas Venner, Thomas Drawbridge. On 28 June, when Josiah [*Josias*] Crooch was driving a cart loaded with coal and drawn by 4 oxen and a horse from Hellingly Park to Glazier's Forge, by misadventure the cart suddenly veered at Warbleton by reason of the ruts in the road there and fell on him, so crushing his body that he immediately died thereof and not otherwise to the jurors' knowledge. The cart, coal, 4 oxen and horse moved to his death and remain with Josiah Crooch jun. of Warbleton, 'husbandman'. The jurors appraised the oxen and horse at £10 and the cart and coal at 40s. KB 9/844, m 73.

[Delivered by the coroner to King's Bench in Trinity 1649. Josiah Crooch jun. was summoned to King's Bench to answer for the deodands. KB 9/844, mm 73, 74d; KB 29/298, m 35.]

406   29 Aug 1648. Upper Beeding. Edward Raynes, gent., county coroner. Jurors: Thomas Whittington, John Backshell, John Marchant, William Snelling, Thomas Riste, Henry Boniface, Richard Morris, Henry Farncombe, John Harland, Robert Wilkins, John Inskipp, John Osborne, Thomas Denman. On 20 Aug John Manning late of Upper Beeding, gent., feloniously killed Daniel Rogers late of Rudgwick, gent., at Upper Beeding with 'a small crabbed sticke' worth ¼d which he held in his right hand, giving him a wound on the left eye 1 inch deep and ½ inch wide of which he languished at Upper Beeding until 25 Aug and then died. Manning had no goods or chattels, lands or tenements in Sussex at the time of the felony or ever after to the jurors' knowledge. ASSI 35/89/2, m 17.

[Delivered with **400**. At the assizes Manning pleaded not guilty but was convicted; he had no chattels. He then successfully pleaded benefit of clergy and was bailed to appear at the next assizes; in the meantime he was to procure a pardon for branding on the hand. ASSI 35/89/2, mm 14, 17, 32d.]

407   8 Sept 1648. Peasmarsh. George Courthope, gent., Hastings rape coroner. Jurors: James Coochman, Thomas Davie, Richard Humfrey, Richard Mercer, Edward Glover, 'Reignold' Perkins, Thomas Freeman, Francis Sampson, Edward Leeds, William Hoy, Richard Sheppard, John Brabrook. On 4 Sept Thomas Sharvall late of Peasmarsh, 'tanner', feloniously killed Matthew Hards late of Peasmarsh, 'laborer', at Peasmarsh with 'a butt speare' worth 12d which he held in both hands, violently thrusting and striking him on the lower part of the abdomen under the navel and giving him 'a mortall bruise' of which he languished at Peasmarsh until the next day and then died. Sharvall had no goods or chattels, lands or tenements at the time of the felony or ever after to the jurors' knowledge. ASSI 35/90/2, m 22.

[Delivered to East Grinstead assizes on 12 Mar 1649 when an indictment was preferred identical to the inquest verdict except that the charge was murder and the last sentence was omitted. The grand jury, to which John Wood, Aaron Holt and Elizabeth Hardes gave evidence, reduced the charge to manslaughter. Sharvall pleaded not guilty to the indictment as amended but was convicted; he had no chattels. He then successfully pleaded benefit of clergy and was branded on the hand and released. ASSI 35/90/2, mm 18, 21, 22, 42d.]

408   25 Sept 1648. Hurstpierpoint. Edward Raynes, gent., county coroner. Jurors: Richard Whitepaine, William Lashmer, George Scrace, Richard Stanbridge, Robert Hall, William Bennett, Samuel Freind, Richard ?Barre, William Bryant, Thomas Gratwicke, Thomas Reeves, Robert Whitepaine, John

Buckell. Witnesses: Walter Lucas, John Virrall, James Bradford, Peter Bradford, William Lachmer, who entered recognizances in £20 to attend the assizes. On 23 Sept George Moore late of Wivelsfield, gent., John Whitebread late of Wivelsfield, 'husbandman', William Jarvice late of Wivelsfield, 'tanner', Robert Buckell late of Keymer, 'husbandman', Edward Miles late of Clayton, 'husbandman', and Richard Davy late of Lindfield, 'cooper', murdered Richard Bradford late of Hurstpierpoint, 'marriner', at Pyecombe: Moore giving him 'one mortall bruise' on the front of the head with 'a staffe' of no value which he held in both hands, of which he languished at Hurstpierpoint and Pyecombe until the next day and then died at Hurstpierpoint; and the 5 others being feloniously present aiding and abetting him. Afterwards, on 10 Oct [sic] all 6 fled on account of the murder to places unknown to the jurors. None of them had any goods or chattels, lands or tenements at the time of the felony or ever after to the jurors' knowledge. ASSI 35/90/2, mm 17, 17d.

[Delivered with 407. At Lewes quarter sessions on 5 and 6 Oct 1648 a recognizance was entered by Richard Pickham of Ditchling, husbandman, in £80 and by Walter Lucas of Wivelsfield, gent., and Thomas Stephens of Ditchling, yeoman, in £40 each for Pickham's appearance at the next assizes to answer for Bradford's death; and another was entered by Richard Colman of Ditchling, husbandman, in £80 and by the same Stephens and Lucas in £40 each for the like appearance of Colman for the same. At the assizes of 12 Mar 1649 a capias issued to the sheriff ordering him to have Moore, Whitebread, Jarvice, Buckell and Davy at the assizes of 14 July, but they were then still at large. Moore, Jarvice, Buckell and Davy had been outlawed before the assizes of 21 Mar 1650. At the assizes of 22 July 1652 Whitebread, who had been committed to gaol by the coroner, pleaded not guilty but was convicted and hanged; he had no goods. Jarvice had been committed to the county gaol by Thomas Chaloner, esq., JP, for Bradford's murder before the assizes of 17 July 1658 when it was ordered that he be kept in gaol without bail until delivered by due process. He was still in gaol at the assizes of 22 July 1659 when the order was repeated. ASSI 35/90/2, m 17; ASSI 35/90/5, m 30; ASSI 35/93/9, mm 9, 27d, 28; ASSI 35/99/10, mm 15, 15d; ASSI 35/100/6, mm 17, 17d; SRS, LIV, 161.]

409   30 Oct 1648. Stopham. Richard Smith, gent., county coroner. Jurors: Edward Onely, Frank Walker, Theodore Walker, Edward Boley, John Arnopp, James Gardner, John Slater, William Greenefeild, James Amersh, Thomas Hopley, John Lansden, John Spring. Witnesses: Robert Greeneyarde, John Parsons, Joan Edwardes, John Slaughter. On 1 Oct Thomas Bennett late of Pulborough, 'laborer', murdered William Walter at Pulborough: he violently threw him into a stream there with both hands and 'did drowne and choake' him whereby he immediately died. Bennett had no goods or chattels, lands or tenements at that time or ever after to the jurors' knowledge. ASSI 35/90/2, mm 16, 16d.

[Delivered with 407. At the assizes the grand jury presented 2 indictments: one, concerning which Edward Rose, William Bridger and Richard West gave evidence, charged Bennett with feloniously breaking and escaping from Horsham gaol about 1 a.m. on 20 Nov 1648, he having been committed there by George Churchar, esq., JP, on 1 Oct on suspicion of murdering Walter, to be kept in the custody of Richard Luckin, keeper of the gaol under Humphrey Steward, esq., sheriff, until his trial; and the other, concerning which Edmund Streater jun. gave evidence, charged him with feloniously stealing and carrying away 7 hens worth 6d each belonging to Streater at Pulborough on 19 Feb 1649. Bennett was still at large at the time of the assizes of 12 Mar 1649 when a capias therefore issued to the sheriff ordering him to have him at the assizes of 14 July. On 14 July Bennett, who had been recommitted to gaol, pleaded not guilty to the inquest verdict but was convicted and hanged; he had no chattels. ASSI 35/90/2, mm 3, 15, 16; ASSI 35/90/5, mm 12, 30, 38, 38d.]

410   22 Feb 1649. Ticehurst. George Courthop, gent., county coroner. Jurors: William Hartridge, gent., Thomas Nash, John Busse, Alexander Gray, Joseph Fowle, Abraham Hunt, Alexander Sheff, Edward Cliff, John Hoadly, William Peene, Joseph Chapman, Leonard Campain. On 20 Feb, when William Patteson was riding on a mare at Ticehurst on the road between Ticehurst and 'Barrows Mill', by misadventure he fell from the mare which also fell, so crushing Patteson's head that he immediately died thereof and not otherwise to the jurors' knowledge. The mare moved to his death, is worth 10s and remains with John Wood of Burwash, 'husbandman'. KB 9/844, m 72.

[Delivered with 405. Wood was summoned to King's Bench to answer for the mare. KB 9/844, mm 72, 74d; KB 29/298, m 35.]

411   17 Mar 1649. Salehurst. George Courthop, gent., county coroner. Jurors: Stephen Pooke, Richard Weller, Richard Stace, Thomas Moyse, Thomas Apps, Paul Wickham, Ralph Mercer, Thomas Roderick, Roger Shoesmyth, 'Annanias' Booreman, John Synnock, William Dunck. On 12 Mar Thomas Russell late of Salehurst, 'laborer', feloniously hanged himself with 'a rope' worth 1d which he held in both hands, tying one end round 'a barr' in his barn at Salehurst and putting the other round his neck; and so he came to his death and not otherwise to the jurors' knowledge. At that time he possessed 3 cows worth £6 which remain with Thomas Bennet of Hastings, gent., for the use of Thomas Pelham, bt. KB 9/844, m 74.
[Delivered with **405**. Bennet was summoned to King's Bench to answer for the cows. KB 9/844, mm 74, 74d; KB 29/298, m 35.]

412   14 Mar 1650. Birdham. George Coperthwaite, gent., Manhood hundred coroner. Jurors: Thomas Forder, Richard Lee, Richard Holmes, Thomas Poke, Andrew Cheeseman, Richard Burrish, William Davis, Roger Hale, Anthony Hoskins, John Stowell, Roger Higgins, Richard Paddicke, Thomas Hobbs. On 1 Mar William Squire late of Chichester, 'yeoman', came about his necessary business to the dwelling-house of John Gray of Birdham, 'yeoman', and by Gray's permission went into the kitchen of the house where he remained for ½ hour transacting his business. Then, Squire 'being about to goe forth of the said kitchen' holding under 'the right arme a birding peece charged with gunpowder and hayleshott' to shoot small birds, suddenly, by misadventure and against his will the gun 'did discharge and shoote of' and from the force of the gunpowder the lead shot struck Katharine Rumbridger, 'spinster', who was in the kitchen near Squire, on the front of the head and she received a wound 2 inches wide and 3 inches deep of which she immediately died by misadventure and against Squire's will. The gun is worth 5s and remains with [*blank*] Bentham, lord of the manor of Manhood hundred. ASSI 35/91/4, m 97.
[Delivered to East Grinstead assizes on 21 Mar. Squire received a pardon for the death which he pleaded at the assizes of 1 Aug when it was allowed and enrolled. ASSI 35/91/4, m 97.]

413   1 Aug 1650. Wadhurst. George Courthope, gent., county coroner. Jurors: Thomas Skynner, Thomas Wood, William Skynner, John Clarke, William Burges, Thomas Pritchett, Abraham Fowler, William Kitchenham sen., William Smyth, Robert Russell, John Coleman, William Hosmer, Thomas Gunter, Nicholas Russell, William Trice. On 30 July, when Francis Smyth late of Frant, 'carpenter', and John May of Frant, 'carpenter', were together at Riverhall in Wadhurst 'workinge' a piece of wood, with May 'standing' behind Smyth's back, and Smyth was 'lifting up his right legg' on 'the blow' of May, by misadventure and against May's will he struck Smyth on 'ye right legg' with 'an axe' which he held in both hands, giving him a wound 1 inch deep and 2 inches long of which he died at Wadhurst within ½ hour. Thus he was killed by misadventure only and not through any felony or otherwise. ASSI 35/91/10, m 109.
[Delivered to East Grinstead assizes on 1 Aug.]

414   30 Sept 1650. Rye. Samuel Landsdale, gent., Rye mayor and coroner. Jurors. Richard Beale; Stephen Dad, John Field, Thomas Wellard; Thomas Stonestreete, Thomas Liscoe; Thomas Seers, Anthony Knight, Stephen Bruffe, Richard Flinstone; Mark Carpenter, Henry Martin, Edward Blaker. About 4 p.m. on 28 Sept 'Hanna Amite, servant to Mr Thomas Greenfield, was delyvered of a man child and did convay the same into the house of office standing in the garden belonging to the dwelling house of the said Mr Greenfield, being in Rye, and there was found dead'. Verdict, murder.
[*Verdict in English.*] RYE 1/14, f 4v.
[At the Rye sessions of the peace on ?2 Dec the grand jury presented an indictment which charged Hannah Amiott of Rye, spinster, with murdering her new-born male child. She pleaded not guilty but was convicted and, having nothing to say on her behalf, was sentenced to be hanged; she had no goods or chattels, lands or tenements to the jurors' knowledge. RYE 1/14, ff 14v–15.]

415   9 Oct 1650. Rye. Samuel Landsdale, gent., Rye mayor and coroner. Jurors: Thomas Boys; Thomas Ducke, Mark Woodfort, Daniel Packer, Robert Wood; William Gates, Thomas Wellard, Joseph Martin, Miles Wilding; Stephen Braffe, Robert Buscod, Edmund Waters. About 5 p.m. on 8 Oct John Boult murdered Jacob Vanbever [*once changed to* Boinart], a stranger, late of 'Melslin' in Brabant [?Malines *or* the lordship of Melin], with a knife, stabbing him in the left breast, and fled. He was 'seized upon by John Dubbins and William Dyer'. [*Jurors and verdict in English.*] RYE 1/14, f 6v.
[On 2 Dec a recognizance was entered before the mayor and jurats by Boult in £40 and by John Cooper and John Collins in £20 each for Boult's appearance at the next general sessions of the peace at Rye and for his good behaviour in the meantime. At the next sessions (*undated*) the grand jury presented an indictment which charged Boult, styled gent., with murder. He pleaded not guilty to the indictment and was acquitted of murder but convicted of manslaughter; he had no goods or chattels, lands or tenements to the trial jurors' knowledge. He then successfully pleaded benefit of clergy and was branded on the right hand. On 1 Dec 1651 Cooper and Collins, who had been bound for Boult's appearance on that day, were released on an affidavit made before the mayor and jurats by an unnamed man of Ostend that Boult had drowned. RYE 1/14, ff 14, 15, 43.]

416   3 Dec 1650. Eastbourne. Edward Raynes, gent., county coroner. Jurors: John Holland, John Worge, Richard Crunden, Thomas Ladds, Nicholas Foord, Thomas Store, Thomas Reedes, John Tutt, John Hutchins, George Berricke, John Bodle, Francis Hicks. On 18 Nov Alice Bassett late of Eastbourne, 'spinster', gave birth at Eastbourne to a live male child which by the laws of England 'was a bastard' and immediately afterwards murdered him there: she took him in both hands, threw him into 'a pond' full of water and 'did drowne and choake' him whereby he immediately died. Bassett had no goods or chattels, lands or tenements at that time or ever after to the jurors' knowledge. ASSI 35/92/9, m 26.
[Delivered to East Grinstead assizes on 15 Mar 1651 when Bassett, who had been committed to gaol by the coroner, pleaded not guilty but was convicted and hanged; she had no chattels. ASSI 35/92/9, mm 21, 26, 30, 30d.]

417   28 Dec 1650. Cliffe. Edward Raynes, gent., county coroner. Jurors: Thomas Parsons, George Shoulder, John West, Thomas Goldham, Robert Pollard, George Goldham, James Russell, William Cooper, Richard White, Daniel Crony, Andrew Browne, Thomas Barnes, Nicholas Tull. On 25 Dec Susan Hockham late of Cliffe, 'spinster', gave birth at Cliffe to a live male child which by the laws of England 'was a bastard' and immediately afterwards murdered him there: she took him in both hands, placed him and left him between 2 linen [*lineas*] 'sheetes' on 'a bed' in the dwelling-house of Ann Moore, widow, and 'did choake and strangle' him between the said woollen [*laneas*] sheets whereby he died. Hockham had no goods or chattels, lands or tenements at that time or ever after to the jurors' knowledge. ASSI 35/92/9, m 25.
[Delivered with **416**. At the assizes Hockham, who had been committed to gaol by the coroner, pleaded not guilty and was acquitted; she had not fled and was therefore discharged, paying her fees. ASSI 35/92/9, mm 21, 25, 30, 30d.]

418   11 Mar 1651. Hailsham. Edward Raynes, gent., county coroner. Jurors: John Reade, William Poole, John Gravett, Thomas Bodle, Abraham Bodle, John Catt, Thomas Frencham, William Lulham, Ellis Swane, Thomas Tutt, William Alfrey, Thomas Everest, John Pardon. On 6 Mar Elizabeth Freakes late of Hailsham, 'spinster', gave birth at Hailsham to a live female child which by the laws of England 'was a bastard' and later that day she murdered her there, taking her in both hands, throwing her into 'a pond' full of water and drowning her whereby she immediately died. Freakes had no goods or chattels, lands or tenements at that time or ever after to the jurors' knowledge. ASSI 35/92/9, m 24.
[Delivered with **416**. At the assizes Freakes pleaded not guilty but was convicted and hanged; she had no chattels. ASSI 35/92/9, mm 21, 24, 30d.]

419   Same date, place, coroner and jurors (in the same order) as **418**. On 24 Dec 1650 John Huggett of Hailsham, 'laborer', came to the barn of John Pollington of Hailsham, 'yeoman', at Hailsham, went in and, seeing a gun 'charged with gunpowder and hayleshott', took it in both hands. While holding it, he pulled 'the cocke' of the gun, intending only 'to strike fire', but Pollington's son James, aged 6,

was coming towards the barn 'out of the sight' of Huggett and the gun suddenly, by mischance and against Huggett's will 'did shoote of and discharge' and the lead shot was fired upon James by the force of the gunpowder, giving him a wound in the left side of the chest 2 inches wide and 3 inches deep of which he immediately died by misadventure and against Huggett's will and not otherwise. The gun is worth 2s 6d and remains with Roger Harris of Hailsham, 'freemason'. ASSI 35/92/11, m 48.
[Delivered with 416. At the assizes an indictment was preferred which charged Huggett with feloniously killing James Pollington at Hailsham on 24 Dec with a gun which he held in both hands and which he discharged at James, giving him a wound as in the inquest verdict of which he immediately died; but the grand jury, to which John Pollington gave evidence, rejected it. ASSI 35/92/11, m 46.]

420   21 May 1651. Cuckfield. Edward Raynes, gent., county coroner. Jurors: Thomas Challoner, gent., Edward Wickham, Thomas Jenkin, Thomas Tompson, Thomas Holford, Thomas Hurst, Thomas Cheale, Thomas Brotherton, John Wood, David Ellis, Edward Virgoe, Stephen Wood, William Wassell. Witnesses: Robert Vincent, Margaret his wife, Ann Mitchell, Thomas Burtenshaw, George Denman, Ann Tasker. On 19 May William Burrell late of Cuckfield, husbandman, feloniously killed Thomas Tasker late of Cuckfield, labourer, at Cuckfield, giving him a bruise on the face and nose with his right hand of which he immediately died. Burrell had no goods or chattels, lands or tenements at that time or ever after to the jurors' knowledge. [*English.*] ASSI 35/92/10, mm 10, 10d.
[Delivered to East Grinstead assizes on 14 July when an indictment was preferred identical to the inquest verdict except that the charge was murder, Burrell was called a labourer and the last sentence was omitted. The grand jury, to which the same 6 witnesses gave evidence (Burtenshaw being called jun.), reduced the charge to manslaughter. Burrell pleaded not guilty to the inquest verdict but was convicted; he had no goods. He then successfully pleaded benefit of clergy and was branded on the hand and released, paying 10s 4d. ASSI 35/92/10, mm 3, 9, 10, 25d.]

421   6 Aug 1651. Petworth. Richard Ailwin, gent., county coroner. Jurors of Petworth: Geoffrey Daughtry, Thomas Morris, Robert Hillman, Nicholas Goodier, John Hasling jun., Henry Sandham, William Hurst, Henry Dammer, James Earlye, Robert Trew, Richard Wyatt, John Mason, Richard Fellery, Nicholas Lucus. Witnesses: Thomas Holland, Henry Beale, Geoffrey Daughtry. On 9 July Mary Barwick jun. late of Petworth, spinster, gave birth at Petworth to a live female child which by the laws of England was a bastard and later on the same day murdered her there, taking her in both hands and strangling her whereby she immediately died. Later on the same day Mary Barwick sen. late of Petworth, spinster, alias Mary wife of Christopher Barwick late of Petworth, labourer, feloniously received, comforted and supported Mary jun., knowing that she had committed the murder. Afterwards Mary jun. fled on account of the murder [to a] place unknown to the jurors. She had [no lands or] tenements, goods or chattels at the time of the murder or ever after to the jurors' knowledge. [*English; damaged.*] ASSI 35/93/8, m 22.
[Delivered to East Grinstead assizes on 13 Mar 1652 when the grand jury, to which Geoffrey Daughtry gave evidence, presented an indictment which charged both women with murder: Mary jun. with strangling the child shortly after giving birth, as in the inquest verdict, and Mary sen., whose husband was styled yeoman, with being feloniously present aiding and abetting her, the last 3 sentences of the inquest verdict were omitted. Mary jun. pleaded not guilty to the indictment and was acquitted; she had not fled and was released, paying her fees. Mary sen. had not been committed to gaol. ASSI 35/93/8, mm 5, 21, 22, 24, 24d.]

422   15 Sept 1651. Chichester. Richard Bragge and Thomas Wheeler, Chichester city coroners. Jurors: William Burry, Edward Floud, Leonard Madgewicke, Thomas Pollard Thomas Barber, George Jenninges sen., Roger Eyles, Gabriel Gauge, Thomas Bartholmew, John Butcher, Richard Phillips, John Mose, Thomas Ghost, Robert Barnes, George Jenninges jun., William Driver, William Smith. 'A litle after sunsett' on 13 Sept, when Edward Short of Burpham, yeoman, was riding very fast on a light grey nag in East Street in Chichester, the nag violently knocked over Joan wife of William Heyward, husbandman, who was walking home there, grievously beating, bruising and wounding her head and face with some or one of its feet of which she languished for 3 hours or thereabouts and then died. Thus Short with his nag killed her by misfortune. The nag moved to her death and is worth 50s. Short had no other goods or chattels at the time of the killing or ever after to the jurors' knowledge. [*English*.] ASSI 35/93/8, m 18.

[Delivered with **421**. At the assizes an indictment was preferred which charged Short and Owen and Robert Ludgater, all 3 called late of Chichester, yeomen, with murdering Joan Heyward at Chichester on 13 Sept: Short forcing a light grey horse worth 50s, on which he was riding, to run violently over her and to trample on her head, face and body, whereby she was so wounded that she immediately died; and the Ludgaters being feloniously present aiding and abetting him. The grand jury reduced the charge against Short to manslaughter and rejected that against the Ludgaters. Short pleaded not guilty to the indictment as amended and was acquitted; he had not fled. He was to apply for a pardon in respect of the inquest verdict. ASSI 35/93/8, mm 5, 18, 19.]

423   29 Sept 1651. Rye. Thomas Greenefeild, gent., Rye mayor and coroner, and the jurats. Jurors: Thomas Morphet, Edward Greeneway, Mark Woodford, John Feild, Henry Marten, Benjamin Blyst, John Kinge, Moses Peadle, Thomas Kennet, Nicholas Kennard, Stephen Bruffe, Bartholomew Breades. About 3 or 4 p.m. on 27 Sept, when Hannah daughter of John Foster of Rye, mariner, 'lay in the Lower Street at the doore of Roger Gilford, senior', she was killed by misadventure by the horses and beer cart of Mark Davis and Thomas Hunter which were going by. The jurors appraised the horses, cart and 'lodinge' at £3 10s. [*English*.] RYE 1/14, f 39.

[There is another, much reduced, version of the inquest which omits the time and date and merely states that Hannah Foster, a child, 'laye in the strete and was killed by the cartwhell, the horses drawing of it, for which wee find the horses and the cart; and wee pryse the horses, cart and loding at' £3 10s. On 29 Sept John Gilberd of Rye, mariner, gave evidence before the mayor and Messrs Spye, Bennet and John Greenefeilde, almost certainly at the inquest, that about 3 or 4 p.m. on 27 Sept he saw Hannah daughter of John Foster lying in Lower Street against the door of Roger Gilford sen. and the near wheel of the beer cart of Mark Davis and Thomas Hunter passed by and injured her head; Thomas Joyner was driving the cart and John Patcham, the master brewer, called to him, telling him to stop the cart because he had killed Hannah, and Joyner tried to stop it.

At the Rye sessions of the peace on 1 Dec an indictment was preferred which charged Thomas Joyner of Rye, carter, with murdering Hannah Foster, spinster: while driving 3 horses with a beer cart worth £3 10s in Lower Street in Rye at 4 p.m. on 27 Sept and seeing her lying on the ground, he gave her a wound on the back of the head with the near wheel of the cart and broke her skull, of which she died about 8 p.m. on the same day. John Gilbert and John Patcham gave evidence to the grand jury which reduced the charge to chance medley. Joyner pleaded not guilty to the indictment as amended but was convicted of homicide by chance medley and misadventure; he had not fled and had no goods or chattels, lands or tenements in Rye to the trial jurors' knowledge. He entered a recognizance in £100 and Mark Davis, beerbrewer, and Thomas Hunter, baker, both of Rye, in £50 each to prosecute his pardon. RYE 1/14, ff 42–43; RYE 47/146, unnumbered documents.]

424   22 Sept 1652. Rye. Alan Grebell, gent., deputy of William Burwash, gent., Rye mayor and coroner, and the jurats. Jurors: Daniel Packer, Samuel Stephenson, Daniel Miller, Nicholas Kennard, Thomas Seere, Moses Peadle, John Diggenson, Robert Wood, John Guildford, Edmund Harris, Robert Pet, Mark Carpenter, John Bones. Between 10 and 11 a.m. on 21 Sept, when John Wright was in a frigate called 'the Merlin' on the sea before Rye, Peter Warren, gent., captain of the frigate, came and murdered him with a pistol 'charged with powder and bullet' worth 12d which he held in his right hand, striking him on the back on the left side of the 'reines' [*sc.* reins, the kidneys or loins], and the pistol discharged and gave him a wound right through the body, the bullet entering on the left side of the reins and coming out on the left side of the belly, a little below the navel, of which he died there about 5 or 6 hours later. At the time of the felony Warren had no goods or chattels, lands or tenements in Rye or elsewhere to the jurors' knowledge. [*English*.] RYE 47/147, no 3; RYE 1/14, f 72. [*Described in HMC, XIII, App. IV, 219.*]

[There is a third, much reduced, version of the inquest verdict which merely states that Wright died of the wound given him by the captain with the shot, that it was wilful murder and that Warren had no goods or chattels, lands or tenements. There is also a small piece of paper containing what appear to be shorthand versions of part of the following evidence taken on the day of the inquest and presumably at the inquest.

Before the deputy mayor and Thomas Palmer, Thomas Greenefeild and Alexander Bennet, jurats, Captain Peter Warren, commander of the frigate 'Marline', said that on 21 Sept on board the frigate Wright contradicted him and called him coward. Although he often told him to be silent, he would not, whereupon Warren, being angered, shot him with a pistol of which he died about 5 hours later. Before the deputy mayor, the same 3 jurats and also John Spye and Thomas Miller, George Crapnel, master of the frigate, said that he saw Warren discharge a pistol at Wright's back of which Wright died about 5 hours later; but he did not know what was the cause of the dispute between them, only that some in the frigate said that Wright had given Warren 'some crosse language'. Paul Bayly, purser of the frigate, said that when he was on the deck of the frigate with Warren and Wright, some words arose between them and Warren told Wright to hold his tongue or he would pistol him. Wright replied 'Sir, I have done', and as he and Bayly were turning away from Warren, Warren shot Wright of which he shortly afterwards died. Henry Gosner also heard Wright say to Warren 'Sir, I have done' and said that Warren pistolled him as he was turning away. Robert Burrough said that when he was in his cabin in the frigate he heard Warren say after Wright was shot that he killed him because he would not fight, although Burrough had earlier heard Wright say that he would fight. David Knowles, boatswain, said that he did not see Warren pistol Wright, but he saw Wright fall down after being shot and then saw Warren kick him and say 'Throw him over boord. Here is powder and shot to kill another'. Knowles asked who shot Wright and Warren replied that it was he. Knowles then took the pistol out of his hand because Warren said that he did not care if he killed 20 more. John Rumney, carpenter, said that he saw Warren present his pistol at Wright twice and, being near them, put aside the pistol; but later, as Wright turned to go away from Warren, Warren shot him in the back. Rumney, turning round, saw Wright fall down and then took him by the hand, whereupon Warren said 'Hange him, dog, throw him over boord'. Afterwards, when Warren was in his cabin, Rumney said to him 'Captain, you have done a sad accident', to which Warren replied 'Hange it, I doe not care if I kill twenty more, I will answere it'.

On the day of the inquest the mayor and jurats wrote to the Council of State, informing it that the Merlin had arrived at Rye on the previous night, and that morning several of its officers had complained to them that Warren, their captain, had killed Wright, a passenger in the frigate, and had presented Warren as a prisoner, asking for him to be secured until further orders. Having taken several examinations, the mayor and jurats had committed him to custody, but could proceed no further because the killing took place outside their jurisdiction and the offender was a military man. They therefore asked for further direction.

James Harrington, president of the Council of State, replied on 24 Sept that the Council, having considered the letter and also a certificate from the frigate's officers about the murder, had decided that Warren should be brought to London under safe custody for speedy trial and had sent 4 of the Council's messengers to convey him. The mayor and jurats were to deliver him to them. The Council had also written to the master of the Merlin to appoint at least 3 eye-witnesses of the murder to give evidence before the judges of the Admiralty, before whom the case would be tried, and asked the mayor and jurats to send to the master on the subject in order that fit witnesses should be sent. If convenient, the witnesses should come with the captain to assist the messengers and to be ready in London for the trial which was to be held speedily.

On 25 Sept Anthony Compton, Edward Tyson, Henry Byard and Thomas Baker, deputies of Edward Dendy, esq., the Council's serjeant at arms, were ordered to go to Rye, take Warren into their custody and bring him to the Council. On 29 Sept the mayor and jurats of Rye wrote again to the Council, saying that they had delivered Warren to the 4 messengers; had asked the master of the Merlin if Henry Gosner, steward, David Knowles, boatswain, and John Rumney, carpenter, who were eye-witnesses of the event and could say most about it, might go with them; and enclosed a copy of the evidence given on 22 Sept by Gosner, Knowles and Rumney, the transcript having been checked against the original by Samuel Jeakes, recorder of Rye, and found to be accurate.

On 30 Sept the Council ordered that a warrant should be drawn up for the committal of Warren to Newgate to await trial; and that a letter should be sent to the Admiralty judges telling them of the committal, enclosing the examinations of the witnesses and urging them to bring Warren to trial speedily because the witnesses were staying in town to give evidence and, being officers of the ship, they could not for long be spared from their duties. On 2 Oct the Council informed the keeper of Newgate that by its warrant for Warren's close imprisonment it intended no greater restraint than was necessary for his safe custody for trial. On the same day it ordered that the mayor of Rye should be told to deliver to Warren's wife Eleanor such of his goods as were taken into the mayor's keeping on his arrest. Also on 2 Oct John Rumney of Chatham in Kent, mariner, aged 24 or thereabouts, Henry Gosnell of London, steward of the Merlin, and David Knowles, its boatswain, entered recognizances in £50 each in the dining chamber before William Clerk and John Exton, doctors of law and judges of the High Court of Admiralty, and in the presence of Samuel Howe, notary public, to appear before the Admiralty judges at Southwark between 8 and 10 a.m. on 7 Oct to give evidence against Warren.

Warren himself was examined before Clerk and Exton on 6 Oct. He said that about 3 weeks before, by the order of Captain Moulton, one of the commissioners of the navy, John Wright and others were embarked at Portsmouth on the frigate Merlin, which belonged to the state and of which he (Warren) was then captain, to be taken to the Downs or elsewhere to the fleet under the command of General Blake; and Warren was ordered by Moulton to set sail from Portsmouth to discover the Dutch fleet and to notify the Council of State and Blake accordingly. He therefore set sail from Portsmouth on 19 Sept. On 21 Sept they discovered 48 ships of the Dutch fleet between

Beachy Head and Fairlight, the Merlin being about 2 leagues to the windward of the Dutch and with a fresh gale blowing so that she could approach and retreat from them at pleasure. Warren said that he ordered his men to 'bear away towards the headmost ship' of the Dutch fleet to gain further intelligence about it, and ordered his gunner to prepare a broadside and his corporal to put his soldiers into a warlike posture. Wright then came up to Warren and asked him what he intended to do and made other remarks, to which Warren replied 'What have you to doe with it? Begone. You have nothinge to doe here. Meddle with your owne busines'. As they drew nearer to the Dutch fleet one of its ships shot at the Merlin and she returned fire, the 2 ships being about 4 miles apart. Wright afterwards came up to Warren 3 or 4 times and each time opposed his orders. He also had private conference with other passengers, and some of the Merlin's company began to join him, so that Warren feared that he would start a mutiny on the frigate. He therefore told Wright to be quiet and hold his peace or else he would pistol him, having his pistol then in his hand. As Warren turned away, Wright came behind him and swore by God that 'for all your bravado and vapouring you are a coward'. Warren turned back, Wright having turned his back on him, and the pistol that Warren was holding, being half bent and with the cock up, accidentally and not by his will and intention went off and shot Wright through the back and Wright died of the wound in the frigate at sea within 6 or 7 hours. Warren added that Wright was shot about 10 a.m. on 21 Sept in the frigate on the high and open sea and that he immediately fell down. Asked if David Knowles, the boatswain, on seeing Wright fall, asked who had pistolled him and if Warren answered that he had, Warren denied having said any such thing to Knowles, but confessed that Knowles snatched the pistol out of his hand and that, when Wright fell down, some of the passengers and some of his frigate's company laid hands upon him (Warren), imprisoned him in his cabin and, as soon as Wright had died, put both his legs into the bilboes and so kept him prisoner until he was carried as a prisoner ashore.

The grand jury, to which Gosnell, Knowles and Rumney gave evidence, presented an indictment which charged Peter Warren late of Horsleydown in Surrey, mariner, late captain of the frigate Merlin in the service of the Commonwealth, with murdering John Wright: on 21 Sept, in the frigate on the high and open sea, he maliciously reviled and threatened Wright, a subject of the Commonwealth who was retained in its service as an officer of and in its fleet and a master's mate of the frigate 'Freindshipp', part of the fleet, and who had been put aboard the Merlin as a passenger to be taken to the fleet to perform his duties; and Warren publicly and maliciously swore that he would kill and pistol Wright and several times presented his pistol against him; later he discharged his pistol upon Wright, shooting him in the body and killing him; and having shot him and seeing him fall down mortally wounded, Warren further vented his malice against him, saying 'Hange him dogg, throwe him overboard' and that he did not care if he killed 20 more, with other malicious words.

Warren pleaded not guilty to the indictment and was acquitted. Warren had died before 21 Oct, on which day the Council ordered that a petition of his widow Eleanor be referred to the Admiralty Committee, which was to report. The petition presumably related to Warren's goods, and the Rye assembly of 22 Nov ordered that those which were then in the mayor's custody should be delivered to his widow or her assigns on the payment of the charges. HCA 1/8, nos 38–40; HCA 1/50, ff 169v–171v; RYE 1/14, f 73v; RYE 47/147, nos 2, 4; RYE 47/148, unnumbered documents; SP 18/24, no 140; SP 25/33, pp 30, 33, 57, 70; SP 25/34, p 53; *CSPD 1651–1652*, 415–417, 419, 424, 427, 450.]

425 26 Mar 1653. Rye. Alan Grebell, gent., deputy of William Burwash, gent., Rye mayor and coroner, and the jurats. Jurors: Thomas Willard, Edward Harre, Edmund Waters, Daniel Miller, Nicholas Kennard, James Godsmarke, Henry Martin, Moses Peadle, John Smith, Richard Winter, James Parker, Joseph Radfoord, Mark Carpenter. About 11 a.m. on 25 Mar Wegsert Mensemts 'happened to fall downe' the Gun Garden Cliff in Rye, striking his head on a rock and breaking the front of his skull over the right eye, of which he immediately died. At that time he had in his possession 12d and 'certaine other implements' worth 12d, but no other goods or chattels, lands or tenements in Rye to the jurors' knowledge. [*English.*] RYE 1/14, f 82v.

426 30 May 1653. Rye. William Burwash, gent., Rye mayor and coroner, and the jurats. Jurors: Richard Boys, John Collens, Thomas Willard, Edward Dearinge, Benjamin Blyst, Henry Martin, Moses Peadle, John Smith, John Boanes, William Todde, George Woolvin, John Frencham. Between noon and 1 p.m. on 29 May, when Robert son of Robert Daniell of Hastings was in a cock-boat on the water in or near the new dock at the Strand, he 'suddenly happened to fall over boord, and soe was drowned' in the sea by misadventure. [*English.*] RYE 1/14, f 85.

427 9 July 1653. Rudgwick. Richard Ailwin, gent., county coroner. Jurors: George Naldred, Henry

Stackman, Matthew Napper, Thomas Greenefeild, Humphrey Willett, William Man, Richard Overington, John Bucke, William Jorden, William Sherborne, John Overington, John Studman, Richard Thorneden, 'Farthinando' Grantham. On 6 July Edward Cooper late of Rudgwick, gent., feloniously killed William Slaughter, then one of the bailiffs of William Wilson, esq., sheriff, while he was executing his office of bailiff, at Rudgwick with a 'prong' worth 4d which he held in both hands, giving him a wound on the nose ½ inch wide and 3½ inches deep of which he immediately died. Cooper then immediately fled on account of the felony to a place unknown to the jurors. He had no goods or chattels, lands or tenements in Sussex or elsewhere at that time or ever after to the jurors' knowledge apart from those mentioned in the schedule annexed [*now missing*]. [*English.*] ASSI 35/94/10, m 1.

[Delivered to East Grinstead assizes on 21 July when an indictment was preferred which charged Edward and John Cooper, gents, and Edward Songhurst, labourer, all late of Rudgwick, with murdering Slaughter on 6 July while he was executing his office: Edward Cooper striking him with a prong of iron and wood worth 4d (details as in the inquest verdict); and John Cooper and Songhurst being feloniously present aiding and abetting him. The grand jury, to which Henry Allen, Alexander Luxford, John Hill, John Hurst, William Man, John Hayward, William Moore, Leonard Crooke and Anthony Hilton gave evidence, reduced the charge against Edward Cooper to manslaughter and rejected that against John Cooper and Songhurst. The last 2, who had been committed to gaol by Richard Yates, William Freeman and Edward Michell, esqs, JPs, were delivered by proclamation, paying their fees. Edward Cooper was presumably still at large. ASSI 35/94/10, mm 1, 2, 23, 23d.]

428   30 Sept 1653. Cuckfield. Edward Raynes, gent., county coroner. Jurors: Richard Burt, Thomas Jenkyn, Richard Vynall, Thomas Burtenshaw, David Ellis, Thomas Holford, Ninian Burt, Robert Hall, John Jenner, John Bartlett, George Blunden, Samuel Blunden. Witnesses: Margaret Hockham alias Ansty, Joan Beast, William Garston, William Stone. On 27 Sept Thomas Ludbiter late of Clayton, husbandman, murdered Thomas Gasson late of Cuckfield, husbandman, at Clayton with a wooden 'haying prong' which had 2 'iron speanes' fastened to one end [*sc.* a wooden hay-fork with 2 iron prongs] worth 6d which he held in both hands, violently striking him with one of the speans on the front of the head 'neere unto the toppe of the left brow' and giving him a wound 1 inch deep and ¹/8 inch wide of which he languished at Clayton and Cuckfield until the next day and then died at Cuckfield. Ludbiter had no goods or chattels, lands or tenements at the time of the felony or ever after to the jurors' knowledge and he did not flee on account of the felony. [*English.*] ASSI 35/95/9, mm 10, 10d.

[Delivered to East Grinstead assizes on 2 Mar 1654 when Ludbiter, who had been committed to gaol by warrant of Thomas Challonor, esq., JP, pleaded not guilty and was acquitted; he had not fled. Gasson, called Thomas son to John Garston of Bridge in the register, was buried at Cuckfield on the day of the inquest. ASSI 35/95/9, mm 2, 10, 22; SRS, XIII, 176.]

429   7 Nov 1653. Rye. Alan Grebell, gent., deputy of William Burwash, gent., Rye mayor and coroner, and the jurats. Jurors: Mark Woodford, Henry Whitewoode, Edward Dering, Nicholas Kennard, John Smith, Henry Martin, Moses Peadle, Edmund Waters, Mark Carpenter, Joseph Radford, John Bones, Andrew Dunckc. Between 10 and 11 p.m. or thereabouts on 5 Nov, when it was dark, Richard Chiswell went down the lane commonly called 'Dirrickes Lane' to the cliff at the end of the lane against Watchbell Street in Rye 'and there happened to fall downe the said cliffe', breaking his skull on the forehead above the right eye, whereby he immediately died by misadventure. At that time he had no goods or chattels, lands or tenements in Rye to the jurors' knowledge. [*English.*] RYE 1/14, f 110v.

430   10 Jan 1654. Rye. Alan Grebell, gent., deputy of William Burwash, esq., Rye mayor and coroner, and the jurats. Jurors: Edward Beale, Mark Woodford, Richard Boys, Richard Laurence, Edmund Waters, Anthony Knight, Mark Carpenter, 'Woolfram' Eedes, Benjamin Blyst, John Bones, Henry Martin, Joseph Radford, Richard Hendley. Between 1 and 2 p.m. or thereabouts on 10 Jan, when John Gee was aboard a ship of war called 'the Grace' of Faversham in Rye harbour, John Buckland, the ship's gunner, who was also on board, happened to discharge a pistol, which was loaded with powder and bullet, out of the cabin door, the bullet accidentally hitting Gee on the inside of the right knee and passing through the knee, whereby and from the 'large effussion of blood which followed thereupon' he suddenly died. Thus Buckland was guilty of his death by chance medley and not otherwise to the jurors' knowledge. [*English*.] RYE 1/14, f 114.

[On the same day a recognizance was entered before the same deputy and jurats by John Buckland of Rye, mariner, in £40 and by Roger Gilford, mariner, and Henry Martin, pewterer, both of Rye, in £20 each for Buckland's appearance at the next general sessions of the peace at Rye to answer for the death and before the Admiralty of the Cinque Ports or the High Court of Admiralty if required. At the sessions of the peace on 4 Dec a bill of indictment was preferred which charged Buckland with the manslaughter of Gee by misfortune, alleging that between 1 and 2 p.m. on 10 Jan, when John Buckland of Rye, seaman, was in the company of John Gee of Rye, yeoman, at Rye, he discharged a pistol which was loaded with powder and bullet and by misfortune Gee was struck on the inside of the right knee, the bullet passing through the knee, whereby and from the large effusion of blood which followed he died at Rye on the same day; but the grand jury rejected the charge and Buckland was therefore released by proclamation. RYE 1/14, ff 114v, 151v–152; RYE 47/152, unnumbered document.]

431   13 May 1654. Wadhurst. George Courthope, gent., county coroner. Jurors: Joseph Swatlinge, James Bellingham, John May, Thomas Drowley, Stephen Kinge, William Shoesmith, Thomas Luck jun., Robert Austin, John Wickham, William Palmer, John Grayburne, Walter Buss, William Luckhurst, Richard Burges. On 9 May Susan late wife of John Savidge of Wadhurst, labourer, died a natural death at Wadhurst and not otherwise to the jurors' knowledge. [*English*.] KB 9/865, m 23.

[Delivered with **433** and on to King's Bench in Easter 1655. At Horsham assizes on 28 July 1654 an indictment was preferred which charged John Savidge with murdering Susan at Wadhurst on 30 Apr by giving her a bruise on the left side of the head with his right hand of which she languished at Wadhurst until 9 May and then died. The grand jury, to which James Wilcocke, William Gater, John Beale, Mary Jarrett and Thomas and Richard Waters gave evidence, rejected the charge. An identical indictment was preferred at the assizes of 14 Mar 1655 and again the grand jury, to which Thomas Waters gave evidence, rejected it. ASSI 35/95/12, m 52; ASSI 35/96/11, m 130; KB 9/865, m 25d; KB 29/304, m 11d.]

432   28 May 1654. Billingshurst. Richard Allwine, gent., county coroner. Jurors: Richard Jupp, Reuben Baker, John Davis, Lawrence Dobs, Richard Greenefeild, Edward Gray, Henry Mower, Thomas Lover, Benjamin Caught, Henry Remnant, Henry Pyper, Nathaniel Haylor, Thomas Haybitell. Witnesses: William Skyllman, Thomas Deane, Thomas Lover, Thomas Heybeetle, Lawrence Dobbs, Edward Grey, Henry Remnant, Richard Greinfeild, Nathaniel Haylor, Richard Juppe, Benjamin Caught, John Davis, Thomas Rice, John Greinfeild, William Greenefeild, Richard Cooper, William Clayton. On 16 May John Elliott of Itchingfield, yeoman, feloniously killed William Greenfeild at Itchingfield with a staff worth 1d which he held in his right hand, giving him a bruise on the left side of the head of which he languished at Itchingfield until the next day and then died. Elliott had no goods or chattels, lands or tenements at the time of the felony or ever after to the jurors' knowledge. [*English*.] ASSI 35/95/10, mm 11, 11d.

[Delivered to Horsham assizes on 28 July when an indictment was preferred which charged Elliott, called a labourer, with murdering Greenfeild, the details otherwise being as in the inquest verdict but with the last sentence omitted. The grand jury, to which Mary Grinvell, Joan Cheseman, Henry Piper, Matthew Grinvell, Moses Brookes, Richard Cooper, Elizabeth Hill, Joan Lee, Solomon Nye, William Clayton, John Muncke, Edward Sayers, William Grinvell, John Grinfield, Thomas Rice, John Davis, William Skylman, Thomas Deane, Thomas Haybettle, Thomas Lover and Richard Greenefeild gave evidence, reduced the charge to manslaughter. Elliott pleaded not guilty to the inquest verdict and was acquitted; he had not fled and was therefore discharged. ASSI 35/95/10, mm 7, 10, 11, 23d.]

433   27 Oct 1654. Lewes. Edward Raynes, gent., county coroner. Jurors: John Greene, Henry Rose, Samuel White, Edward Greene, Edward Burkin, John Davey, Richard Paine, George Worrall, Ambrose Gallaway, Lawrence Townsend, Edward Baker, Richard Burser, Richard Page. Witnesses: Stephen Dennett, William Goreing, John Wales, Richard Crunden. On 21 Oct Thomas Vaughan late of Lewes, cooper, aged 15½ or thereabouts, feloniously killed John Walles late of Lewes, shoemaker, aged 16 or thereabouts, at Lewes, violently striking him on the face and head 'with both his hands clinched', of which he languished at Lewes until 26 Oct and then died. Vaughan had no goods or chattels, lands or tenements in Sussex at the time of the felony or ever after to the jurors' knowledge. [*English.*] ASSI 35/96/9, mm 4, 4d.

[Delivered to East Grinstead assizes on 14 Mar 1655 when an indictment was preferred identical to the inquest verdict except that the charge was murder and the last sentence was omitted. The grand jury, to which the same 4 witnesses gave evidence, rejected the indictment. Vaughan pleaded not guilty to the inquest verdict and was acquitted, the trial jury finding that Walles had died a natural death. Vaughan had not fled and so was discharged, paying his fees. ASSI 35/96/9, mm 2, 4, 19d; ASSI 35/96/11, m 129.]

434   23 Dec 1654. Rye. Alexander Bennet, esq., Rye mayor and coroner, and the jurats. Jurors: Edmund Ellis, John Collens, Thomas Hunter, Richard Downer, Gideon Kettell, Abraham Hanson, Richard Laurence, John Jones, John Smith, John Peadell jun., Henry Martin, Edward Whiting, Richard Flintstone. Between 8 and 9 p.m. on 22 Dec Jasper Grant killed Peter Seizoun in Market Ward, Rye, with a knife which he held in his right hand, giving him a wound in the lower part of the throat, on the right side just above the 'channell bone' [*sc.* channel-bone, cannel-bone or neck-bone], 2 inches deep and 1 inch wide or thereabouts of which he died at Rye about 3 hours later. Thus Grant was guilty of his death by manslaughter and not otherwise to the jurors' knowledge. At the time of the felony he had no goods or chattels, lands or tenements in Rye to their knowledge. [*English.*] RYE 1/14, f 153v.

[On 25 Dec Andrew Reyly and Hendricke de Rosson entered a recognizance before the mayor and jurats in £20 each to appear at the Rye sessions of the peace on 15 Feb 1655, and at other times as required, to give evidence against Grant, a prisoner in Rye gaol. RYE 1/14, f 154.]

435   8 Mar 1655. Cuckfield. Edward Raynes, gent., county coroner. Jurors: John Jenner, Robert Vincent, Thomas Tompset, Edmund King, Walter Gallier, Lionel Gatford, Stephen Wood, Thomas Wynpenny, Thomas Jenkin, Stephen Stanner, Richard Jarrett, Richard King, John Godsmarke. Witness: Frances Carr of Cuckfield, spinster. On 7 Mar Edmund Tipton late of Cuckfield, gent., feloniously killed Mary Heath late of Cuckfield, spinster, at Cuckfield with a knife of iron and steel worth 2d which he held in his left hand, giving her a wound on the right thigh 1½ inches deep, 1 inch long and ¼ inch wide of which she immediately died. Tipton had no goods or chattels, lands or tenements in Sussex at the time of the felony or ever after to the jurors' knowledge. [*English.*] ASSI 35/96/9, mm 7, 7d.

[Delivered with **433**. At the assizes an indictment was preferred identical to the inquest verdict except that the charge was murder and the last sentence was omitted. The grand jury, to which the same witness gave evidence, reduced the charge to manslaughter. Tipton pleaded not guilty to both the indictment as amended and the inquest verdict but was convicted; he had no goods. He then successfully pleaded benefit of clergy and was branded on the hand and released, paying his fees. ASSI 35/96/9, mm 5–7, 19d.]

436   9 Oct 1655. Rye. Alexander Bennet, esq., Rye mayor and coroner, and the jurats. Jurors: Edward Lanes, John Collins, Edmund Waters, Thomas Burdet, John Smith, Joseph Radford, Martin Perry, William Todde, Nicholas Kennard, John Peadle jun., Gideon Kettle, James Miller, Thomas Willard, Aaron Peadle. Between 3 and 4 p.m. or thereabouts on 8 Oct, when Elizabeth daughter of Samuel Bunce of Rye, miller, was walking with another child in the common carriage-way near the Landgate and Thomas Tutty's 'budge cart', drawn by 5 horses, was coming out of the gate, although George Breades, the carter, did all in his power to restrain them, the horses 'kept on their course' because of 'the descent of the ground there' and one of them knocked Elizabeth down and 'the offward wheele' of the cart by misadventure went over her head whereby she immediately died. The jurors appraised the 5 horses and cart at £3. [*English.*] RYE 1/14, f 188v.

[At the Rye sessions of the peace on 3 Dec Elizabeth wife of Samuel Bunce preferred a bill of indictment which charged George Breades of Rye, carter, with murder, but the grand jury reduced the charge to manslaughter by misadventure. Breades pleaded not guilty to the indictment as amended but was convicted; he had not fled for the killing and had no goods or chattels in Rye to the trial jurors' knowledge. He therefore found pledges to sue his pardon, viz Bartholomew Breads and Joseph Radford who were present in court, and was released. At the Rye assembly of 11 Jan 1656 Tutty paid the £3 for the horses and cart which were forfeit to Rye corporation as deodand, but asked the assembly to return the money to him; it ordered that 40s of the sum should be returned to him, which was done. RYE 1/14, ff 194v–195, 196, 198v.]

437 20 Nov 1655. Edburton. Edward Raines, gent., county coroner. Jurors: John Backshell, John Carver, John Merchant, Abraham Prior, John Ingram, John Inskip, Henry Farnecombe, Gerard Morris, Thomas Owlder, Henry Ascoll, John Harland, 'Jonas' Cooter. Witnesses: Mary Scrace, Richard Morris, Joan French, Elizabeth Morris, John Inskipp, Bernard Holden, John Haslegrove, John Smyth, Cicely Wheeler. On 5 Nov Thomas Goffe and John Newarke, both late of Steyning, husbandmen, feloniously killed Walter Covert late of Edburton, gent., at Edburton: Goffe taking him in both hands and throwing him 'over a certaine pannell of pales' onto the ground on the other side of them upon 'the reines of the backe' and giving him 'one mortall bruise' of which he languished at Edburton until 16 Nov and then died; and Newarke being feloniously present aiding and abetting him. Goffe and Newarke had no goods or chattels, lands or tenements in Sussex at the time of the felony or ever after to the jurors' knowledge. [*English.*] ASSI 35/97/7, mm 2, 2d.
[Delivered to East Grinstead assizes on 11 Mar 1656 when the grand jury, to which the same 9 witnesses gave evidence, presented an indictment identical to the inquest verdict except that the charge was murder and the last sentence was omitted. Newarke, who had been committed to gaol by the coroner, and Goffe both pleaded not guilty to the indictment but were convicted and hanged; they had no goods. Covert was buried at Edburton on 22 Nov 1655. ASSI 35/97/7, mm 1–3, 18, 18d; *Edburton reg.*, 49.]

438 22 July 1656. Hastings. William Parker, gent., deputy of Thomas Delves, esq., Hastings mayor and coroner. Jurors: Robert Bursey, Edward Hildring, Thomas Lovell, Richard Amyett, Martin Harrison, Henry Tyherst, William Philipp, Thomas Austen, John Webb, Thomas Payne, Henry Newman, Richard Baker jun. Inquest on view of a dead bastard child of Elizabeth Cruttenden, late maidservant of Thomas Waller, gent., secretly buried. 'Goeing upp to the house of Thomas Waller, gent., scituat in the parish of Mary Magdalen and digging in the gardein of the said house under the ground cell of an outhouse there by the directions of one Joane Stedman, widdow, about a two foote under the said cell they found in a cloath the bones of a young child, the scull with haire uppon and one of the kidneyes not consumed, there lately buyried; but whose the said child was and howe it came to its death the jurors aforesaid knowe not'. [*English.*] HASTINGS C/A(c) 3, unnumbered folio.

439 24 Nov 1656. Rye. Thomas Marshall, esq., Rye mayor and coroner, and the jurats. Jurors: Richard Hendley, Edmund Waters, Thomas Willard, John Smith, Abraham Hanson, Nicholas Kennard, Aaron Peadle, Thomas Seer, Henry Martin, Peter Collens, William Todde, Richard Neakes. On the morning of 23 Nov Elizabeth Beecraft gave birth alone and without help to a female bastard child which, 'not being carefully preserved', died. [*English.*] RYE 1/14, f 221.
[On 26 Nov Beecraft was examined before the mayor and Thomas Greenefield and Thomas Miller, jurats, and said that on the morning of 23 Nov she gave birth in her mistress's chamber, but did not know about what time, whether the child was male or female, or whether it was born alive or dead; and some time later she got out of bed, took the child, which was then dead, out of the bed and therefore wrapped it in a cloth, carried it downstairs and laid it in a settle. She added that no one ever advised her to conceal the birth. At the Rye sessions of the peace on 1 Dec a bill of indictment was preferred which charged Elizabeth Beecraft of Rye, spinster, with giving birth at Rye on 23 Nov to a live female bastard child and afterwards on the same day murdering her by taking her in both hands, putting her in a linen sheet worth 12d and strangling her with it whereby she immediately died. The grand jury, to which Ellen Benbrigge, Mary Hardier, Barbara Cockram and Margery Laurence gave evidence, affirmed the bill. Beecraft pleaded not guilty and was acquitted; she had not fled for the death. It was therefore awarded that she should find 2 sureties at the next sessions and then be discharged; in the meantime she was returned to gaol. RYE 1/14, ff 222v–223; RYE 47/156, unnumbered documents.]

440 15 Dec 1656. Worth. Edward Raynes, gent., county coroner. Jurors: Henry Fawkener, Henry Snashall, 'Theophilus' Martin, Thomas Smith, John Haythorne, Richard Martin, Stephen Cooper, 'Sidrake' Baldwin, William Jenner, William Wickenden, Richard Gardiner, Nicholas Gardiner, Thomas Childerston. Witnesses: Benjamin Reynolds, Nicholas Netlingham, John Penfold jun., Edward Penfold, Robert Osborne, John Feild, James Salter, Richard Akeherst, Mercy Saunders, Alice Saunders, Elizabeth Saunders, Elizabeth Haynes, Francis Humfry. On 2 Dec John Bowyer late of Lingfield in Surrey, gent., feloniously killed Edward Saunders late of Worth, husbandman, at Worth, 'punching, thrusting and strikeing' him with his right hand and elbow 'uppon the stomacke and left side of the breast', of which he languished at Worth until 8 Dec and then died. Bowyer had no goods or chattels, lands or tenements in Sussex at the time of the felony or ever after to the jurors' knowledge. [*English.*] ASSI 35/98/9, mm 19, 19d.

[Delivered to East Grinstead assizes on 21 Mar 1657 when an indictment was preferred identical to the inquest verdict except that the charge was murder, Bowyer was called late of Worth, gent., and the last sentence was omitted. The grand jury, to which the same 13 witnesses gave evidence (the last called Frances Humfry), rejected the indictment. Bowyer pleaded not guilty to the inquest verdict and was acquitted; he had not fled and so was released, paying his fees. ASSI 35/98/9, mm 13, 19, 30d; ASSI 35/98/11, m 74.]

441   3 Feb 1657. Northchapel in Petworth. John Peachey, gent., county coroner. Jurors: Thomas Ayling, William Combs, William Dennett, John Hollier, Matthew Pennicod, Nicholas Goodyer, Richard Bainard, 'Emery' Puttocke, Daniel Palmer, John Beane, 'Kalebb' Paine, Nicholas Bettesworth, John Wymball, William Rixall, John Lickfold. Witnesses: Thomas Curtis, Ann Miles, Richard Booker. On 28 Jan William Miles late of Northchapel, labourer, murdered Nicholas Miles at Northchapel with a knife of iron and steel worth 2d which he held in his right hand, giving him a wound 'in and uppon the lower parte of the left side of the stomacke' 1 inch long and 2 inches deep of which he languished at Northchapel until 1 Feb and then died. As soon as he had committed the felony William Miles fled on that account to places yet unknown to the jurors. He had no goods or chattels, lands or tenements at that time or ever after to the jurors' knowledge. [*English.*] ASSI 35/98/9, mm 1, 1d.

[Delivered with **440**. At the time of the assizes William Miles was still at large. At the assizes of 26 Mar 1658 the grand jury, to which Thomas Curtis, Edward Miles, John Haslyn jun. and Richard Booker gave evidence, presented an indictment identical to the inquest verdict but without the last 2 sentences. Miles pleaded not guilty to the indictment at the assizes of 17 July 1658 but was convicted and hanged; he had no goods. ASSI 35/98/9, m 1; ASSI 35/99/9, m 2; ASSI 35/99/10, mm 3, 15d.]

442   10 Mar 1657. Lurgashall. John Peachey, gent., county coroner. Jurors: Edward Lickfold, John Christmas, Thomas Chalcroft, Thomas Feilder, John Launder, William Maiden, Andrew Spassett, Anthony Ayling, John Hoggsflesh, Henry Ede, Robert Farndon, John Hooke, William Challwyn, James Langley, John Cowper, Nathaniel Spranke, Henry Chalwyn, Geoffrey Collier, Edward Lickford. Witnesses: John Cooper alias Stening, John Pennicodd, Ann Marden, Mary Boxall, Henry Chalwyn. On 7 Mar Ann Comber late of Lurgashall, spinster alias widow, gave birth to a live male child at Lurgashall which by the laws of England was a bastard and later on the same day she took him into both her hands, threw him into a pit 'filled with water, mudd and other filth' in 'Myne Pitt Feild' in Lurgashall and 'did choake, drowne and stifle' him therein, of which he immediately died. Thus she murdered him on the said 28 Nov [*sic*]. She had no goods or chattels, lands or tenements in Sussex at the time of the felony or ever after to the jurors' knowledge. [*English; damaged.*] ASSI 35/98/9, mm 4, 4d.

[Delivered with **440**. At the assizes the grand jury, to which the same witnesses except for Pennicodd gave evidence, presented an indictment which charged Comber with giving birth and murdering the child on 7 Mar, as in the inquest verdict, and John Puttocke late of Lurgashall, labourer, with being feloniously present aiding and abetting her, so that they both murdered the child on the said 28 Nov; the last sentence of the inquest verdict was omitted. Comber and Puttocke, who had been committed to gaol for the murder by Edward Michell, esq., JP, pleaded not guilty to the indictment. Comber was convicted and hanged; she had no goods. Puttocke was acquitted; he had not fled. At the same assizes the grand jury presented an indictment which charged Puttocke with having unlawful sexual intercourse with Comber at Lurgashall on 10 Apr 1656, she then being a widow and unmarried. He confessed to the indictment and was committed to the county gaol for 3 months. ASSI 35/98/9, mm 2–5, 30, 30d.]

443   4 Apr 1657. Rotherfield. Robert Shoebridge, gent., Rotherfield hundred coroner. Jurors: Robert Tyndall, gent., John Cheesman, Edmund Holmsby, Nicholas Filtnes, John Stapley, Thomas Lockyer, Thomas Ovenden, James Ovenden, William Clarke, Alexander Pococke, James Dalby, John Whatley. Witnesses: John Avery, William Crowherst, Dorothy Martyn, John Crowherst, Thomas

Alchorne. On 2 Apr Henry Tompsett of Rotherfield, labourer, feloniously killed Thomas Hemsley late of Uckfield, labourer, at Rotherfield with 'a payer of tonges' worth 1s which he held in both hands, violently striking him on the left side of the head of which he immediately died. Tompsett had no goods or chattels, lands or tenements in Sussex at that time or ever after to the jurors' knowledge. [*English*.] ASSI 35/98/10, mm 5, 5d.
[Delivered to East Grinstead assizes on 11 July when an indictment was preferred identical to the inquest verdict except that the charge was murder and the last sentence was omitted. The grand jury, to which the same 5 witnesses gave evidence, rejected the indictment. Tompsett, who had been committed to gaol by the coroner, pleaded not guilty to the inquest verdict but was convicted; he had no goods. He then successfully pleaded benefit of clergy and was branded and released. ASSI 35/98/10, mm 3, 5, 17; ASSI 35/98/12, m 53.]

444   10 June 1657. Rye. Thomas Marshall, esq., Rye mayor and coroner, and the jurats. Jurors: Mark Woodford, Alan Soale, Edmund Waters, John Smith, Edward Harrey, Bartholomew Breads, James Cradocke, Alan Eedes, Thomas Seere, Gideon Kettle, Thomas Burdit, Edward Waters, Thomas Sharpe, Thomas Copeland. Between 4 and 6 p.m. on 9 June John Wootton of Rye, butcher, son of William Wootton of Rye, butcher, feloniously hanged himself with a small cord fastened to an iron nail in one of the rooms of his father's house, dying immediately. At that time he had no goods or chattels, lands or tenements in Rye or elsewhere to the jurors' knowledge. [*English*.] RYE 1/14, f 238.

445   27 July 1657. Mayfield. Edward Raynes, gent., county coroner. Jurors: John Chilly, 'Nathan' Taylor, 'Jabeze' Warnet, William Daw, Samuel Atwells, Thomas Shepperd, John Smyth, Richard Oxley, Edward Chapman, Thomas Symons, John Fowle. On 23 July Frances wife of John Edwards of Mayfield, gent., while of unsound mind killed their natural son Thomas, who was asleep in bed in John's dwelling-house in Mayfield, with a wooden bar of a door of the house which she held in both hands, violently striking him on the right side of the head and giving him a wound 2 inches long and ½ inch deep of which he immediately died. [*English*.] KB 9/877, m 180.
[Delivered to East Grinstead assizes on 26 Mar and on to King's Bench in Easter 1658. At the same assizes an indictment was preferred which charged Frances Edwards late of Mayfield, spinster, alias Frances wife of John Edwards late of Mayfield, gent., with murdering Thomas Edwards (relationship not given) at Mayfield on 23 July 1657 with a wooden bar of a door worth 2d which she held in both hands, giving him a wound on the right side of the head 2 inches long and ½ inch deep of which he immediately died. The grand jury, to which Thomas Houghton, William Barham, Abraham Stolion and Frances Edwards gave evidence, rejected the indictment. ASSI 35/99/11, m 96; KB 9/877, m 196d.]

446   10 Dec 1657. Rye. Thomas Marshall, esq., Rye mayor and coroner, and the jurats. Jurors: George Wattell, Edward Lane, Edmund Waters, Nicholas Kennard, William Oake, Henry Martin, Moses Peadle, William Hurlstone, Thomas Bishop jun., Joseph Radford, James Miller, Thomas Sharpe. Between 3 and 5 p.m. on 9 Dec, when Philip Swaine, aged 4¾ or thereabouts, son of Philip Swaine of Rye, seaman, was in 'the backside' of the house in which William Hurlestone lives in Watchbell Street in Rye, where a herring barrel about half full of water stood, and was playing with the ice on the water, he reached into the barrel and 'suddenly and unawares pitched' into the water and was drowned. [*English*.] RYE 1/14, f 256.

447   26 May 1658. Storrington. John Peachey, gent., county coroner. Jurors: John Duppa, Thomas Badcocke, Richard Duppa, John Greene, Anthony Duke, John Bridger, Anthony Seale, George Palmer, Joseph Hamond, Richard Greene, Thomas Alcocke, John Holfold, Samuel Ledbetter, Richard Parham, Richard Turner, Richard Streater, John Brooker, Thomas Clarke, Nathaniel Blundell, John Andrew, Richard Edsaw. Witnesses: Mary Bennett, Henry Bennett, Mary Jupe, William Slaughter, Elizabeth Arthur, Susan Slaughter. On 9 May John Scutt late of Storrington, yeoman, and 'Dionis' Scutt late of Storrington, spinster, alias 'Dionis' wife of the said John Scutt feloniously killed Ann Bennett, spinster, at Storrington: John kicking her with both feet in 'the middle parte of the backe' and giving her 'one mortall bruise' of which she languished at Storrington until 13 May and then died; and 'Dionis' being feloniously present aiding and abetting him. John and 'Dionis' had no goods or chattels, lands or tenements in Sussex or elsewhere at the time of the felony or ever after to the jurors' knowledge. [*English.*] ASSI 35/99/10, mm 4, 4d.

[Delivered to East Grinstead assizes on 17 July when an indictment was preferred identical to the inquest verdict except that the charge was murder, 'Dionis' was merely called John's wife and the last sentence was omitted. The grand jury, to which the same 6 witnesses gave evidence, rejected the indictment. The Scutts pleaded not guilty to the inquest verdict and were acquitted, the trial jury finding that Bennett had died a natural death. They had not fled and so were released, paying their fees. ASSI 35/99/10, mm 3, 4, 15d; ASSI 35/99/12, m 100.]

448   21 June 1658. Halnaker in Boxgrove. John Peachey, gent., county coroner. Jurors of Halnaker and the 5 neighbouring townships, viz Westhampnett, Oving, Pagham, Merston and Aldingbourne: Richard Trunnell, Robert Ameares, Henry Deacon, Henry Peachey, Thomas Gibbons, William Hamond, … Awsten, Thomas Hamond jun., John Burrey, Thomas Greene, Thomas Yonge, John Stampe. Between 3 and 4 p.m. on 13 June William Morley, kt, who for the previous 17 years 'was divers times taken and laboured of and with certaine fitts and turnes of the frenzey, lunacy and madnes', was again seized with such a fit at Halnaker and at 4 p.m., while still labouring with it, struck himself in the middle of the throat with a knife of iron and steel worth 2d which he held in his right hand, giving himself a wound 2 inches long and 1 inch wide of which he languished at Halnaker until 20 June and then died and not otherwise. [*English; faded.*] KB 9/879, m 426.

[Delivered into King's Bench by the coroner in Michaelmas. KB 9/879, m 426d; KB 29/307, m 85.]

449   26 Nov 1658. Lewes. Edward Raynes, gent., county coroner. Jurors: Edward Baily, Thomas Norton, Edward Barret, John Draper, Richard Hollingdale, Henry Seeres, Lancelot Michel, Samuel White, Thomas White, Richard Purser, Henry Hutchen, John Vandike, Edward Floore. Witnesses: John Sternes, John Evans. On 22 Nov Thomas Rawlins late of Lewes, cordwainer, murdered Jeremy Clerke late of Lewes, labourer, at Lewes with 'an earthen pott' of no value which he held in his left hand, violently throwing it against him and giving him 'one mortall bruise' on the right side of the head of which he languished at Lewes until 25 Nov and then died. Rawlins had no goods or chattels, lands or tenements in Sussex or elsewhere at the time of the felony or ever after to the jurors' knowledge. [*English.*] ASSI 35/100/6, mm 7, 7d.

[Delivered to East Grinstead assizes on 22 July 1659 when Rawlins, who had been committed to gaol by the coroner on the day of the inquest, pleaded not guilty and was acquitted of murder but convicted of manslaughter; he had no goods. He then successfully pleaded benefit of clergy and was branded and released, paying his fees. ASSI 35/100/6, mm 2, 7, 17, 17d.]

450   1 Jan 1659. Arundel. John Peachey, gent., county coroner. Jurors: George Penfold, John Albery, William Pellett, John Highland, Justinian Chaundler, Anthony Greene, Thomas Mattocke, Thomas Druett, Henry Owden, Richard Nevell, James Briant, Thomas Smyth, George Hopkin, Thomas Payne, Christopher Elliott, Robert Linkhorne, William Townesend, George Edwards, Thomas Withers, William Stoakes. Witness: Josiah Horscroft. On 28 Dec 1658 John Mason late of Arundel, hempdresser, murdered Richard Pescod at Arundel with 'a certeyne rope made of hempe and flax' worth 1d which he held in his right hand, striking him violently on 'the middle parte of the backe' and giving him 'one mortall bruise' of which he languished at Arundel until the next day and then died. Mason had no goods or chattels, lands or tenements in Sussex or elsewhere at the time of the felony or ever after to the jurors' knowledge. [*English.*] ASSI 35/100/6, mm 6, 6d.

[Delivered with **449**. At the assizes Mason, who had been committed to gaol by Thomas Colbrook, mayor of Arundel, on 3 Jan for murdering Pescod, his apprentice, pleaded not guilty and was acquitted of murder but convicted of manslaughter; he had no goods. He then successfully pleaded benefit of clergy and was branded and released, paying his fees. ASSI 35/100/6, mm 2, 6, 17, 17d.]

451   4 July 1659. Uckfield. Robert Shoebridge, gent., Loxfield Dorset half-hundred coroner. Jurors of the half-hundred: John Peckham, John Tyler, John Bridger, ?Bartholomew Vyne, Thomas Holman,

John Smyth, William Gouldsmyth, Edward Isted, Gregory Rose, Thomas Relfe, John Earle, John Walker, … Russell. On 1 July, when Thomas son of John Daw of [Mayfield], husbandman, was alone on the common and public highway at Framfield driving 6 black oxen which were fastened to a cart loaded with chalk, by misadventure he suddenly fell to the ground and the oxen drew the cart forward so that its further wheel ran over his head, giving him a bruise of which he immediately died. The oxen, cart and wheel moved to his death. The oxen are worth £9 10s and the cart and chalk [10s]; they are all with Henry Brissenden of Mayfield, yeoman. [*English; damaged.*] KB 9/884, m 40.
[Delivered into King's Bench by the coroner in Hilary 1660. Brissenden was summoned to King's Bench to answer for the deodands but there was no further process against him. KB 9/884, m 39d; KB 29/308, m 138d.]

452   15 Nov 1659. Rye. Thomas Marshall, esq., deputy of Thomas Greenefield, esq., Rye mayor and coroner, and the jurats. Jurors: Richard Hendley, John Collens, John Peadle jun., Robert Pett, Bartholomew Breads, Aaron Peadle, Michael Savary, Michael Bacon, Mark Woodford jun., Thomas Willard, John Porter, Richard Tew. Between 2 and 4 p.m. on 12 Nov, when William, aged about 2, son of Nicholas Earle of Rye, seaman, was in 'the backside' of his father's dwelling-house in Lower Street in Rye, where stood a tub containing about 3 or 4 gallons of water, and was playing with a dish in the water, he 'suddenly and unawares pitched' into the tub and was drowned. [*English.*] RYE 1/14, f 316.

453   19 July 1661. Herstmonceux. William Cooke, gent., Hastings rape coroner. Jurors: Richard Jeffery, John Isted, Richard Freind, Samuel Hood, John Eastone, William Turner, Thomas Wenham, Benjamin Mott j[un.], Abraham Sherwin, William Draper, William Richards, John Richards, Thomas Barnott. About 2 p.m. on 27 June, when James Feild late of Herstmonceux, gent., was alone on 'the bancke of a certaine little pond' full of a large amount of ?stagnant water [*aquatimus*] and other filth near 'the hoppehouse' in 'a certaine parke' commonly called Herstmonceux Park in Herstmonceux, he feloniously threw himself from the bank into the pond and drowned himself in the stagnant water and other filth, dying immediately. At that time he had goods and chattels worth £71, viz 27 'bullocks' worth 40s each, 4 'colts' worth 20s each, 4 'mares' worth 20s each, 2 'horses' worth 40s each and 5 'quarters of wheate' worth 20s a quarter, all of which are with John Pelham, bt, lord of the honor and barony of the rape. KB 9/890, m 34.
[Delivered into King's Bench by the coroner in Hilary 1662. Pelham was summoned to King's Bench to answer for the goods and chattels; he entered a special plea in Trinity 1664. KB 9/890, m 34; KB 29/312, m 11.]

454   13 Aug 1661. Chailey. Edward Raynes, gent., county coroner. Jurors: John Newnham, John Chatfeild sen., John Sawyer, Thomas Hooke, Richard Vynall, John Chatfeild jun., John Hin…, Thomas Slaughter, William Sawyer, John Combridge, William Copperd, Richard Page, Robert Shepperd. On 9 Aug 'a nagge' belonging to Edward Keeleing of Chailey, esq., by misadventure violently struck Thomas Reade late of Chailey, 'laborer', 'with his hindmost foote' on 'the forepart of the head', giving him a wound 3 inches long and 1 inch wide of which he languished at Chailey until 12 Aug and then died. The gelding moved to his death and is deodand; it is worth 40s and is now with Keeleing. KB 9/900, m 83.
[Delivered into King's Bench by the coroner in Easter 1665. Keeleing was summoned to King's Bench to answer for the gelding; he had licence to imparl in Michaelmas 1668. KB 9/900, m 83d; KB 29/316, m 54.]

455   12 Mar 1662. Uckfield. Edward Raynes, gent., county coroner. Jurors: David Austen, gent., John Everist, Robert Drowst, Henry Medhurst, George Weller, Abraham Cooper, John Russell, Henry Durrant, Francis Jenkins, 'Faintnot' Batchellor, Isaac Alchorne, James Cottington. On 7 Mar Thomasin Pollington late of Framfield, 'spinster', gave birth at Framfield to a live female child which by the laws of England 'was a bastard' and afterwards on the same day she murdered her there with a knife or iron and steel worth 2d which she held drawn in her right hand, giving her a wound on the right side of 'the necke' 1½ inches long and ½ inch deep of which she immediately died. After committing the felony Pollington fled to places unknown to the jurors. She had no goods or chattels, lands or tenements in

Sussex or elsewhere at the time of the felony or flight or ever after to the jurors' knowledge. ASSI 35/103/8, m 5.

[Delivered to Horsham assizes on 10 July when Pollington confessed to the murder and was hanged. ASSI 35/103/8, mm 5, 29d.]

456 28 Mar 1662. Ticehurst. William Cooke, gent., Hastings rape coroner. Jurors of the rape: John Dunsteere, John Barham, Arthur Cockshott, George Besbidge, Nicholas Busse, Richard Burchet, Thomas Ollive, Richard Welden, Thomas Roper, William Hunt sen., Thomas Bryant, Robert Moore, Charles Tyler. On 8 Mar Dorothy Wood late of Ticehurst, 'spinster', gave birth at Ticehurst to 2 live female children which by the laws of England 'were bastards' and afterwards on the same day she murdered them there: immediately after their birth she took them in both hands, 'did putt and cast' them into 'a pitt' full of water, mud and other filth and 'did choake and drowne' them in it whence they immediately died. Wood had no goods or chattels, lands or tenements in Sussex or elsewhere at the time of the felony or ever after to the jurors' knowledge. The inquest was held on view of both bodies. ASSI 35/103/8, m 2.

[Delivered with **455**. At the assizes the grand jury, to which Bartholomew and Ann Thorpe, William Butler and Mary Cliffe gave evidence, presented an indictment identical to the inquest verdict except that it gave the date of the births and murders as 4 Mar and omitted the last sentence. Wood pleaded not guilty to the indictment but was convicted and sentenced to be hanged; she had no chattels. She then pleaded pregnancy and was found to be pregnant by a jury of matrons and remanded in gaol without bail. At the assizes of 10 Mar 1663 she was again remanded in gaol without bail. ASSI 35/103/8, mm 1, 2, 6, 7, 29d; ASSI 35/104/9, m 35d.]

457 23 May 1662 [?*recte* 1661]. Plumpton. Edward Raynes, gent., county coroner. Jurors: Daniel Rolt, Richard Stanbridge, John Hurst, Thomas Wood, John Parker, John Lashmer, Thomas Bromfeild, Edward Stanbridge, Richard Homewood, William Gibbs, Walter Sturt, John Burtenshawe. On 22 May, when Joshua Verrall late of Plumpton, 'weaver', was riding on 'a nagge' of 'browne bay' colour at Wivelsfield, by misadventure the gelding suddenly and violently threw him to the ground whereby he 'was soe hurt and bruised' that he immediately died. The gelding moved to his death and is deodand; it is worth 50s and is now with John Challoner of Lindfield, esq. KB 9/891, m 105.

[Delivered into King's Bench by the coroner in Easter 1662, on Wednesday after the quindene of Easter (16 Apr). The date of the inquest must therefore be wrong, and as May is repeated in the body of the verdict the regnal year was probably given as 14, in error for 13, Charles II. There are no entries for either year in the Plumpton parish register and no bishop's transcript. Challoner was summoned to King's Bench to answer for the gelding; there was no further process against him. KB 9/891, mm 105, 105d; KB 29/312, m 47; PAR 446/1/1/1.]

458 16 Aug 1662. Waldron. Edward Raynes, gent., county coroner. Jurors: John Chilley, William Gower, 'Moremercy' Curtis, Thomas Phipps, William Tieherst, Nicholas Brackfeild, John Heathfeild, 'Isaac' Moise, John Durrant, John Goodman, John Gower, 'Isaac' Cooke. On 13 Aug, when William Dyke late of Waldron, esq., was holding 'a birding peece charged with gunpowder and haileshot' in both hands at Waldron, by misadventure and against his will the gun suddenly discharged and the lead shot struck him on the right side of the neck, giving him a wound 4 inches deep and 1 inch wide of which he immediately died. The gun moved to his death and is deodand; it is worth 5s and is now with James Berwicke of Waldron, 'husbandman'. KB 9/900, m 143.

[Delivered with **454**. Berwicke was summoned to King's Bench to answer for the gun; he was later outlawed. KB 9/900, m 157d; KB 29/316, m 51d.]

459 1 Sept 1662. Upper Beeding. Edward Raynes, gent., county coroner. Jurors: Samuel Lucke, Richard Beckshell, George Withers, John Ingram, John Lucas, John Merchant, Henry Boniface, John Hills, Frank Champion, Samuel Rogers, Thomas Wood, John Refford, Thomas Andrewes. On 30 Aug, when Elizabeth Beckshell late of Upper Beeding, 'spinster', was riding in 'a wagon' drawn by 6 oxen, the wagon was suddenly thrown to the ground by the violent movement of the oxen, whereby Beckshell's body was severely 'bruised' and she immediately died by misadventure. The wagon and oxen moved to her death and are deodand. The wagon is worth £2 and the oxen £20; they now all remain with John Beckshell of Upper Beeding, 'tanner'. KB 9/893, m 17.

[Delivered into King's Bench by the coroner in Michaelmas. John Beckshell was summoned to King's Bench to answer for the deodands; he had died before there was further process. KB 9/893, mm 17, 37d; KB 29/312, mm 114d, 115.]

460   7 Mar 1663. Hastings. William Parker, esq., Hastings mayor and coroner. Jurors: Thomas Sargent sen., Robert Bartholmew, 'Martin' Harison, George Oliver, Nicholas Hutchins, Robert Phipps, John Darlie, Lawrence Iham, Robert Thetcher, Richard Cooke, John Webb, Richard Lowen, Peter Grover. On 6 Mar Thomas Penbuckle of Hastings, 'fisherman', aged 15, got into a fishing boat called 'a hookebote' [*sc.* a boat from which men fished with lines and hooks] on Stonebeach in Hastings, took 'a capstone barr' of wood worth 4d which he found in it and threw it from the boat, not knowing or seeing that anyone was near it; but Mark White, aged 4, the poor son of Rachel White of Hastings, widow, was near, although out of Penbuckle's sight, and the end of the bar fell and struck him on the head, giving him a wound of which he languished until 2 a.m. on the next day and then died of that misadventure and not otherwise. Penbuckle had no goods or chattels in Hastings or anywhere else on 6 Mar or ever after. HASTINGS C/A(a) 2, f 101v.

461   29 June 1663. Lindfield. Edward Raynes, gent., county coroner. Jurors: William Batchellor, Francis West jun., James Long, Thomas Garston, Thomas Sayers, James Wisby, Thomas Comber, Henry Kidder, Thomas Gunter, John Fayerhall, Richard Harland, John Hother. Witness: John Martin. On 21 June Margaret Buck late of Lindfield, 'spinster', gave birth at Lindfield to a live male child which by the laws of England 'was a bastard' and immediately afterwards she murdered him there, strangling him with both her hands whence he immediately died. Buck had no goods or chattels, lands or tenements in Sussex or elsewhere at the time of the felony or ever after to the jurors' knowledge. ASSI 35/104/10, mm 12, 12d.

[Delivered to East Grinstead assizes on 4 Aug when Buck pleaded not guilty and was acquitted; she had not fled and was released, paying her fees. ASSI 35/104/10, mm 11, 12, 23d.]

462   21 June 1664. Southease. Edward Raynes, gent., county coroner. Jurors: John Martin sen., John Martin jun., William Brackpoole, Thomas Ade, Richard Gurre, John Ballard, Daniel Boult, William Ade, Richard Ade, John Funnell, William Washer, Thomas Funnell. On 19 June, when Francis Bryan late of Southease, 'yeoman', and Jonathan Hancocke of Southease, clerk, who were neighbours and close friends, were together at Southease trying to catch 'a nagge' belonging to Hancocke which was grazing in the close of John Willard of Southease, clerk, the gelding suddenly ran near to Hancocke who threw 'a sticke' towards it, intending thereby to impede and catch it, but the stick, not 'hitting' the gelding, suddenly, by misadventure and against Hancocke's will 'did hitt' Bryan in the corner of his left eye near the top of the nose, whereby he received a wound 1 inch deep and ¼ inch wide of which he languished at Southease until the next day and then died. Thus Hancocke killed him by misadventure and against his will. He had no goods or chattels, lands or tenements at the time of Bryan's death or ever after to the jurors' knowledge. ASSI 35/105/9, m 2.

[Delivered to Horsham assizes on 28 July when an indictment was preferred which charged Hancocke with murdering Bryan at Southease on 19 June with a stick of no value which he held in his right hand and threw at Bryan, giving him a wound in the corner of the left eye near the top of the nose 1 inch deep and ¼ inch wide of which he languished at Southease until the next day and then died. The grand jury, to which William Bryan gave evidence, rejected the indictment and Hancocke confessed to the inquest verdict. ASSI 35/105/9, m 2; ASSI 35/105/11, m 80.]

463   30 June 1664. Mayfield. George Courthop, gent., Loxfield Camden half-hundred coroner. Jurors of the half-hundred and county: Thomas Sands sen., Solomon Foster, John Foster, Edward Burges, John Ollive sen., John Ollive jun., Thomas Bunce, John Tompkin, William Gallett, John Pococke, John Saxpes, Nicholas Drawbridge, Richard Woodman, John Relfe, 'Wyatt' Partridge. On 19 May Richard Parkes died a natural death at Mayfield. KB 9/898, m 54.

[Delivered into King's Bench by the coroner in Michaelmas. KB 9/898, m 62d; KB 29/314, m 165.]

464 21 July 1664. Wadhurst. George Courthop, gent., Loxfield Camden half-hundred coroner. Jurors of the half-hundred and county: William English, gent., Thomas Markwicke, gent., Richard Wickham, Thomas Baldocke, Thomas West, Thomas Norton, Robert Adds, John Grayborne, Robert Bird, John Crowhurst, Michael Guilbert, Stephen Wickinge. About 9 a.m. on 17 July, when Richard Jerman was climbing a pear tree growing in Edward Moore's orchard at Wadhurst to pick 'peares', the branch on which he was standing suddenly broke from the tree by reason of the weight of his body and fell to the ground together with Jerman who by misadventure fell on his head and from 'that fallinge downe' his neck was broken whereby he immediately died. The branch moved to his death, is worth ½d and remains with Moore. KB 9/898, m 57.
[Delivered with **463**. KB 9/898, m 62d; KB 29/314, m 165.]

465 15 Apr 1665. Rotherfield. Robert Shoebridge, gent., Rotherfield hundred coroner. Jurors of the hundred: Thomas Cripps, Thomas Maynard, Nicholas Feltnes, Thomas Weller, John Barber, Thomas May, George Wells, William Harmer, Thomas Hooke, Alexander Pococke, Richard Wisedome, John Dulvy, William Lockyer. On 29 Mar Charles Harvey alias Jermyn late of Frant, 'husbandman', feloniously killed James Alchorne at Frant with 'a woodden batt' worth ½d which he held in his right hand, throwing it at him, striking him on the left side of the head a little above the ear and giving him 'a mortall bruise' of which he languished at Frant until 10 Apr and then died. At the time of the felony Harvey had no goods or chattels, lands or tenements in the hundred or elsewhere to the jurors' knowledge. ASSI 35/106/10, m 1.
[Delivered to Horsham assizes on 1 July when the grand jury, to which Thomas and Katharine Alchorne, Francis Owen, John Vaughan, John Cheeseman, Nicholas Manwood, John Parker, John Brookes and John Poeton gave evidence, presented an indictment identical to the inquest verdict except that the charge was murder and the last sentence was omitted. Harvey pleaded not guilty to the indictment and was acquitted of murder but convicted of manslaughter; he had no chattels. He then pleaded benefit of clergy and was remanded in gaol without bail. At the assizes of 22 Mar 1666 he proved his clergy and was branded and released, paying his fees. ASSI 35/106/10, mm 1, 10, 11, 25d; ASSI 35/107/7, m 20d.]

466 18 July 1665. Petworth. John Peachy, gent., county coroner. Jurors: John Aylwyn, Henry Goble, John Barnard, John Haslyn jun., Richard Barnard, Daniel Watsfeild, Henry Lutman, Richard Mason sen., Richard Mason jun., Thomas Phillipps, Daniel Morris jun., 'Emeri' Puttocke, Thomas Purchice, John Letfold, Peter Newyn, William Lanne, John Ward, Thomas Lillington, Henry Donner. About 3 p.m. on 16 July Henry Beale late of Petworth, 'wheelewright', murdered his natural daughter Susan, aged ½ year, at Petworth, striking her on the chest with his right hand and giving her 'a mortall bruise' of which she languished at Petworth until 4 p.m. and then died. He had no goods or chattels, lands or tenements in Sussex or elsewhere at the time of the felony or ever after to the jurors' knowledge. ASSI 35/107/7, m 1.
[Delivered to Horsham assizes on 22 Mar 1666 when the grand jury, to which John Greene, Thomas Lillington and Sarah Bunne gave evidence, presented an indictment which charged Beale, called a labourer, with murdering Susan, aged 15 (or 50) weeks, at Petworth on 16 July 1665, when she was lying asleep in a cradle in his dwelling-house, by clutching her in both hands, violently striking her on the chest, stomach and abdomen and giving her a bruise of which she immediately died. Beale pleaded not guilty to the indictment but was convicted and hanged; he had no chattels. ASSI 35/107/7, mm 1, 2, 6, 20d.]

467 24 July 1665. Hastings. John Cox, esq., Hastings mayor and coroner. Jurors: James Batchellor, Stephen Tompsett, Robert Phipps, William Farr, John Webb, Herbert Lunsford, Edward Stapley, Edward Beverstock, Robert Davys, James Shingleton, Robert Cooper, Francis Norwood. Witnesses: Thomas Browne, William Hayward. At 1 p.m. on 23 July, when Nicholas Jarrett late of Hastings, 'butcher', aged 20, was washing and swimming of his own free will in 'le Priorie Pond' in Hastings, which was very deep, he was suddenly gripped by a convulsion or spasm in the shin by reason of which he could swim no further from the failure of the sinews of the shin whence he was lame and, turning himself onto his back, a short time later he was drowned in the middle of the pond, there being no one near to come to his aid and save him. HASTINGS C/B(k) 1; HASTINGS C/A(a) 2, f 108v.

468   3 Nov 1665. Uckfield. Edward Raynes, gent., county coroner. Jurors: Robert Turner, John Baker, Thomas Cheeseman, Richard Hugget, gent., John Olive, William Olive, Robert Petit, John Alchorne, Richard Burges, Ralph Chatfeild, Robert Drowst. On 18 Oct Agnes Rivers late of Withyham, 'spinster', feloniously threw herself into the water in 'a marlepitt' on the land of Michael Turner of Withyham, 'yeoman', at Withyham and drowned herself. At that time she had goods and chattels worth 17s 6d which were appraised on 21 Nov [*?recte* Oct] by Robert Turner, John Baker and Isaac Peckham and which remain with John Baker of Withyham, 'yeoman', viz 'ready money in her purse 2s, item for her wareing apparrell 13s, itcm for an old bible and old box 2s 6d'. [*Inventory mainly in English.*] KB 9/904, mm 158, 159.
[Delivered into King's Bench by the coroner in Easter 1666. Baker was summoned to King's Bench to answer for the goods and chattels; no further process against him is noted on the Controlment Roll. At Horsham assizes on 22 Mar 1666 an indictment was preferred which charged Michael Turner late of Withyham, labourer, Dorothy his wife alias Dorothy Turner late of Withyham, spinster, and Ann Baker late of Withyham, spinster, alias Ann wife of John Baker late of Withyham, labourer, with murdering Ann Rivers at Withyham on 21 Oct 1665: Michael Turner taking her violently in both hands, throwing her into a marl pit full of water, gravel, mud and other filth and drowning her, whereby she immediately died; and Dorothy Turner and Baker being feloniously present aiding and abetting him. The grand jury, to which Isaac Peckham, Ann Waters, John Pulman and Elizabeth Swanne gave evidence, rejected the indictment. ASSI 35/107/9, m 68; KB 9/904, m 158d; KB 29/317, m 36d.]

469   2 Mar 1666. Higham, a member of the Cinque Port of Hastings. John Cox, esq., Hastings mayor and coroner. Jurors: Thomas Franke, gent., Thomas Winter, William Batcheller, John Webb, Thomas Lasher, John Salmon, Robert Phipps, Edward Stapley, Thomas Labie, Richard Watts, George Joy, Edward Beverstock. About 4 p.m. on 1 Mar Alice Smyth late of Winchelsea, widow, aged 60 or thereabouts, went into the close or piece of land belonging to Thomas Farnham of Winchelsea, jurat, called Brewers Marsh at Higham and feloniously got into a ditch containing water in the farthest part of the close and drowned herself in the mixture of water and mud and so came to her death, there appearing to be no other cause. HASTINGS C/A(a) 2, f 109v.

470   28 May 1666. Birdham. Edmund Crispe, gent., Manhood hundred coroner. Jurors: Richard Zoutch, John Jolliffe, William Spring, Stephen Corpes, John Voake, Andrew Cheeseman, John Christmasse, Richard Holmes, Edward Lee, John Stephens, Edward Hasler, John Richards, John Alemoor, William Busby, Richard Densley, Thomas Dennis. On 20 May Henry Austen, a youth, late of West Wittering died a natural death at Birdham. KB 9/905, m 54.
[Delivered into King's Bench by the coroner in Michaelmas. KB 9/905, m 67d; KB 29/317, m 132d.]

471   20 June 1666. Sutton. John Peachey, gent., county coroner. Jurors: William Garrett, John Roads, William Langley, Stephen Leggat sen., Richard Churcher, James Booker, Austin [*Augustus*] Floate, John Spicer, William Symonds, Thomas Heather, Thomas Beale, Stephen Leggat jun., John Andreis, Thomas Lockett, John Filp, John Richman. About 3 a.m. on 26 May Robert Turner alias May of Sutton, 'yoman', died a natural death at Sutton. KB 9/905, m 53.
[Delivered into King's Bench by the coroner in Michaelmas. KB 9/905, m 67d; KB 29/317, m 132d.]

472   28 Sept 1666. West Firle. Edward Raynes, gent., county coroner. Jurors: John Waker, Thomas Rowe, John Colvill, Thomas Arnold, Thomas Waker, Richard Whiteinge, John Vynall, James Bunce, Edward Whiteinge, Thomas Teeling, Nicholas Lee, Nathaniel Tourle. Witnesses: Joan Baker, widow, Joan Harmer, widow, Joan wife of Michael Harmer. On 26 Sept Joan Harmer late of West Firle, 'spinster', gave birth at West Firle to a live male child which by the laws of England 'was a bastard' and immediately afterwards murdered him there, strangling him with both hands whereby he immediately died. She had no goods or chattels, lands or tenements in Sussex or elsewhere at that time or ever after to the jurors' knowledge. ASSI 35/108/7, mm 11, 11d.

[Delivered to Horsham assizes on 7 Mar 1667 when Harmer pleaded not guilty and was acquitted; she had not fled and so was released, paying her fees. ASSI 35/108/7, mm 4, 11, 20d.]

473 17 Dec 1666. Catsfield. John Purfeild, gent., Hastings rape coroner. Jurors of the rape: Thomas Fuller, gent., Henry Evans, William Tampkin, Thomas Snepp, John Brattle, George Miller, Edward Goodman, Thomas Highland, John Holford, Thomas Jenner, Richard Crackbone, Richard Mugredge, Robert Thomas, James Berricke, Richard Combes. About 9 a.m. on 16 Dec Stephen Harmer of Catsfield, 'laborer', apprentice of John Grayling of Catsfield, 'blacksmith', was ordered by Grayling to carry immediately into 'the kitchen' of his dwelling-house in Catsfield 'a great logg' of wood belonging to Grayling and lying near his house for burning in the kitchen. Harmer immediately took the log in both hands, lifted it onto his right shoulder and carried it into the kitchen. The log was very heavy and 'did crush' his shoulder so that Harmer, because he could not put it down from his shoulder gently and could not otherwise escape the great 'crushing' of his shoulder without mutilation of his limbs and peril of immediate death, decided to throw the log backwards onto the floor of the kitchen; and lest any injury should thereby result to anyone, before throwing it he twice at least gave notice of his intention in a loud voice to everyone then in the kitchen, requesting them urgently to stand aside for their own safety. After that he threw the log backwards from his shoulder towards the kitchen floor. At that moment Grayling's natural daughter Ann, aged 3, ran [behind] Harmer's back and under the log which suddenly fell on the right side of her head and 'did bruise' her so gravely that she immediately died. Thus Harmer killed her suddenly, by mischance and against his knowledge and will and not otherwise. The log moved to her death, is worth 2d and remains with Grayling. Harmer had no goods or chattels in Sussex at the time of the death or ever after to the jurors' knowledge. [*Damaged.*] ASSI 35/108/8, m 2.

[Delivered to East Grinstead assizes on 5 Sept 1667 when an indictment was preferred which charged Harmer with murdering Ann Grayling at Catsfield on 16 Dec 1666 with 'a great blocke of wood' worth 1d which he held on his left shoulder and threw from it onto the right side of her head, giving her a bruise of which she immediately died. The grand jury, to which Richard Oxley and John Grayling gave evidence, rejected the indictment. ASSI 35/108/10, m 29.]

474 24 Dec 1666. Westbourne. John Peachy, gent., county coroner. Jurors: Robert Witcher, John Hale, William Hale, George Sherlocke, Richard Sowter, Thomas Stent, Ralph Churcher, Thomas Page, John Levett, William Baker, John Passenger, Nicholas Stephens, Nicholas Mill, John Sherryer, Thomas Pay. Witnesses: Sarah Foster, Eleanor Churcher, Richard Silverlock, Mary Tangley, John Levett, Edward Gibbs, Mary Churcher, Mary Goodson. On 22 Dec Thomas Goffe, 'laborer', Florence [*Florentius*] Marryr, 'laborer', 'Darby' Bryan, 'laborer', and Arthur Kaverner, 'laborer', all late of Westbourne, murdered Henry Ryce late of Westbourne, 'laborer', at Westbourne: Goffe 'did strike and thrust in' the right side of his chest near the nipple with 'a rapier drawne' made of iron and steel and worth 12d which he held in his right hand, giving him a wound 1 inch wide and 3 inches deep of which he immediately died; and Marryr, Bryan and Kaverner were feloniously present aiding and abetting him. Immediately afterwards Goffe and Marryr fled to places unknown to the jurors. All 4 had no goods or chattels, lands or tenements in Sussex or elsewhere at the time of the felony or ever after to the jurors' knowledge. ASSI 35/108/7, mm 3, 3d.

[Delivered with **472**. At the assizes Goffe, Bryan and Kaverner were remanded in gaol, as they were again at the assizes of 5 Sept 1667. At the assizes of 28 Feb 1668 all 3 pleaded not guilty. Kaverner was acquitted; he had not fled and so was released, paying his fees. Goffe and Bryan were acquitted of murder but convicted of manslaughter; they had no chattels. They then successfully pleaded benefit of clergy, were branded on their hands and were ordered to be kept in gaol without bail for 11 months unless within that time they should find sureties for their good behaviour or be transported overseas; they were still in gaol at and after the assizes of 2 July 1668 but had been released before that of 12 Mar 1669. ASSI 35/108/7, mm 3, 20d; ASSI 35/108/8, mm 23, 28d; ASSI 35/109/5, m 23d; ASSI 35/109/6, m 16d; ASSI 35/110/5, m 19d.]

475   20 Apr 1667. Hastings. [*Coroner omitted.*] Jurors to inquire into the death of an unknown child: James Batcheller, John Lunsford, Thomas Penbuckle, Richard Watts, Thomas Stapley, John Darley, George Labey, Richard Lowen, Peter Grover, Robert Cooper, George Oliver, John Webb.
    13 May. Witnesses: 'Old Widdow' Winckfeild, Sarah wife of George Wales, Rachel wife of [*forename omitted*] Elmes, Elizabeth wife of John Sargent, Dorothy wife of Robert Winckfeild, Joan Stedman, 'Goodwife' Morgan. 'The verdit of the coroner's quest given us in charg concerning the death of a child. Wee have made diligent search and enquirie theireof and canne finde no discovery theireof and this wee say all'. [*Verdict in English.*] HASTINGS C/B(k) 2, 3.
[The jurors empanelled on 20 Apr are all marked as sworn, but Darley and Labey are also marked as sick and Lunsford and Watts alone as having appeared. There is a note on the panel that the jurors were discharged on 13 May. The verdict is signed by Darley; Batcheller's and Lunsford's names are written beneath his in the hand of the verdict. A jury of 13 women was empanelled on 27 Apr. They were all sworn and are noted as having appeared. They returned that they knew nothing. The women were Sarah wife of George Wales, Ann wife of Simon Waters, Joan wife of Matthew Butler, Elizabeth wife of Thomas Grover, Mary wife of Thomas Meadow, Joan Hide, widow, Elizabeth wife of John Sargent, Alice Meadow, widow, Mary Sargent, widow, Jane wife of James Batcheller, Dorothy wife of James Chowle, Bridget wife of Thomas Staplus, Ann wife of John Darley. HASTINGS C/B(k) 2, 3.]

476   27 Aug 1667. West Lavant. John Peatchey, gent., county coroner. Jurors: John Greenefeild, 'Derby' Lurry, William Crowcher, Arthur Randall, John Starr sen., John Apps, Thomas Peter, Thomas Young jun., John Greenefeild jun., John Starr jun., Roger Tuffe, John Standen, Roger Stephens, Richard Bettesworth. Witnesses: Thomas Stamp, William Peachey, John Stamp [jun]. On 12 Aug John Compton late of West Lavant, 'laborer', feloniously killed John Stampe sen. at West Lavant with 'a woodden stake' of no value which he held in both hands: he 'did beate and strike' him on the left side of the head, giving him 'a mortall wound' 4 inches wide and ½ inch deep of which he languished at West Lavant until 25 Aug and then died. Compton had no goods or chattels, lands or tenements in Sussex or elsewhere at the time of the felony or ever after to the jurors' knowledge. ASSI 35/108/8, mm 12, 12d.
[Delivered with **473**. At the assizes an indictment was preferred which charged John and Richard Compton of West Lavant, labourers, with murdering Stampe at West Lavant on 12 Aug: John striking him on the left side of the head with a wooden stick of no value which he held in his right hand and giving him a wound 4 inches wide and ½ inch deep of which he languished at West Lavant until 25 Aug and then died; and Richard being feloniously present aiding and abetting him. The grand jury, to which the same 3 witnesses gave evidence, reduced the charge against John Compton to manslaughter and rejected that against Richard. John Compton pleaded not guilty to the inquest verdict but was convicted; he had no chattels. He then successfully pleaded benefit of clergy and was branded on the hand and released, paying his fees. ASSI 35/108/8, mm 3, 6, 12, 28d.]

477   26 Sept 1667. Withyham. Edward Raynes, gent., county coroner. Jurors: Robert Baker, John Woodgate, Thomas Bennet, William Peereles, William Saunders, Jeremy [*Jeremia*] Medherst, William Barnes, Robert Saxbies, George Huntly, William Picket, Thomas Aynscombe, William Fidge, William Harmer. On 7 Sept George Morley of Withyham, 'laborer', son of William Morley of Withyham, 'yeoman', 'espying' some crows in a close recently sown with wheat near his father's dwelling-house, immediately hurried into the house to load 'a birding peece' which was inside 'with gunpowder and haile shott', intending to shoot and kill the crows. He tried 'to reach downe' the gun from 'the mantletree' in his father's kitchen on which it was lying in order to load it, the gun 'being charged' by some other person, unknown to the jurors, 'with gunpowder and haile shott'. George, not knowing that, took the gun in both hands and moved the smaller end of it a little backwards in order to reach it down and 'the cocke', which was of iron and had a flint fixed in it, suddenly 'slipped downe' upon the steel of the gun and set fire to the gunpowder in the gun whereby from the force of the gunpowder the lead shot was fired from the gun and by misadventure struck and penetrated Mary Russell late of Withyham, 'spinster', William Morley's servant, who was then sitting in the kitchen near George, in the left side of the chest near 'the left pappe', giving her a wound 1 inch wide and 2 inches deep of which she languished at Withyham until 9 Sept and then [died. Thus] George killed her suddenly, by mischance and against his will and not otherwise. The gun is worth 6s 8d, moved to Russell's death and remains with William Morley. George Morley had no goods or chattels in Sussex or elsewhere at the time of the death or ever after to the jurors' knowledge. [*Damaged.*] ASSI 35/108/8, m 1.

[This inquest is now in the same file as **473**, but it could not have been delivered to the assizes of 5 Sept 1667. Mary Russell was buried at Withyham on 12 Sept, which suggests that the dates given for both death and inquest are correct although the inquest was said to have been held on view of her body. The record of the inquest was probably delivered to the following East Grinstead assizes of 28 Feb 1668 and later (perhaps quite recently) misplaced into the earlier file. The indictments files of both assizes are broken and the second is now incomplete. At whichever assizes he attended George Morley confessed to the inquest verdict. ASSI 35/108/8, m 1; ASSI 35/109/5; EP II/16/202A.]

478   11 Feb 1668. Maresfield. Edward Raynes, gent., county coroner. Jurors: William Prior, John Mason, Martin Hoth, Richard Comber, David Martin, Thomas Smith, Edward Seale, Henry Paine, John Bridgland, Adrian Duffeild, William Picket, William Smith, John Jarret. Witnesses: Ann wife of John Coulstocke, Mary wife of John Tailor. On 2 Jan Jane Dobson late of Maresfield, 'spinster', gave birth at Maresfield to a live male child which by the laws of England 'was a bastard' and, as soon as he was born, murdered him there, taking him in both hands and strangling him by the neck and throat whereby he immediately died. She had no goods or chattels, lands or tenements in Sussex or elsewhere at that time or ever after to the jurors' knowledge. ASSI 35/109/5, mm 8, 8d.

[Delivered to East Grinstead assizes on 28 Feb when Dobson pleaded not guilty but was convicted and hanged; she had no chattels. ASSI 35/109/5, mm 8, 23d.]

479   23 Mar 1670. Goring. John Howes, gent., coroner of Arundel and Bramber rapes. Jurors: Edmund Negus, gent., Robert Dugles, Thomas Aylwin, gent., Henry Francklyn, Thomas Grinder, John Mustian, John Boley, John Wyatt, William Jupp, Henry Campion, George Isted, Thomas Curtis. Witnesses: Ann Watersfeild, Joan Longe, Elizabeth Breade. On 11 Mar Ann Gates late of Goring, widow, 'was delivered of a child', a male bastard, secretly at Goring and secretly 'hid and conceald' him, but whether he was alive or dead at the time of the delivery the jurors do not know. Gates had no goods or chattels, lands or tenements in Sussex to their knowledge. ASSI 35/111/6, mm 1, 1d.

[Delivered to Horsham assizes on 7 July when the grand jury, to which the same 3 witnesses gave evidence, presented an indictment which charged Gates with murdering her male bastard at Goring on 20 Mar, the day of his birth, taking him in both hands as soon as he was born alive and strangling him by gripping him by the neck and throat whereby he immediately died. Gates pleaded not guilty to the indictment but was convicted and hanged; she had no chattels. It is uncertain which date of death is correct. Both days are given as words (*undecimo* and *vicesimo*), not small roman numerals. The inquest verdict gives 11 Mar as a Friday, which it was, and so the date in the indictment is more likely to be wrong. The baby's burial is not entered in the Goring parish register. ASSI 35/111/6, mm 1, 3, 6, 47d; PAR 92/1/1/1.]

480   30 Mar 1670. Stoughton. John Peachey, gent., county coroner. Jurors: John Baily, George White, Richard Randoll, William Good, Edward Page, Thomas Jenman, William Jenman, William Symmes, John Read, Nicholas Boyer, William Russell, William Letchlow. Witnesses: Arthur Bayley, John Wheeler, Edward Locke, Richard Clewer. On 25 Mar Mary Smyth late of Stoughton, 'spinster', alias Mary wife of Lawrence Smyth late of Stoughton, 'yeoman', feloniously killed John Smyth late of Stoughton, her natural son, at Stoughton with 'an earthen drinking cupp' worth 1d which she held in her right hand, striking him violently on the head of which he languished at Stoughton until 27 Mar and then died. Mary had no goods or chattels, lands or tenements in Sussex or elsewhere at the time of the felony or ever after to the jurors' knowledge. ASSI 35/111/6, mm 2, 2d.

[Delivered with **479**. At the assizes the grand jury, to which the same 4 witnesses gave evidence, presented an indictment identical to the inquest verdict except that the charge was murder, John was described as the natural son of Mary and Lawrence, who was styled labourer, and the last sentence was omitted. Mary pleaded not guilty to the indictment and was acquitted of murder but convicted of manslaughter by misfortune; she was remanded in gaol until she found sureties to prosecute her pardon of course at the next assizes. ASSI 35/111/6, mm 2, 3, 5, 47d.]

481   22 Sept 1670. Heyshott in Arundel rape. John Howes, gent., coroner of Arundel and Bramber

rapes. Jurors of Arundel rape: John Sturt, Robert Austin, William Elmes, Robert Todman, Andrew Tippe, John Phillipps, Adam Coles, Richard Mills, William Roper, Richard Redman, Thomas Marchant, Thomas Wakeford, John Hopkins, William Lokyer, Thomas Booker, George Roper. On 20 Sept Bernard White late of Heyshott, 'laborer', feloniously killed John Smyth late of Heyshott, 'wheelwright', at Heyshott with 'a rapier drawne' made of iron and steel and worth 3s which he held in his right hand and with which he 'did strike and thrust in' the left side of his body near the left breast, giving him a wound ½ inch wide and 4 inches deep of which he immediately died. Afterwards White fled to places unknown to the jurors. He had no goods or chattels, lands or tenements in Sussex or elsewhere at the time of the felony or flight or ever after to the jurors' knowledge. ASSI 35/112/6, m 1.
[Delivered to East Grinstead assizes on 27 Mar 1671 when the grand jury, to which Henry Beacon, Richard Cribborne, William Oakeley, Thomas Hockley and John Haynes gave evidence, presented an indictment identical to the inquest verdict except that the charge was murder and the last 2 sentences were omitted. White pleaded not guilty to the indictment but was convicted and hanged; he had no chattels. ASSI 35/112/6, mm 1, 3, 9, 88d.]

482   10 Feb 1671. Hastings. Thomas Jarrett, Hastings mayor and coroner. Jurors: Mark Moore, John Bailif, Richard Sargent, Thomas Faulkner, Thomas Winter, William Sargent, Thomas Peck, Edward Cooper, Robert Phillip, James Belton, William Farr, John Webb, William Philcox, Thomas Stapley, Thomas Thacker, Richard Smith, Henry Oliver. Between 1 and 2 p.m. on 10 Feb Ralph Stedman, ?boatman [*naupegus*], aged about 14, climbed into a new boat in the parish of St Mary in the castle, Hastings, which was then built there, fixed a cord worth ½d to the ?top rung [*rotund*'] of a ladder which was standing in the boat with his own hands, tied it with a slip-knot [*nodo elapso*] round his neck and feloniously hanged himself. He remained hanging there until found dead shortly afterwards by the said John Webb. At the time of the felony Stedman had no goods or chattels to the jurors' knowledge. The jurors requested that this inquest be enrolled of record in the common register of Hastings according to custom. The ½d for the cord accrues to the town as deodand according to law and custom. HASTINGS C/A(a) 2, f 128.

483   27 Feb 1671. Horsham. Alexander Luxford, gent., county coroner. Jurors: Peter Waterton, William Weller, Henry Waller, Leonard Booker, John Curtis, William Bridger, John Picke, Richard Bryant, Nicholas Best, Robert Savage, John Hayler, Edmund Lintott, John Clarke, Samuel Hunt, Robert Lutman, Edward Slater, James Burstow. On 25 Feb William Bywood, aged 77, who had recently been committed to Horsham gaol by John Baker, esq., JP, for stealing a 'fatt hogg', died a natural death there. KB 9/918, m 174.
[Delivered into King's Bench by the coroner in Easter. ASSI 35/112/6, m 88d; KB 9/918, m 200d; KB 29/324, m 74.]

484   4 Dec 1671. Horsham. Alexander Luxford, gent., county coroner. Jurors: Richard Wood, Robert Saridge, Henry Patching, Henry Pinfold, Michael Longmer, William Perkins, Richard Briant, James Baker, John Voyce, John Browne, Edward Balchin, Alexander Pilfold, Walter Fletcher, John Jenden, Thomas Forman. Witnesses: Richard Huggatt, Stephen Clowser, Jane Peters, Thomas Michell, John Bristow, Elizabeth Naldrett, [widow]. On 19 Nov Michael Bridges late of Horsham, 'laborer', feloniously killed Benjamin Jeale at Horsham, violently throwing him to the ground and striking and kicking him on the head, shoulders, arms, chest, sides, back and abdomen with his hands, arms, legs, knees and feet, of which he languished at Horsham until 11 p.m. on the next day and then died. After committing the felony Bridges fled to places unknown to the jurors. He had no goods or chattels, lands or tenements in Sussex or elsewhere at the time of the felony or flight or ever after to the jurors' knowledge. ASSI 35/113/8, mm 4, 4d.
[Delivered to East Grinstead assizes on 16 Mar 1672 when the grand jury, to which the same 6 witnesses gave evidence, presented an indictment identical to the inquest verdict except that the charge was murder and the time of death and the last 2 sentences were omitted. Bridges pleaded not guilty to the indictment and was acquitted; he had not fled and so was released, paying his fees. ASSI 35/113/8, mm 4, 5, 8, 83d.]

485 11 Mar 1672. Ringmer. Alexander Luxford, gent., county coroner. Jurors: James Plumer, Henry Plumer, Thomas Flave, Matthew Adds, Abel Parson, Daniel Panckhurst, John Tayler, Henry Page, John Marten, John Newenden, William Carter, Thomas Plumer, John Beecher, John Foord, Anthony Bannister, 'Newton' Sheppard, Richard Stonehouse, Thomas Fitzherbert, Gregory Wilding. About 11 p.m. on 6 Mar John Graycoate late of Ringmer, 'laborer', murdered Jane Salter late of Ringmer, widow, at Ringmer: he took her in both hands and violently 'did hold and gripe' her in the neck and throat and strangled her, whereby she immediately died. After committing the felony Graycoate fled to places unknown to the jurors. He had no goods or chattels, lands or tenements in Sussex or elsewhere at the time of the felony or flight or ever after to the jurors' knowledge. ASSI 35/113/8, m 2. [Delivered with **484**. Graycoate was outlawed at Lewes on 12 Dec by Luxford and John Peachey, esq., county coroners, on a writ of exigent issued at Horsham assizes on 27 July. ASSI 35/114/7, m 41.]

486 22 July 1672. Hurstpierpoint. Alexander Luxford, gent., county coroner. Jurors: Robert W..., John Marchant, Richard Chatfeild, John Bernard, Thomas Weckham, Thomas Moore, Richard Herriott, Thomas Bull, James Hodsell, John Buckwell, Robert Dyar, John Freind, John Parker, Thomas ?Roper. Witnesses: William Skynner, Elizabeth Farley, Eleanor Mackrell. About 11 a.m. on 17 July Elizabeth wife of Thomas Faulkner of Hurstpierpoint, 'husbandman', feloniously killed Margery Glassington, 'spinster', aged 12, her husband's servant, at Hurstpierpoint with 'a small stick' of no value which she held in her right hand and with her hands, arms, legs, knees and feet violently striking and kicking her on the head, shoulders, chest, stomach, sides, back and abdomen of which she languished at Hurstpierpoint until 6 p.m. on the same day and then died. At the time of the felony Faulkner had no goods or chattels, lands or tenements in Sussex or elsewhere to the jurors' knowledge. [*Damaged.*] ASSI 35/113/9, mm 1, 1d.
[Delivered to Horsham assizes on 27 July when the grand jury, to which the same 3 witnesses gave evidence, presented an indictment identical to the inquest verdict except that the charge was murder, Faulkner was called Elizabeth Faulkner late of Hurstpierpoint, spinster, alias Elizabeth wife of Thomas Faulkner late of Hurstpierpoint, husbandman, Glassington was called the servant of both Thomas and Elizabeth and the last sentence was omitted. Faulkner pleaded not guilty to the indictment at the East Grinstead assizes of 14 Mar 1673 and was acquitted; she had not fled and so was released, paying her fees. ASSI 35/113/9, mm 1, 2; ASSI 35/114/7, mm 5, 76d.]

487 24 Sept 1672. Horsham. Alexander Luxford, gent., county coroner. Jurors: George Mills, Richard English, John Spurr, Walter Longhurst, Robert Terrey, William Ede, Thomas Ede, Thomas Comber, John Hyll, John Smith, John Willett, Edward Heavery, Alexander Watson, Thomas Worsfold, Edward Stenning, Thomas Jackman, Richard Myles. About 10 p.m. on 19 Sept William Graycoate, 'laborer', Thomas Tallman, 'laborer', and Richard Blacke, 'laborer', all late of Horsham, murdered William Ellis late of Roffey in Horsham, 'yeoman', at Horsham: Graycoate violently striking him on the head, shoulders, arms, chest, sides and back with a 'great staffe' worth 1d which he held in both hands, of which he languished at Horsham until 1 a.m. on 22 Sept and then died; and Tallman and Blacke being feloniously present aiding and abetting him. After committing the felony all 3 fled to places unknown to the jurors. They had no goods or chattels, lands or tenements in Sussex or elsewhere at the time of the felony or flight or ever after to the jurors' knowledge. ASSI 35/114/7, m 3.
[Delivered to East Grinstead assizes on 14 Mar 1673 when Graycoate, Tallman and Blacke were still at large. A capias was therefore issued for them which was returned to the assizes of 10 July endorsed that they were not found in the sheriff's bailiwick. A writ of exigent then issued on which all 3 were outlawed at Lewes on 13 Nov by Luxford and John Peachey, esq., county coroners. At the assizes of 14 Mar the grand jury, to which Mary Taylor, Alice Steere and Joan Oziver gave evidence, presented an indictment which charged John and Henry Sheppard, James Vilewood, Ralph Coote, John Bristow, Edward Lucey and Edmund Capen, all late of Horsham, labourers, with murdering Ellis about 10 p.m. on 19 Sept 1672 at Horsham: John Sheppard violently striking him on the head, shoulders, arms, chest, sides and back with a great staff worth 1d which he held in both hands, of which he languished at Horsham until 1 a.m. on 22 Sept and then died; and the 6 others being feloniously present aiding and abetting him. All 7 pleaded not guilty and were acquitted; they had not fled. The 2 Sheppards and Capen were released, paying their fees. Vilewood, Coote, Bristow and Lucey, being drunk and disorderly persons, were sentenced to a week's hard labour in the Arundel house

of correction and then to be released, paying their fees. ASSI 35/114/7, mm 3, 5, 8, 76d; ASSI 35/114/8, m 11; ASSI 35/115/8, m 22.]

488   2 Oct 1672. Petworth. John Howes, gent., coroner of Arundel and Bramber rapes. Jurors: Robert Paine, 'Caleb' Paine, Nicholas Goodyer, John Hollyard, Geoffrey Horton, William Eade, Robert True, Richard Taylor, Arthur Shaftoe, Thomas Trevett, Richard Hale, Robert Lambert, Nicholas Coates, Thomas Woods, Hugh Eaton, Philip Keeler, Robert Grover, John Hamon, John Beane, Thomas Lucas, Nicholas Alderton, Ambrose Hood. About 6 a.m. on 30 Sept Henry Bulstroad late of Petworth, gent., murdered John Dawtrey, esq., at Petworth with 'a sword drawne' made of iron and steel worth 2s 6d which he held in his right hand: he 'did strike and thrust in' the left side of his body near the navel, giving him 'a mortall wound' 1 inch wide and 6 inches deep of which he languished at Petworth until 9 p.m. on the same day and then died. After committing the felony Bulstroad fled to places unknown to the jurors. He had no goods or chattels, lands or tenements in Sussex or elsewhere at the time of the felony or flight to the jurors' knowledge. ASSI 35/114/7, m 2.
[Delivered with **487**. Attached is a letter of 7 Oct 1673 from H Finch (*sc.* Heneage Finch, bt, keeper of the seals), to Thomas Leigh, esq., clerk of assize for Sussex, or his deputy, asking for a copy of the inquest to be made and delivered to the bearer, William Peachey. At the assizes of 14 Mar 1673 the grand jury, to which Richard Burnell, John Scutt, John Cooke, Samuel Morris, William Rose and James South gave evidence, presented an indictment identical to the inquest verdict but without the last 2 sentences. Bulstroad was still at large and a capias was therefore issued for him which was returned to the assizes of 10 July endorsed that he was not found in the sheriff's bailiwick. A writ of exigent then issued on which he was outlawed at Lewes on 13 Nov by John Peachey, esq., and Alexander Luxford, gent., county coroners. At the assizes of 2 Apr 1674 Bulstroad pleaded a pardon for the murder and outlawry which was allowed and he was released, paying his fees. ASSI 35/114/7, mm 2, 4; ASSI 35/114/8, m 11; ASSI 35/115/8, mm 22, 30d.]

489   6 Dec 1673. East Grinstead. Alexander Luxford, gent., county coroner. Jurors: Thomas Bodle, Richard Freebody, John Mathewes, Thomas Bowra, Nicholas Cripps, Thomas Wood, Thomas Cooper, John Underhill, Andrew Ledgen, John Willett, William Taylor, Thomas Bromley, Arthur Harmand, Stephen Head, John Rice. Witnesses: Robert Alchorne, Edward Elmore. On 5 Dec John Graycoat late of East Grinstead, 'laborer', murdered 'Younge' Rolfe at East Grinstead with 'a wooden staffe' worth ½d which he held in his right hand, striking him violently on the head, shoulders, arms, chest, sides and back of which he immediately died. After committing the felony Graycoat fled to places unknown to the jurors. He had no goods or chattels, lands or tenements in Sussex or elsewhere at the time of the felony or flight or ever after to the jurors' knowledge. ASSI 35/115/8, mm 1, 1d.
[Delivered to East Grinstead assizes on 2 Apr 1674 when the grand jury, to which Mary Rolfe, Joseph Puxtey, Thomas Bromley, John Bennett, John Heasman, Robert Alchorne, Edward Elmor and Charles Hood gave evidence, presented an indictment identical to the inquest verdict except that the man charged with the murder was John Glide late of East Grinstead, labourer, and the last 2 sentences were omitted. Glide pleaded not guilty but was convicted and hanged; he had no chattels. ASSI 35/115/8, mm 1, 2, 5, 30d.]

490   9 Feb 1674. Hastings. John Lunsford, Hastings mayor and coroner. Jurors: Robert Phipps, Richard Baker, Thomas Stapley, Thomas Paine, William Philcox, Thomas Baker, Richard Laurence, Thomas Dighton, William Stevenson, Bartholomew Lovelace, Richard Smith, Nicholas Hutchens. Between 4 and 5 p.m., as is supposed, on 7 Feb Edward Brooke late of Hastings, fisherman, aged about 16, went into a close or parcel of land near the sea in the parish of St Mary Magdalen, Hastings, climbed a small oak tree worth 4d which was growing there, fixed a cord worth 2d to one of its branches with his own hands, tied it with a slip-knot round his neck and feloniously hanged himself. He remained hanging there until found dead the next day by John Glasier. At the time of the felony Brooke had no goods or chattels to the jurors' knowledge. The jurors requested that this inquest be enrolled of record in the common register of Hastings according to custom. The 2d for the cord accrues to the town as deodand according to law and custom. HASTINGS C/A(a) 2, f 138v.

491 2 May 1674. All Saints' parish, Chichester. John Peachey, esq., county coroner. Jurors: Ellis [*Elizeus*] Gad, Richard Lillyatt, John Butler, William Jenings, William Dawes, Robert Hasler, William Jelley, William Lilliatt, Robert Newnington, William West, Joseph Farnden, Henry Newman, Jeremy [*Jeremia*] Leggatt, James Drewett, Robert Scarlett, John Gittins, William Turner. Witnesses: Richard Baker and [*blank*] his wife, William Meeres, John May, Ann Bishopp, [*blank*] Doncaster. On 1 May Alice Playfoote late of the parish of St Peter the Great in Sussex, 'spinster', alias Alice wife of Ralph Playfoote late of St Peter the Great, 'laborer', murdered Elizabeth Stoner in St Peter the Great, violently striking and kicking her on the head, face, shoulders, arms, chest, sides and back with her hands, arms, legs and feet, of which she languished in St Peter the Great until the next day and then died. Alice had no goods or chattels, lands or tenements in Sussex or elsewhere at the time of the felony or ever after to the jurors' knowledge. ASSI 35/115/9, mm 4, 4d.
[Delivered to East Grinstead assizes on 23 July when the grand jury, to which Jane wife of Richard Baker, William Meeres, John May, Ann Bishopp, Sarah Stoner, Joan ?Peere and possibly Richard Baker and (*blank*) Doncaster gave evidence, presented an indictment identical to the inquest verdict but without the last sentence. Alice Playfoote pleaded not guilty to both the indictment and the inquest verdict and was acquitted, the trial jury finding that Stone had died a natural death; she had not fled and so was released, paying her fees. ASSI 35/115/9, mm 3–5, 33d.]

492 11 Feb 1676. Rye. Michael Cadman, esq., Rye mayor and coroner. Jurors of Rye: Thomas Knight, Cornelius Peadle, Giles Davis, John Breads, William Richardson, Daniel Miller, William Buteler, John Weight, John King, Nicholas Earle, Thomas Tailor, John Frierson. About 9 a.m. on 11 Feb Mark Skinner of Lydd in Kent, 'cordwainer', came to David Hales's dwelling-house in Baddings ward in Rye and seemed to be healthy in body and mind, but a very little later he went out into Hales's garden, suddenly fell to the ground and immediately died a natural death and not otherwise to the jurors' knowledge. RYE 32/3.

493 11 May 1676. Parish of St Peter the Less, Chichester. William Baldwyn jun., gent., Chichester city coroner. Jurors of Chichester: John Bartholmew, John Deare, Nathaniel Fulford, Thomas Baker, William Lewis, Richard Godman, George Butterley, Aaron Bennett, William Deeare, George Wheeler, John Farhill, Thomas Barber, Nicholas Watkins, Joseph Perkins, Richard Joanes. At midnight on 9 May Walter Littleton of All Saints' parish, Chichester, gent., murdered John Gipps late of St Peter the Less, gent., in All Saints' parish with 'a rapier draune' worth 20s which he held in his right hand, giving him a wound on 'the left side' of the abdomen 6 inches deep and ½ inch wide of which he languished in St Peter the Less until 9 p.m. on the next day and then died. Littleton had no goods or chattels, lands or tenements in the city or its liberties or elsewhere at the time of the felony or ever after to the jurors' knowledge. ASSI 35/117/10, m 2.
[Delivered to East Grinstead assizes on 17 July when the grand jury, to which Ann Bennett, Mary and Robert Floid, Francis Coaches and William Peachey gave evidence, presented an indictment substantially the same as the inquest verdict but stating that the rapier was made of iron and steel and that Gipps languished in the parishes of All Saints and St Peter the Less, dying in the latter, and omitting the hours of the assault and death and the last sentence. Littleton pleaded not guilty to the indictment and was acquitted of murder but convicted of manslaughter; he had no chattels. He then produced a royal warrant for a stay of judgment and found good sureties to appear at the next assizes and in the meantime to be of good behaviour. A writ of mittatis of 26 May had summoned the inquest into King's Bench in Trinity; and a letter of 13 Feb 1677 from Thomas Jones (kt, justice of King's Bench), to the clerk of assize or his deputy asked that a copy of the indictment and proceedings be delivered to the bearer. ASSI 35/117/10, mm 1, 2, 8, 13, 14, 36d.]

494 28 May 1676. Hastings. William Parker sen., Hastings mayor and coroner. Jurors: Robert Bursey, Thomas Meadow sen., Richard Baker, Robert Phipps, William Batcheller, John Webb, Thomas Hurt, George Harison, Samuel Pacey, John Shosmith, Mark West, Henry Stevenson, Richard King, Thomas Baker, Thomas Whinyeates, William Stone. Between 11 a.m. and noon on 27 May, when John Wright, aged about 2, son of John Wright late of Hastings, 'fisherman', deceased, was playing with other children on 'le paviament' in the road in All Saints' parish, Hastings, and 'a waggon' belonging to Richard Carpenter loaded with bundles of sticks [*fasciculi*], drawn by 4 oxen, the whole being worth £20, and driven by Thomas Davys and John Padiham was passing near the pavement where they were playing, Wright suddenly and by mischance stumbled and fell from the pavement under the wagon and as he lay on the ground one of its rear wheels ran over his face and head, giving him a wound of which he immediately died by misadventure. The jurors requested that this inquest be recorded in the common book of Hastings according to ancient and approved custom. HASTINGS C/A(a) 2, f 155.

495   3 Oct 1677. East Grinstead. Alexander Luxford, gent., county coroner. Jurors: John Cripps, Richard Johnson, George Drewry, John Eastland, Richard Martin, Thomas Chapman, Toby Showen, Benjamin Page, John Head, Edward Head, George Tinett, Isaac Peirce, John Langridge, John Gibson, William Withers, Michael Richardson, Francis [*Francus*] Ridgwell. Witnesses: John Colgate, William Wythers, Henry Colgate, John Willett, William Wright. On 30 Sept Thomas Reynolds of East Grinstead, 'warrener', murdered Stephen Colgate late of Godstone in Surrey, 'cordwayner', at East Grinstead with 'a spade staffe' worth 4d which he held in both hands, violently striking him on the right side of the head and giving him 'a mortall bruise' a little above the right ear of which he languished at East Grinstead until the next day and then died. At the time of the felony Reynolds possessed 'a mare' coloured 'chesnutt' and worth 40s and £9 7s in money. The mare and £9 remain with Richard Martin of East Grinstead, 'inneholder', and the 7s with Henry Colgate of East Grinstead, 'husbandman', to whose hands they respectively came. At that time Reynolds had no other goods or chattels or any lands or tenements to the jurors' knowledge. ASSI 35/119/8, mm 11, 11d.
[Delivered to East Grinstead assizes on 16 Mar 1678 when Reynolds pleaded not guilty and was acquitted of murder but convicted of manslaughter; he had no chattels. He then successfully pleaded benefit of clergy and was branded on the hand and ordered to remain in gaol until he found sureties for his appearance at the next assizes and in the meantime to be of good behaviour. There is no record of his appearing at the assizes of 20 July. ASSI 35/119/8, mm 1, 11, 38d.]

496   22 Dec 1677. Worth. Alexander Luxford, gent., county coroner. Jurors: William Halcombe, John Baldin, Richard Boone, John Streater, James Dimmocke, Stephen Mose, John Brooker, John Steare, Benjamin Culpeper, Henry West, Thomas Brooker, Thomas Wood, William Jeale, Thomas Greene, John Locke, Richard Blake. Witnesses: Alice Brooker, Thomas Colton, Jane Locke. On 8 Dec Elizabeth Baker late of Worth, 'spinster', gave birth at Worth to a live male child which by the laws of England 'was a bastard' and immediately afterwards she murdered him there: she took him in both hands, 'did hold and gripe' him violently by the neck and throat and strangled him whereby he immediately died. Baker had no goods or chattels, lands or tenements in Sussex or elsewhere at the time of the felony or ever after to the jurors' knowledge. ASSI 35/119/8, mm 13, 13d.
[Delivered with **495**. At the assizes Baker pleaded not guilty but was convicted and sentenced to be hanged; she had no chattels. At the assizes of 20 July 1678 and 27 Mar 1679 she was remanded in gaol without bail. At Horsham assizes on 24 July 1679 she produced a pardon which was allowed and she was released, paying her fees. ASSI 35/119/8, mm 1, 13, 38d; ASSI 35/119/9, m 31d; ASSI 35/120/7, m 38d; ASSI 35/120/8, m 41d.]

497   21 Jan 1678. Edburton. Alexander Luxford, gent., county coroner. Jurors: Thomas Osborne, William Marchant, William Osborne, William Hobbs, William Stukes, Robert Gower, Thomas Elliott, Henry Lansdale, Thomas Fowle, Thomas Harrison, George Lashmer, George Inskipp, Richard English, John Mersh, Richard Lipscombe, Robert Freind, William Smith, Richard Jorden, Richard Nunham, Robert Young, James Nasher, Richard Brucker, Thomas Sansome. Witnesses: John Coulstocke, Richard Inskipp, Henry Osborne, Elizabeth Osborne, Richard Lipscombe, William Marchant, Elizabeth Lipscombe, Rachel Cooper. On 17 Jan Margaret Pollard late of Edburton, 'spinster', gave birth at Edburton to a live male child which by the laws of England 'was a bastard' and afterwards, on the same day, she, William Pollard late of Edburton, 'laborer', and Jane his wife alias Jane Pollard late of Edburton, 'spinster', murdered him there: Margaret violently striking him on the back of the head with 'a bedstaffe' worth 1d which she held in her right hand and giving him 'one mortall bruise' of which he immediately died; and William and Jane being feloniously present aiding and abetting her. None of the 3 had any goods or chattels, lands or tenements at the time of the felony or ever after to the jurors' knowledge. ASSI 35/119/8, mm 12, 12d.

[Delivered with **495**. By the time of the assizes William Pollard had died a natural death in gaol, as found by an inquest, now missing but returned into King's Bench in Hilary 1678, presumably by the coroner. Margaret and Jane pleaded not guilty. Margaret was acquitted; she had not fled and so was released, paying her fees. Jane was convicted and hanged; she had no chattels. ASSI 35/119/8, mm 1, 12, 38d; KB 11/3, Hilary 29–30 Charles II; KB 29/336, m 54d.]

498   4 Mar 1678. Hastings. Thomas Carleton, Hastings mayor and coroner. Jurors: John Bailie, George Fellowes, Thomas Hurt, John Page, Stephen Gibbons, Zachary [*Zacharius*] Harison, John Turpen, Richard Baker, Thomas Gurr, Thomas Whinyeates, Peter Grover, Thomas Carswell. Between 2 and 4 p.m. on 3 Mar, when William Parker, aged about 3, son of William Parker jun. of Hastings, gent., was 'with somme others of his playfellowes' near the uncovered draw-well of Richard Ellis of Hastings near All Saints' churchyard, he 'happened to fall therein and, the well being deepe and none present that were able to helpe' him, he died, 'which the said jury verily beleive, there appearing noe other woundes to, uppon or about ye body' 'but only ye bruise with the greatnes of ye fall into the said well'. The jurors requested that this inquest be recorded in the common book of Hastings according to ancient custom. [*Verdict in English.*] HASTINGS C/A(a) 2, f 166v.

499   4 Jan 1679. Hastings. Thomas Lovell, Hastings mayor and coroner. Jurors: Robert Bursey, John Bailif, Richard Lowen, Philip Griffen, Henry Oliver, Thomas Gur, James Winter, John Page, Thomas Whinyeates, Peter Grover, John Barber, John Gurr, John Russell, Edward Wild, John Evernden. On 3 Jan Francis Stephens late of Hastings, 'carpenter', aged about 28, died a natural death from hectic fever [*sc.* consumption] in Hastings gaol where he was detained in a plea of debt at the suit of William Parker of Hastings, jurat, for failing to find pledges for the defence of the plea. The jurors requested that this inquest be entered and enrolled among the coroner's records. HASTINGS C/A(a) 2, f 170v.

500   29 Jan 1679. Framfield. Alexander Luxford, gent., county coroner. Jurors: Richard Praule, John Delves, Thomas Peckham, Thomas Delves, John Weller, Thomas Butler, Josiah Bonnicke, John Jenner, Robert Towner, John Johnson, Roger Tester, Richard Weaver, John Ford, John Dobell, William Shoveler. Witnesses: John Smith, Susan Tester, Mary Collins. On 23 Jan Ann Batchelor late of Framfield, 'spinster', gave birth at Framfield to a live male child which by the laws of England 'was a bastard' and immediately afterwards murdered him there: she took him in both hands, 'did hold and gripe' him violently by the neck and throat and strangled him whereby he immediately died. At that time she had no goods or chattels, lands or tenements in Sussex or elsewhere to the jurors' knowledge. ASSI 35/120/7, mm 29, 29d.

[Delivered to East Grinstead assizes on 27 Mar when Batchelor pleaded not guilty and was acquitted; she had not fled and so was discharged, paying her fees. ASSI 35/120/7, mm 25, 29, 38d.]

501   12 July 1679. Patching. John Howes, gent., Arundel rape coroner. Jurors of the rape: Henry Morton, Robert Busbey, Edward Drewett, William Drewett, John Merchant, Robert Roakes, Edward Goodier, Henry Short, Richard Charles, Robert Fullicke, John Soale, John Grinfeild, George Fullicke. On 4 May Ann Taylor late of Patching, 'spinster', gave birth at Patching to a live male child which by the law of England 'was a bastard' and on the same day murdered him there: she took him in both hands, 'did throw and cast' him into 'a pond' full of water, gravel, mud and other filth in John Drewett's close, commonly called 'le backside', in Patching and 'did choake and drowne' him in it whereby he immediately died. She had no goods or chattels, lands or tenements within the liberty or elsewhere at that time or ever after to the jurors' knowledge. ASSI 35/120/8, m 1.

[Delivered to Horsham assizes on 24 July when the grand jury, to which John and Robert Drewett, Hannah Pescod,

Robert Roakes and Henry Morton gave evidence, presented an indictment identical to the inquest verdict but without the last sentence. Taylor pleaded not guilty to the indictment but was convicted and sentenced to be hanged; she had no chattels. At the Horsham assizes of 18 Mar 1680 she pleaded a pardon for the murder which was allowed and she was released, paying her fees. ASSI 35/120/8, mm 9, 12, 41d; ASSI 35/121/6, m 38d.]

502   8 Mar 1680. Brede. Richard Coleman, Brede liberty coroner. Jurors of Brede and 3 neighbouring townships in Sussex and the liberty: George Tilden, gent., William Cogger, gent., Samuel Cartwright, Thomas Cruttenden, Henry Cradock, Edward Brooker, Samuel Furminger, John Baker, Thomas Fuller, Solomon Wilmshurst, Francis Jarvis, Edward Cox, John Burges, Francis Marten, Christopher Cruttall, Thomas Parkes, John Tayler. About 8 a.m. on 6 Mar Thomas Fuller of Brede, 'labourer', feloniously killed his son Richard at Brede with 'a cudgell' worth 1d which he held in his right hand, striking him on the head, shoulders, arms, sides, thighs, shins and back and giving him several wounds and bruises on the thighs, shins and back of which he languished at Brede until the next day and then died. What goods or chattels, lands or tenements Thomas had at the time of the felony the jurors do not know. ASSI 35/121/6, m 10.
[This inquest, whose verdict began as manslaughter and seems to have been changed, mainly by interlineation, into murder and then changed back, mainly by erasure, to manslaughter, was delivered to Horsham assizes on 18 Mar when the grand jury, to which Susan Bird, Ann Trafficke and Joan Taylor gave evidence, presented an indictment which charged Thomas Fuller with murdering his natural son Richard at Brede on 6 Mar with a wooden stick of no value which he held in his right hand, violently striking him on the head, shoulders, arms, sides, chest and back of which he languished at Brede until the next day and then died. Fuller pleaded not guilty to the indictment and was acquitted of murder but convicted of manslaughter. He then successfully pleaded benefit of clergy and was branded on the hand, but was remanded in gaol without bail until safely conveyed to the house of correction for East Sussex at Lewes where he was to be kept at hard labour until 1 Mar 1681 and then released, paying his fees. ASSI 35/121/6, mm 9–11, 38d.]

503   12 June 1680. Fittleworth. John Howes, gent., Arundel rape coroner. Jurors: John Duke, John Pearly, John Fowler, John Bozard, Anthony Searle, Henry King, Thomas Waite, Richard Frye, Richard Sendall, John Downer, John Hale, William Lutter, John Mosse, Thomas Andrew, Samuel Harwood, William Mills, William Weller. On 8 June Edmund Lucas late of Fittleworth, 'laborer', feloniously killed Thomas Crowcher at Fittleworth with 'a ploughstaffe' of no value which he held in his right hand: he violently threw it at Crowcher and 'did strike' him on the right side of the head a little under the ear, giving him 'a mortall bruise' of which he immediately died. Lucas had no goods or chattels, lands or tenements within the liberty or elsewhere at that time or ever after to the jurors' knowledge. ASSI 35/121/7, m 2.
[Delivered to Horsham assizes on 22 July when the grand jury, to which Thomas Edsaw and Robert Tanner gave evidence, presented an indictment identical to the inquest verdict except that the charge was murder and the last sentence was omitted. Lucas pleaded not guilty to the indictment and was acquitted of murder but convicted of manslaughter. He then successfully pleaded benefit of clergy and was branded on the hand and released, paying his fees. ASSI 35/121/7, mm 3, 5, 41d.]

504   17 Aug 1680. Hastings. Samuel Smersall, Hastings mayor and coroner. Jurors: Thomas Swayne, physician, Richard Baker, Robert Phipps, Thomas Carswell, Michael Wamsly, Henry Oliver, Robert Gerey, Edward Wild, Mark Barry, Edward Williams, Thomas Baker, Mark Wright. On 16 Aug, when Thomas Hurt late of Hastings, 'ropemaker', was standing near 'a capstone to wind up boates' which was on Stonebeach by 'le Fishmarket Place' in Hastings with 'a capstone barr' of wood fixed onto 'the capstone', 'the said capstone' suddenly and unexpectedly caused 'the said capstone barr' to go round violently and in its circular movement it struck Hurt on the head and arm, giving him several wounds of which he died by misadventure within an hour. The bar is worth 18d. The jurors requested that this inquest be enrolled of record in the common register of Hastings according to custom. HASTINGS C/A(a) 2, f 184.

505   17 Oct 1680. Oving. John Peachey, esq., county coroner. Jurors: William Cox, gent., Thomas

Arundell, gent., Thomas Nash, gent., Joseph Hartly, George Bower, Richard Christmas, Richard Pococke, John Holloway, Simon Simkin, Thomas Cooper, William Collick, James May, Thomas Meares, John Goffe, Richard Hartly, William Hartly, Henry Gadly, Richard Hamond, John Netherway, Samuel Bennett. Witnesses: John Cobby, Thomas Hatcher, Mary Cockwell, Mary Burnett, William Peachey, William Neve. About 11 p.m. on 15 Oct John Terrey, 'laborer', Thomas Compton, 'laborer', and Daniel Tailor, 'laborer', all late of Oving, feloniously killed Richard Neve at Oving: Terrey violently striking him on the left side of head with 'a staffe' of wood worth ½d which he held in both hands and giving him 'one mortall bruise' of which he languished at Oving until 10 a.m. on the next day and then died; and Compton and Tailor being feloniously present aiding and abetting him. None of the 3 had any goods or chattels, lands or tenements at the time of the felony or ever after to the jurors' knowledge. ASSI 35/122/7, mm 7, 7d.
[Delivered to East Grinstead assizes on 11 Mar 1681 when all 3 pleaded not guilty and were acquitted, the trial jury finding that Neve came to his death by the hands of John Noakes; they had not fled and so were released, paying their fees. ASSI 35/122/7, mm 6, 7, 44d.]

506   4 Feb 1682. Amberley. John Howes, gent., Arundel rape coroner. Jurors of the rape: Richard Sergeant, William Francklyn, Thomas Symonds, Thomas Deane, Richard Elliott, William Francis, George Rose sen., George Rose jun., John Duke, Roger Searle, Richard Chambers, John Sotcher, John Ireland, Nathaniel Blundell. On 3 Feb Mary Gardiner late of Amberley, 'spinster', was delivered at Amberley of a female child which at the time 'of the bringing forth' was premature and dead and so died a natural death. KB 11/7, Trinity 34 Charles II, unnumbered membrane.
[Delivered to King's Bench, presumably by the coroner, in Trinity. In King's Bench it was classified as a natural death. At East Grinstead assizes on 20 Mar the grand jury, to which Elizabeth Mitchell, Mary Collson and Ann Chambers gave evidence, presented an indictment which charged Gardiner with giving birth to a live female bastard child at Amberley on 3 Feb and immediately afterwards murdering her by taking her in both hands, gripping her by the neck and throat and strangling her whereby she immediately died. Gardiner pleaded not guilty and was acquitted; she had not fled and so was released, paying her fees. ASSI 35/123/7, mm 3, 9, 48d; KB 11/7, Trinity 34 Charles II, unnumbered membrane; KB 29/341, m 151.]

507   13 Mar 1683. Findon. John Howes, gent., Arundel rape coroner. Jurors of the rape and county: William Lasseter, John Grevatt, Richard Nightingale, Edward Davis, John Bennett, Edward Scotchford, Walter Geele, 'Druery' Cheile, Christopher Lanse, John Stringer, John Stone, Robert Page, Thomas Carpenter, Thomas Hayne. Witnesses: Alice Homer, Margaret Sturt, Joan Stone, Edward Scotchford. On 12 Mar Elizabeth Bennett late of Findon, 'spinster', gave birth to a live male child at Findon which by the law of England 'was a bastard' and immediately afterwards murdered him there: she took him in both hands, 'did hold and gripe' him violently by the neck and throat and strangled him whereby he immediately died. Bennett had no goods or chattels, lands or tenements in the rape or elsewhere at that time or ever after to the jurors' knowledge. ASSI 35/124/7, mm 10, 10d.
[Delivered to East Grinstead assizes on 23 July when the grand jury, to which the same 4 witnesses gave evidence, presented an indictment identical to the inquest verdict but without the last sentence. Bennett pleaded not guilty to both the inquest verdict and the indictment and was acquitted; she had not fled and so was released, paying her fees. ASSI 35/124/7, mm 6, 9, 10, 47d.]

508   ... [1684. Withyham.] ... Jurors: ...nman, Robert Freind, Thomas ..., ...am, Richard Tompsett, Joseph Dartnall, Alexander ..., Thomas ...   Witnesses: Thomas Sands, ... Taylor, ... Austen, ... Willett, ...llingham, ... Gaynsfo[rd], ...tigott, ...rst. On 18 Nov William Taylor murdered Mary Baker at Withyham: having mixed 'white mercury', which he knew to be a deadly poison, with 'beere', he [gave] it to her to drink as good and wholesome beer, with the intention of [poisoning] her, whereby she died. Taylor had no goods [or chattels, lands or tenements] at the time of the felony or ever after to the jurors' knowledge. [*Damaged.*] ASSI 35/126/9, mm 26, 26d.
[Delivered to East Grinstead assizes on 16 Mar 1685.]

509   ... [1685]. ... near Chichester.   ... [Jurors of Sussex]: ...mford, John Freind, George ..., ...
Splawfoot, Edward Smith. Witnesses: James Par... [On 8 Feb] John Fisher feloniously [killed] John
Garrard [in the parish] ... with 'a rapier drawne' made of iron and steel worth 5s [which] he held [in] his
right [hand] and 'did strike and thrust in' the left side of the chest near the breast, [giving him] a
wound 1 inch [wide] and 3 inches deep of which he [immediately died]. ... [*Damaged.*] ASSI 35/126/9,
mm 28, 28d.
[Delivered with **508**. At the assizes the grand jury, to which Edward Freem..., Nicholas Clowde..., James Park...,
James ?Pude..., Mary Und... and Frances G... gave evidence, presented an indictment, also badly damaged but
apparently identical to the inquest verdict except that the charge was murder. At the summer assizes Fisher pleaded
not guilty to the inquest verdict but must have been convicted: he then successfully pleaded benefit of clergy.
ASSI 35/126/1, m 24; ASSI 35/126/9, mm 27, 28.]

510   23 Mar 1685. Lindfield. Alexander Luxford, gent., county coroner. Jurors: John Weeker,
Thomas Jenner, Thomas Holman, Thomas Brigden, John Holman, Thomas Hunt, William Older, John
Combridge, William Rowland, Thomas Midmor, John Beard, Thomas Denman, Clement Scrace, Thomas
Marchant, John Lushmor, John Snell, John Jenner. On 22 Mar, when John Attersole late of Lindfield,
weaver, who was then not of sound mind but 'franticke' and 'distracted' in mind and senses, was
alone near 'Blackbrooke' stream in Lindfield, he suddenly threw himself into the stream and drowned
under the water, dying immediately. KB 11/11, Trinity 1 James II, unnumbered membrane.
[Delivered into King's Bench by the coroner in Trinity. The sheriff was ordered by a writ of 8 July to inquire by a jury
if Attersole drowned himself feloniously or otherwise and, if feloniously, what goods and chattels he had at that time,
what was their value and in whose keeping they remain; and to make the return to King's Bench in Michaelmas.
There being no further process recorded in King's Bench, the sheriff's inquisition, which is now missing, presumably
agreed with the inquest verdict. KB 11/11, Trinity I James II, dorse of Ditchling inquest (**511**); KB 29/344, mm 89,
119.]

511   3 Apr 1685. Ditchling. Alexander Luxford, gent., county coroner. Jurors: Thomas Geere,
Nicholas Marchant, Richard Webb, Thomas Limbrest, Thomas Gates, Richard Morris, Henry Monke,
John Geering, Thomas Loocker, William Becheley, James Eales, Edward Harrowden, James Hubbard,
Richard Cottingham, Henry Jordan, Edward Gatland, John Copper. About 4 a.m. on 1 Apr, when
Thomas Browne late of Ditchling, 'wheelewright', who was then not of sound mind but 'franticke' and
'distracted' in mind and senses, was alone near a pit which was full of water in his close in Ditchling,
he suddenly threw himself into the pit and drowned under the water, dying immediately. KB 11/11,
Trinity 1 James II, unnumbered membrane.
[Delivered with **510**. The sheriff was ordered by a writ of 8 July to inquire by a jury if Browne drowned himself
feloniously or otherwise and, if feloniously, what goods and chattels he had at that time, what was their value and in
whose keeping they remain; and to make the return to King's Bench in Michaelmas. The sheriff's inquisition, which
is now missing, returned a verdict of felo de se, and in Michaelmas Joseph Browne of Ditchling, yeoman, was
summoned to King's Bench to answer for Thomas Browne's goods and chattels worth £132 16s 6d which had come
to his hands; process against him ceased in Hilary 1686 by order of the attorney general. KB 11/11, Trinity 1
James II, dorse of this inquest; KB 29/344, mm 89, 119, 142d.]

512   24 Aug 1685. Slinfold. Alexander Luxford, gent., [county] coroner. Jurors: Thomas Haylor,
John Briggs, Thomas Whale, John Constable, Philip Constable, John Smith, John Halland, Richard
Nicholl, ..., John Peacock, William Rice, John Ireland, Thomas Lucy, Edward Awlard, Joshua Turner,
John Nicholl, John Swan. Witnesses: Edward Chelsham, Jane Chelsham, John Roberts, John Buckle.
On 20 Aug Richard Jones late of Slinfold, 'laborer', murdered his daughter Elizabeth, aged 8 weeks, at
Slinfold, violently striking her with his right hand on the left side of the head and giving her 'one
mortall bruise' of which she immediately died. Jones had no goods or chattels, lands or [tenements in
Sussex] or elsewhere [at the time] of the felony to the jurors' knowledge. [*Damaged.*] ASSI 35/126/1,
mm 14, 14d.
[Delivered to the Sussex summer assizes when the grand jury, to which the same 4 witnesses and Jane Luckins gave
evidence, presented an indictment which charged Richard Jones and Elizabeth his wife alias Elizabeth Jones late of

Slinfold, spinster, with murdering his daughter: Richard killing her as in the inquest verdict with the omission of the last sentence, and Elizabeth being feloniously present aiding and abetting him. They both pleaded not guilty to the indictment. Richard was acquitted of murder but convicted of manslaughter; he had no chattels. He then successfully pleaded benefit of clergy and was branded. Elizabeth was acquitted; she had not fled. ASSI 35/126/1, mm 14, 15, 24.]

513   5 Jan 1686. Ringmer. Alexander Luxford, gent., county coroner. Jurors: William Parker, John ...ior, Richard Stonehouse, Anthony Banister, Stephen Martin, Henry Weller, John Pentecost, Walter Harmor, ..., Matthew Hards, John Peckham, Edward Page, John Page, William Cobb. On 31 Dec 1685 John Pockney of Ringmer, 'laborer', feloniously killed John Wheatley [at] Ringmer with 'a sticke' of wood of no value which he held in his right hand, violently striking him on the right side [of the head] of which he languished at Ringmer [until 1] Jan and then died. Pockney had no goods or chattels, lands or tenements in Sussex at the time of the felony or ever after [to] the jurors' [knowledge]. [*Damaged.*] ASSI 35/127/9, m 9.
[Delivered to East Grinstead assizes on 22 Mar 1686 when the grand jury, to which William Weller, Thomas Peirce, Philip Potlands, Richard Hollands, Edward Wheatly, Henry Hopkins and the coroner gave evidence, presented an indictment identical to the inquest verdict except that the charge was murder and the last sentence was omitted. Pockney pleaded not guilty to the indictment and was acquitted of murder but convicted of manslaughter. ASSI 35/127/9, m 10.]

514   27 Jan 1686. Lewes. Alexander Luxford, [gent.], county coroner. Jurors: Herbert Springatt, William Rose, Isaac Butler, Benjamin Harman, Richard ..., ...terman, Nicholas Glasbrooke, John Baker, Henry Owden, Thomas Harman, Thomas Whiskey, Edward ..., John Rapley, Richard Carden, Edward Inskipp. On 23 Jan Katharine Dodson late of Lewes, 'spinster', alias Katharine wife of ... [Dodson late] of Lewes, 'tailer', murdered Ann Pockney, 'spinster', aged 14, then her servant, at Lewes with ['a g]reat sticke' of no value which she held in her right hand, striking her violently on the shoulders, sides, back and abdomen of which she languished at Lewes until the next day and then died. Dodson had no goods or chattels, lands or tenements in Sussex or elsewhere [at the time] of the felony [or ever after] to the jurors' knowledge. [*Damaged.*] ASSI 35/127/9, m 11.
[Delivered with **513**. At the assizes the grand jury, to which 'Faintnot' Batchlor, John Parham, Thomas Waterman, Peter Garton, John Hinckly, John Colwell, Joan Horsted and ?Sarah Garton gave evidence, presented an indictment identical to the inquest verdict but without the last sentence. Dodson pleaded not guilty to the indictment but was convicted and hanged; she had no chattels. ASSI 35/127/9, mm 2, 11.]

515   ?1 Feb 1686. West Chiltington. Henry Chatfeild, gent., coroner of Arundel and Bramber rapes. Jurors: Thomas Badcocke, Henry Coale, ..., Richard Whittington, John Champion, Robert Searle, Edward Harroden, Henry Harwood, Richard Tully, William Tully, ..., Thomas Grant, George Penfold, John Edsawe, John Norman, Edward Norman, George ...d. Witnesses: John Searle, John Tully, Thomas Humfry, Nicholas Ward, Thomas Soane, Mary Soane. On 24 Dec 1685 Richard Fivens late of Storrington, 'laborer', feloniously killed Thomas Soane at Storrington, violently striking him on the head with his right hand of which he languished [at] Storrington until 18 Jan and then died at West Chiltington. Fivens had no goods or chattels, lands [or tenements in] the rapes or elsewhere at the time [of the felony] or ever after to the jurors' knowledge. [*Damaged.*] ASSI 35/127/9, mm 7, 7d.
[Delivered with **513**. At the assizes a bill of indictment was preferred which charged Richard and Edward Fivens late of Storrington, labourers, with murdering Soane: Richard killing him as in the inquest verdict, but Soane being said to have languished at Storrington and West Chiltington and the last sentence being omitted; and Edward being feloniously present aiding and abetting him. The grand jury, to which the same 6 witnesses gave evidence, affirmed the charge against Richard but rejected that against Edward. Richard pleaded not guilty to the indictment and was acquitted, the trial jury finding that Soane died a natural death. ASSI 35/127/9, m 8.]

516   21 July 1686. Sedlescombe. John Purfeild, gent., Hastings rape coroner. Jurors of the rape: Henry Henly, William Springet, Thomas Snow, Joseph Bigg, 'Barnabas' Frencham, John Brett, Thomas Darby sen., Robert Bissenden, William Croft, Robert Spice, James Paine, Thomas Glover, Henry Sheather jun., Daniel Piper, Edward Coleman. On 3 July Margery Barham of Sedlescombe, 'spinster', gave birth

at Sedlescombe to a live male child which by the laws of England 'was a bastard' and immediately
afterwards she murdered him there: she took him in both hands, 'did hold and gripe' him violently by
the neck and throat and strangled him whereby he immediately died. Barham had no goods or
chattels, lands or tenements in the rape or elsewhere at that time or ever after to the jurors' knowledge.
ASSI 35/127/10, m 2.
[Delivered to East Grinstead assizes on 22 July when the grand jury, to which Mary Langham, Bridget Piper, Mary
Olliver, Susan and Thomas Darby and Ann Stephens gave evidence, presented an indictment which charged Barham
with giving birth to a live male bastard child at Sedlescombe on 3 July and, in order to conceal her offence and escape
punishment, with murdering him there immediately afterwards, taking him in both hands, throwing him into a well
full of water and drowning him whereby he immediately died; and with trying to conceal the private and secret
drowning in order that it might not be known whether the child was born alive or dead. It also charged Thomas Brazier
and John Coife, labourers, both late of Sedlescombe, with feloniously harbouring, aiding and comforting Barham at
Sedlescombe on 8 July, knowing that she had committed the murder. All 3 pleaded not guilty to the indictment.
Barham was acquitted; she had not fled but was remanded in custody to find good sureties for her appearance at the
next assizes and to be of good behaviour in the meantime, and then to be released, paying her fees. Brazier and Coife,
being accessories after the fact, were released on the acquittal of the principal, paying their fees. ASSI 35/127/10,
mm 2–4, 9d.]

517   5 Nov 1686. Piddinghoe. Alexander Luxford, gent., county coroner. Jurors: William de la
Chambre, John Burtenshawe, William Washer, Nicholas Hudson, Henry Rogers, James Gatland, George
Peckham, John Ellis, Anthony Ade, William Cole, John Martin, John Peckham, John Baker, John
Funnell, James Ford, John Chatfeild, Robert Howell, Thomas Peckham, William Ade. On 1 Nov Thomas
Carr, 'laborer', and Richard Finch, 'laborer', both late of Piddinghoe, murdered Edward Sanders at
Piddinghoe: Carr 'did beat and strike' him violently on the left side of the head with 'a spade staffe'
worth 10d which he held in both hands, giving him 'one mortall bruise' of which he immediately died;
and Finch was feloniously present aiding and abetting him. Carr and Finch had no goods or chattels,
lands or tenements in Sussex or elsewhere at that time or ever after to the jurors' knowledge.
ASSI 35/128/8, m 7.
[Delivered to East Grinstead assizes on 28 Feb 1687 when the grand jury, to which Stephen Russell, William French,
John Crouch and John Sanders gave evidence, presented an indictment identical to the inquest verdict except that it
added that Carr struck Sanders on the left side of the head near the temple, giving him a wound, bruise and fracture of
the skull, and omitted the last sentence. Carr and Finch pleaded not guilty to the indictment. Carr was acquitted of
murder but convicted of manslaughter; he had no chattels. He then successfully pleaded benefit of clergy and was
branded. Finch was acquitted; he had not fled. ASSI 35/128/8, mm 6–8.]

518   13 Dec 1686. Frant. Thomas Hooper, gent., Rotherfield hundred coroner. Jurors of the hundred:
Thomas May, Thomas Moone, Thomas Budgen, William Smith, Thomas Clarke, John Hosmer, William
Willett, John May, Frank [*Francus*] Johnson, John Carley, John Knight, William Appleby. On 6 Dec
Mary Peirce of Frant, 'spinster', gave birth at Frant to a live male child which by the laws of England
'was a bastard' and as soon as he was born she murdered him there: she took him in both hands and
'did hold and gripe' him violently on the neck and throat, strangling him whereby he immediately died.
She had no goods or chattels, lands or tenements within the liberty or elsewhere at that time or ever
after to the jurors' knowledge. ASSI 35/128/8, m 4.
[Delivered with **517**. At the assizes the grand jury, to which William and Mary Russell gave evidence, presented an
indictment identical to the inquest verdict but without the last sentence and calling Peirce late of Frant. Peirce
pleaded not guilty to both the inquest verdict and the indictment and was acquitted; she had not fled. ASSI 35/128/8,
mm 1, 4, 5.]

519   5 Apr 1687. Ninfield. John Purfeild, gent., Hastings rape coroner. Jurors: Philip Blackman,
Thomas Blackman, Nathaniel Mills, William Vigor, Thomas Squier, William Brooks, William Coleman,
Thomas Crowhurst, Anthony Combridge, Thomas Bray, Alexander Martin, Nicholas Dubry [*or* Duboy],
Daniel White, Thomas Parker, Thomas Horscroft, Robert Saunders, Robert Frend, James Roberts,
John Easton. On 27 Mar Mary wife of Thomas Jenner late of Ninfield, 'laborer', murdered Elizabeth

Hamond, aged 17, her husband's servant, at Ninfield with 'a horsewhipp' worth 4d which she held in her right hand, violently striking her on the head, shoulders, chest, stomach, back, sides and abdomen of which she languished at Ninfield until 30 Mar and then died. Mary Jenner had no goods or chattels, lands or tenements in the rape or elsewhere at the time of the felony or ever after to the jurors' knowledge. ASSI 35/128/9, m 6.

[Delivered to Lewes assizes on 14 July when the grand jury, to which Adrian Hamond, Mary Austen, Mary Longley and Joan Jenner gave evidence, presented an indictment identical to the inquest verdict but without the last sentence. Mary pleaded not guilty to both the inquest verdict and the indictment and was acquitted, the trial jury finding that Hamond had died a natural death; Mary had not fled. Hamond was buried at Ninfield on the day of the inquest, the parish register recording that she had 'died by her dame's much beating her with a horsse flash, the crowner being sett upon her and the jury, finding by the ill looks of the ded corps and by the wittnesses, gave there opinion that the dame was giltty of her death', whereupon she was sent to gaol and acquitted at the next assizes. ASSI 35/128/9, mm 4, 6, 7; PAR 430/1/1/1; *SAC*, XVII, 62.]

520   17 Sept 1688. St Michael's parish, Lewes. Alexander Luxford, gent., county coroner. Jurors: Simon Snell, James Miller, James Bridger, William Pellatt, Andrew Lawrence, John Delves, William Rose, Samuel Yorkton, John Elphick, John Shanck, Thomas ?Earle, John Rapley, Isaac Ginn, Nathaniel Russell, Herbert Stiles, Walter Willard, John Artridge, Christopher Yockehurst, Robert Colgate. Witnesses: Thomas Medl[ey], gent., James Graves, gent., John Olive, Nicholas As[hdo]une, John Nutt. On 14 Sept Archibald Clinkard late of St Michael's parish, 'laborer', murdered Thomas Nutt, gent., in St Michael's with 'a rapier' of iron and steel worth 5s which he held drawn in his right hand. He 'did strike and thrust in' the rapier into Nutt's right side a little below the breast, giving him a wound ½ inch wide and 6 inches deep of which he languished at St Michael's until the next day and then died. After committing the felony Clinkard fled to places unknown to the jurors. He had no goods or chattels, lands or tenements in Sussex or elsewhere at the time of the felony or flight or ever after to their knowledge. [*Damaged.*] ASSI 94/4, mm 3, 3d.

[Delivered to Horsham assizes on 20 July 1689 when the grand jury, to which the same 5 witnesses gave evidence, presented an indictment identical to the inquest verdict except that it added that the wound was near Nutt's short ribs and omitted the fact that the rapier was of iron and steel and the last 2 sentences. At the time of the assizes Clinkard was still at large. ASSI 94/4, mm 3, 4.]

APPENDIX I

Inquests delivered to King's Bench but no longer extant

521 Delivered to East Grinstead assizes on 27 Feb and on to King's Bench in Easter 1615: at least one suicide and at least one death by misadventure, that of John Smythe. Thomas Dykes of Ninfield was summoned to King's Bench to answer for a roan mare which was the cause of Smythe's death and had come to his hands. He was outlawed at Lewes on 30 Mar 1626. His heirs were then summoned to King's Bench and when the sheriff returned that there was no heir his executors were summoned. Process ceased in Trinity 1631. KB 29/259, mm 4d–5d.

522 Delivered to King's Bench in Michaelmas 1617, probably by the coroner: the deaths by misadventure of Grace Thatcher and Henry Ashdowne in Holmestrow hundred, Lewes rape. George Coles, deputy almoner of Sussex, was summoned to King's Bench to answer for a bullock, a cart and barley worth £3 6s 8d which were the cause of Thatcher's death and had come to his hands. He had licence to imparl in Trinity 1619. KB 29/263, m 114.

523 Delivered to East Grinstead assizes on 17 July and on to King's Bench in Michaelmas 1620: the suicide of John Smythe, aged 13, in Manhood hundred. KB 29/269, m 89.

524 Delivered to King's Bench in Michaelmas 1623, probably by the coroner or coroners: the deaths by misadventure of Edmund Clement late of Rogate, yeoman, and John Parker, aged 8. William Clement of Durford abbey, gent., was summoned to King's Bench to answer for the wall and roof of a bedroom worth 10s which were the cause of Edmund Clement's death and had come to his hands. He was discharged in Trinity 1624 because the deputy almoner acknowledged satisfaction. KB 29/272, m 96d.

525 Delivered to King's Bench in Hilary 1632, probably by the coroner or coroners: the death by misadventure of Thomas Kinge and the suicide of Elizabeth Perrin, spinster. KB 29/280, m 132.

526 Delivered to King's Bench in Trinity 1632, probably by the coroner: the death by misadventure of John Drewe. Edward Thurland, gent., Bramber rape bailiff, was summoned to King's Bench to answer for a mare with its trappings worth £3 which was the cause of Drewe's death and had come to his hands. He had licence to imparl in Michaelmas 1640. KB 29/281, m 51d.

527 Delivered to King's Bench in Easter 1633, probably by the coroner: the death by misadventure of Thomas Snatt. Thomas Button of Wivelsfield, yeoman, was summoned to King's Bench to answer for 2 bullocks and a cart with its load worth £3 10s which were the cause of Snatt's death and had come to his hands. He was discharged in Easter 1633 because the deputy almoner acknowledged satisfaction. KB 29/282, m 6.

528 Delivered to King's Bench in Michaelmas 1635, probably by the coroner or coroners: the deaths by misadventure of William Barnes late of Southover, cooper, and John Hardinge late of Preston, labourer. Henry Sparks of Southover, yeoman, was summoned to King's Bench to answer for 4 horses and a cart and wheels worth £4 which were the cause of Barnes's death and had come to his hands. He was outlawed at Chichester on 29 Sept 1636. Thomas Sherley of Preston, esq., was similarly summoned to answer for 3 oxen and a cart with a load of barley worth £8 which were the cause of Hardinge's death and had come to his hands. He had licence to imparl in Hilary 1636. KB 29/284, m 123.

529   Delivered to King's Bench in Michaelmas 1635, probably by the coroner, but not with the inquests of **528**: the deaths by misadventure of John Hareforde, John Whiskey and John Bennett in Bramber rape.   John Elliott, constable of Broadwater and of Brightford hundred, was summoned to King's Bench to answer for 3 horses, a mare and a cart and appurtenances worth 40s which were the cause of Hareforde's death and had come to his hands.   He was discharged in Easter 1636 because the deputy almoner acknowledged satisfaction.   Thomas Kytchen, constable of the whole of Brighton, was similarly summoned to answer for a fishing boat worth 40s which was the cause of Whiskey's death and had come to his hands.   He was discharged in Easter 1636 because the deputy almoner acknowledged satisfaction.   KB 29/284, m 115.
[Whiskey, who had been killed under Foorde's boat, was buried at Brighton on 25 Aug 1635. *Par. reg. of Brighton*, 193.]

530   Delivered to East Grinstead assizes on 29 Feb and on to King's Bench in Easter 1636: the death by misadventure of John Ellis, aged about 9, the natural deaths of Andrew Hills and John Ede, prisoners in Horsham gaol, and possibly one or more of the other natural deaths.   KB 29/285, mm 11, 11d.
[John Ede may be the John Ide who was in Horsham gaol at the East Grinstead assizes of 17 July 1634, having been committed there by Richard Lewkener, esq., JP, as an approver. ASSI 35/76/10, m 46.]

531   Delivered to King's Bench in Easter 1637, probably by the coroners: the suicide of Thomas Hover, the deaths by misadventure of Richard Butcher sen. and George Seager late of Pevensey, clerk, and at least one natural death.   Benjamin Streater of Warminghurst was summoned to King's Bench to answer for Hover's goods and chattels worth 31s 5d which had come to his hands.   He was outlawed at ?Chichester on 19 Feb 1638.   Richard Butcher of Hurstpierpoint, son of Richard Butcher sen., was similarly summoned to answer for an oak worth 4s which was the cause of his father's death and had come to his hands.   He was outlawed at ?Chichester on 19 Feb 1638.   George Carleton of Westham, gent., was also summoned to answer for a gelding worth 20s which was the cause of Seager's death and had come to his hands.   He was discharged in Trinity 1637 because the deputy almoner acknowledged satisfaction.   KB 29/286, mm 7, 11d.

532   Delivered to King's Bench in Michaelmas 1637, probably by the coroners: the suicides of Margaret Beldam, widow, and Drew Stapley late of Worth in Lewes rape, esq.   Thomas Challenor of Lindfield, esq., was summoned to King's Bench to answer for Beldam's goods and chattels worth ?£53 17s 8d which had come to his hands.   He had licence to imparl in Hilary 1638.   Thomas Sherley of Preston, esq., was similarly summoned to answer for Stapley's goods and chattels worth £246 5s 5d which had come to his hands.   Process continued until at least Hilary 1640.   Francis Keene, gent., deputy almoner, was also summoned to answer for Stapley's goods and chattels worth £34 3s 4d which had come to his hands.   He was discharged in Hilary 1638 because he was the deputy almoner and had received the money for the use of the High Almoner.   KB 29/286, mm 123d, 127d, 128.

533   Delivered to East Grinstead assizes on 5 July and on to King's Bench in Michaelmas 1638: at least one natural death.   KB 29/287, m 119d.

534   Delivered to Horsham assizes on 4 Mar and on to King's Bench in Easter 1622: at least one death by misadventure, that of Thomas Gunter of Burwash, labourer.   KB 29/312, m 43.

535   Delivered to Horsham assizes on 1 July 1665 and on to King's Bench in Hilary 1666: at least one death by misadventure.   KB 29/317, m 3.

536   Delivered to King's Bench in Trinity 1666, probably by the coroner: at least one death by misadventure, that of John Birch.   Brian Bickley of Chidham, esq., was summoned to King's Bench to answer for a horse worth £5 which was the cause of Birch's death and had come to his hands. He had licence to imparl in Michaelmas 1666. KB 29/317, mm 74, 74d, 144d.

537   Delivered to King's Bench in Trinity 1668, probably by the coroner: the suicide of Thomas Winchester late of Kingston near Lewes who had hanged himself. Edmund Tipton late of Lewes, gent., was summoned to King's Bench to answer for 2 cows worth £4, formerly Winchester's, which had come to his hands. He was discharged in Hilary 1669 because the almoner acknowledged satisfaction. KB 29/321, m 81d.

538   Delivered to King's Bench in Hilary 1671, probably by the coroner: the death by misadventure of George Haselden late of Wadhurst, husbandman. Ann Sanders of Wadhurst, widow, was summoned to King's Bench to answer for 6 oxen and a cart loaded with oats worth £10 which were the cause of Haselden's death and had come to her hands. She had licence to imparl in Hilary 1672. KB 29/324, m 9d.

539   Delivered to Horsham assizes on 27 July and on to King's Bench in Michaelmas 1672: the natural death of William Westbrooke. KB 29/325, m 164d.

540   Delivered to King's Bench in Hilary 1682, probably by the coroner: the suicide of Robert Brinckhurst late of Lewes, cutler. KB 29/341, m 4.
[At Horsham assizes on 18 Mar 1680 a bill of indictment had been preferred, charging Robert Brinckhurst, Thomas Lester and Samuel Driver, all late of St Michael's parish in Lewes, labourers, with murdering William Moore, late of the same parish, draper. They knew that Moore was greatly troubled with 'a stinking breath' of which he was trying to be cured, and on 8 Nov 1679 Brinckhurst, on the advice of Lester and Driver, obtained some yellow arsenic in St Michael's parish, all 3 knowing it to be a deadly poison, and wrote a letter in the name of John Newton, a close friend of Moore's, which stated that the arsenic was good and wholesome medicine suitable for the cure of bad breath. On the same day Lester, on the advice of Brinckhurst and Driver, delivered the letter and poison to Moore in St Michael's, intending to murder him. On 17 Nov Driver, on the advice of Brinckhurst and Lester, wrote another letter in Newton's name, urging Moore to take the poison mixed with sugar at once, immediately before he went to bed, and on the same day Brinckhurst delivered it to Moore in St Michael's. Moore, believing the arsenic to be wholesome medicine, ate it on 18 Nov whereby he became so ill in the body, stomach, liver and abdomen that he languished at St Michael's until 23 Nov and then died. The grand jury, to which John Newton, William Read and John Apps gave evidence, affirmed the charge against Brinckhurst, but rejected that against Lester and Driver. It is not known if Brinckhurst ever stood trial. ASSI 35/121/6, m 40.]

541   Delivered to the Sussex summer assizes and on to King's Bench in Michaelmas 1688: at least one natural death. KB 29/347, m 183d.

APPENDIX II

Evidence concerning an autopsy probably given at an inquest

542 11 July 1618. Rye. Richard Gibbson, gent., mayor, and Richard Fowtrell, Thomas Ensinge, Matthew Young, Mark Thomas, John Palmer and Joseph Benbrick, jurats. John Kevell of Rye, surgeon, deposed that on 3 July, after the dead body of Joan late wife of Thomas Myles of Rye, baker, which had a dead female child in the womb, had been opened, he found that the child's skull was broken in one place and bruised in another and that the right side of the head near the ear was bruised in 3 places and the skin was off, but he did not know how Joan or the child came to their deaths. Walter Baker of Rye, surgeon, deposed exactly as Kevell concerning the view of the child, but he was not present at the opening of Joan's body. Margaret wife of William Coaker of Rye, tailor, deposed that she was present at the opening of Joan's body and that the child was taken out of her body dead; that she was with Joan throughout her troubles and the child was dead in her body, but how long before Joan's death she did not know; and that Joan had taken hurt before her troubles, but how she did not know and Joan did not say anything about that during her troubles to the witness's knowledge. Dorothy wife of Robert Allen of Rye, labourer, deposed that she was appointed nurse to Joan and was with her throughout her troubles; and that she heard her say that her husband's brother Francis took her and shook her about 3 days before her troubles, set her down upon the brake and set his knee against the side of her belly. RYE 47/94, unnumbered document.
[A bill of indictment was preferred which charged Francis Myles late of Winchelsea, baker, with feloniously killing Joan late wife of Thomas Myles of Rye, baker, who was then pregnant with a female child, in the market-place at Rye on 12 July 1618, throwing her upon a piece of wood called a brake and then striking her on the abdomen with his knee, giving her a wound on the abdomen of which she languished at Rye until 19 July and then died. The grand jury rejected the indictment. 25 more witnesses are listed as due to testify, either to the grand jury or at the inquest or both; one defaulted. RYE 47/94, unnumbered documents.]

INDEX OF PERSONS

Arabic numbers refer to entries, small roman numbers to pages.

The following abbreviations are used for the most frequently occurring forenames:

Alex	Alexander	Edm	Edmund	Jas	James	Nic	Nicholas
And	Andrew	Edw	Edward	Jn	John	Phil	Philip
Ant	Anthony	Eliz	Elizabeth	Jos	Joseph	Reyn	Reynold
Arn	Arnold	Fran	Francis	Kath	Katharine	Ric	Richard
Art	Arthur	Fred	Frederick	Lawr	Lawrence	Rob	Robert
Bart	Bartholomew	Geo	George	Len	Leonard	Rog	Roger
Ben	Benjamin	Geof	Geoffrey	Margt	Margaret	Sam	Samuel
Chas	Charles	Gil	Gilbert	Margy	Margery	Ste	Stephen
Chris	Christopher	Greg	Gregory	Mat	Matthew	Thos	Thomas
Clem	Clement	Hen	Henry	Mic	Michael	Wal	Walter
Dan	Daniel	Hum	Humphrey	Nat	Nathaniel	Wm	William

Bassage, Jas, 181

Bassett (Basset), Abraham, 377; Alice, 416; Thos, 353

Bastard, Edw, 84

Batcheler, Batcheller, Batchellor, Batchelor, Batchlor
    see Bachelor

Bate see Bates

Bateman, Wm, 106

Bates (Bate, Baytes), Abraham, 96; Chris, 99; Thos,
    263

Bathurst, Thos, 306

Batnor (Batner), Ste, 371, 375

Batter, Jn, 298; Ric, 298

Baverstock (Beverstock, Beverstocke), Edw, 467, 469;
    Wm, 198, 286

Bawcomb, Bawcombe, Bawcumbe see Balcombe

Bayley, Baylie see Bailey

Baylif see Bailiff

Bayly, Baylye see Bailey

Baynard (Bainard), Ric, 441

Baytes see Bates

Beach, Hen, 394; Ric, 190

Beachley see Betchley

Beacon, Hen, 481

Beale (Bealle), Edw, 379, 430; Geof, 16; Hen, 6, 16;
    Hen, 421, 466; Jn, 16; Jn, 431; Ric, 38; Ric, 414;
    Rob, 16; Rob, 204; Susan, 466; Thos, 42, 246;
    Thos, 205; Thos, 355; Thos, 471

Bean (Beane), Jn, 240; Jn, 441, 488; Ste, 240

Beard, Jn, 126; Jn, 510; Thos, 292; Wm, 74, 139

Beaser see Bezer

Beast see Best

Becheley, Bechely see Betchley

Beck, And, 240

Beckett, Gil, 140

Beckshell see Backshall

Bedham see Beldam

Beecher, Ant, 231, 355; Jn, 485; Thos, 128; Wm, 278

Beeching (Beechinge), Ste, 101

Beecroft (Beecraft), Eliz, 439

Beeding (Beedinge), Edw, 55; Edw, 326

Begeler, Ric, 151

Begley see Bagley

Belchamber (Bellchamber), Ben, 275, 280; Thos, 68;
    Wm, 40

Beldam (Bedham, Beldham), Hen, 39; Jn, 341; Margt,
    532; Nic, 293; Rob, 293

Bell, Nic, 63, constable, 34

Bellchamber see Belchamber

Bellingham, Edw, kt, sheriff, 102; Jas, 431; Thos, 345

Belton, Jas, 482

Benbrick, Benbricke, Benbrigge see Bainbridge

Benge, Rob, 108; Wm, 71, 92

Benjamin (Benjamyn), Jn, 61

Bennester see Bannister

Bennett (Bennet, Bennitt), Aaron, 493; Alex, jurat,
    423, 424, mayor and coroner, xxxix, 434, 436;

Ann, 447; Ann, 493; Edm, 188; Edw, 150; Eliz,
    507; Geo, 67; Hen, 447; Jn, 62; Jn, 111; Jn, 183;
    Jn, 204; Jn, 281; Jn, 489; Jn, 507; Jn, 529; Mary,
    447; Mat, 371; Nic, 50, 66; Peter, 154, 288; Phil,
    338; Randal, 33; Ric, 36; Ric, 126; Sam, 505; Thos,
    57; Thos, 62, 68, 98; Thos, 101; Thos, 239; Thos,
    332, 346; Thos, 409; Thos, 411; Thos, 477; Wm,
    199; Wm, 219; Wm, 336; Wm, 408

Bennyfold, Hen, 301

Benson, Jn, 58

Bensted see Binsted

Bent, Clem, 44

Bentham, …, 412

Benton, Jas, 380

Benyeare, Peter, 290

Beresford (Berisford), Hugh, mayor and coroner, xxxix,
    385

Berkeley, Eliz, Lady Berkeley (Barckley), xliv, 223;
    Hen, Lord Berkeley, xliv

Berkshire (Barckshire, Barksheire, Barkshere), Jn, 301;
    Wm, 45; Wm, 217

Bernard see Barnard

Berricke see Berwick

Berrisson, Wm, 197

Berry see Bury

Berwick (Barwick, Berricke, Berwicke), Chris, 421;
    Geo, 416; Jas, 458; Jas, (?same), 473; Mary, 421;
    Mary, 421; Thos, 281

Besbeech (Besbidge), Geo, 456

Best (Beast, Beste), Geo, 61; Joan, 428; Nic, 483; Rob,
    250, 312, 318, 319, 323, 372

Betchley (Beachley, Becheley, Bechely), Edm, 23; Edw,
    121; Edw, (?same), 296; Ric, 129; Wm, 511

Betser (Bettser, Betzer), Jn, 139; Thos, 217

Betsworth see Bettesworth

Bett see Betts

Bettesworth (Betsworth, Bettisworth), Jn, 226, 326;
    Nic, 301; Nic, 441; Peter, kt, 301; Ric, 476

Betts (Bett), Jn, 131; Jn, 315; Thos, 81, 296

Bettser, Betzer see Betser

Beverstock, Beverstocke see Baverstock

Bexhell (Bexell), Jn, 161

Bexley (Bexlie, Bexly), Jn, 31, 202; Jn, 344

Beyond the Moon, Jn, (fictitious), xxi, xxiii, 295

Bezer (Beaser), Chris, 119, 141

Bickley, Brian, 536

Biddenden (Byddenden), Thos, 324

Bigg see Biggs

Biggar (Biggard), Hen, 31

Biggs (Bigg, Bigges), Jn, 284; Jn, 320; Jos, 516; Ric,
    67, 172; Ric, 274; cf. Bugg

Bilk (Bylke), Thos, 132

Billett (Billet), Jn, 217, 226

Billinghurst, Thos, 65

Binckes see Binks

Binden, Jn, 75

Boult *see* Bolt

Bound *see* Bond

Boune *see* Boon

Bourne (Aburne, Boorne, Borne), Edw, 379; Geo, 236; Hen, 290; Jn, 361; Ric, 283; Ric, 342

Bowell, Wm, 245, 334

Bowers (Bower), Geo, 505; Rob, 66

Bowley (Boley), Edw, 409; Jn, 479

Bowra *see* Boorer

Bowyer (Boyer), Hen, JP, 7; Jn, 440; Nic, 238, 260, 358; Nic, 480; Rob, 54; Rob, (?*same*), 370; Thos, JP, 250

Boxall (Boxhall), Mary, 442; Wm, 13

Boxer, Solomon, 379

Boxhall *see* Boxall

Boycatt *see* Boycott

Boyce (Boys), Jn, 220; Ric, 426, 430; Ric, mayor and coroner, xxxviii, 248, 252; Simon, 277; Thos, 415; Wm, 126

Boycott (Boycatt), Jas, 321; Jn, 66

Boyer *see* Bowyer

Boys *see* Boyce

Bozard *see* Bossard

Braban (Braband), Wm, 162

Brabie *see* Braby

Brabrook *see* Braybrooke

Braby (Brabie, Brabye), Dan, 91; Jn, 70, 91, 187; Thos, 26

Brace, Hen, 67

Brackfield (Brackfeild), Nic, 458; *cf.* Brookfield

Brackpole, Brackpoole *see* Brapool

Brad *see* Bradd

Bradbridge *see* Broadbridge

Bradbury, Geo, 11, 21, 24, 100, 103

Bradd (Brad), Ant, 132, 315; Jn, 315; Rob, 379; Thos, 380

Bradfield (Bradfold, Bradford), Jas, 408; Peter, 408; Ric, 408; Rob, 345; Rog, 198

Bradley (Bradlie), Edw, 53

Bradman (Brodman), Wm, 349

Bradway *see* Broadway

Braffe *see* Bruff

Bragg (Bragge), Edw, 200; Ric, coroner, xxxvii, 422

Braker *see* Brooker

Bran *see* Brann

Brand (Brende), Ric, 201

Brann (Bran), Alice, 236; Jn, 236; Ric, 236

?Brann, Hen, 244

Brapool (Brackpole, Brackpoole, Brapley), Nic, 389; Wm, 110; Wm, 309; Wm, 462

Brasier *see* Brazier

Brattle, Jn, 473

Bray (Braye), Jn, 405; Ric, 56; Ric, 61; Rob, 297; Thos, 134; Thos, 198; Thos, 397; Thos, 519

Braybrooke (Brabrook), Jn, 407

Braye *see* Bray

Brazier (Brasier), Thos, 334; Thos, 516

Breach, 'Abedindus', 354

Breacher (Brecher), Thos, 236

Breade, Breades *see* Breeds

Breadon *see* Bredon

Breads *see* Breeds

Brecher *see* Breacher

Bredham, Adam, 295

Bredon (Breadon), Jn, 255; Jn, 271

Breeds (Breade, Breades, Breads, Broudes), Bart, 382, 423, 436, 444, 452; Eliz, 479; Geo, 436; Jn, 492

Brende *see* Brand

Brett, Jn, 516; Jn, mayor and coroner, xxxviii, 277; Nic, 247; Thos, 243

Brewster (Bruster), Ant, 63

Brian, Briant, Briantt *see* Bryant

Bridaye *see* Priday

Bridger (Briger, Brigger), Chris, 20; Chris, 63; Chris, 229; Edm, 41; Edm, (?*same*), 55; Edw, 386; Edw, 392; Jas, 520; Jn, 63; Jn, 65, 93, 217; Jn, 156, 275; Jn, 193, 273; Jn, 447; Jn, 451; Nic, 45; Nic, 112, 226; Ric, xxiv, 205, 226, 229; Ric, xxiv, 229; Ric, xxiv, 229; Rob, 93; Thos, 205; Thos, 295; Thos, 327; Thos, 336; Valentine, 94, 95; Wm, 118, 185, 210, 213; Wm, 409, 483

Bridges *see* Briggs

Bridgland, Jn, 478

Brigden, Edw, 222; Jn, 9; Thos, 510

Briger, Brigger *see* Bridger

Briggs (Bridges), Alex, 328, 333, 353; Jn, 177; Jn, 512; Mic, 484; Rob, 38

Brigham (Brighames), Thos, 67

Bright, Ant, 60

Brightridge (Brithredge), Ric, 191; Thos, 241

Brimsted (Brymsted), Jn, 11

Brinckhurst *see* Brinkhurst

Brinckwell *see* Brinkwell

Brinkhurst (Brinckhurst), Rob, 540

Brinkwell (Brinckwell), Alice, 275; Alice, alias Alice Munday, 275; Edw, 275; Jn, 120; Wm, 275

Brisenden (Bissenden, Brissenden), Hen, 451; Rob, 516

Brishant *see* Brissant

Brishe *see* Brush

Brisher *see* Brusher

Brissant (Brishant), Ste, 90

Brissenden *see* Brisenden

Brisser *see* Brusher

Bristow (Bristo, Bristoe, Bristowe, Brystow, Brystowe), Edw, 17, 29, 30, 43, 74, 143, 167, 169, 189, 195, 250, 267; Fran, 172; Jn, 484, 487; Ric, 239

Brithredge *see* Brightridge

Britton (Britten), Edw, 162

Broad (Broade), Goddard, 202

Broadbridge (Bradbridge), Jn, 35; Rob, 144

Broade *see* Broad

Broadway (Bradway), Thos, 321

Hodder (Hoder, Hother), Ben, 148, 211; Jn, 461; Rog, 23; Thos, 73

Hode *see* Hoad

Hodelye *see* Hoadley

Hoder *see* Hodder

Hodges (Hogges), Geo, 375; Thos, 122, 124

Hodgkins, Abraham, 392

Hodly *see* Hoadley

Hodsoll (Hodsell), Jas, 486

Hogben (Hogbeane), Wm, 72

Hogesfleshe *see* Hogsflesh

Hogges *see* Hodges

Hogsflesh (Hogesfleshe, Hoggesflesh, Hoggsflesh, Hogsfleashe, Hogsflcshe), Jn, 320; Jn, 442; Ric, 13; Thos, 181; Wm, 226

Holben (Hobbeame, Hobben, Hobeame, Holbeane), Hen, 61; Jn, 170; Jn, 396; Wm, 373

Holcum *see* Hockham

Holden (Holdyn), Bernard, 437; Jn, 250, 267, 281, 307, 318, 319, 372; Jn, 349

Holford (Holfold, Holforde), Eliz, 202; Jn, 447; Jn, 473; Thos, 328, 420, 428

Holland (Halland, Hollandes, Hollands), David, 377; Edw, 146; Edw, 224; Jn, 10; Jn, 228; Jn, 256, 271, 416; Jn, 304; Jn, 512; Ric, 513; Rob, 125, 364; Thos, 143; Thos, 421; Walwin, 291, 305; Wm, 87, 88, 145, 232; Wm, 256; Wm, chamberlain and coroner, xxxvii, 5

Hollas, Hollest *see* Hollis

Hollick (Hollicke, Hollock), Wm, 61; Wm, 374, 381

Holliday (Holydaye), Peter, 314; Thos, 279

Hollier (Halliard, Helliard, Hillard, Hollyard, Hollyer), Jn, 20; Jn, 193; Jn, 441, 488; Wm, 42; Wm, 50

Hollingdale (Hollingall), Ric, 449; Thos, 209

Hollis (Hollas, Hollest, Hollys), Jn, 93, 112; Ralph, 112; Rog, 65; Rog, 292; Wm, 60, 239

Hollock *see* Hollick

Holloway, Jn, 505; Thos, 213

Hollyard *see* Hollier

Hollybon *see* Hallybone

Hollyer *see* Hollier

Holman, Jn, 510; Thos, 101; Thos, 451; Thos, 510; Wm, 363

Holmes, Nat, 154; Ric, 142, 470; Thos, chamberlain and coroner, xxxvii, 15, 18, 144

Holmewood *see* Homewood

Holmsby *see* Homsby

Holmwood *see* Homewood

Holt (Holte), Aaron, 407; Hen, 142; Jn, 142; Wm, 101

Holydaye *see* Holliday

Homer, Alice, 507

Homesby, Homesbye *see* Homsby

Homewood (Holmewood, Holmwood), Hen, 128; Hen, 134; Joan, 54; Joan, 54; Mic, 311; Ric, 54; Ric, 54; Ric, 457; Rob, 213; Thos, 54

Homsby (Holmsby, Homesby, Homesbye), Edm, 332, 354, 443; Jn, 155

Honeywood (Honiwood, Honnywood, Honywood), Rob, 169; Rob, (?*same*), 285, 307, 372, 386

Honnor *see* Honour

Honnywood *see* Honeywood

Honour (Honnor), Jn, 142

Honysed *see* Hunnisett

Honywood *see* Honeywood

Hood, Hoode *see* Hoad

Hook (Hooke), Edw, 186, 235; Jn, 442; Ric, 82; Thos, 454; Thos, 465

Hooker, Edw, 244; Jn, 244

Hooper, Jn, 255; Thos, coroner, xxxvi, 518

Hopkins (Hopkin), Geo, 450; Hen, 513; Jn, 35, 226; Jn, 481; Ste, 91

Hopley, Thos, 409

Hore *see* Hoare

Horley (Horly, Horlye), Jas, 253; Ric, 218; Rob, bailiff, 87; Rog, 22; Thos, 98, 183; Thos, 192; Thos, 401

Hornden *see* Harnden

Horscroft (Horscrofte), Josiah, 450; Ric, 191; Rob, 207; Silas, 197; Thos, 519

Horsley (Hersley), Jn, 256

Horsted, Joan, 514

Horton, Geof, 488

Hoskin (Hoskins, Hoskyn), Ant, 412; Ric, 83

Hosmer, Abraham, 337; Edw, 71; Geo, 145; Jn, 518; Thos, 276, 282; Wm, 413

Hoth *see* Hoad

Hother *see* Hodder

Hothly *see* Hoadley

Houghton, Thos, 445; Thos, (?*same*), coroner, xvii, xix, xx, xxxvi, 249, 262, 263, 268, 278, 306

Hounsell (Hownsell), Jn, 304; Jn, 304; Mark, 387; *cf.* Hussell

Hover, Thos, 531

Howard (Howarde), Hen, duke of Norfolk, xliii; Hen, duke of Norfolk, xliii; Hen, earl of Arundel and Surrey, xliii; Lancelot, 14; Thos, duke of Norfolk, xliii, 1–3, 7, 8, 14, 17, 23, 29, 30, 33, 39, 43, 47–49, 52, 56, 58, 73, 74, 77, 78, 81, 84, 85, 98; Thos, duke of Norfolk, xliii; Thos, earl of Arundel and Surrey, xliii, 34, 40, 60, 62, 69, 94, 115, 158, 168, 206, 207, 210, 213, 215, 217, 226, 229, 295, 362, earl marshal, 261, 322, 323, 338, 371

Howcombe *see* Hockham

Howe, Sam, notary public, 424; *cf.* Howes

Howell, ..., 272; Edw, 225; Hen, 149, 171; Jn, 139; Jn, 151, 153; Jn, 340; Jn, 340; Jn, 394; Ric, 151, 272; Rob, 126; Rob, 517

Howes, Jn, coroner, xviii, xxv, xxxvi, 479, 481, 488, 501, 503, 506, 507; *cf.* Howe; Hughes

Howett *see* Hewitt

Howlett, Jn, 266

Hownsell *see* Hounsell

Jn, 461; Jn, 462, 517; Jn, 485; Jos, 415; Lancelot, 172; Mat, 259; Peter, 159; Ric, 138; Ric, 166; Ric, 244; Ric, 311; Ric, 440; Ric, 495; Rob, 4, 69; Rob, 31; Rob, 232, 249, 262; Rob, 402; Rog, 135; Rog, 223; Rog, 310; Ste, 513; Theophilus, 440; Thos, 5, 28; Thos, 79; Thos, 126; Thos, 160, 176, 214; Thos, 163; Thos, 274; Thos, 374; Wm, 86; Wm, 189; Wm, 225, 237, 271

Mascall (Mascull, Maskall), Jn, 26; Thos, 39

Mason, Jn, 108; Jn, 421; Jn, 450; Jn, 478; Ric, 466; Ric, 466; Ste, 254, 330; Thos, 66

Masters (Mayster), Edw, 129; Edw, (?*same*), 136, 245; Jn, 294; Ninian, 309; Rob, 69

Matcham (Maicham), Wm, 20

Mates (Meates), Ben, 371

Matthews (Mathew, Mathewe, Mathewes, Mathy, Mattheu, Matthew), Abraham, 243; Ant, 361; Geo, 355; Geo, coroner, xxxvii, 244; Hen, 334; Jn, 166; Jn, 211; Jn, 489; Oliver, 5; Ric, bailiff, 37, 41, 55, 102; Ste, 186; Thos, 101; Thos, 334; Thos, 370; Thos, 370; Wm, 366

Mattock (Mattocke), Thos, 450

Mauncer, Maunser *see* Manser

Maxwell, Thos, 227, 330

May (Maye), Jas, 505; Jasper, 58; Jn, 105, 249; Jn, 106, 168; Jn, 176, 214; Jn, 413, 431; Jn, 491; Jn, 518; Ric, 278; Rob, alias Rob Turner, 471; Thos, 53; Thos, 71; Thos, 276, 282, 331, 346, 354; Thos, 465; Thos, (?*same*), 518; Thos, kt, xliii, 87, JP, 74, 145; Wm, 71; Wm, 71, 203, 337, 354

Mayfield (Mayfeild), Jn, 346

Maynard (Maynarde, Maynerd, Maynord), Art, 276, 290, 332, 346, 354; Joan, 92; Jn, 155, 203, 276, 282, 290, 346; Jn, 164, 203; Jn, 331, 332, 346; Nehemiah, 243; Nic, 146; Ric, 92; Ric, 344; Rob, 219, 228; Thos, 79, 92, 99, 130, 146, 155; Thos, 249, 290, 346; Thos, 465; Wm, 105

Mayster *see* Masters

Mead (Meade), Jas, 401; Ric, 341

Meadows (Meadow), Alice, 475; Mary, 475; Thos, 475, 494

Meakin (Mekins), Geo, 172

Meares *see* Meers

Mearshe *see* Marsh

Meates *see* Mates

Medhurst (Medherst), Ant, 388; Hen, 455; Jeremy, 477; Jn, 191, 192; Jn, 325

Medley, Thos, 520

Meek (Meekes), Ben, 267, 279, 318, 319, 322, 323

Meers (Ameares, Amearse, Ameeres, Ameers, Amerrs, Meares, Meere, Meeres, Mere), Edw, 83; Edw, 258; Hen, 237; Nic, 12; Rob, 207; Rob, 448; Thos, 207; Thos, 505; Wm, 193; Wm, 491; *cf.* Mare

Mekins *see* Meakin

Mellearshe *see* Mellish

Meller *see* Miller

Mellish (Mellearshe, Mellyshe), Jn, 185; Thos, 60; Wm, 45

Melsam, Melsham *see* Milsom

Mensemts, Wegsert, 425

Mepham (Meppham), Ric, 27

Mercer (Merser, Mersher), Ralph, 411; Ric, 407; Wm, 109; Wm, 336

Merchant *see* Marchant

Mere *see* Meers

Merie *see* Merry

Merriall *see* Murrell

Merry (Merie), Jas, 57; Jn, 223; Wm, 33

Merryweather, Alice, 356; Eliz, 356; Jn, 356; Nic, 356; Nic, 356; Wm, 356

Mersall *see* Marshall

Merser *see* Mercer

Mersh, Mershe *see* Marsh

Mersher *see* Mercer

Messent (Messance), Adrian, 357

Miall (Mighell, Mihell, Mihill, Myhell), ..., 309; Edw, 149; Edw, constable, 190; Geo, (*probably same as Geo Mitchell*), 53; Hen, 394; Thos, 394; *cf.* Miles; Mitchell

Michel *see* Mitchell

Michelborne (Michilborne), Ric, kt, JP, 353; Thos, 18, 104; Wm, 77

Michell *see* Mitchell

Michener *see* Mitchener

Michilborne *see* Michelborne

Middlemore, Thos, 331, 337

Middleton (Midleton), Jn, 199; Peter, 93; Thos, JP, 372, 375

Midmore (Midmor), Thos, 510

Mighell, Mihell, Mihill *see* Miall

Miles (Myles), Ann, 441; Edw, 408; Edw, 441; Fran, 542; Hen, 60; Hen, 157; Joan, 542; Jn, 174; Jn, 275; Nic, 441; Ric, 129; Ric, 487; Thos, 542; Wm, 441; *cf.* Miall; Mills

Mill *see* Mills

Millard (Millerd, Millward), Hen, 247; Jn, 349

Miller (Meller, Myller), Chas, 189; Dan, 424, 425, 492; Edw, 234, 238; Geo, 473; Gil, 19; Jas, 246, 260; Jas, 436, 446; Jas, 520; Jn, 137; Thos, jurat, 424, 439

Mills (Mill, Milles, Mylles, Mylls), Geo, 487; Hen, 70, 91, 187; Hen, 135; Jas, 125; Jn, 60, 120; Jn, 90, 258; Jn, 180; Nat, 519; Nic, 474; Ralph, 266; Ric, 481; Ric, deputy mayor and coroner, xxxviii, 288, 289, mayor and coroner, xxxviii, 347; Rob, 248, 269, 299; Rob, 370; Thos, 10; Thos, 37; Thos, 208; Thos, 208; Wm, 503; Wm, JP, 233; *cf.* Miles

Millward *see* Millard

Milsom (Melsam, Melsham), Ant, 193; Wm, 150

Mitchell (Michel, Michell, Mitchel), Ann, 420; Edw, 386; Edw, JP, 427, 442; Eliz, 506; Geo, (*probably same as Geo Miall*), 67; Hen, 169; Hen, 329; Jn,

Newen *see* Newing
Newenden, Jn, 485
Newill *see* Newell
Newing (Newen, Newyn), Jn, 9; Peter, 466
Newington, ..., 170; Jn, 313
Newman, Hen, 119; Hen, 438; Hen, 491; Jn, 182; Jn, 230; Jn, 276; Wm, 146
Newnham (Newnam, Newneham, Nunham), Jn, 353; Jn, 403; Jn, 454; Ric, 497
Newnington *see* Nunnington
Nework *see* Newark
Newton, Ann, 171; Jas, 347, 358, 376, 379, 382, 383; Jn, 540; Nic, 211; Ric, 166, 380; Thomasin, 29; Wm, 355, 380
Newyn *see* Newing
Niblett (Niblet), Jane, 372; Mat, 312, 316, 317; Ric, 196
Nicholas, Edw, 184; Edw, 357; Jn, 132; Jn, 350; Wm, 225, 237
Nicholls (Nicholl, Nicholles, Nycholles), Jn, 219; Jn, 512; Ric, 512; Wal, 169
Nicholson (Nicollsone, Nicolson), Jn, 25; Jn, 83; Jn, 223; Jn, 288, 304
Nightingale (Nitingall, Nytingall), Jn, 26; Ric, 507
Ninn (Nyn, Nynne) alias Barber, Geo, 146; *cf.* Nunn
Nitingall *see* Nightingale
Noakes, Jn, (*fictitious*), 505; Thos, 109; *cf.* Neakes
Noble, Jn, 229
Nonington *see* Nunnington
Norfolk (Norff', Norffolc), dukes of *see* Howard
Norman, Edw, 515; Joan, 129; Jn, 515; Ric, 2; Ric, 31; Ric, 129; Ric, 357; Thos, 137; Wm, 329
Norris (Norrys), Hen, 24; Jn, 75; Ric, 40; Wm, 206; Wm, 206
North (Northe), Edw, 91
Northumberland (Northumbria), earl of *see* Percy
Norton, Ant, 260; Jn, 328; Lawr, 343; Ninian, 334; Ric, 253; Thos, 80, 87; Thos, 303, 449; Thos, 464
Norwich, bishop of *see* Harsnett, Sam
Norwood, Fran, 467
Novell, Denis, 194
Nowell, Jn, mayor and coroner, xxxviii, 304, 308, 315; Wm, 106; *cf.* Newell
Nowers (Nower), Edw, 66
Nunham *see* Newnham
?Nunn, ..., 286; *cf.* Ninn
Nunnington (Newnington, Nonington), Ric, 18; Rob, 28; Rob, 491
Nurse (Nursse), Mark, 148; Martha, 148
Nutfield (Nutfeild), Jn, 39
Nutt, Jn, 520; Thos, 520
Nye (Ny), Jn, 364; Ric, 279; Rob, 322; Solomon, 432; Thos, 169
Nyn *see* Ninn

Oake *see* Oakes
Oakeley *see* Oakley
Oakes (Oake, Oke), Thos, 347; Wm, 446
Oakley (Hockley, Oakeley), Thos, 481; Wm, 481
Ockenden, Thos, 142
Oke *see* Oakes
Old (Oulde), Nic, 13; Rose, 13
Older (Oulder, Owlder), Fran, 360; Ric, 157; Rob, 209; Thos, 167; Thos, 437; Wm, 181; Wm, 294; Wm, 510
Olive *see* Olliffe
Oliver (Olliver, Olyver), Ben, 215; Edm, 61; Geo, 178, 266, 305; Geo, 460, 475; Hen, 482, 499, 504; Mary, 516; Ralph, 299; Ric, 20, 115; Thos, 197; Thos, 197, 215; Thos, 197, 255; Wm, 197
Olley (Ollye), Ste, (?*same as Ste Olliffe*), 88
Olliffe (Olive, Ollive, Olyve), Jn, 395, 463; Jn, 395, 463; Jn, 468; Jn, 520; Ste, (?*same as Ste Olley*), 268; Thos, 343; Thos, 456; Wm, 468
Olliver *see* Oliver
Ollye *see* Olley
Olyve *see* Olliffe
Olyver *see* Oliver
Onley (Onely), Edw, 409
Orgill (Orgle, Orgles), And, 82; Nic, 327
Osborne (Osbarne, Osbourne, Usborne), Edw, 129; Eliz, 497; Geo, 44; Hen, 497; Jas, 320; Jn, 320; Jn, 406; Ric, 344; Rob, 440; Ste, 65, 93; Thos, 124; Thos, 365; Thos, 497; Wal, 27; Wm, 497
Ottey (Ottye, Oty), Hen, 400; Jn, 229
Otway, Geo, 316
Oty *see* Ottey
Oughton (Owton), Jn, 52; Jn, 52; *cf.* Uden
Oulde *see* Old
Oulder *see* Older
Outred (Owtred), Dan, 162
Ovenden, Jas, 443; Thos, 443; Wm, 203, 331, 332; Wm, 346
Overington, Jn, 132; Jn, 427; Ric, 125; Ric, 427; Rob, 42, 308
Overy, Ric, 381
Owden *see* Uden
Owen (Owens), Edw, 175; Fran, 465; Rob, 142
Owlder *see* Older
Owton *see* Oughton
Owtred *see* Outred
Oxenbridge, Goddard, 10
Oxley, Ric, 445; Ric, 473
Oziver, Joan, 487

Pace (Paise), Rog, 91
Pacey, Sam, 494
Pack (Packe), Rog, 391
Packer, Dan, 415, 424
Packham *see* Peckham
Paddock (Paddicke), Clem, 37; Ric, 412

INDEX OF PLACES

Places are in Sussex unless otherwise stated.

INDEX OF SUBJECTS

Most subjects are arranged in groups under the following main headings: Accidental death; Accidental homicide and chance medley; Buildings; Clothing; Criminal and other offences; Deodands; Farm equipment and trade tools; Homicide in self defence; Homicide, uncertain; Household articles; Livestock and other fauna; Manslaughter; Murder; Natural death; Occupations and styles; Officials; Punishments; Suicide; Weapons and armour.